# THEY CANNOT BE EXPLAINED.
# THEY CANNOT BE DENIED.

There are marvelous men and women who are blessed with power they cannot see, power that enables them to achieve triumphs in the art of healing the sick and hopeless.

David St. Clair has interviewed eleven of these unusual and important healers, who revealed to him their personalities, methods, accomplishments and even their failures.

Now you can learn about the miraculous and instantaneous battlefield healing of a Vietnam veteran . . . a man whose slipped disc was cured in a witches' coven . . . how singer Della Reese, who was almost killed when she walked through a glass door, saved her life . . . and many other fascinating stories of

*PSYCHIC HEALERS*

# PSYCHIC HEALERS

## DAVID ST. CLAIR

BANTAM BOOKS • TORONTO • NEW YORK • LONDON

RL 6, IL 6-up

PSYCHIC HEALERS

*A Bantam Book / published by arrangement with
Doubleday & Company, Inc.*

*PRINTING HISTORY*

*Doubleday edition published May 1974*
*2nd printing ...... August 1974*
*3rd printing ... September 1974*
*Revised Bantam edition / August 1979*

ISBN 0-553-02056-0

*Published simultaneously in the United States and Canada*

*Bantam Books are published by Bantam Books, Inc. Its trade-
mark, consisting of the words "Bantam Books" and the por-
trayal of a bantam, is Registered in U.S. Patent and Trademark
Office and in other countries. Marca Registrada. Bantam
Books, Inc., 666 Fifth Avenue, New York, New York 10019.*

PRINTED IN THE UNITED STATES OF AMERICA

This book is dedicated to my mother
Ruth Sutton St. Clair . . .
whose hands have the healing gift of love.

# CONTENTS

BG True story 2

Many there were in our garden several

honey.

"Upstairs, in their bedroom," Christopher XI
healing. There are twin beds, some

# PSYCHIC HEALERS

# I
# Dorie D'Angelo

Dorie was frantic with fear. Her husband was dying; doctors in town were unavailable because it was Christmas Eve and all her family was in far-off Canada. She managed to get André onto her massage table before he passed out. Her small hands worked his temples trying to assuage some of the terrible pain in his head.

It was then that she looked up and saw a stranger standing beside her. The man was in his middle fifties, had gray hair, and wore an old-fashioned salt and pepper tweed suit that buttoned almost up to his neck. He had the hint of a flounce tie and wore a pair of rimless glasses that hung on a black silk ribbon, which was pinned to his jacket lapel. "If you are willing to do as I say," he told her, "I can save your husband's life. But you must follow orders."

The white-haired woman shook her head in agreement. Amazingly, she wasn't frightened at this sudden appearance, only grateful that someone had come to help her.

"Now the first thing we must do is relieve the pressure inside his head. I'll need your energy to do this, so follow instructions! Cut off the top of his skull."

"But I don't have a knife that sharp," she protested.

"Don't be silly," he replied irritably. "I didn't say anything about using a knife! Take your finger and

1

run it along his brow, over his ears and across the back of his head. And don't dawdle, woman!"

She ran her finger the way he ordered and recalls: "I saw the top of André's head fall off. And I smelled the terrible stench that came from inside. I could see the brain and see the blood vessels, but no blood was running from where I had made the incision."

Then the stranger showed her some bits of bone that had gotten lodged in André's brain and told her to pick them out. The particles, he said, were from an old accident and had slowly worked themselves into the brain. That was the reason André had been having the terrible headaches and the reason he had passed out that afternoon. Dorie remembered that André had told her of an accident he had had long before they were married. She also remembered that she loved this man too much to be frightened by anything that was happening. She wanted him to get well, that was all she could think of. The fact that she had cut off the top of his skull on orders from a trespassing stranger didn't even enter her mind.

"When the particles were out the man told me to put the head back on, but not too tight because we had to let the air get in. I did just as he bid me. Then he said that he would be back the next afternoon if I wanted him to return. Naturally, I told him I did. And with that he vanished."

For the first time in almost two weeks André slept peacefully. He was still asleep the next day—Christmas Day 1968—when the man appeared again. Again the top of his head was removed and again the pressure was relieved. But this time Dorie had her wits about her and asked him who he was. He wouldn't tell her too much, just that he was "not of this world" and that he had been a medical doctor when he lived "in this world." He said that he was studying more advanced medicine where he was now and that he used these techniques to work on André. "I do not have the energy to do these operations myself," he told her, "that's why I must work through you. I must use your forces and vibrations. I chose you because you are a professional physiotherapist and understand the body and its workings. I also chose you because you are a nurse and know how to take orders from a doctor. If we are to continue you must be obedient and do everything exactly as I tell you." Dorie nodded her head in agreement. "From now on when you want me set a metronome slowly in motion and I will come in on those vibrations. Your husband will be healed." And with that he vanished.

"It was incredible," she recalls; "I felt as if I was in the middle of some grotesque fairy tale, but after a few sessions I had André take an encephalogram and everything was perfect. Those headaches never came back."

Dorie D'Angelo of Carmel, California—now the Reverend Dorie D'Angelo—is a rational, intelligent, normal human, able to discuss almost every subject with sure-footed common sense except this one topic: her incredible spirit doctor.

"I didn't tell anybody about him at first," she says, "because I knew people wouldn't believe me. I believed in the power of my doctor and believed that he could cure people. Good heavens, André was proof enough for that, but it's difficult to talk about such things in a small town."

But that hadn't stopped her. One day previous to her doctor's visit, when on her way to the post office, she looked in an open doorway and saw a woman doubled up over a table. The woman was having a heart attack. Dorie doesn't know what made her go to this woman's rescue, but she entered the house and placed her hands on the woman's chest. "I have healing hands," she told the lady, "and if I put my hands on you and you keep quiet for a few minutes everything is going to be all right." And it was. The woman recovered almost immediately.

Then, several weeks after the doctor had operated

on André, a close friend became terribly ill. Dorie had told her about the doctor but swore her to secrecy. Now the friend wanted Dorie to come over to her home and bring her doctor with her. Dorie went, the doctor appeared, and the friend was cured. After that the news spread quickly and little Dorie D'Angelo became known as a healer. But she doesn't mind; in fact, she loves it for it keeps her active and in the center of things. She loves Carmel and is sure that "the angels" brought her and André together, made them marry and led them out of Toronto, Canada, and into Carmel even though they both had children and grandchildren.

Dorie was born in 1902 and is one of the most energetic septuagenarians I have ever met in my life. The snow-white hair (which she says she has had since her thirties) belies the incredible youth underneath. Her eyes are a twinkling bright blue. Her face is almost free from lines and her voice is clear and lilting. She doesn't smoke, will have an occasional glass of wine, and is not too particular about her diet. She takes vitamins and cleans her face every morning with a mixture of olive oil, lemon juice, and salt. But her youthfulness doesn't come from outside. It's all inside and bursts out to engulf everyone she meets. "I think a great part of it is that I don't feel any older inside. I feel as though I'm just beginning this great adventure of living and just hope that I can stay young all the time so I can keep on going. I never remember I'm my age and so when a child of ten comes in I sort of get a thing going, I want to get down on the floor and play with him. I forget that I'm over seventy years old and the beautiful part is, so does he."

Dorie was just an ordinary housewife in Canada for years. She raised two children and nothing really happened in her life until her daughter's husband came back from World War Two and moved in with them. A cousin took her aside one day and asked her

why she didn't do something to "get out of the house
and let the young people be by themselves for a
while." She didn't know where to go or what to do
but she heard of a college of hydrotherapy and massage and decided "just for fun to go and see what it
was like." She loved it. After two weeks it had become her whole world. The students were all returned servicemen and the professors were European
doctors who were required by law to study and teach
before they could openly practice in Canada. "It was
my thing," she recalls. "One of my teachers looked
like John the Baptist. He had this great mass of hair
and long arms and he would say, 'with hot and cold
water you can cure anything in the whole world.' I
discovered that I had a way of memorizing with pictures and even though the other students were younger and with quicker minds I was really a much better student than they were. We were taught diagnosis
and the curing of illnesses rather than just massage.
We had a condensed chiropractic course so we didn't
have to learn all the muscles but we did have to learn
one third of them and one third of the nerves and so
on. And even though I have small hands they seemed
to be able to expand to meet the work. Of course we
were taught how to throw our weight, so that when I
do massage I use my whole body. I was so proud
when I graduated and had a diploma that said I was
an R.M.G. That means Remedial Massage and Gymnastics. And almost immediately I got a position in a
chiropractic clinic. I was happy and I was useful to
others and because of that I was happy all over
again."

Now Dorie is not one just to sit back and vegetate
into a routine no matter how pleasant she may find
that routine. No sooner was she earning a good living
than she began to experiment with healing devices.
She had read of Dr. Wilhelm Reich's work with the
orgone-accumulator and a book by L. E. Eeman called
Co-Operative Healing. Reich believed that he could

accumulate healing energies in a machine made of lead and felt. Eeman believed he could capture these energies with copper wiring and copper screening. They were successful in treating some symptoms with these machines, on the theory that the metals would hold the energies which could be released into a human body on contact. So Dorie began to experiment too.

I got very excited about these copper wires and I made sets of wires where you hold a handle in your left hand and a handle in your right and then you had a wire that went from your head to your seat and up to the hands. But you'd use other people as generators for this energy. I spent a fortune on copper wires and tubing and made seven sets of those things. I got them together and then invited some friends over and spread them out on the living room rug. Then I made my guests lie down on the wires and concentrate. It was a little like what Dr. Elmer Green is doing now with Alpha Waves by concentrating and making the palms of your hands hot. So there we were clutching these copper handles and making our palms hot and you know we got this tremendous experience. All seven felt the power and all of them felt better afterward. The experiment probably would have lasted longer except that my husband came home unexpectedly from a business trip to find seven people stretched out on his living room rug holding copper handles. He didn't appreciate it and he told me so.

"Anyway, after a while a manufacturer from someplace out West heard about my wires and he came to see me. He said he wanted to start making machines that would heal people. He brought a couple of assistants with him and so I put the wires on the floor and we all lay down on them. Well, the manufacturer became terribly excited because he got a healing! He had had terrible pains in his back and when we were finished the pains were gone. 'All right,' he said to me, 'I'll buy this from you. It's terrific! But where does it plug in?' And I said, 'Well, it doesn't plug in, anywhere.' And then he said, 'Well, how does the electricity run along it?' He takes a look and it was all put together with safety pins. The shock on his face was something. He said that it was impossible because electricity will not cross over on safety pins. And I told him that this kind of energy will jump a quarter of an inch. I'd read that in a book somewhere. Well, the poor man was very disappointed and said, 'I can't sell anything unless it plugs in.' And he went away, so nothing ever came of my wires."

After that she made her own orgone-accumulator. She got window screening and rolls of felt and ran her copper wires through and put handles on either side. She first put this in her mother's bed and made the lady hold the handles to see what would happen. Then she took it to the clinic and tried it out on patients there. She claims it helped them.

Her experiments made only a slight ripple on Canadian medicine, for none of the doctors would listen to her. Once when a psychiatric seminar was held in Toronto she went as a spectator but got so fed up with their intellectualism and the fact that "they weren't even mentioning the power that seemed to come from the wires" that she asked to speak. They granted her ten minutes and she immediately proceeded to tell these learned gentlemen that they were missing the whole basic concept of healing. The applause afterward was sparse to say the least.

Dorie's enthusiasm for her wires diminished when she discovered that often a healing would take place when the wires were not even connected. "I puzzled a great deal over this and finally came to the conclusion that it didn't have anything to do with the wires themselves, that there was a stronger force that did the cures and this force didn't need our man-made apparatus to work with, it had its own methods."

Then she discovered Somatic processing, the theory

that illnesses are held inside the body in memory-pockets of muscles and that by applying pressure to those muscles the memories will be forced out and along with them the traces of illness in the body. The process seemed to work so well that at the clinic one doctor would do physical chiropractic work on a patient and then send him in to Dorie, who would do psychotherapy on him. The results were such that patients were healed much faster and needed to return fewer times. While this was great for the patients the clinic suffered from the lack of the lucrative repeat business.

It was then that she met André. He had been coming to the regular chiropractor and going out a different door so he never met Dorie. Finally, when he failed to respond to normal treatment he was turned over to "this lady with the white hair and the pleasant voice, but I didn't know what she could do for me and I resented her butting in on my case."

"He gave me the worst time I ever got from any patient," she recalls, "but when he left he told me: 'You know what you're doing.' "

"And when I came back I told her something else: I told her she was going to marry me."

"I told him he was crazy. I was separated from my husband and André was divorced from his wife. He was ten years younger than I was and I had no intentions of becoming a housewife all over again. I told him to find another girl and find another therapist."

But André insisted and she insisted right back, but he has just as much masculine charm as she has feminine and eventually won her over. They are still as much in love as the day they were married.

Dorie feels that she was destined to marry André D'Angelo and to have the last name that translates into "of the angels." She has known all along that she has angels protecting her and she talks about her angels (and to her angels) the way one would talk about cherished friends.

"They have always been important in my life" she told me with that twinkle in her blue eyes. "When I found out about the spiritual side of life I began to ask the angels to come to me. When we first arrived in Carmel there was a lecture given by Mortimer Adler. He was here to refute a previous lecture by Julian Huxley, who had talked against the existence of God. Adler was here to defend God, so to speak. Well anyway, at the end of his talk, during the question and answer period, some woman asked him, 'You don't really believe in angels, do you?' And he replied, 'Everyone was born with a guardian angel, and I can tell you a great deal about angels.' So this really excited me, that he believed in angels, because I had thought a lot about them and felt that I had an angel beside me. I could see his head often near me. So I began to really study them and think about them and I discovered that a lot of people knew about angels but didn't talk about them."

"How does one contact their guardian angel?" I asked Dorie. I was sure it must be very difficult.

She assured me that it wasn't. "First you have to believe that you have one near you. That's more than half the answer. We all have some power that we talk to when we are lonely or troubled. The next time you meditate just ask that during the next hour you'd like your angel to come. You may not see him or hear him but you'll get a kind of *feeling*, a feeling that everything is all right and you're not alone. It's a wonderful feeling to know you're not alone. Then when you know he's there just start talking to him. Tell him your problems and ask him to help you solve them. I always place my entire day in their hands. When I get up in the morning, I'll say, 'Well, angels, please look after the whole day for me,' or 'Angels, everything is a big mess, please straighten it out (which is mostly what I say), and I have several appointments all at the same hour, will you do something?' And they always make the day flow smoothly. When I tell others to do this they say they find parking places, get tickets to shows that are sold out, and locate objects and friends they thought were long lost. And the angels protect children in school, too. Children love to have their own angel. Show them how to introduce themselves to their angel and ask that angel to protect them while they are away from home. They take the angels to school with them and they don't get into any quarrels and the teacher loves them."

"That in itself is worth calling on the angels," I said, "but are these angels great fluttery beings with huge wings or what?"

"Your angel becomes how you think of him. Some people see a light, which they figure is the angel. Some people have a feeling of color. I even know one lady who said she heard a bell, a little bell ringing. One girl told me she was once going to commit suicide because she was very ill and unhappy. She shut herself in her room determined to stay there until she died. Suddenly an angel appeared—and she didn't know a thing about angels, she wasn't even thinking about them—and she said this figure appeared in front of her. Funny, it only appeared from the waist up but it had huge feathered wings. This angel told her she had a great deal to do yet in this world and that she would publish a book and be needed by many people. She scoffed but decided not to die just to see if any of it would come true. She wrote down the dates she was given and everything. And you know it all came true exactly like the angel said it would."

"Exactly?"

"Yes. Exactly. Everything that she had been told and on the very days she had been given. Isn't that wonderful? I get so excited when I think of what the angels do for us and all we have to do for them is just to recognize that they are here waiting to help us."

Dorie and André are sure that the angels helped them move from Canada to California. André vividly remembers the day he walked into a toy store in Toronto and bought a Ouija board. He says it was just a plaything but when he sat down with it, words began to come through that were not in his mind at all. "The board told me all sorts of things. It said I would marry again but I was trying to coax Dorie into it so that wasn't really news. Then it said we would leave and go to California together and I knew that was ridiculous. Then it told me I'd own a publishing company and at that I really laughed. I didn't know the slightest thing about printing and frankly, I wasn't the least bit interested."

But they did get married, did move to California, and the D'Angelo Publishing Company is the only bonafide book publisher on the Monterey Peninsula. André and Dorie are its sole owners.

André is a strikingly handsome man with dark hair, tanned complexion, and piercing dark eyes. His small frame is muscular and laden with energy. His deep voice is smooth and clear. And he is no novice to the world of the occult.

"I realized early in life that I had certain psychic abilities," he told me, "but I went the usual route where I turned my back on it. I had a photographic studio in Toronto and got to be very well known because of it and I know now—I didn't realize it at the time—that I was using psychic abilities in my portraits."

He would place the client in one of his plush studios, turn on soft music, and pinpoint soft colored lights. He would talk to the client, watch him carefully as the colored lights changed until the exact mood was set. Then he captured that mood on film. But while he made a great deal of money, this method bothered him.

"After a sitting I would get in my car and go for long drives by myself. I used to worry about what I was doing because during the session I would see all kinds of things about their characters, their aspirations, and all their hang-ups and frustrations. Then later I gave up the studio and started a personality development school. I only taught women. While I was giving the course I didn't pay any attention to them in the personal sense. You know, when you're teaching a group of people you're not looking into their minds. Then the last night would come where I would have to give a student a personality analysis and I'd look at them and suddenly know everything about them and be able to tell them about themselves in depth. What I was doing was giving them a psychic reading. It helped them a great deal but it bothered the hell out of me."

"Well, why should this have bothered you as a professional?" I asked. "After all, you were being paid to take portraits and to improve personalities in your school."

"I didn't like the idea of probing. I felt I was doing something dishonest making people bare their souls to me for a fee. If you'll examine it you'll see that what I was doing was looking into a very private place in them and I didn't particularly like it. Of course it helps me in my publishing business now but whenever I catch myself looking too deeply into a client's soul I pull back and change my pace."

André's biggest project so far is the publishing and promotion of a book written by a man long dead who is still lively enough today to insist on how he wants the book printed and publicized. Back in 1910 an occult classic was published titled *A Dweller on Two Planets*. Its author, Frederick S. Oliver, claimed he had received the entire manuscript through automatic writing from an entity called "Phylos the Tibetan." In the late fifties "Phylos" took control of a woman's hand and started dictating another book. He called this one, *The Growth of a Soul*.

Yet once it was written he didn't seem in any hurry to have it published. The lady was a member of a group of people in northern California who did guided writing (letting spirits control their pens to bring through messages). In December 1971, the group got an unexpected message. "Phylos" was ready to have his latest work printed and the group was directed to give the manuscript to "a publisher in Carmel." A guest of the group, who had attended some of Dorie's healing sessions, said she knew who that publisher was and took the script to André. Then followed several sessions where André would ask questions of "Phylos" and the lady would go off, contact the dead author, and give André his replies. "Phylos" kept telling her—which seemed very odd to the D'Angelos—"don't worry about anything. It's all been set up and André will know what to do."

But André didn't know what to do and each time he would come up with a brilliant idea "Phylos" would reject it. André wanted a deluxe, numbered edition bound in leather. It would sell for fifty dollars a copy and create a fund for publishing more spiritual books. "Phylos" said no and then guided a lady to André who *gave* him three thousand dollars for the project. "Phylos" also told him he would have enough business to take care of the costs of the new machinery and bindery the book would require and André has been engulfed in work, winning every bid he has placed for each new contract. When he complained to "Phylos" that he couldn't do all this new work because of insufficient capital, A friend suddenly came forward with a four-thousand-dollar loan, saying he "knew" the shop needed money temporarily.

"But is this book worth reading?" I asked, for I'd read some of the other so-called "spirit-guided" volumes and they were usually colossal metaphysical bores.

"Oh, yes," Dorie exclaimed. "It's a beautiful book. It's on a caliber with Hermann Hesse and his *Siddharta*. It's one of those books that you won't put down once you start to read it."

I am amazed that Dorie ever has time to read anything. Her hours are so taken up with her healing work that the times I have been with her she hasn't had a moment even to read her mail.

The tiny house in Carmel, cluttered with furniture, books, records, candles, paintings, and dozens of various-sized angels is the place where the D'Angelos live and where Dorie does her healings. It's also the place where her healing group meets once a week to hold services and pray for those who are unable to attend. Those who are ill and can attend are treated to emotional charges of healing powers that are so strong in the room they can almost be tasted.

Dorie should officially be called the Reverend, having been ordained in 1969 by the Universal Church of the Masters. It's a spiritualist church with some two hundred ministers around the United States. Like everything else, she was led to it and found that their creed "was absolutely beautiful. I believe all of it. I was so lucky I found that church."

Scores of people consider themselves lucky they found Dorie. Mrs. Jean W. Sholes of Ukiah, California, is one of them. I wrote and asked her how Dorie had helped her. This is what she replied:

"I am overweight and had a severe gall bladder attack in August and I was in the hospital for about four days. The X rays they took with the dye showed that the gall bladder was not functioning. About two or three weeks later the X rays were taken again and the results the same: diseased gall bladder.

"So I heard about Dorie and went to see her and I tell you that was an experience I'll never forget. After Dorie called her doctor and I was relaxed she talked to him and explained my problem. (And, David, I'll swear on a stack of Bibles that all this is the truth.) Anyway, I was lying on this table and felt fine while Dorie told me everything he was doing. She said he was using a ray to dissolve the gallstones and I felt them just melting away. And I had a small swelling in the thyroid glands and felt something going into the neck. Well, believe it or not, I've lost a lot of fat just under the chin. Okay, one more thing, I had a rather large lump on the back of the neck right at the top of the shoulders. Well, when Dorie's doctor finished it wasn't there and it hasn't come back. I'm able to use my right arm without any trouble. Okay, one more thing now. She told me he gave me new eyes. Well, I can see better but she told me this takes time. I can't say my eyes are perfect as yet, but I'm patient."

There are other letters in Dorie's shoe box of correspondence. A Miss N.T. of San Francisco wrote her:

"This week I have felt much better. Almost all the pain is gone in the area of my neck where you worked and I feel much freer in the chest. The day after I was there I started menstruating and believe that I passed some of the tumor because there was some labor-like pains during the third day and I had a number of large clots. For about 24 hours the area across the top of my back was tingling and I kept remembering that the burden had been removed. I am walking taller and feeling freer as a result of this. I am grateful to you and the good forces for these improvements."

I personally had felt the "tingling" once when I stretched out on Dorie's massage table down in her basement healing room. My back started to tingle and just as I was about to tell her she chuckled and said that her doctor was laughing because here I had been in Brazil for almost fifteen years and had to come to Carmel to have some leaves from the Amazon rubbed into my back. She said "back" and "rubbed" and that was *exactly* the sensation I was experiencing. Yet I was lying on my back and her hands were on my brow. Naturally, I was quite curious about the owner of that other pair of hands.

"Oh, I really don't know too much about him," Dorie confessed. "I've asked his name and he just smiles. I'm pretty sure, however, that he is a Professor Kirk from Scotland. When he speaks he rolls his 'r's' with a Scottish burr and from the way he dresses he must be using clothes from the 1880s. I figured it must be this man because once when I was having trouble understanding what he wanted me to do—and he gets *very* impatient with me sometimes—he told me to go to my bookcase and get a small medical book I had purchased years ago at a book sale. Then he told me what page to turn to and there, really it was, David, there was the disease and the cure he was trying to tell me about."

She showed me the two small volumes, about the size of a pocket Bible, bound in red leather and stamped in gold. They are called, *Papers on Health*, and are authored simply by Professor Kirk, Edinburgh. The printing date of her books reads, "Glasgow, 1892," yet he says in a brief introduction that he wrote them in June of 1876. Unfortunately, there is no illustration of the author in either volume but Dorie is sure she would recognize him if someone would come along with his picture.

"You see him that well?" I asked incredulously.

"Oh, yes. I don't always see his face, but I do always see his hands. They are long and sturdy and he does the most amazing things with them. He will bring along a new instrument or do something with light rays, things doctors today—and especially back then—would never have been able to use. He told me once that he is studying on the spirit plane. Imagine a talented medical man like that still studying! But he is. He said he is testing out the medical equipment of the future on the patients of today. Once he even took me to see his school, but it wasn't like any school I'd ever seen before. There were no walls and all sorts of round machines and strange instruments, you know, like they have in astronomy with curves and lenses and light reflectors. Whether that means he is going to come back and use these things in another life, I don't know. But he wants to practice."

"Does he bring these instruments with him and lay them out on a table or do they just appear?"

"They just appear and I'm usually amazed when I see one of them. Of course I'm always so intent on what he is doing that I don't have sense enough to look around the room all the time. But just recently a girl came to me and said she was in terrible pain and didn't even want me to touch her. She didn't tell me where she was in pain but when my doctor came he looked at her and then looked closely at her heart and then he showed me her arteries and explained that they were filled with some kind of stuff ... you know, like that gray stuff you spit out in the basin after the dentist fills your teeth ..."

"You actually saw her heart and arteries?"

"Oh, yes. When he wants me to see things he makes sure I do. How else would I know what to do if I didn't see the organs myself?"

I couldn't answer that.

"Anyway, he told me that the tubes of her heart were filled with some kind of gray matter and she wasn't getting enough blood. She couldn't get enough oxygen and that's why she thought she was dying. The pressure was so strong it was causing a great deal of pain."

"Did you tell her that?" I asked.

"Oh, no. That would be diagnosing and I don't do that. So anyway, he takes a tiny little instrument out of nowhere and pulls it through the vein or the artery—I don't know which—and takes this stuff out. Now as soon as he does that she starts to breathe deeply and normally and she says, 'I'm all right.' So she stayed all right. It didn't come back."

Another new instrument that she recalls appeared when a woman came to her with something Dorie had never heard of before: reversed menstruation.

"This girl told me that instead of having a normal

menstrual period the blood ran *up* inside the Fallopian tubes and caused the most dreadful pain and pressure. She'd been in the hospital for an examination where they had discovered what it was and had also relieved her of six hundred dollars for the search. She didn't have money or hospitalization and the doctors wanted to operate in the next week and she was terrified at their knives and at their fees. So she gets on the table and my doctor takes a look and then brings out a thing that looks like a long knitting needle with a little kind of scoop on the end and sticks it in the Fallopian tubes and opens up a little place to allow a normal blood flow. Now I think to myself, 'Dorie, you're really imagining things this time!' But the girl goes away happy and calls me back in a few days. She said she had had a normal period for the first time in months and her doctor said she no longer needed an operation. Now here is where the strange part of all this comes in. Her sister lives on the East Coast and without my patient knowing it had the very same trouble with her menstruation. She called her sister and the girl told her that she had been operated on for her problem and the doctor in the East Coast hospital had used a tool exactly as I had described the one *my* doctor had used. Now wasn't that something?"

I had to agree that it was. "You never studied surgery, did you? I mean when you were at that school in Canada."

"Oh, no. We didn't believe in it. Not *their* kind of surgery, anyway," she laughed. "But I was so excited about this tool. The girl told me that instead of being in the hospital she was up on a ladder painting her house. I get thrilled when results like this come back to me."

But people don't always report back to Dorie. Many of them come in desperation, have their healing, and then go away. Those who have been so frantic take their healing for granted. She now asks that they send her a postcard one week later telling her how the operation went. A shoe box is overloaded with these cards of praise.

Dorie doesn't charge a dime for her services. She believes that the doctor is with her to serve humanity and is not in need of any money, but Dorie could use the funds to pay the rent on her small house, buy groceries, and keep her charitable donations going. She does accept the cash she gets but always has a ready place for it to go. Like the other healers in this book, she is far from rich. Rich in material things, that is.

"I'm so wealthy in other ways," she beams. "I have so many friends and people everywhere want to help me. One man was so pleased with what I did for him that he comes over and putters around my plants and shrubs. Another man gave me an organ for my healing services. Imagine, he gave me a real musical organ! A dear lady named Peggy Barrick comes once a week to help me with the housework and put my correspondence in order. She always brings a cake or a casserole with her for André and me. People are so good. They really are! I don't know where all the hatred and wars come from. It's certainly not from the people who come into my life."

Dorie has that "thing," that charisma, that makes you feel you've known her forever just as soon as you've met her. You understand immediately why André was so insistent about marrying her when he first laid eyes on her. Few women have this magic, all of them would like to have it and some of them strive to obtain it. But Dorie has it naturally and it flows from her naturally. She doesn't have a false bone in her body.

The stories she tells and the letters she has to back them up are as fascinating as the lady herself.

"You know, David, a woman who had been reading about me in your book *The Psychic World of California* called me. She said she had been riding in a car with her husband reading your book and when she came to the part about me she told him to stop at the next pay phone. She said that I *had* to help her father. She said he had big lumps behind his knees and the doctors were going to open them on the following Tuesday for an exploratory operation. Oh, how I dislike that word 'exploratory.' I asked her to bring her father to me but she said he was a stubborn man who didn't believe in anything. He was taking all kinds of drugs and was in terrible pain, and anyway, they were three hundred miles away from Carmel. Her father never could make such a long journey even if he agreed to go. Which he wouldn't. She asked me if I would send my doctor to him.

"Well, I told her he had never made house calls before and I didn't know if he would agree to go anywhere else or not, but I was willing to try. I asked her to have her father in bed and asleep that night by 10 P.M. and to call me in a few days. She promised she would.

"So I sat down at ten-thirty with André and we both prayed and asked my doctor to go and help this man. I described him and told my doctor exactly where he would find the man. Well, suddenly, there I was watching the entire operation. I could see him working on the knees and see him pull a lot of fluid out of those big lumps. He took an awfully long time but finally he told me that the operation was over. I prayed extra hard to the angels that night after I got into bed.

"Well, the daughter woke me up by phoning about seven-thirty the next morning . . ."

"The *next* morning?" I interrupted.

"The next morning, and she said, 'My father slept all night and he's much better.' She asked for the doctor again and I sent him one more time but that was all. The next time she called was on the day her father was supposed to have gone into the hospital and instead of that he was outside painting the house."

"You seem to get a lot of houses painted from your therapies."

"Yes, and I wish someone would come and paint mine. Anyway, he was cured and just to be on the safe side I put him on our prayer list."

I was puzzled. "If your doctor is so good why do you have to pray for a patient as well?"

"The power of prayer is a great power and when I pray I feel more secure in what I'm doing. When you're dealing with human beings and their health problems you shouldn't leave any door unopened."

"Are there any cases where your doctor has failed?" I asked.

"Yes, he can't help people who are high on drugs or with a lot of alcohol in their systems. He says it clouds the etheric body and he can't see into it. He also doesn't like to work on mental patients and he refuses to touch teeth."

"Have you ever called him and had him refuse to come at all?"

"Yes, a few times, but this has been when I've disobeyed him."

"How do you mean?"

"Well, sometimes after he has finished with a person he'll say, 'I've done all I can for him there's no use having him come back.' But I'm a soft touch and if someone asks for another appointment I give it to him. So when he sees who is on the table he just doesn't show up."

"Does he always operate alone?" I asked. "Or does he have others with him?"

She smiled. "Sometimes he has two other gentlemen with him. They are distinguished-looking gentlemen like himself, dressed in the style he is. I'm sure they were contemporaries of his on earth. Also, sometimes he appears with some entities that I just call 'beings.' They don't seem to be human yet they have a great deal of power. They look like copper-colored mists in the shape of people. They stand and hold onto the feet of the person. It's as if my physical power is not enough so he has to get another source of power."

"Has anyone ever seen this doctor aside from you yourself?"

"Yes, several people. André never has, poor dear, and he's dying to meet him. He's heard so much about him, you know. But several have seen his face and many have seen his hands. One woman only sees his eyes when she is being worked on."

"What are the simplest things for him to cure?" I was curious because any doctor who could reverse a menstrual flow, drain a knee completely, and do a brain operation must have some things he considers a snap to perform. Her answer surprised me.

"Sinus conditions, allergies, and lungs," she replied without a moment's hesitation.

A friend of mine has been suffering from a collapsed sinus canal for years and has been to some of the best doctors in both North and South America, so I knew that sinus canal work was not that *easy*. And besides, his canal collapsed because of one medical man's lack of knowledge.

"My doctor will fill the sinus area and down the throat into the lungs with something that looks like an ultra-violet light. When this light is there you can smell the ozone. As the person breathes it, then suddenly they can smell it, too. And then it dries. It just dries up. And then they can breathe normally. It seems to be quite a simple thing to do."

"For *him*, maybe," I said, "but go to a doctor today and have him operate on your sinus canals and await the botch-up! What about allergies?" Again I was curious because I was allergic to a certain kind of tangerine when I lived in Brazil and it took weeks of probings and scratch tests on my skin before the doctors figured out what it was. And then they didn't *cure* the allergy, they just told me to stay away from tangerines!

"Well, I had one lady come to me who said she was allergic to her sister's cats and she wanted to visit the sister so much and she couldn't because of those cats. So he operated on her. Then she went to see her sister and wrote me a letter saying she was having a wonderful time and wasn't allergic to the cats any longer. Then there was this ten-year-old boy who is allergic to cats and dogs and he *so* wanted to have a dog for his own. And I told his father that wouldn't be any problem at all. When he got on the table my doctor thought for a while and then made what looked like little screens of fine spun glass. The screens were so fine that air could get through, yet the dog and cat hairs couldn't. And he put this inside the bridge of the little boy's nose and then he put one in the back of the throat where the air goes down the windpipe. He also put about a teaspoon of white crystals into the little boy's bloodstream because he said he had a deficiency of a certain kind of mineral. He put this in because it would stop the reaction to the allergy. I thought it was all very interesting because I'd never seen him do anything like this before. But even more amazing the little boy told me that while he was on the table he saw a glass blower making something out of fine glass and said, 'I think that was what your doctor was using.' You know, I often think that all this is my imagination, but I just couldn't imagine such things as fine glass screens and special minerals. I just couldn't!

"Sometimes he uses a lot of light, different colors for different conditions. He uses a great deal of that lovely purple light. He says the light has a vibration that is effective. Sometimes he uses sound vibrations to break things up like gallstones or those little arthritic lumps in people's arms. Sometimes he will break up a lump and then put a little oil on it to lubricate it so its passage out of the body will be easier."

I asked her if she has ever had her doctor do any plastic surgery and she said that she has never called him for cosmetic surgery but there is a man who comes to her to get rid of ugly skin blemishes on his face. Her doctor applies an "odd ointment like the white of eggs not beaten up or cooked, kind of gluey." And when a person has a psychological problem associated with the illness her doctor takes a pencil-thin instrument that's made of light and shines it around the brain in a pattern. "I'm sure it's symbolical, but he *removes* the damaging pattern that was there. The person always accepts this, they *feel* it happening. And so they will say the next time they come back, 'Oh, that doesn't bother me anymore.' They say they can really see that thing going around inside their head."

While her doctor seems to be a medical man for all seasons I wondered what would happen if he was called upon to stop the flow of blood. So I asked: "Dorie, suppose there was an automobile accident in front of your house and a man's arm was severely cut. Could your doctor stop his bleeding?"

She thought for a moment, her gaze going far off somewhere, then she smiled. "It depends on how bad he was. But certainly while I was waiting for the human doctor to arrive I would call my doctor because I know these cases can be helped. I know that you can really help any kind of an accident very fast."

"But," I insisted, "would you be able to stanch the flow of blood?"

"Perhaps," she replied, with that same sure-of-her-sources smile. "Now this sounds ridiculous, but the blood may stop and even disappear inside the body. I don't know how or why, David, but I know it can happen. It happened to me. I'd fallen up a flight of stone steps and scraped my shin. *Up* the flight, you see, so it took all the skin off my leg. The blood was coming out in huge drops down my leg and my ankle felt as if it was sprained. Oh, it was a mess. Now I was all alone and lying on those steps thinking nobody will find me, you know, so frightened and so in pain, so I crawled back into the house and as I was lying down I thought, 'Okay, Dorie, if you're ever going to work these things on yourself, let it be now.

"So I reached down with one hand and grabbed my leg and began to tell my body that it was aching terribly down there. It really was, so I didn't have to exaggerate too much. But I complained and cried and carried on about the pain and all the healing energy in my body went rushing to my scraped shinbone. I could feel it pouring into that one area. All of a sudden the pain stopped. I looked at my leg and the blood had disappeared! The lumps were down, and my ankle, which should have been swollen, was normal size. Now, I don't know *why* this works, but the blood went back inside my body and all the bruised places returned to normal."

"Can anyone heal themselves this way or do you have to have Dorie D'Angelos' special doctor's touch?"

"Oh, my doctor had nothing to do with this. This happened when I was still living in Canada. I hadn't met my doctor then. You know, when you're cooking and the grease comes up and burns you? Well, you'll have a blister, but if you can catch it fast enough the blister goes right down. I never put a bandage on my blisters anymore, I just hold them real, real tight and sometimes hold the blister under the cold water tap while I'm doing it. If you hold it long enough—even after the pain is gone—you'll be completely healed. André told you about his fingers, didn't he?"

He had indeed. It seems that André was doing something down at the printing shop when a wire snapped back and slashed across three fingers of his right hand. Instantly the blood began to well up from the three deep cuts. He knew they were deep and the pain was terrific but since he was all alone and had no way to get to a doctor, he remembered Dorie's self-treatment and grabbed his right hand with his left. He squeezed for all he was worth, telling his body it pained twice as bad as it really did. He hung on for about fifteen minutes after the bleeding had stopped. Today there is not even a thin line to tell you where the deep gashes had been.

Dorie teaches all the children that come to her how to do this self-healing. "Suppose they get hurt in the schoolyard. Well, I tell them squeeze the hurt and call your angel in. And, boy, they heal up so fast there are no bruises or sprained ankles at all. Children are wonderful receptacles for healing."

I had another question: "Suppose a small baby, unable to understand about angels and healing, falls and is cut. And the mother can't explain to him . . ."

"I think the mother *can* explain no matter how small the child. Words are not the only way to communicate, you know. A mother's mind is strong enough to somehow get the picture to the child of the pain going away. Because when you are treating children you always take away pain. A mother's love and concern is worth more than a hundred pills and injection needles."

"Dorie, why do you think you have been given this gift of healing?"

"Oh, I haven't any gift. Please don't make me out as somebody special. I'm just an instrument. God is doing the work. It has nothing to do with me. Anyone who will allow themselves to become an instrument of God's power can do what I do. My doctor has to have me because he needs the power, vibration, magnetism, or whatever it is that comes out of my hands. He works up a condition in my body and uses it to change the person's physical structure. I'm never tired because he is flowing energy *through* me, not taking it *from* me. Do you understand the difference?

"Without him or without the angels or without Jesus, I can't do anything. If someone said, 'Heal me,' then I'd have to ask inside for one of those people to come. Dorie has no power. God does."

# "God's Been My Friend"
## (Della Reese)

Miss Della Reese, one of America's most popular and talented singers, was almost killed in 1971 when she walked through a pair of glass doors at her summer vacation home. By all normal calculations she should be dead now, yet she survived and considers the experience a great "help."

Oral Roberts, the minister, teacher, and healer from Tulsa, Oklahoma, had Miss Reese on his "Oral Roberts Presents" program one Sunday morning to tell his viewers what happened. It is the story of another healing. One more reason to "believe."

"God's been my friend for a very long time," said Della. "He really loves me very much. We had plate glass doors. I thought the doors were open but my daughter had closed them. I hit the door full force and it split across in two pieces. I fell over the bottom half of the door and couldn't get myself up. Then some force from behind me—I know it was from behind me—reached in and grabbed me by the forehead and pulled me up. Just as He pulled me out of the way the top half of the glass fell. If I had been there just a second longer, it would have guillotined me in two. I had a thousand stitches and lost seven pints of blood and they said that maybe I wouldn't walk or if I did walk, maybe my leg would be stiff because I'd severed my knee cap. They said I wasn't going to make it but they didn't know what they were talking about. Because He was right there and I was getting better all the time and the doctors didn't even know it."

"What did you do?" asked Oral Roberts.

"Well, I'm one of those who believes that if you just let go and let God, it'll be all right. I didn't do anything. I just kept my faith and He did everything that had to be done. Everything they said couldn't be done He did. They said I'd never walk straight. I walk as good as you do.

"They said I'd never really be the same. I feel better now than I felt before it happened. It helped me physically and it helped me mentally. I think that God has a way of setting you down so you pay some attention to what He's trying to say. I think that's what that was all about. He's corrected a lot of things and physically I feel great."

"What do you call this?" asked Mr. Roberts. "Trust in God?"

"I don't know whether it's faith or trust or belief or . . . I'm not too hung up on words. You see, I don't know what the name of it is. I know that I have it and He knows I've got it and we get along good because of it."

# II
# Charles Cassidy

Charles Cassidy has the power. Make no mistake about it. There is something that runs through him that is able to cure, and he is able to call upon it and make it work in almost every case. I myself saw him place his hand on two different people and each time watched as their bodies began to glow with the power he sent into them. The man has it.

And yet to look at him or talk to him you'd think he was anything but a healer or a spiritual man. He looks amazingly like Archie Bunker of "All in the Family" and he even talks from the corner of his mouth, with a slight Brooklyn accent. But unlike Archie, Cassidy doesn't speak ill of anyone. He works day and night—in a church and in his home—helping anyone who comes to him, providing they can get an appointment. He never charges for his services but will, like all the other healers, accept whatever is given him. With his amazing healing record and the offers he has had from well-heeled patrons he could be one of the wealthiest men in the healing business today. But he isn't. He makes enough to live on, to send his two teen-age boys to school and support his wife Alice. The man is not greedy. He's one of those *avis rara:* a man dedicated to helping others.

A charming English lady, Suzanne Crayson, first told me about Cassidy. I was off writing *The Psychic*

*World of California* when she sent me a letter asking me how could I have not included Charles Cassidy in my collection of psychics and healers in that book. A close personal friend, she had been keenly interested in whom I had interviewed as I researched it. She herself had gone to several healers for a rare hereditary disease that is making her bones gradually dissolve. Cassidy was the first man to give her energy and to take away the pain. She wrote that "his touch was like an electric shock" and added "he is far superior to any other healer I've ever visited."

The reason I hadn't included him in my previous book was that, quite simply, I'd never heard of him. He is not a man who seeks publicity. He does not like to lecture to groups, to brag about his abilities, or to talk to reporters. He doesn't consider what he does anything special. He has it and that's it.

Charles and Alice Cassidy came to Los Angeles from New York in 1956. They had met while working in the same office, had fallen in love, and had wanted to get away from the bad weather on the East Coast. After a brief stopover in Phoenix, they decided to go on to Los Angeles.

Alice got a job immediately, but it was more difficult for Charles. Work was scarce and employers thought he was just out for the winter. Finally, he was given a job in a cemetery. He loved it and in a year and a half worked himself up from clerk to foreman. In 1972 he started doing his healings on a full-time basis.

The Cassidys live in a two-story house in an inner court of other similar houses. It is not in the best area in town but it's not the worst either. It's halfway between Hollywood and the downtown commercial district. The house is scattered with mementos of their life together, with oil paintings people have given them, and with other canvases that Alice has painted. There are also angels and pine trees and little mobiles that Alice makes as a hobby and sells for a church at Christmas time. The downstairs is comfortable and homey.

Upstairs, in their bedroom, Charles does his healing. There are twin beds, some paintings on the wall, a dresser, and two lamps. He brings the clients up into this room, asks them to take off their shoes, and has them lie down on one of the beds.

Then he'll lean against the far wall, cigarette in hand, and out of the corner of his mouth will tell the person (if he is a newcomer) what to expect.

"I don't work like any other healer," he'll say. "So if you have any preconceived notions, forget 'em. I don't sing songs, I don't chant, I don't light candles or burn incense. Let the others do that. I don't say prayers either. I just act as a channel for the power that comes through me. Now don't ask me where this power comes from because I don't know. There is a higher intelligence and that's where it comes from, maybe, but don't ask me to prove it. And another thing. I work alone. I don't have any spirit guides in the room with me or any band of angels helping me or anything like that. I just put my hand on you and the power comes.

"Now sometimes strange things happen to the people who are getting this power. Strange things in their minds or strange things to their bodies. I won't tell you what sort of things because then you'd accuse me of planting an idea in your head. All I want from you is to tell me when you are feeling anything out of the ordinary. Anything at all. Understand?"

The patient will, from his flat-on-his-back position, mutter an okay.

"Now I'll probably talk about lots of things and you do the same. If you want to talk, go ahead. Nothing sacred here. No fancy words or comportment. Just relax and be yourself. Okay?"

Again the patient mutters an okay.

"Now the only thing I ask is that for the next two

minutes you don't say a word. I'm going to sit on the other bed and I want two minutes of silence from you. Then I'll move over and place my left hand on your solar plexus. When I do that you can start to talk."

There is another okay and Cassidy sits on the edge of the other bed. He lowers his head and places the thumb and forefinger of his left hand on his closed eyes. For two full minutes this gray-haired, green-eyed, round-bellied Archie Bunkerish-looking man communicates with something, somewhere. His presence is so domineering that the patient on the bed wouldn't dare as much as cough during this time. True to his word, there is no music, no candles, and no "stage setting." It's just that one solitary unpretentious man.

Before I went for my first interview with him I had met him at a dinner party and had taken a Brazilian friend of mine to see him. He had a bad knee that two chiropractors had worked on to no avail. An osteopathic surgeon had told him he "needed" an operation. He asked me to take him to a healer. I took him to Cassidy.

He stretched out on the bed and after the silence Cassidy moved and sat beside him. He put his left hand on my friend's abdomen—even though he knew it was the knee that needed work. Now I have been in many "psychic" places and seen many "psychic" things, but I was not prepared to see a current of light run down Cassidy's arm and into my friend's body. I was not prepared to see his body light up like a white neon tube and stay that way while I rubbed my eyes, glanced around the room to see if other things were glowing, and fidgeted into another position on the only chair in the room.

He told Cassidy, at various times during the healing, that he felt himself growing taller, that he felt fingers working on his knee (Cassidy's hand was on his abdomen), and at one point felt "a screwdriver screwing something into my knee cap." And, that night, his knee was better than it had been for weeks. He never needed the operation. So I was prepared well in advance for the kind of answers I wanted from Cassidy, but he began by telling me how to write the book.

"First thing I want you to remember," he said in his corner-of-the-mouth Bunker-style, "is not to get people's hopes up that a miracle will happen to them. I am a healer, not a miracle worker. No one consistently produces miracles. They work within laws. Sometimes the phenomena appears to be a miracle, but nine times out of ten it isn't."

His wife Alice came into the living room with a tray of coffee, which she put on a near-by table. She is slender and brown-haired. She and Charles made beautiful point-counterpoint during the two lengthy interviews I had with them. I was glad she was there because, sometimes, to get an answer from her self-effacing husband was like pulling a tooth. He doesn't mind talking about what he does. He just doesn't like to talk about himself.

Alice added to what he had said. "You can say anything in print, but you have a responsibility to your readers not to word things in such a way so that someone thinks 'if I get into that presence, that presence is God and I'll be immediately cured' or 'if I go to that person he will immediately solve my problems.'"

I agreed with her and recalled some of the desperate letters I received as a result of my book *Drum and Candle*, with people wanting to mortgage everything and fly to Brazil for a miracle-healing. But here was a man whom I had personally seen effect a cure. If he *couldn't* cure someone, was it because of that person's karma?

"I don't put any limitations on healing," he told me, settling back into the sofa with a cigarette in one hand and a cup of coffee in another. "In other words,

I believe anybody can be healed. I get very good results, as you know. I get results that used to startle me. They don't startle me anymore. I just had a terminal case of atherosclerosis. You know, when fat globules pile up in the connective tissues of the arteries. I gave him twenty treatments and he's as good as new."

"Twenty treatments?" I asked. "How old was the patient?"

"It was a man of sixty-five. He was a professor at one of the universities. One of the big ones here. He came to me after he had been to a lot of other doctors and they had all told him he hadn't a chance of getting well. They 'encouraged' him by letting him know he would become senile and then have a very quick death. His veins were so clogged, you know. He told me he was already doing very strange things in his personal life that scared him. He saw senility just around the corner. I would say that he was really a desperate man.

"Well, I went to work on him and he complained that he felt a terrible burning inside him. He couldn't stand to take the treatment too long. He said the heat was incredible. Well, now he's much improved and is back lecturing again. His doctors put him into a hospital and ran all sorts of tests but they can't figure out how this change could have taken place."

"Were you surprised when this burning started?" I asked.

"I'm never surprised at anything. It's not me that is doing the work. But I told him he would get better. I knew he would."

"How do you know?" I asked. "Does some little voice tell you or do you just feel?"

"I feel. Sometimes I hear. Sometimes I see pictures. I don't tell that to the average person. The average person who is dangerously ill, you have to figure out beforehand. Certain people you don't say anything to. Certain ones you talk to. Others come to you scared.

Now many people become frightened of this. I've had many, many people frightened. Many people come to you after they've been to twenty, thirty healers. They've been to hypnotists, all kinds. I worked on a woman today. She's got cancer of the face. Never saw her before. I looked at her and asked her if she felt anything *before* I touched her. As soon as she told me what she felt—and I hadn't laid a hand on her yet—I knew curing her would be a cinch. I knew. Even without touching her. She was getting a sharp reaction.

"And healers fool themselves. There are many healers in this town as you probably know. They're not frauds in the strict sense of the word but they fool themselves. They embroider. Many people think that heat has a lot to do with this. In other words a person will come to you and say they've been to such and such a healer and the heat from his hand was terrific. But that doesn't mean anything, because you can put a hot water bottle in bed with you and feel *heat*. Right? It's what happens. It's not just the heat. So a lot of people who can generate heat in their hands think they're healers. But they're not."

"But when you heal, does your hand get hot?"

"Yes. Sometimes it burns. This man with the atherosclerosis, he screamed from the burn. Not from my hand but from what was passing through me. It gets abnormally hot to the person. To me, it just feels warm. Now people with cancer, too, will burn like a match. This man would scream and tell me to stop. I would stop momentarily and then go back. Now the manifestation in this thing that really freaks people out is, like in this man, I would touch his neck where the stoppage was most prevalent and he would burn. Then I'd switch and touch his knee and he felt nothing. That's how quick it turns on and off. Which I don't guide or control."

"The power backed off," put in Alice, "when it wasn't needed at the knee."

"There's an intelligence guiding this. I've discussed this subject many times with the people at the Southern California Society for Psychical Research and they say there's no intelligence. They call it a consciousness."

"It's a play on words," said Alice.

"There's an intelligence behind this," Cassidy repeated.

"Let's get back to my first question. What about the people you and other healers cannot heal? Does that mean they are fated for that particular illness? Do you believe in Karma?"

He skirted the issue by pausing and looking at his wife. "I have to be completely honest with you," he said. "I have never run into one I couldn't help."

"That's quite a statement," I said.

"That's quite a statement, yes, but Alice will back me up on it. For various reasons people don't get healed, but I don't think it has anything to do with what you call Karma."

"Why?" and this was very important.

"Okay. I will cite an example for you. I worked with a man in the Valley here that had a very deadly ailment. In fact, he was at the point of suicide. From the pain. His wife contacted me through somebody else and I went and saw the guy. The guy immediately wanted to know what kind of books I'd read on the subject. Immediately wanted me to know how much he knew. Now, I'm a very unorthodox healer. You've seen me work, you know I talk and smoke cigarettes when I work on 'em, etc. But it turns a lot of them off. Okay. I went to this guy three times. I know what I could have done for him, but they didn't want me to come back. In their opinion, I was not an esoteric healer."

"And it had nothing to do with smoking," put in Alice, "because they both smoked."

"I was just not an esoteric healer. That's all. Okay. I don't dress it up. I don't put on a different act when

I'm working. I'm the same guy then as I am now. A lot of people want mystery. Now I worked with a woman who had a tumor on her foot . . ."

I pulled in the reins, delighted that he was talking, but not wanting him to get ahead of himself. "Let's go back to the man first. What eventually happened? You were not able to help him because he refused . . ."

"No. They just didn't like the way I operated. I wasn't esoteric."

"But you went to him three times."

"But his wife stopped me from coming back. I don't know how much he improved during those treatments because he was in such pain and was usually highly drugged. It's difficult to work with a drugged person."

"Charles did relieve the pain," said Alice, "but the man couldn't tell him very much of what was happening."

"Most of the people that I work with, I can't tell them what I feel. What I feel inwardly. I can't go up to a person and say, 'Look, you're dying of cancer and have to stick with me because I can cure you.' I can't tell them that. So a lot of people quit for various reasons. I had a woman come to me for a very major problem. Mary W. . . . something. I was doing tremendous with her. She called me up one day and said she wasn't coming back. I asked her why. She said she had told the neighbors about what I was doing and they said she was crazy."

"And yet she herself knew she was getting better," I said.

"That's right," he replied. "Physically. You could see it."

"Well," I added, "this book is for the Mary W.'s of the world. And the message should be, 'to hell with what the neighbors think.'"

"Either they know all about it or else they fall into the middle road of thinking they know most of what healing is about or else they get influenced by a friend who will tell them, 'What are you doing? Calling on the aid of the devil?'"

"The devil?" I was amazed.

"Don't be surprised. You've got people who'll not come to you even though they know they're dying. Because they think you're working for the devil. Now there are a couple of Christian religions in this country that believe in healing, but only through the touch of Jesus. Anybody else's touch is the touch of the devil. And you got another type. I don't know if you ever ran into these kind or not, but this type believes that in order to be cured of one ailment they have to receive another in its place. I call them traders. Now how about that? Did you ever run into anybody like that?"

"In other words, you would take away their cancer but give them T.B.?"

"That's right. They want to know, what are you going to give me for this? Like we're going to barter over a car or a TV or something. A lady came to me with tumors. Her husband had told her these guys can do this but watch out what he's going to give you in place of that tumor. Now as far as regards Karma, I only think about things like that when I work with people."

Alice leaned forward as I was about to ask a question and asked me one. "Wait a minute," she said, "before you get any further, what is your definition of Karma?"

"My definition is," I started, "something that you have to experience in this lifetime because of a happening in a previous lifetime. I believe in reincarnation."

"This is not for the book," Alice said. "We don't."

"Why isn't it for the book?" I asked. "Many people don't believe in it."

"Well," she explained, "many, many people he works with believe in reincarnation and many do not. He doesn't want to get embroiled in any controversy, so he just tells them it doesn't matter what you were in a previous life, it's what you are in this life that counts. Which is true."

"Put it in this way," Charles spoke up; "that I myself don't pay any attention to past lives because this is the life that counts. Obviously, if you want to take the definition of Karma as the law of cause and effect, naturally, anybody who has an illness is reflecting a cause."

"But not necessarily of a previous life?" I asked.

"No." They both answered together.

"The people who come to me and are firm believers in reincarnation, I don't try to upset with my own views. They're sick and didn't come to hear me tear down their ideas. So I skirt the issue very easily. This is what you're concerned with right now. Not Egypt or Italy or the Roman Empire, but right now. That's why you're here.

"Now another thing I run into," he continued, "are people who are very involved in metaphysics. They are metaphysical intellectuals. They start letting me know that they know all about what I'm doing. So I listen to them for about five minutes, then I turn them off. I say, 'Of course, you realize I'm beyond all that.' They say, 'Oh. Yes.' And it shuts them up."

"If not," I said, "you'd sit and listen all day to what Madame Blavatsky said about something or other."

"Right. They go on and on, and it doesn't have any bearing on the problem that brought them to me in the first place."

"While we are on problems," I ventured, "what do you consider your 'problem' cases?"

"Mental ones. No question about it. I try to skirt those. They're very hard." When I asked why, he continued, "I have a theory on them. And I'm sure I'm right because I've seen it evolve over the years. I believe that if I have to take something *from* you, it's easy."

"Like a growth," added Alice.

"That's easy. I'm taking away something that don't belong there. The hardest thing is to put something back that you don't have. That you need. Like erosion of a bone or a disintegrated hip socket. To put something back or rebuild something, that takes time. The easiest is taking something away. I'm not afraid of cancer. That's taking away something. There is nothing I back off from. But a mental problem, now, that's because something that should be there, isn't. Do you follow me?"

I nodded.

"I have worked with Huntington's Chorea. Have you ever heard of it? No? It's a genetic thing. It affects them mentally through the nervous system. That's all I know about it. I have worked with scleroderma, which is strangulation by your own skin. I have worked with osteomyelitis, a deadly bone ailment. Marrow of the bones. I have worked with leukemia and aplastic anemia, which is kin to leukemia. I have worked with brain blood clots. I just finished working with a guy who went blind from three blood clots on the brain. Now he can see. I have worked with double vision and cataracts. Those are the easy ones. Now I'll tell you the hard ones. I've worked with Addison's disease. I've worked with bleeding ulcers. Emphysema. I've worked with almost everything. Most of the common things people have."

When I asked about Parkinson's Disease and tuberculosis he admitted he'd never had a case of either of them, yet he did say that he's cured bone cancer and "innumerable women with female problems. Tumors of the uterus, they're easy."

That very morning the Los Angeles *Times* had had a front page photo of ex-movie star Shirley Temple. She'd had a breast removed. It had been cancerous.

"I saw that, too," Cassidy said sadly. "How I wish she had come to me before she went into surgery. I've worked with a breast cancer case. It dissipated immediately. Ten minutes."

"That was a case that people would call a miracle," said Alice. "Right in front of his eyes. It vanished. The woman almost went out of her mind. Just one treatment."

"I worked with a girl who had a birth defect. She was thirty-two years old and all her life one foot was shorter than the other, one hip higher than the other. She straightened out. And she, in the beginning, was a nonbeliever. She believes now!" He laughed, remembering. "She went through all kinds of weird experiences while I was working on her. She felt like she was swelling. She felt like her legs were being pulled. Once when she was walking down the street she fell because her whole style of walking started changing.

"Before I forget ... there are many people who go through a surgical procedure when I touch them that really flips them out. They describe a cutting, a stitching. Especially tumor cases. One gal came to me with a prolapsed bladder, whatever the hell that is ..."

"Her bladder," explained Alice, "was right under the pelvic bone, on top of her uterus. Apparently there was some muscular weakness and it had fallen down and she was in a bad way."

Her husband nodded. "She was facing major surgery and was very frightened. Well, she got cured, but she didn't tell me she also had a tumor in her uterus. She didn't tell me that; she just told me about the bladder. So one night when I was working on her she suddenly started burning and then she described going from hot to cold almost like an anesthesia or a numbness. Then she felt a cutting and a stitching."

"While this was going on, what was your hand doing?" I interrupted.

"Touching."

"Nothing more? You didn't know what she was feeling? No? So, if she hadn't told you, you never would have known that she was undergoing these various sensations?"

"I felt nothing," he replied.

"Then," I continued, "it wasn't the case of a spirit guide standing beside you saying, 'Charles, now we are opening this, now we're stitching that . . .'"

"No. Nothing like that at all. Most of the time I work from the solar plexus. Seldom does my hand go anywhere else but to the chest or a knee or the neck. I had another woman who came to me with a thyroid condition. Surgery facing her. This was weird. She described an operating room. She saw herself in this operating room and being operated on, but she was conscious. She also made me stop in the middle of the treatment because she said she was choking on her own blood."

"She was talking quite plainly," added Alice, "but that was the sensation she was having."

"Now, another thing. For many people my hand goes inside their body. And that must be weird. Yet I've never been on the receiving end of any of this. I have no idea what these people are feeling. Only what they tell me. But that hand going inside their body must be a very weird experience." He turned to his wife. "Do you remember that boy that came here from Washington, D.C.? He was facing heart surgery. This kid described my hand doing something to his heart between beats. Inside his heart. Between beats!"

"Where was your hand?" I asked.

"Just on his chest. Sitting lightly over the heart area." He lit another cigarette. "Now I want to stress that my hand does *not* go into the patient's body. What goes into the body is an *extension* of this hand. This hand extends itself into your body because it has to go into you. If it has to perform surgery then it has to get inside your body. Right? Science has proven that we all have a magnetic field around us. An occult person calls it an aura. It's the same thing. My aura extends, or my magnetic field extends, or my etheric body extends—whatever name you want to give it—itself to go into yours. If you need surgery."

"Sometimes it goes in even when he doesn't know a person needs surgery," said Alice. "He worked with a doctor last week . . ."

"Yeah, and he's afraid I'm going to tell everybody his name because he's a doctor . . ."

"But it was in a group just for the purpose of demonstration and yet this doctor said, right in front of everybody, 'Your hand is inside my chest.' Now I was there, too, and all I could see was Charles's hand on the man's chest."

Cassidy chuckled, remembering the doctor's face. "Now another phenomenon that happens, and I run into this every day, is a person will feel himself getting taller. There was a little lady here yesterday—just under five feet—and she told me, 'I feel as if I'm seven feet tall.' Now the theory here, I think, is that, of course, their physical body is not getting longer but their etheric body, or their aura, is. It's getting longer because it's getting charged. The thing that's been around them all their lives is suddenly increased by about a foot. So, therefore, they feel taller."

He shifted position on the sofa. He is an active man and not used to remaining in one spot. "I was working with a lady today that I've been working on for quite awhile and she came into the room and she said to me, 'Now, you're going to think I'm crazy,' and I said, 'No, I'm not,' and she said, 'As soon as I walk into this room I can feel the force moving right toward me and you're not even touching me.' I said, 'That's natural.'"

Alice refilled my coffee cup. "One night," she said, "a woman came over here who can't drive so she had a friend bring her. So while the patient was upstairs, I sat down here and chitty-chatted with the friend. I'd never seen her before. As the patient was ready to go, the friend said to me, 'You know, I had such a bad toothache when I came in here. I haven't been able to eat all day long. And now it's gone.' The next day she went to her dentist to have root canal work done and her tooth was still numb. So numb that the dentist worked on her without having to use any novocain. I thought that was interesting."

I had to agree that it was.

"Another thing that brings people out," said Cassidy, "is they will see colors when I work on them. And they don't tell you because they figure you'll think they're nuts. But you can't say to them beforehand, lady or mister, do you see colors, because they'll think you planted the idea in their minds. So you have to be very quiet in what you say. You keep asking them, 'Okay now, tell me what's happening. Tell me.' Because I work by past performances. Like a guy doping horses. You look at a horse and see what he did in New York. What he did in Chicago. It's the same thing with this. Past performances. You go on how other patients with the same problem reacted.

"And then there are the explainers . . ."

"The explainers?" I asked.

"Yeah. People who explain all this stuff to themselves so they can accept it. Because they don't want to really accept the truth of it. A member of a family gets cured and all the others will explain it as 'coincidence.' It would have happened if the person had stayed home on the couch. Some people get very cold. Others get very hot. The cold ones say I must have a window open. The hot ones say that I've turned up the furnace. They keep hammering away to come up with an explanation. And also, I'm sure I told you, there are people who come to you and get so completely frightened they never come back."

"Frightened of what?" I wanted to know. "Do they think there is a ghost in the room?"

"They believe that I am not an ordinary person and they figure if they are dealing with an *un*-ordinary person, then God only knows what's liable to happen. A physical therapist woman—I guess that's a high-class way of saying a massager—came to me with emphysema. Medical science has no way to cure it so far. She didn't get a treatment; she came with another lady. Anyway, when they left the other lady said, 'Oh, Mr. Cassidy, I'm so glad someone like you can do these things,' and went on and on and got me embarrassed and she said she'd call me for an appointment for herself. But she never did. The patient told me she was afraid of me. Afraid of my magical powers. Isn't that a laugh? She'd rather continue with her illness than get a little iron in her backbone and come here for a treatment. She thought I was not an ordinary person."

"Charles Cassidy." I asked most solemnly, "are you an ordinary person?"

"Absolutely."

"Why?" I continued. "What you do is *not* ordinary."

"No, what I do is not ordinary. But *I* am an ordinary guy. I believe . . . I believe . . . that many, many people can do what I do. And they don't know it. I believe that half the people in state mental institutions are psychic. They have the abilities but don't know how to handle it."

"You know," I said, "people like you used to be thrown in jail or stoned to death or drowned at the bottom of a well for doing what you do."

"I know that," he said calmly.

"In another era you would have been killed for your powers," I went on.

"He's an extraordinary human being," Alice put in quickly.

"I'm just an ordinary human being," he protested.

"Because of his unboundless patience with people. He has compassion for everyone, whether he knows them or not. He wants to help the world."

"Now will you not talk that way?" he asked her,

and moved across the room to straighten a picture that wasn't the least bit awry.

"Now you've embarrassed him," I said.

"He can't take praise," she said, "but it's the truth."

He continued with his back to us, fussing with nothing.

"Charles," I said, "can this force heal a person who is not anywhere near you? Can you heal someone in Chicago, for example?"

Now that the conversation had gone back to what he did rather than what he was, he rejoined it eagerly. "Absolutely. I work with a hundred people every night and they are scattered all over the world."

"Absent healing," explained Alice.

"But how?" I asked, for I hadn't been expecting this. "Do you have a list? How long do you take with each one?"

"I blanket them all for fifteen minutes." He was back on the sofa. "But I don't go into meditation or anything like that. I line all these people up beforehand and I tell them, look when it's 9 P.M. California time, you sit down, relax, and think of me sending you lots of healing energy. I don't care what time it is in London. That's their problem. If it means they got to get up at five o'clock in the morning, then that's when they gotta get up.

"And I'll tell you something else that can be done with this. I can send this to a person and as soon as they feel it they can touch somebody else and *they'll* feel it. I did this with a woman in Detroit. I had worked with her personally and she told me her cat was ill. So I told her to hold the cat on her lap and to watch his reaction when she touched him at nine o'clock California time. As soon as it hit nine the cat would leap up and jump off her lap. 'Cause he got a jolt. She got it first and then transferred it to him. And he was cured.

"Now I have another theory about this. The smaller the person the easier it is to cure them. Children are much easier than adults. It isn't because they are children and are more willing to believe or any of that baloney; it's because they are small. The smaller the unit the easier it is."

"The easier it is to fill it with energy," I said. "A water glass is easier to fill than a washtub. Because of its size."

"Right," he said, "because it's a small unit. I once reached in and took a canary from the bottom of its cage. It was so ill it couldn't even hop onto its perch. All I did was hold it. In a minute it was happy and singing. Completely cured. The lady who owned it began to scream and cry worse than the bird ever did."

We talked about politics and a famous television star who came to him for a treatment, and I glanced at his watch to see that it was two minutes after nine. "I hate to remind you," I said, "but weren't you supposed to blanket the world at nine?"

"So?" he replied.

"He's been doing it," said Alice. "Can't you feel it? Think about yourself for a minute."

I thought and then recalled that just before his watch hand said nine I felt a shock run down my hand from the recorder microphone I was holding. It was as if something had short circuited. I remembered that I'd been surprised at the sensation for my recorder had never done that to me before. I told them about the shock.

"I can do this and talk about baseball or movies at the same time. It turns a lot of people off because they think it ain't spiritual to do healing and mundane things at the same time. They figure the spiritual should get my undivided attention."

"But he can literally divide his mind," his wife added. "He discovered this a long time ago. Picture his mind as a blank screen. Well, he can put two pictures on it divided half and half without any trouble."

Cassidy brushed away her explanation and said, "I

have an interesting story to tell you. A girl came in about seven or eight months ago. She's left-handed and she's an artist, and she has a cyst on some part of her wrist that makes it very painful when she moves her hand. Now she didn't have it removed because there was danger that surgery would also touch some nerves and that she didn't want. Now she also had some trouble with her ovaries and an old injury to her tail bone. But she didn't tell me about those things. She was only interested in getting rid of that cyst.

"Well, as soon as I touched her she began to complain of a pain in her tail bone but nothing at her cyst. Then the next treatment she felt various sensations in her female organs but still nothing with the cyst. Finally, when she was cured in both the other places, the intelligence went to work and took care of the cyst."

"Why?" I asked.

"Because they were the more important areas. The cyst was minor. The intelligence is not concerned with how she makes her money. She was concerned, but the intelligence wasn't. She was worried about her wrist. The intelligence knew the other areas were more important to her over-all health."

Another "why" question. "Why does this force sometimes make people feel pain or a burning sensation or ill at ease? Does it have to have this reaction?"

"In the beginning it stirs things up. It intensifies their problem. If you had a boil on your arm and a surgeon removed it without anesthesia, it's going to hurt. Now the intelligence doesn't make it hurt that bad, but it has to let you know that something is happening so that the rest of the body knows it and so that you know it, too. Anybody who comes to me with an ulcer, within five or ten minutes, they're going to throw up. Because the power is moving through them."

"If we can stop here for a moment," I said. "I have

a thought. The girl came to you for a cyst and you didn't know there was anything else wrong so you sat down with the intention of curing only the cyst. Right?" He nodded. "But the energy went first to her tail bone and then to her uterus and only lastly did it go to the cyst." Again Cassidy nodded. "So that means you have no *control* over this power."

"Right. I never said I did have control. I am used merely as a channel. They need me, for some reason, to send their power—this intelligence—from them into the patient. I'm merely the go-between."

"Have you ever sat down and tried to analyze where this power is coming from?"

"In the beginning we spent endless hours discussing it," Alice said. "We'd lie awake nights trying to figure it out. Finally, we just accepted it as something we could never really define. We had to, or it would have made us both basket cases."

"But I have a conclusion." He got up and walked to the other side of the room, then turned and pointed at me. "My conclusion is that this is a force that is outside my body. It may be only two inches away from me or it may be two hundred thousand miles away. And I can tap it. I've discussed this with others and they've said it comes from inside me. Well, I don't buy that because if it came from inside me then I'd be exhausted when I finished a healing. And I'm not! I can do twenty healings a day if necessary and not be tired. I've done as high as twenty-seven in one day."

"Do you feel it coming in to you?"

"Yeah. Right here," and he touched the right-hand side of his face. "It comes when I call it and sometimes, when there is someone in the room that needs a healing and I don't know anything about it, it will come *without* me calling it. It will just suddenly be there. And I'll feel it."

"If you decided one night not to bother with the

people on your healing list and refused to call in the power at nine, would it come anyway?"

"Probably. I don't know. It is an intelligence. It *knows* those people out there are waiting for it."

"How do you call it in? What special words or ritual do you have?"

"I don't really say anything. I just clear my mind. Very briefly. You've seen me before I gave a healing; you know about the two minutes of silence. Well, that's the time I need to clear my mind. Sometimes I'll say, 'I'm ready,' or, 'Okay, where is it?' or something like that. And it comes."

"If this is energy and nothing else but energy, then couldn't you do things like taking your hand and cutting a hole in the sofa? Just with your hands, if it is really nothing more than pure energy?"

"I've never tried that, no. But if this is pure energy, then I ought to be able to move your coffee cup, like they do in Russia. But I've never tried that either. I won't try it because it takes that woman four hours. Hell, I go through twenty people in four hours."

"If this is only energy, then do you think you could pick up a spliced wire and rejoin it through this energy?"

"No, I don't think so."

"Then it goes beyond the energy that lights these lamps."

"Yes," he said, "it goes way beyond. I always tell people, when they question me, it's beyond medicine, beyond science, and beyond comprehension."

"I think what David's getting at," Alice broke in, "is where you really believe this source is."

I could tell he didn't want to say it, but his wife's insistence left him no other choice. "It comes from some sort of divine source. That's the only way I can sum it up. I don't try to explain it anymore. I just accept it."

Charles Cassidy—this extraordinary man—was quite an ordinary man for the first twenty-four years of his

life. He was born in New York City, on September
29, 1919. He had two brothers and a sister and went
to the Roman Catholic church almost every Sunday.
He attended parochial schools and swears that he
never had a psychic experience when he was a child
and that no one in his family (in spite of the lep-
rechauns his grandparents must have known about
in Ireland) was the least bit psychic.

He was drafted into the army and wound up in a
hospital bed in North Africa. Malaria. The year was
1943. He had a very high fever and lost a great deal
of weight. But that wasn't what bothered him. The
pictures were what was bothering him.

"When I closed my eyes I saw pictures, like on a
televison screen. I called them newsreels. The pictures could be of anything and most of them had
nothing to do with me. But they were so startling
they would shake me up. Now they weren't my
imagination. I know when I'm imagining things.
These pictures would just suddenly appear and jolt
me. Sometimes they were in color. Sometimes they
were accompanied by sound. I was really frightened."

Yet when he confided in a hospital nurse about
them she just laughed and warned him not to tell the
doctors about it or they'd put him in the psycho
ward. So he never told anyone about them. Not even
Alice after they were married. He thought, by this
time, that everyone saw pictures and didn't feel they
were important enough to discuss. And he was always
just a little wary of that psycho-ward attitude.

It was while he was working in the Los Angeles
cemetery that his psychic knowledge began to grow.
He overheard Alice talking with a friend who had
been to a medium in their neighborhood and the
friend was amazed that the medium had been able to
tell her her mother's name. Cassidy thought that was
indeed something and decided if he went to that
medium and she gave him *his* mother's name, then he
would believe.

So over he went on the night the medium held open house, paid his fifty-cents admission, and took a back-row seat. The medium was doing billet readings, giving answers to questions that were in sealed envelopes. Cassidy didn't write anything because he didn't have any questions. He was just curious.

"So the medium looks at me and she laughs. She laughs and says to me, 'I see you walking through tombstones and going into an office.' Boy, she hit it right on the head because I was working in the cemetery and I was always in and out of the office. Then she told me some other things that really wigged me out and then she made a prediction. I scoffed at this one because I didn't know how or why it could ever come true. She told me that sometime in the future I would be in great demand. That people would be coming from all over the United States to see me. I laughed then, but I ain't laughing now. She hit it right on the button."

That night, on their way home, Charles told Alice that he thought he could do what the medium had done. When Alice asked him to explain, he said that all the woman did was close her eyes, concentrate, and get a picture and it was this picture that she told about. "The only difference between her and me is that she can control it and I can't control mine."

"You can't control *what?*" Alice demanded, and then and there the whole story of his malaria and his "newsreel pictures" came to light.

Alice had read enough books on ESP, mind control, and psychic matters to understand what he was talking about, even though he didn't have a clue. When they got back to the house she asked him to concentrate on a picture and to tell her what it was. She would write it down and they would see if it later made any sense.

"So I did. I shut my eyes and the very first thing I get is a picture of some old man I ain't never seen in my life before and he's out in the middle of a field and marking off something with a shovel. I told her what I saw but it didn't make no more sense to her than it did to me.

"The next day I'm in the barbershop waiting to have my hair cut when I look up and there sits that old guy right in front of me, in the barber's chair! I recognized him immediately. So when he gets finished and is paying his bill the barber asks him, 'What are you going to do this weekend?' and he replies, 'I'm going out to the desert and I'm going to lay out a piece of land for my son to build a house on!' "

"Then he came home all excited," Alice said. "That was the start. He knew then that those pictures meant something and he was fascinated enough by them to want to continue."

They both started reading more on the subject and even wrote to Dr. Rhine at Duke University to tell him of their discoveries but they got a rather formal note in reply and decided not to bother scientists anymore. They did tell a third party, a friend named Renée, of their experiments and would send her copies of all they wrote concerning his pictures. Charles remembers one quite vividly.

"I got a picture of three men and a woman. They were sitting in the kitchen of a small apartment and they were plotting something. Even though they were speaking in Arabic, I knew they were up to no good and that they were planning some sort of trouble. Well, three days later Renée calls our attention to a story in the newspaper about the police in Beirut, Lebanon, looking for three men and a woman who were plotting to overthrow the government. Now I thought this was all very interesting but I was just getting things at random, and I started trying to control it.

"I didn't ask Jesus or Buddha or Krishna or anybody for help in controlling this. I just said, 'Whoever's out there, I want it.' I was sure that I was tapping into a stream of intelligence that knew everything. All I had to do was to tune myself in.

"You see, I also believe that, like the Bible says, coming events cast their shadows. When that clicked with me I figured the logical thing was to dope the outcome of a horse race. So I did it."

"Did you make any money at it?" I asked.

"Darn right, I did. The first time we tried it the evidence was right there. We got the winners but they came through symbolically. For instance, I got something about my sons. Or many sons. And that was the name of the horse that won; Many Sons. Then I had a picture about the sea and something about sailing. So we looked and there was a horse called Sea Clipper and we played him and he won. I used to tune into things that were to come in the far future, like the Kentucky Derby for instance. Two weeks in advance I saw the race being run in front of me. I saw the horse who was first, second, and third. I knew the names of the second and third places but the crowd was making so much noise I couldn't hear the name of the winner. So I drew a picture for Alice and showed her exactly how each number would finish. And this was before I had even seen a list of the possible contenders in that race."

"Well, now, many people consider this immoral," I said.

"Yeah. I know. But I don't. They say I'm wasting my talent. Well, I don't do this every day and I don't do it to cheat or defraud anybody. I think if I did use it to cheat someone, *then* it would be immoral. But what's a horse race? Everybody is betting anyway. What's the difference if I have an inside tip from the race track or from the stream of intelligence?"

"If you suddenly became very, very rich by picking all the horses in an important race, do you think you could continue to tap the intelligence for future races or would they take this ability away from you?"

He shook his head. "I don't think they'd care one way or another. I'm sure that right now there are many psychics that play the horses and they do it with this ability you're talking about. What we would be doing would be legal in the eyes of the law. We would never go to a bookie or anything connected with the underworld. But I haven't thought about doing this on a full-time basis because, frankly, I don't have the time. I have my healings to do and a family to support. If I had the time, I'd be doing it, however. I don't think there is anything wrong in it, but this 'intelligence' wants me for more serious things."

"Let's get away from the horses and back to patients," I said. "When did you first know you could heal?"

"Well, Alice here had a reoccurring throat ailment. She was always going to the doctor and he was always taking away the pain but he never took away the cause. And it wasn't just the fact that all that running around didn't do any good, but Alice would get depressed when she'd feel the pains coming on again.

"So one night she says, 'My God, this damn throat is starting up again!' So just like the hand of God was stepping in, I looked at her and said, 'Gee, I'm sorry to see how you're feeling. I wish I could do something for you.' And she said, 'Maybe you can, because from the books I've read, with your abilities you ought to be able to heal people, too. Why don't you try it?' I said, 'What am I supposed to do?' and that started it."

"He touched my throat and meditated on it. I didn't feel anything and neither did he. We both passed it off as a foolish experiment and went to sleep. And then the next morning I woke up and the pains were gone. And they've never come back."

"Once I knew I could do this then I'd start working with her on other things; I'd call it into me and she could feel it when I touched her."

"How did you call it in?"

"I don't know."

"If you didn't call it in the first time," I persisted, "why did you think you had to call it in after that?"

"I don't know why," he said simply, "it just came to me."

"He gets answers to things like that," Alice said. "Once when we had trouble with our old car and we took it to the garage the man checked it over and couldn't find anything wrong with it, but there was a rattle inside that we could all hear when it moved. So one night Charles got the answer that there was a pencil rattling around loose inside the dashboard. He went out, looked where the intelligence had told him, and there was a pencil that one of the kids had pushed in there."

"Yeah, and once when I was having trouble with a watch I bought, and had had it in and out of repair shops, the intelligence told me to bang it on the wall."

"Your watch?"

"Yeah. So I did. I banged it against the wall and it worked perfectly after that."

Charles Cassidy's abilities have been tested by Dr. Thelma Moss at U.C.L.A.'s Parapsychology Laboratory as well as the Southern California Society for Psychical Research. This was done by Dr. Barbara Brown at the Sepulveda Veterans Hospital. The tests showed that "something" was at work when he placed his hands on a patient, but they didn't go into enough detail for any positive conclusions. Maybe there aren't any, scientifically speaking, at this time.

Cassidy became Practitioner Cassidy late in 1972 when he was taken into a healing church in Los Angeles. He doesn't preach. He is listed as one of their "practitioners" and can be found there doing healings two or three times a week.

He continues to do his healings in his home in the evenings for friends, old clients, or those who can't make it to the church during the day.

Being a practitioner of the church has great meaning for Cassidy because one of the tenets of the church is healing through the laying on of hands. Also, many people are looking for "charisma or spirituality" and feel better about receiving his help now that he is actively a part of a church. That and the fact that he is a working member of TRY Foundation, a charitable organization dedicated to helping others "try" to help themselves.

"I don't know into what category you're going to put me in your book but I'm not a faith healer. Okay? Science has called what I do *magnetic* healing, but you don't have to put a name to it unless you want to."

"Yet you yourself are spiritual, aren't you?" I asked, as I gathered my paraphernalia together.

"No, I'm not."

"Yes, he is," insisted Alice.

"Okay," he grinned, "maybe I am ... a little."

"Is he becoming more spiritual the longer he does this?" I asked his wife.

"No, he's always been a very humble, very spiritual person. He is the essence of spirituality. I've met many, many people who think they are spiritual but they lack the things that Charles has. He's modest and he's also very honest. He can't say no to anybody who calls on him, no matter what the hour or how much he will have to change his own plans. He is truly his brother's keeper."

"One thing before you go," he said. "I want you to put in the book that faith has nothing to do with getting healed. A man who doesn't believe in anything can come here and I'll heal him.

"He doesn't need faith. *I* have the faith. I have the faith that I can heal him. That's what faith healing is all about. The *healer* has to have the faith. You got that?"

I nodded.

"Good. Because it's important."

And I knew it was.

# The Mysterious Handprint

The young man was rushed to the hospital with pneumonia. He had been taken ill while miles out on the Texas ranch where he worked. Not having heard from him for a couple of days, a fellow worker rode out to his secluded cabin and found him unconscious on the floor.

The hospital doctors said there wasn't too much they could do for him and put him in an oxygen tent after filling him with antibiotics. They placed him on the critical list and someone thought to telephone his mother.

The woman called her friends and a prayer chain was set up. For two days there was someone, somewhere, praying for the young man's recovery. The hospital hung a "no visitors" sign on his door.

On the morning of the third day the nurse made her customary check in his room. She was shocked to see his oxygen tent on the floor and the young man sitting on the edge of the bed.

He had been unconscious when they brought him there and seemed dazed to find himself in a hospital bed. The nurse hastily summoned the doctors, but the young man refused to have the oxygen tent replaced.

"I am okay now," he told them. "I was sleeping, I guess, and heard a voice telling me to wake up. When I opened my eyes I saw an arm coming down from the middle of that thing you had me under and I felt an open hand pressing on my chest. I tried to pull the arm away, but the voice said it was there to help me. It said it was making me well. Then that tent thing came off and fell over by itself."

The doctors ran the proper tests. His lungs were clear. His pneumonia had vanished.

And on his chest was the reddened imprint of a hand and five fingers.

# III
# Rosita Rodriguez

There is no psychic healer more controversial in the world today than Tony Agpaoa of the Philippine Islands. His methods are unique, his demonstrations bloody and upsetting, his cures fantastic. And his critics are vociferous.

He is small, dark, and oriental. His bedside manner is nonexistent and his methods are anything but orthodox. He has been accused of fraud, of performing magic, and of deception. His detractors have never been able to prove anything against him even though they've tried. And oh, how they've tried.

Tony is as unorthodox as they come. His *modus operandi* is quite simple. He asks the patient to stretch out on a table, raises their blouse or shirt (or lowers their trousers or skirt) so the flesh above the afflicted area is exposed. While an assistant stands ready with cotton and a basin of water he presses his finger tips into the area. Immediately the flesh opens and he slips his hands inside the wound. Blood pours out to congeal about six inches from the opening. His fingers search for the tumor, fibrous matter, or foreign object that must be removed. Once he has it, he snatches it out, removes both hands, and the wound closes over. Quickly the "incision" is swabbed with a piece of wet cotton. Away comes the bood and away goes the scar.

The operation is over. Usual running time: two to seven minutes.

The patient has felt no pain.

There has been no anesthetic.

There is no scar.

There has been no attempt at sterilization.

There are usually no postoperative aftereffects.

The operations have been described with such superlatives as "fantastic" "unbelievable," "incredibly rapid," "one hundred per cent effective," and "incredible."

Naturally, the American Medical Association has looked askance at Tony's methods and has banned him from working in the United States. The British Medical Association allows him over there, but he may not open bodies. In other places, such as India, Mexico, etc., he does things his way.

Plane loads of Americans have gone over to his hilltop town of Baguio with all sorts of ailments and afflictions. The majority of them return healed. Crutches are left behind as are thick eyeglasses, trusses, and wheel chairs. He is not one hundred per cent effective with all who seek him out but then what medical doctor is? Those who have gone there and have returned in the same condition have been the ones who are most vindictive against him. They've seen what he did for others and can't understand why he didn't do the same for them. He believes that Karma can hinder his healing techniques as it does for all other healers.

I had heard of Tony Agpaoa long before I'd met anyone who had undergone one of his operations. In Brazil, as I watched the now-deceased healer Arigó at work, I knew that there was a man in the Philippines who could do the same thing. I read about Tony in several magazines and in the prestigious *Psychic News* of London. Then I met Mr. and Mrs. Ray Makela of Palo Alto, California. They had gone to see Tony and they had a movie film to prove it.

The Makelas are not "kooks" who run from occult group to witchcraft coven looking for thrills but are two normal people who were told by American doctors that there was nothing more they could do for them.

Mrs. Makela could not breathe through her nose. When she was a teen-ager the tubes in her nose had grown shut. She could take in oxygen only by breathing with her mouth. Doctors at the best West Coast hospitals told her they "could operate but we can't guarantee the results." She was also told that her forehead would probably be heavily scarred. Mr. Makela had a back problem. During World War Two he had injured his spine and could not bend from the waist or reach up over his head without excruciating pain. Doctors recommended an operation that would remove a "disc or two" but couldn't guarantee the results. The Makelas have a young married daughter who had two large unsightly tumors on her neck and shoulder. While not cancerous, their roots went deep into her flesh and, because of a heart condition, local doctors didn't want to take the chance and operate.

The Makelas heard of the Philippine surgeon, wrote to him, made an appointment, and managed to scrape up money for the fares. Mrs. Makela was the first one on the table. Her husband's hand held a small 8 mm. movie camera loaded with color film. In these pictures you can see Tony smiling at the woman as she glances up rather worriedly at his hands. While she says something to him, his fingers suddenly part the flesh between her eyebrows. The blood runs down her face. His hands work quickly and he pulls out small round bits of something that shine like fat globules and puts them into a basin an assistant holds. You note that he wears no gloves nor mask over his mouth. He's peering into the open wound, breathing in there, naked fingernails prodding. Mrs. Makela says something and Tony laughs. Then his hands come out and he swabs the already closed wound with some wet cotton. He wipes away the blood. There is no scar. Mrs. Makela puts her hand up to where, just seconds before, bone and muscle had been exposed. Then she smiles and gets nimbly off the table. Her operation didn't take any longer than it took you to read about it.

Then Ray, her husband, got on the table. He was shirtless. Tony's hands darted at his spinal column and a gaping wound opened. Immediately the Filipino's fingers were inside, working rapidly and giving off flashes of light. (I claim the light from his fingers is energy; skeptics claim it's simply reflection from the naked bulb hanging overhead.) Out came the hands, the wound closed as if it were on a zipper, and the scar was swabbed away. For good measure Tony then operated on Ray Makela's hemorrhoids and that operation took less than three minutes.

Their daughter then sat on the table. Tony had wrapped her in a sheet with her shoulders exposed. The lumps on her neck and shoulder were quite visible. The flesh on her neck opened on contact and his fingers pulled out some long fibrous matter. He swabbed the opening and it closed immediately. This was repeated on her shoulder and when he finished wiping away the congealed blood it was more than evident that both lumps—which had been there just minutes before—were completely gone.

The operations on these three people, performed with no pain and a minimum of fuss, did not take longer than fifteen minutes in all. In the most advanced U.S. hospital a team of doctors and nurses performing these operations would have taken several hours. And there would have been pain. There would have been scars. There would have been drugs and postoperative shock. As it happened, the Makelas put on their bathing suits and went swimming in the sea that afternoon.

"Impossible," say the critics. "Fraud" shout several doctors. "Hypnotism" charge others. Yet the Makelas were cured. Mrs. Makela now breathes normally for the first time in years. Mr. Makela has no pain when he bends over or reaches up. Their daughter now buys clothes to show off her smooth shoulders, not clothes especially chosen to hide the ugly lumps.

"The film was doctored," continue the critics. "The camera was made to lie." Yet the Makelas took their own camera and film to the Philippines. No one else handled it. They returned and had the film developed in California. It didn't get any special processing; it was just sent through the Kodak mill. The only place it could have been tampered with was at the Kodak plant and why in the world would *Kodak* go to the expense of doctoring up an amateur film? The Makelas had no reason to doctor the film, either. They don't need celluloid proof they were healed. They *know* they were healed. (The Makelas are not the only people who have filmed Tony at work. Amateur movies of him at work abound all over the United States. Several scientific films on Tony have also been made, many of them played back in slow motion trying to catch him in some sort of chicanery. One investigator told me: "If he's not the greatest psychic surgeon in the world, then he is the world's greatest sleight-of-hand artist.")

In several cases people have managed to bring back the tumors and foreign objects that Tony has removed from their bodies for laboratory analysis. Often these objects have been declared mineral or animal rather than human. Here critics think they have "facts" to prove that Tony is practicing sleight of hand rather than medicine. Yet a Swiss parapsychologist once handed Tony a vial of human blood and asked him to concentrate on it. Tony held the vial in his hands, sending his energy through it. On analysis by a laboratory that knew nothing of where the blood had been it was declared "animal" blood. Tony's hand had actually changed the chemical content of the specimen.

Because of stiff AMA pressures Tony is not permitted to enter the United States. If you want him to work on you, you have to go to the Philippines, so when I learned that there was a lady in Chicago practicing Tony's brand of healing, I was very interested in meeting her.

They told me her name was Rosita Rodriguez. They said she was Tony's number-one pupil. That she had been trained by Tony personally and that she did his kind of operation. They also said that in order to get around the law she practiced in the office of the Panamanian Consulate in Chicago. That way she was technically not on United States soil.

I phoned Mrs. Rodriguez from Los Angeles and she agreed (much to my delight and surprise) to see me, but she lived in Oak Park, Illinois, not Chicago proper. I was rather startled that she had a low voice with a slight Germanic accent. I couldn't understand how a Philippine woman could sound like that but I put it down to a bad connection. Could I watch her work? Of course. Could I take pictures? No reason why not. I flew out to Oak Park.

The house she lives in is like all the others on the block of middle-class, two-story wooden houses. I grew up in one just like it in Warren, Ohio. It was snowing that morning and as I walked up the wooden steps a cat, who was waiting at the door, arched his back and glared at me. Cats usually like me, and I didn't know whether to take this as a good "omen" or not. Inside a two-tone chime sounded as I pushed the bell. There was a few seconds' pause and the heavy wooden door opened.

Instead of seeing a small, round, dark oriental woman, I was looking at a quite attractive fair-skinned, auburn-haired, tall, elegant lady. "I'm here to see Mrs. Rosita Rodriguez," I said. "I have an appointment."

"I know you do," she said in the same voice I recognized from the phone call. "I'm Rosita. Come in, please." The cat dashed in ahead of me.

I stepped in and she closed the door. As I took off my heavy coat she said, "I know what you're going to say. You didn't expect me to look like I do. Right?"

I laughed. "Right! With a name like Rosita Rodriguez I was expecting someone who looked like Tony Agpaoa."

She took me into the dining room where coffee and cookies were waiting. I plugged in the tape recorder as she served. "You've very light for a Filipino," I said.

"But I'm not a Filipino," she replied. "I am Austrian."

"With that name?"

"With that name. When I was born my parents named me Rosa. But a few days later my mother abandoned me in the hospital and I was put in an orphanage. Then when I was three years old a foster family took me. They decided to baptize me and gave me the name Rosita. I took their last name of Wendlik. Then later I married a Mexican-American named Rodriguez, and that's the story. My name seemed to fit in perfectly with the people I met in the Philippines. I speak Spanish and could communicate with them. It's funny," she smiled, "but I never really felt at home anywhere until I went to the Philippines."

She had done a lot of traveling before that, both in the world and in her dreams. "When I was ten years old I had this reoccurring dream that I was working with an old man in a hospital in some tropical country. I assumed it was Africa from the color of the patient's skins. I wasn't just a nurse, but a full-fledged medical doctor, and he was doing marvelous things for the people there. Eventually this dream crystallized into my thinking that I wanted to be a doctor. Then when I was twelve my parents sent me to Italy on a three month program where children of the war would get a chance to see how others lived. As fate would have it, the man whose family I stayed with was a doctor. He was a marvelous man and answered all my questions about medicine and healing. He also showed me a picture of a man in Africa named Dr. Schweitzer. It was the *same* man that had been in my dreams! That made me all the more certain that my lifework was to be helping people through medicine. I studied Latin and Greek and went to premed school and managed to get in a year and a half of medical school. I never did get to Dr. Schweitzer's clinic but he was always a guiding light for me."

Then she let her heart rule her head and fell in love with an American. They made plans to be married and she came over to the States. The affair fell flat but she had her permanent visa. She got a job in a clinic and soon met Mr. Rodriguez. Married, the two of them and a doctor set out for Mexico where a primitive tribe needed their assistance.

"The Mexican government will deny that this tribe even exists," she said, "but we saw them and we worked with them. They are the Taramara Indians and they live in caves along the sides of a cliff. They are so primitive that they wear loin-cloths and speak almost no Spanish. There is a small hospital there, run by six European nuns, but it is badly equipped and can't begin to aid the 125,000 Indians in the area. We were faced with problems like you wouldn't believe. Operations, under terrible conditions, were made more difficult by the fact that we didn't speak the nuns' language very well and during surgery communication has to be rapid and concise. We were able to do only fifty or sixty cases in a week. Those people were dying and we couldn't help them. Everybody needed something."

After they returned to the States she read an article about a man in the Philippines named Brother Terte. It told how he performed surgery with his bare hands and that there was no need for operating rooms, surgical equipment, anesthetics, or sterilization. The operations took only minutes instead of hours and the patients suffered nothing. "I felt that if what Brother Terte was doing in this primitive area was real, and if there was some way I could learn it, that it would be the answer to our problems down in Mexico. So I began a correspondence with Brother Terte and he told me if I came to the Philippines, he would teach me what he knew.

"About that time my mother was very ill with cancer. She was in Europe and I was in the United States. I asked Brother Terte to send her healing from the Philippines. She had a type of cancer where she would have died in great pain but he sent her absent healing, and she didn't have to take any drugs. She passed away in her sleep, never knowing what she died of. He told me he couldn't save her life, but he could save her suffering. He did."

Rosita began going to various psychic groups, studying their philosophies and reading everything she could find on the subject. When she heard that another Philippine healer, Tony Agpaoa, was coming to Chicago she read everything she could on him. "People were flocking to him like crazy," she recalls, "but because of the law he didn't open up any bodies; he worked only with magnetic healing. He placed his hands on the person and caused his energy to work inside the body, but his fingers never went in and he never drew blood.

"I took my mother-in-law to see him. She had a bad heart and her doctors had given her only six months to live. Tony had her lie down on a massage table and he covered her with a sheet. I didn't know then what he was doing because his hands were under the sheet all the time, but knowing what I know now I understand. There are some instances when magnetic healing has to be done very intently and when you have to concentrate that much power sometimes the person performing the operation is not always in complete control. I mean the healing may happen in a way they hadn't planned. It worked, because my mother-in-law is still alive and very healthy and that was in 1966. The doctors had given her six months to live, if you remember.

"The next day I brought in my little boy. He had a growth on his foot. It was painful and the doctors didn't want to operate because he was so little. Tony took a little bit of skin off the top and in three weeks the growth just peeled off.

"I had a problem too. Sinus. It was a chronic condition that was so bad that I had to take drugs around the clock. If I didn't and forgot my pill, in two hours I'd be deathly sick. I also had an arthritic vertebra in my back near my neck and it had gotten to the point where I'd lost mobility and would have to turn my entire body rather than just my head. The headaches were excruciating. Sometimes so bad that I'd black out. I'd been to hospitals and they'd told me that the vertebra was arthritic but they couldn't see how it was affecting me to that degree."

"What did Tony do?" I asked.

"It was a strange thing. He just manipulated a little bit back there and then he massaged the areas around my sinus. That's all. No operation, nothing. I had an appointment the next day and when I saw him I told him the sinus pains hadn't come back. He told me to throw away the pills. I waited a few days and then got rid of them forever. Then because my neck was hurting worse than it ever had, he gave me another manipulation. He said the pains would be gone forever. And they were. Just as quick as that. I've never had another headache because of it and I've never been back to a doctor for it."

During Tony's lunch break Rosita explained her medical background and asked if he thought she could learn to do what he did. He told her that he thought she'd make an excellent student and set a date for her arrival in the Philippines. She told him she'd try to make it by then.

"What do you mean *try?*" he asked her.

"I don't have the money," she explained. "I'll try to have it by then, but I'm not sure I'll be able to."

"Don't worry about the money," he replied. "You reserve the ticket and make your plans."

Two days before the flight was to leave, Rosita still lacked over half the money for the trip, yet she went ahead with her packing. The bell rang and when she opened the door, there stood a friend. "I know you want to go to the Philippines," she said, "and don't have all the cash you need. Here, take this." She shoved a packet of bills into Rosita's hand.

"I didn't want to take it," Mrs. Rodriguez recalls, "but I did because it was a sign that something was working for me over there."

Rosita expected to sit in a classroom, study books, and discuss healing techniques. There was none of that. Tony told her to make herself at home, to wander in and out the rooms he was operating in and to use his large library as she chose. Finally after a few days Rosita confronted Tony. "When am I going to start doing something?" she asked. "You're already doing it," was his cryptic reply. "Just relax and in time things will come."

She began to assist him at the operating table by holding the pan of water and handing him a wad of cotton. When he would go into the lowlands to treat villagers, she would accompany him. Once she went with him into the jungle to stop an epidemic of dysentery among a tribe of head-hunters. On their trips and during their breaks he would discuss his philosophy and his interpretation of the Bible. (Tony is an ordained minister of the Philippine Spiritualist Church.) "I got quite a bit of insight into the New Testament," Rosita recalls, "but after a few weeks of this I said, 'I'm trying to figure out what you're doing. I haven't got it yet, but there must be a way.'" He told her to "concentrate and meditate." "That was all the direction he ever gave me," she says, "just concentrate and meditate."

"When did Tony finally tell you you were ready?" I asked.

"We had many sessions where I would put my hands on people and he would make suggestions and show me the Yin and Yang theory and how to use it. He did teach me the mechanics of what he did. He showed me what and where meridians are, how to find them and how to concentrate healing energy into them. He finally allowed me to take a few patients of my own, always native women, and I'd cure them by the laying on of hands and his version of magnetic healing. It was really spectacular what happened to one woman. She came in a wheel chair. When she went out she was walking and pushing her own chair. Another woman was cured of breast cancer, and I did it only with magnetic healing.

"Then a native woman came to me for a uterus problem. She was hemorrhaging badly. I had her get onto the table and I pulled her skirt down so I could see her flesh. I swabbed her with some wet cotton and placed a wad of dry cotton right over the area that was giving her the most pain. I began to press on her abdomen with my finger tips when suddenly the cotton began turning red. I looked and saw that my fingers had gone into her body. I could see the opening they had made and could see the muscles and the blood. Some blood ran from the wound but congealed before it had time to spill off her belly. I put my other hand into the wound the way I'd seen Tony do so many times and began moving my fingers to attract the diseased tissue. I could feel her body heat. I was surprised and elated. I had wanted this for so long that I had decided it never would happen. That very day I'd told myself that it didn't matter if I never opened up a body because I could be of help in other ways. I guess that *not* trying for it finally made it happen. After that I worked with Tony for several months. I knew I had 'made it' and he knew it too. I was his first successful non-Filipino student and I became his assistant and Gal Friday."

She also became his missionary to the United States where she is dedicated to proving his philosophy through healing. She has divorced Mr. Rodriguez, the father of her four children (Rosita, Ricardo, Gregory, and Julio) but still sees him occasionally. He is also a healer, working with the Mexican community in the Chicago area. Rosita is a determined woman with the very difficult goal she set for herself. Surrounded by her children, her helpers, and all the people who clamor for healings, she somehow manages to remain apart, almost aloof. Maybe it's the way she carries herself. Maybe it's the way she speaks with such assurance. Maybe it's just the "woman" in her being pushed into the background in order that her healing mission be first and foremost. She is quite attractive and quite feminine in spite of her responsibilities and her being in command. I asked her if she thought of marrying again.

"My life wouldn't be fair to a man," she said. "I'm called out of bed at two in the morning because someone has something wrong with them. I travel a great deal, sometimes for weeks at a time. I'll go off suddenly to the Philippines or India or some such place and a husband has the right to expect certain things from a wife that I cannot give him. A certain amount of companionship and a certain amount of devotion to him and his problems. So, I guess I'll just skip that chapter for the rest of this lifetime."

"Wouldn't it be nice to have someone to depend on?" I asked.

She smiled. "I have someone to depend on. I don't look to people anymore. I look higher."

"Does that mean you've given up a so-called normal life?" I asked. "Does that also mean that you've given up other things such as meat, cigarettes, and alcohol? Is that part of this Philippine philosophy?"

"The philosophy entails good living but doesn't demand that you give up anything that you don't want to. Good living is a matter of understanding the philosophy, doing good to others, living a life that projects love, and doing everything with that love as a force behind it. The things you do on a personal level don't even count except for the excesses which interfere with your spiritual life. These people who pound on the fact that you're not allowed to dance, smoke, drink, or other things are preaching asceticism. We are not an ascetic group. This is probably the most misunderstood thing in our philosophy. The churches have led people to believe that if they are involved in spiritual matters they have to be ascetics. They make them believe they have to go through all sorts of personal tortures and withdrawals. A forced fasting or forcing yourself to give up cigarettes because you are 'spiritual' is of no use at all. When true spiritual enlightenment comes, the body changes its desires and eliminates these things naturally."

"By naturally," I interrupted, "you mean that the mind doesn't *force* itself to give up bourbon but automatically decides to do it without any outside coercion."

"That's right. You don't have to tell yourself 'I'm not going to drink bourbon anymore.' You don't have to make up your mind to eliminate something harmful. The desire will leave on its own accord. I was originally a Roman Catholic," she said, "and we had certain fast days and fast periods and they were observed and I was living under the delusion that all these saints and nuns who were doing these things were really doing it for themselves and were going to heaven because of it. I found out differently down in Puerto Rico. Tony was there working and a woman here in Chicago wanted to go there. She paid my way and as soon as I got there Tony put me to work. I had been nervous about the trip and hadn't eaten at all the day before. I couldn't eat on the plane and when I arrived Tony didn't give me time to think about food. But I didn't have an appetite. I thought it was nerves. But I was wrong. It was something else. Anyway I worked with Tony for six days and didn't eat one bite of food. Yet I had more energy than I ever had before. I worked in a crowd of people, all those hours, and didn't get dizzy or any of the other things that usually happened to me when I went without food. Finally I was beginning to feel kind of weird and I told Tony, 'I don't know why you're doing this but you can turn it off now.' So he laughed and gave me half a grapefruit but said to eat nothing else until the next day.

"Now this changed my way of thinking about what and how much I had to eat because I found that I lost no weight and I was in better health. People had told me that Tony had fasted for fifty-three days before he came to the United States the first time, but he sure didn't look like it with that little pot belly.

"I tell people in my classes that yes, if you want to attain the Kingdom of God you have to give up some things. You have to give up sickness and poverty and misery."

"You talk about God now," I spoke up, "but did you believe in God when you were a nurse and a surgeon's assistant?"

"I've always believed in God. I've always *known*. Even when I was very little I remember asking my mother why they had all those pictures of that old man and called him God, because that wasn't God."

"I've discovered," I said, "that most of the psychics I interviewed believe in God. Some of them have started out as agnostics but almost all of them eventually came to believe in a Supreme Being. Many of them have become spiritual."

She nodded her head in agreement. "While all psychics and healers are not working on a spiritual plane this doesn't stop them from learning and growing in that direction. One thing people here in the United

States have got to understand is that there are psychic healers and spiritual healers and there is no way you can combine the two and say it's the same thing. Healing is not desirable of itself because the body goes sooner or later anyway. Healing is only a *demonstration* to the people who need to know that there is a God and that this God is at work and what this God does.

"We can all heal ourselves. We don't need to run to others for it. It's quite simple. You stand in front of a mirror and then knowing what you are saying, you say 'I am God.' Then you say, 'God, I am healed.' It is a command. It has to be said with conviction. Again, this is a case of *knowing* rather than believing. I've done this in a large audience and when several cures have taken place the believers become the knowers."

"And you think everyone can do this?" I asked.

"Of course they can. It is basic psychology. It's like in the Hawaiian Kahuna where the lower self gets the message and reacts. In this case the subconscious gets the message and sends it to the parts of the body that need healing. We have to learn to utilize this stuff. What good is psychology if we don't use it?"

"How do you answer the critics who say that this is nothing but curing hypochondriacs?"

"This is not hypochondria," she said emphatically. "Many of the illnesses that have been cured this way have been diagnosed by medical doctors as being tumors, arthritis, ulcers, etc. Yes, of course, we bring these illnesses on ourselves, so it's only natural that we can also take them away by ourselves."

I wanted to get back to practical applications so I asked her to describe what occurs when the hand opens the body. "Is the theory that the one hand cuts the body and holds the incision open while the other hand goes in and works? If you remove the hand, does the incision automatically close up?"

"Yes," she answered, "you have to have one hand in

there to keep it open, but both hands are involved in going in."

"And when you are in there," I persisted, "do your fingers search for the tumor or foreign matter or does the 'intelligence' of this energy go in and do what's necessary?"

"For someone who hasn't seen an operation personally," she laughed, "you have a pretty good idea of what goes on. Yes, once inside we move our fingers and the energy brings the things into our hands. We try to help this energy as much as possible by making the incision as close to the diseased area as we can. The more primitive healers only work in one area. I remember when I saw Marcello at work he opened only one spot on each of his patients. I thought it was funny that all those people had the same thing wrong with them. He would touch that area, stick in his fingers, and in a few seconds bring something out. He later explained that he had no knowledge of anatomy and that the intelligent power he was channeling would bring the diseased organ or cancerous growth to him. His fingers were acting like a magnet no matter where the disease lay in the body. The more knowledgeable healers, like Tony, go to the area closer to the illness. That doesn't necessarily mean that he knows what a surgeon knows about the human anatomy. Often he has no idea what he is looking for but the powers guide his hand and channel their energies into the right places.

"And while I'm on the subject let me tell you that Tony's energy is the energy of love. We work with love, that's all we work with. It's so high that a person can pick it up physically. When his patients experience this overwhelming love they are not prepared to understand what it is. They don't know it's his higher self touching them and they can only identify it with physical love or emotional love. That's the only type of love they are familiar with, and there is no end to their imagination. Tony treats everyone the same and some of his women patients get very distraught when they attempt to reciprocate this love feeling. We have to guard against these kind of reactions."

The phone rang and she jumped up to answer it. When she came back I asked her a question that had been puzzling me for most of the interview. "Why is it necessary for Tony to open the body?" I asked.

Instead of being vexed by the question (as I had supposed), she smiled. "I'm glad you asked that. It's *not* necessary. I gave you three case histories including my own where he did not open the body but brought about a complete cure in my case, my son's case, and an almost complete cure in my mother-in-law's case. He's healed hundreds and hundreds of people in this country without opening the body. And he heals many over there without opening the body.

"You have to understand that when a person spends fifteen hundred to two thousand dollars to make a trip eleven thousand miles away to see a little bit of blood in order to be convinced that they were healed, Tony *has* to open the body. It was originally meant for the primitive peoples, but the Americans stumbled onto this and decided that this was *it*. They all want the show of blood. Tony isn't the only psychic surgeon over there but all of them are forced by their patients to turn on the gore. Some of his patients over here complained he didn't do anything for them until a few days later they found out they'd been healed.

"It's a strange thing about this power of Tony's. The normal blood clotting process takes about eight to ten minutes. Over there the blood clots within seconds and we think it's the result of the power that is working. The minute it hits the air it clots. Some medical doctors who've seen this say it's a lot of baloney and that he has palmed the clots somehow. But nobody has found any clots concealed on his per-

son before an operation and he has been searched
and checked out by some of the best.

"Maybe the main difference between the Philippine
healers and the others around the world is that we
know what we are doing; the others are merely stumbling in the dark unsure where their power comes
from or how they channel it. Even if a patient doesn't
have 'faith' he can be cured, where with many other
healers 'faith' is a determining factor. In this day and
age people should *know*, they shouldn't have to believe because believing is such a shaky thing."

"There is a big difference between 'I believe' and 'I
know,'" I said.

"You'd better believe it!" she laughed.

And our interview was over for the morning.

That afternoon Rosita introduced me to her number-one helper and fellow healer Tom Hanauer. The
two make a striking couple. He is six feet four, with
broad shoulders and dark hair (combed into a mod
fashion) flecked with gray. His face is a study in
strong angles and positive lines. A Korean veteran, he
looks like a combination of Rod Taylor and Rock
Hudson. While he could have any number of females
flocking around him, he has, like Rosita, dedicated his
energies to his healing mission.

Tom became interested in psychic matters when
the Bridey Murphy story was news. While in service
he studied theories on reincarnation and it made
sense to him. Then he started reading books on other
metaphysical subjects and became interested in
healing. In 1968 he attended a lecture Rosita was giving and saw a film about Tony Agpaoa and his operations. After the lecture he introduced himself and
asked if he could be of some help to her and possibly
learn to heal in the Philippine manner. They've been
together ever since, going to the islands and working
directly with Tony as well as working and teaching in
the Chicago area.

"I didn't feel that Tony and Rosita were telling me

anything new," he recalls about his training with them, "it was just *relearning* what I already knew deep inside. The very first time I saw Tony he had a small, ancient Filipino woman on the operating table and he was going to pull her teeth. But he turned to me and told me to do it!

"I said I didn't know how but he insisted it was quite simple. You put your fingers on the tooth and pull. He showed me how to do one and then I yanked out all the others. It was a strange sensation and one I hadn't been expecting because I'd only gotten off the plane that morning, but the woman didn't seem to be in pain and I didn't feel anything either. The only difficulty was getting my big fingers inside her little mouth."

Tom was quick to add that he doesn't pull teeth here in the United States because the American Dental Association would be down on him like a ton of bricks.

"It's not unusual for people to learn Tony's methods almost at once if they are ready for it," Rosita said. "There was a medical doctor from Canada over there and he observed Tony for several days. He decided that most of what was happening was mental so he returned to Canada and started putting some of those laws into practice. He still operates in the normal way but he uses fewer clamps in surgery than he did before. His assistants wonder why arteries bleed less for him than they do for other doctors on the hospital staff. He tells them he is 'talking' to the tissue. Canadian law demands that a certain amount of antibiotics be administered after each operation as a precaution against infection. Other doctors give massive doses of the drugs but he gives the barest legal minimum. He is able to control infection with what he learned from Tony."

"How much sense does that make to you," I asked, "that he is 'talking' to the tissue?"

"A great deal," she said, "because he is. He is in

contact with the tissues. To give you an example, a lady in Kansas telephoned me at 3 A.M. one morning asking for emergency help. She had bad leg ulcers and they were hemorrhaging. She was panic-stricken and didn't know what to do. So over the phone I communicated with the bleeding tissues and stopped it."

"We had a funny one last week," said Tom. "Rosita worked on a lady who had polyps growing in her sinus canals. They usually shrink and go away normally but the next day the lady sneezed into a handkerchief and blew the polyps out."

I wondered if the cures are always that rapid.

"The cures are not that rapid," said Rosita, "but the healing power goes to work instantly."

"Let me give you an example," spoke up Tom. "About two years ago we had a mother call us. Her oldest son had a kidney problem and because of this problem the doctors had given him large amounts of cortisone and he was hospitalized because of it. The cortisone had begun to eat into the bones and both hip sockets were affected. He couldn't walk. We worked on him and told him to stay off the cortisone. We went to his house once a week for two months and then every other week and finally just once a month for the last five months. Seven months after we began treating him he had X rays taken and the bones had regenerated and filled in."

"Why was it necessary to go back so often," I questioned. "If the power is all that strong why didn't it just go zap and cure him?"

"It does go zap! Once the healing process has started it is a continual thing but our visits instilled the faith in him that we were still concerned and working for him. People don't understand this power and think they have to keep coming back. We give them a psychological booster shot but it's really not necessary. Once the power is in there it works until the body is restored to health. Many times a patient will turn off this power by negative thinking and so he has to come back for another dose of it. You see, we are also dealing with the minds of these people not just with the flesh and the blood. Often we give a person a time period, telling them they'll be feeling better 'within a few days' or 'within a month' and that's all they need."

"Well, is this power, this energy, something you can turn on and turn off whenever you wish or is it something that comes when you don't expect it?" I stumbled for what I wanted to ask. "What I mean is, do you have to call the power into you and can you direct it?"

"It's always there," said Rosita. "It never goes anyplace. It works in strange ways. Supposing we have a patient and she wakes during the night and is in pain and she begins to *think* of our energy going into her. Well, even though we are asleep that energy will go to her and treat her."

"We don't know too much about this energy," Tom added, "except that it works. People have reported we have been there with them even though we didn't know they had been ill and had called for us. Most have sensed us there but some have actually seen us there. We use an oil in our healing work that people identify with. We treated a man and rubbed this oil on him. We told him that two nights later we would send energy to him while he was asleep. Well, the wife called us on the morning of the third day to tell us that she had been awakened by the overpowering scent of this oil. She could smell it for about five minutes."

"We've had many people tell us that," put in Rosita. "This is how we are aware that our healing presence has been felt."

I asked for a list of the diseases they have cured and they said it would be easier to give me a list of things they haven't cured. They've taken care of everything from diabetes to broken bones to cancer to blindness to arthritis.

"Supposing someone in Denver asks you for a healing. What are the mechanics involved? Do you tell that person to sit and concentrate at nine that night and then you sit down at nine and begin sending him energy?"

"That would be a good way to do it," Tom answered, "but it's not necessary. It's not like a television set that's plugged in and tuned to the right channel at the right time. This energy has no time or space limitations. Let me tell you about a man who was in an automobile accident. He had blowout fractures around his eyes, a broken jaw, two vertebrae were cracked in his neck, he had a concussion, glass in his eyes, a couple of broken ribs, and bruises all over his body. He was taken to a hospital where they X-rayed him and put him into bed with braces and things on his arms and legs. They weren't sure what they were going to do so they didn't put any casts or anything on him. They wanted to give him more shots the next morning. That was when four of us started sending him absent healing. The next day back to X ray he went, but they couldn't believe it. The fractures were gone, he didn't have a broken neck any more, there was no more glass in his eyes, the concussion had cleared up, the blowout fractures around the eyes were reduced to almost nothing, his bruises were reduced, and he was feeling great. It was a spectacular thing that had happened but there were four of us working on his healing. None of us knew the man or met him personally."

"Tom's father was rushed to the hospital with hemorrhaging," said Rosita, "and the doctors were going to operate on him the next day. Tom's mother called and told us and we went to work sending him absent healing. The following day the X rays were negative and the bleeding had stopped. No surgery was needed."

"When you are healing," I asked Tom, "do you have the feeling that there is someone beside you? Is there a spirit guide with you?"

He shook his head. "No outside entity works alongside of us or through us. The only entity is God Himself. Those who have spirits with them are doing bonafide healings, but it's not *our* way of doing it. We have been taught our philosophy by spirit guides, yes, but they are not beside us when we are healing."

"Do you feel the power coming into you?"

"Not really. In the beginning when you first start working you feel all kinds of things but after you've been working in it for a while your vibrations start rising and you get used to this higher vibration level. At times we can feel an increase in power coming through us but the God power is always there. It is not something that can be stopped and set aside for another day. Even if the healer doesn't feel it, it doesn't mean that it isn't there."

"How do you know when you've given enough healing?" I asked.

"A patient won't take on any more than is necessary. The time spent with a patient depends on what's wrong with him and usually runs from two to fifteen minutes. If someone comes in with three or four things wrong with him, then we have to take time out for each one."

"Do you get a message saying 'they are healed' and you know they don't need anything else?"

"Not really. It's more of an intuitive thing. Like we also just know when we are doing some good."

"We also know if it's a karmic thing," added Rosita, "but we try to help anyhow. Even Tony, if he knows he can't help someone, will tell them 'I'll pray for you' rather than tell them there is nothing he can do."

"Now that you brought up Tony's doing good for people," I said, "what is the *real* story behind his not being allowed into the United States? Was he accused of fraud as the rumors have it or of taking money for a healing he never accomplished? Everyone has his own story of this and I'd like the real one."

She sighed and looked at Tom. "It's a long story but I'll tell it to you. If it can be of help to Tony then it's worth having it printed. You can check the facts if you want to. I'll give you the names and addresses of all the parties concerned. It's no great secret but it has become a great annoyance because it's badly limited his healing ministry.

"It all started when a construction worker named Joe Ruffner fell off a scaffold and broke his spine in several places. This happened in Wyandotte, Michigan, in 1956. He was taken to a veterans' hospital and they operated on him. They operated on him and treated him for *twelve* years and were able to do nothing for him. They were unable to get him to walk. He couldn't move his arms. He was completely paralyzed. He had been on narcotics for so long that they had lost their effect and his pain was unbearable. The doctors told him the only thing they could do for him was to sever his spinal cord.

"At this he balked. He drew the line on this drastic surgery. Then he heard about Tony in the Philippines and wrote to him. He told Tony what was wrong but added he didn't have any money to pay him. Tony wrote back and said he only lacked faith and that with faith he would somewhere find the cash for the airplane ticket. Tony said he wouldn't charge him for the operation.

"So Joe told his parish priest about Tony's offer and much to his amazement the priest talked the congregation into taking up a collection and sending Joe over to the Philippines. Faith had paid for the trip.

"The first time Tony worked on him he told him to get up off the table and stand on his own two feet. Joe said it was impossible that he hadn't been able to stand for twelve years. Tony insisted and slowly he sat up, swung his legs off the table, and stood up.

Then Tony said, 'Okay. Walk!' Joe took a few steps and with just a little bit of help was able to walk across the room and back.

"He had several other operations after that and when his plane arrived back in the United States he walked down the steps and ran to embrace his sobbing wife.

"He went back to the veterans' hospital and told them he was cured. He asked to be taken off the disability paychecks and given a medical release so he could get a job and earn his own money. The doctors refused. They said he wasn't cured, that there was no way he could be cured even though they saw him walking and using his arms. So they took X rays and showed him that *nothing* had changed. His spinal column was still broken. Joe insisted that he was cured. He ran up and down a staircase for them, he threw and caught a ball for them. He tried to convince them that no matter what the bones showed, the nerves were perfect again and he was cured.

"While he was battling for a medical release, word traveled fast in his church group that he had gone to Tony and been cured. Others in the area wanted to be cured also and they asked Joe to organize a trip over for them. He made the necessary arrangements with Tony and got a charter flight deal with a Canadian airline. The flight left Canada with people in wheel chairs, on crutches, and with great hopes.

"But the American Medical Association heard about this load of sick Americans they could not cure heading over to a foreign faith healer and they were furious. They notified the Philippine Medical Association and demanded action be taken. The patients who had come so far didn't care what the AMA or the PMA thought. They wanted to be cured. And almost all of them were!

"When they returned to the United States the AMA was right after them. What did Tony do? What cures did he effect? How much money did he swindle out

of them? And so on. Most of the 110 people on that
flight told the AMA to bug off, but there were a few
who hadn't been healed or else who had had their illness return after they had arrived back in the States.
The AMA got these few to sign statements against
Tony.

"But what they really were jubilant about was that
they thought they had a case against him for transporting U.S. funds across the border because the
money for the charter flight had been sent from
Michigan to Canada. If Joe had been able to get an
American flight they wouldn't have had a leg to stand
on."

Rosita sighed. "You must remember that it wasn't
Tony's idea to set up the flight or to choose a Canadian airline over an American one. He was in the
Philippines and all the arrangements were made here
in the States. Well, the next time that Tony arrived in
San Francisco he was arrested. He was accused of
transporting funds across the border. We immediately
got him a lawyer and put up bail. The lawyer proved
that the money was sent by check from one bank to
another and that everything was perfectly legal.
While this was being decided some of his more loyal
followers decided to make a test case out of it, to
make the AMA accept Tony here in the United States
once and for all. There was publicity in the papers
and the poor man was dragged around and discussed
both pro and con. With all this publicity and all this
uproar Tony felt lost and very much a foreigner in a
strange land. So he did a silly thing, he skipped the
country. He jumped bail.

"There had been no evidence against him on any of
the counts and the case would have been thrown out
if it had come to court. But Tony didn't want to wait
for the slow-moving judicial system to operate. He
went back to his own country and because he jumped
bail he is, technically, a fugitive to be arrested whenever he returns.

"That's the story," she said softly. "The damage has been done. Tony's name has been blackened. The AMA is delighted it all happened. It makes them look lily-white and it keeps Tony from coming over here and curing the people that the AMA is unable to cure. It keeps the cash in their pockets because Tony doesn't charge for his work. It's all donations."

(Later I heard another story from a woman who had been operated on by Tony and how the AMA had closed down a Chicago doctor who dared to cure his patients with "unorthodox" methods. In 1960 Mrs. Ann Best of St. Louis, Missouri, was operated on. They opened her up, discovered she had cancer, and closed her again. They gave her six months to live. She heard about a Dr. Ivy, an American in Chicago, who had invented something he called Krebiozen as a treatment against cancer. He claimed that this drug went to the cancerous area and surrounded it with a kind of hard shell. While it didn't eliminate the cancer from the body it stopped its growth. Mrs. Best saw Dr. Ivy and began taking the drug. *Seven years later* she decided to go to the Philippines and have Tony take out the encapsulated cancer. [Remember, please, that before Krebiozen she had been given just *six months* to live.] "I saw my abdomen open from hip to hip," she told me, "and I saw this thing come out. I was wide awake and watched every move he made. It didn't hurt but I did feel him pulling something away from something else. When he took his fingers out it closed very fast. I couldn't believe it. That afternoon I put on a bathing suit and went swimming in the sea." Mrs. Best's doctors in St. Louis still can't understand what is keeping her alive and have been pressuring her to allow them to perform an exploratory operation on her to find out why she *isn't* dead! She refuses, of course, and she has decided to let them "stew in their own juices" for a while before she tells them about her trip to the Philippines. Dr. Ivy? He went through hell, thanks to the pressures of the AMA and is no longer permitted to prescribe his drug to anyone.)

"I have to keep within the law myself," said Rosita. "I refuse to open the body here in the States. I've been offered safe places to do this and even a conference room at the Conrad Hilton with the FBI standing guard, but I have refused. I tell people that if they want to see blood that badly they can pay my way to the Philippines and I'll do it for them over there. We are doing here exactly what Tony does but the body doesn't open. We work on the physical body touching the spiritual. We have worked on the so-called etheric body but ours is more physical than etheric. Most other healers work the other way around but our work on the physical regulates the spiritual."

As the afternoon turned into evening people needing cures and operations began to ring the front doorbell. Rosita Junior would answer it, write down the name of the person calling (most of them had appointments weeks in advance), and ask them to sit in the living room. Soon the room was filled with people of all ages and with all sorts of complaints. As I sat at the table in the dining room and looked into the living room it was like watching a scene from a play. Bodies of various sizes and shapes were scattered around on a battered sofa or in a couple of old overstuffed chairs. The television was on and David Cassidy of the "Partridge Family" was singing about young love. Rosita's two small boys were in the room watching the show, one of them stretched out full on the floor, the other draped over a chair arm. Two cats wandered in and wandered out. Then they meowed at the door wanting to go outside. They came bounding in from the cold each time a newcomer opened the door. The phone rang constantly. Letters were piled on the dining room table and atop the buffet. Christmas cards still hung from the doorway even though it was February and a 1972 calendar hung on a wall even though it was 1973. Rosita came out from the back room and embraced one person, shook hands with another, and was introduced to a third. Tom came out a few times to offer words of comfort or to explain to a husband what was being done for his wife. Rosita Junior, looking very pretty, served coffee, chatted with some school chums, and dashed into the back room to help with the healings. It was all disorganized yet moved smoothly. It reminded me of the home of a Mexican healer I had visited some months before. There, too, it was coffee, herbs, conversation, music, prayers, and suffering.

Rosita came and asked me if I wanted to watch them at work. Naturally, I jumped at the chance, for she doesn't allow most people to observe.

A woman was lying on a padded massage table, her skirts pulled up way past her knees. Tom was standing by her head, holding it in his two large hands while Rosita Junior held the woman's ankles. Rosita Senior (someone once dubbed her the Reverend Mother in order to differentiate her from her daughter) was rubbing a heavily scented oil into the woman's upper legs. It smelled like Vicks but the label was in Chinese characters. Rosita would rub and then raise her hands just a little and hold them steady over the oiled area. Then she would frown and bring her hands down for more circular massaging. The woman closed her eyes as Tom rubbed some of the oil into her forehead and then placed his palm down over her face.

From previous visits with healers I knew that he was sending energy into the body and down the right side and that Rosita Junior, at the woman's feet, was acting as a conduit to keep the energy moving up the left side while her mother attended to the business of healing.

Another lady came into the room and stood beside me. I asked her if she was also going to have a healing. She said yes and that the woman on the table was a friend that she had brought. She told me her name was Milazzo and that Rosita had cured her son. It seems that the boy had developed a growth on his front upper gum about the size of a pea. She took him to a dentist who said it wasn't an impacted tooth and advised her to see a dental surgeon. The surgeon said it was a cyst and that it definitely had to be operated on. She made an appointment for the next week but the doctor warned her that the anesthetic would only be local because her son had to be awake and sit with his mouth open. He said it usually was quite painful.

Mrs. Milazzo said that she was worried about submitting her son Randy to such an operation, but it was obviously going to be necessary. Then the day before the appointment he came down with a fever and a sore throat. The operation was postponed and set up for the next week. During that time a friend told her of a boy who had the same thing on his gum and when the surgeon opened it, it was cancerous. Mrs. Milazzo was really worried now. Once again, on the day before the operation, Randy came down with a fever and a sore throat and once again the operation was postponed and a new date set.

"The surgeon was upset with me but there was nothing I could do about it. Then I heard about Rosita and I brought Randy over here. She put him on the table and touched his lip. He said there was a 'zizzling' feeling but the cyst was still there. Rosita said it would come out by itself in two days. Just two days later while he was eating dinner he suddenly grabbed for his mouth and dashed into the bathroom. He spat out the food but also the matter that was inside the cyst. There was no pain at all."

She took her son to a new dental surgeon and asked for a routine checkup. The man X-rayed and could find nothing wrong. She insisted he carefully examine Randy's upper front gum. The surgeon, after the second look, insisted there was nothing wrong there.

Now she waited for her friend to get off the table

so she could be next. She had a stiff neck and wanted to see what Rosita could do for it.

I went back into the dining room. New faces had appeared in the living room and Rosita Junior was greeting them and trying to answer the phone at the same time. The cats still wanted in and then wanted out and someone had mercifully turned down the television set. (Rosita Junior is a healer in her own right and often takes over when her mother is not there. She has healed people over the phone and her most memorable case was a complete healing of a woman who suffered with psoriasis for twelve years.)

I started a conversation with a middle-aged woman who was next in line for treatment. She was visibly nervous and kept fiddling with the dark sunglasses she wore. "I have to wear these things even in the house," she said. "I've had some kind of a virus for the past fifteen years that makes any light hurt my eyes. I've been everywhere," she sighed. "I was afraid to come here because I don't know what they will do to me, but when you get into such despair even though you don't believe it you figure it can't hurt to go and try." I comforted her telling her they wouldn't do anything to her and that the most she could expect would be to have her forehead massaged with some strong-smelling oil.

Rosita Junior came for her and led her into the back room. I returned to my notes and tape recorder at the table. In less than five minutes she was out. She came straight toward me holding her sunglasses in her hand.

"I can look at a light bulb now!" she shouted at me as she stared directly into the chandelier over the table. "I can look at those bulbs without my glasses! I'm serious! It doesn't pain my eyes! It's fantastic!" She was almost crying. "My eyes don't burn any more! Those people are a gift from God!"

# "God Has Healed Me"

Anna Belle Kness lives in Van Buren, Missouri. She has had many healings in her long lifetime and sent the following to me giving me permission to publish it but admonishing, "I do not want you to cut it or add anything to it, please." I haven't.

## Injured Back Healed

### BY ANNA B. KNESS

I am now near 85 years old. When I was 5 years old I fell off a horse my brother Jim had put me on and landed on my back. I just felt like my back was broken.

I had back trouble right in my spine for years. Never was rid of that awful misery & pain.

In 1968 I went to St. Louis to The A. A. Allen of Miracle Valley, Ariz. revival and was prayed for one night at 11 o'clock. I did not feel God's Power upon me and I told my friend I'm not healed yet, my back is just killing me. But the next fore noon I was lying down on my back on the bed resting when the most wonderful feeling began to surge thru and over my body. It was 11 a.m. just 12 hours after A. A. Allen had prayed for me. I soon got up & I said to my friend God has healed me I felt Him do it and I've not got a pain. I know I'm healed after being in constant misery for 76 years And it's never returned. I've not had the back ache since I was healed.

# IV
# Harold Plume

The first time I saw the Reverend Harold Plume of
Monterey, California, I saw him stick his hand
straight into his patient's body! The hand vanished. I
was sure I saw it go straight in, disappear from sight
and come back again. This hand has been seen by
hundreds, photographed by skeptics, and even filmed
by a CBS television studio crew that was so shocked
by what they captured that they refused to show the
film.

The first I'd heard of him was when a lady in San
Francisco told me that she had a growth on the inside
of her rib cage. The doctors said surgery was required and cautioned that it might be necessary, because of the location of the growth, to cut through
the ribs to get at it. She did not want that kind of operation and then a friend took her to Reverend
Plume.

She said that she was seated on a chair and the reverend placed his hand on her rib cage. She was fully
clothed. Then she said she felt a funny sensation as if
something was moving inside of her. She glanced
down and was sure that she saw his fingers moving
into her body. After that she just shut her eyes and
prayed. A visit to her own doctor a few days later
confirmed what she thought: the growth was gone.

The Reverend Plume is an amazing little man. He

has snow-white hair, bright flashing eyes, and a sense of humor that startles those who expect a man of God to be sanctimonious. He speaks with an accent that borders on Cockney even though he was born and raised in Iver, Buckinghamshire, England. He moves quickly, laughs often, and can't just tell a story, he must get up and act it out. When there are three or more people in his stories they become all the more hilarious as he jumps from one character to another.

He has been a soldier, a factory worker, and a shop manager, all this before becoming an ordained minister of the Church of the Good Shepherd in London.

He also had the good fortune of marrying a wonderful woman named Bertha, who acts as his foil, his pianist, and his brake. It is Bertha who steps in when she thinks a story is going too far. It is Bertha who writes the letters and chases disrespectful clients from the church. It is Bertha who plays and sings for each service and is there to encourage him when things look dark. They like to joke that she is a Taurus and he a Scorpio and while her tough head and his stinging tail can never meet to hurt each other—just watch out if this strange creature advances on you.

Harold Plume's psychic activity goes all the way back to the age of three. Scenes would be played out before his eyes after his mother had put him to bed and turned out the light. They were scenes of people crying, begging, and pleading for some sort of help. He remembers that he would become terrified by these unwanted specters and would call for his mother. She was a very practical person and assumed he was just afraid of the dark. She never believed that he actually saw those visions.

Often during the day, as he grew older, these people would come to him. They would moan their troubles and try to make contact and if he ever answered and his mother heard she would scold him. If the people appeared when she was having company for tea she would blush and laugh that "Harold is talking to his imaginary playmates again." When the visitors had departed, Harold heard about it.

Finally his mother took him to a local doctor. By this time he was fourteen years old. The doctor was an old German who talked to Harold and then suggested that he be sent on a holiday for a while, away from that house and those surroundings. Harold insists that the doctor "knew more of what was happening than he wanted to let on to my mother. He was a very wise man."

His mother sent him to visit his favorite aunt, and nothing could have pleased him more. He loved this particular aunt and loved the little village she lived in and he'd wander the streets and back lanes thinking of his spirit friends and hoping that nothing would happen to make his mother send for him.

One afternoon he walked into the dining room to have tea with his uncle and aunt and her aged mother when he stopped short. "What's the matter, child?" his aunt asked. Harold paused, then knowing the consequences of his coming remark, said meekly, "There's a man sitting in my chair."

If this had been at his own home, his mother would have sent him to his room immediately, but his aunt leaned forward and encouraged him. "What's he look like, love?"

For the first time in his life someone was interested in his visions and he described the man who was still sitting and smiling at him. "And he says his first name is Clarence and he says he's your father!"

Neither of the ladies spoke but took their tea and talked of village affairs. When the uncle excused himself and returned to his job, the two women grabbed Harold and raced upstairs with him. They told him he had given a perfect description of the aunt's father. They lifted up the mattress of one of the beds and there were the first psychic books he had ever seen.

While Harold read the books eagerly, his aunt sat

down and wrote his mother of the amazing talents of her little boy. Harold asked her not to post the letter because "there'll be a telegram." Indeed there was. An irate telegram from his mother ordering him back home immediately.

It was after this that she took him to the vicar. Harold remembers that the old man with the turned collar removed book after book from his library shelves and quoted long passages to him. Finally he stared hard at the boy and said, "You know, Harold, this is evil."

And Harold said, "If that's the case, do you believe in the law of attraction?" He knows now that he was being controlled by a spirit force as he asked that question because he had never heard of the law of attraction himself. "If that's the case then I must be evil, because only if I am evil will I attract evil."

The vicar replied that while Harold was *attracting* evil he himself was not evil. "Then a gracious God will never allow evil to come to me," he replied emphatically.

The old man sighed and closed the books. "I have no answer for what's happening to you," he said. "I'll pray for you."

Harold thanked him and left with his mother. He began making plans to get out on his own. He wanted to be his own boss. When he was sixteen he moved to London and found a job. Then he began to read everything connected with spirits and spiritualism and sat with the top mediums of the day. More and more he became convinced that he had the ability to act as a channel for the spirit world but then he met Bertha and decided it was more important to become a husband and a father than it was to chase after ghosts. He rented a small house in a middle-class neighborhood and settled down. Or so he thought.

Next door lived a man named Tommy Atkins. He was a well-known spiritualist medium and highly respected in London circles. Soon Harold was talking for hours with this man, listening to him, reading his books, and learning everything he could about trance, apports, clairvoyance, and healing. Finally Mr. Atkins decided that the young man was ready to become a professional medium.

But Harold wasn't so sure. While he had been able to go into trance and give people information about their health and their jobs and their family who had passed on he didn't know if it was spirit that was giving him this information or his own mind. He knew almost everyone in the neighborhood and was unsure if he wasn't just remembering things he'd heard about them. Atkins put him to the test.

"So one day into the séance walks the whole bloomin' fire department of a near-by town! One by one Tommy presents them to me and asks, 'Did you ever see this bloke before?' and, of course, I had to say no. I'd never seen any of them before. So I went into trance and gave them all messages and advice from their family and friends in spirit. They were quite impressed," he remembers, then adds, "and so was I!" Soon he began to serve spiritualist churches all over England but making just enough money to cover his traveling expenses.

Being a church worker doesn't necessarily mean that you have a steady income, as Harold soon found out. He was asked to preach at various small churches, did "platform" readings and an occasional lecture, but to earn his keep he worked in a store. After work and on the weekends he and Bertha would have their own spirit sessions at home. It was at one of these, while he was in trance, that Hoo Fang appeared.

Hoo Fang claimed to be a Chinese doctor who had died some twenty-five hundred years ago. He said he worked with a group of other doctors in the spirit world and his aim was someday to have Harold's vibrations so high that he would be able to perform operations with Harold. But Harold wasn't that interested in healing—not until the first one happened in his own family.

This healing through Hoo Fang came directly and surprisingly to the Plumes. Bertha was expecting their first child (they now have six daughters) and she developed a serious kidney infection. Doctors wanted to operate and take out the diseased organ, saying that it would cost the life of the baby but if allowed to remain it might even cost the life of the mother. Bertha, always independent, didn't want anything to do with medical doctors. She told Harold to ask Hoo Fang for guidance.

The Chinese physician came through upon being called and asked Harold to trust him. When the young worried husband promised, the spirit asked him to go and place his finger tips on Bertha's body. He wanted the fingers placed directly over the area of the infection. Harold was in semi-trance at this stage, fully aware of what was happening yet still under enough to be a channel for Hoo Fang. Harold placed the fingers of one hand on the area and Hoo Fang ordered, "Push!"

Harold pushed and to his amazement saw his fingers slide effortlessly into his wife's body. He saw his fingers disappear, and Bertha jumped at the sensation.

Through Harold's voice box, Hoo Fang explained that what he was doing was using Harold's physical body and cosmic energy to dematerialize his fingers as well as the area where Bertha's disease was located. This high vibration would dematerialize the diseased tissue of her kidney. Harold felt his fingers rub against a swelled inner organ. Bertha said she felt it too.

At Hoo Fang's orders, Harold slid his hand out slowly. There was no hole in Bertha's body. There was no blood. There was no pain. And, most importantly, there was no more diseased tissue in her kidney.

News of an operation like this in the spiritualist movement travels fast and soon Reverend Plume was besieged with clients wanting healings. The British are more open about such happenings than we Americans are and take them for granted even though they consider them miracles. Once a British spiritualist accepts the power of the spirit intervention nothing is impossible to his way of thinking. Reverend Plume's name was news in the psychic publications and he traveled on the lecture circuit for the National Association of Spiritualists, holding services and demonstrating his healings.

Another incredible healing took place when Ann, their fourth child, was born in 1940. In England, in those days, the mother rested while a midwife took care of the baby until the mother was well enough to do it herself. After ten days the midwife turned the little girl over to Bertha and went away.

"So the day after the midwife went home," says Reverend Plume, "Bertha was washing the baby and she called me and she said, 'You know, there's something wrong with Ann. Something wrong with her rear end.' What do you mean? I asked, and she said, 'She doesn't have any opening back there. She's no anus!' So I said, 'Don't be silly and I called a neighbor lady in and we both looked and sure enough there was no opening. So I marched straight to the midwife and marched back with her and when she turned the baby over and took a closer look she began to fret that she would lose her job when this was reported. But I told her I wasn't going to report her to anybody, but I just wanted her to see it too. So our doctor came, a lady doctor that Bertha liked, and she took just one look and said that Ann would have to have immediate surgery."

"Now all these days," said Bertha, "the stuff that we'd been feeding the child was coming out as liquid and passing through the urinary canal. Being a baby she hadn't had any real food, you know."

"So later the doctor calls and says she's found the perfect surgeon to do the job. He was one of the most famous doctors at Windsor Hospital. That's the one that's near the Queen, you know. She said that everything was ready for Ann to be examined the following Tuesday.

"Well, I was a bit leery about this operation and being as Hoo Fang said he was a doctor I thought we'd better consult him. So I went into trance and he comes in and he says, 'It's perfectly all right, take her. And I'll tell you the exact words the surgeon will say. He will say, "It calls for finer hands than I have got or any surgeon in this hospital." ' So Bertha took Ann over there and after he got through examining her he said, 'This is the most mysterious case I've ever seen, and I'm going to discharge myself from it because it calls for finer hands than I have got or any surgeon in this hospital.' The very words that Hoo Fang had said would be said! So we came back and held another meeting and he came through again. I want to state right here that I didn't have the confidence in this spirit that Bertha had. I just wasn't sure because it was coming through *me*, don't you see? Anyway, Hoo Fang told us that night that 'no doctor on this earth will ever touch her.'

"Well, when I came out of it and Bertha told me what he'd said, I said, 'Well, it's all very good for *him* to say that but you know as well as I do that she'll have to have some surgery of some sort and soon. You see, there I was arguing with the voice that was coming through me. Well, three days later the lady doctor sends for me and said that she had made arrangements at the Great Ormond Street Hospital. And I said 'wonderful!' because it was the best children's hospital in London. The doctor said to take Ann in on Saturday.

"So I goes home and tells Bertha and she says, 'Humph! You mean to say you're going to go against Hoo Fang's advice?' Well, I had prayed and asked for guidance and I was sure that Great Ormond Street was the answer. But Bertha wanted to ask Hoo Fang about it, so into trance I went.

"Now you've got to remember that I was delighted that we were going to put Ann in this particular hospital but when Hoo Fang came through he said that under no circumstances should we take her there on Saturday. He said he wouldn't give us the reason why just then but that we would know on Monday. So with Bertha almost with a gun at my head not to have her child go to that hospital I canceled the call for the ambulance.

"I'll never forget that day as long as I live for I was certain I was signing the death warrant for my tiny little daughter. When the lady doctor found out about it she was furious. She came to see me and when I told her it was on orders from Hoo Fang she said she didn't go along with anything psychic and it was all nonsense. She also said she should report me to the authorities and all that but she did give me until Monday to take Ann to the hospital.

"Saturday came and went and so did Sunday. Then on Monday we heard over the radio that German bombs had blitzed the Great Ormond Street Hospital and that all the children had been evacuated. There were beds in the streets and alleys and everyplace. It was awful and Ann would have been in the middle of all that if we had taken her there on Saturday! Then the lady doctor came around and said that she thought it was a lucky 'coincidence' that we hadn't taken her after all.

"Right after that I lost my job at the shop where I worked and searched for days until I finally got another position in a factory that shipped things out for export. How I got that job is a long story involving the spirits but I won't go into it now. Anyway, in there I met a man who was the chemist of the place and he was very interested in Ann's case and became even more so when Bertha took the baby to show him. Now all this time, remember, Ann is eating and healthy and still has no anus to pass her heavy stuff.

"The lady doctor became more and more demanding and really threatening now to report me to all the authorities. She thought I was being negligent to my daughter. She insisted that I have surgery on Ann and immediately. But Ann wasn't suffering and Hoo Fang had said no doctor on this earth would ever touch her and I was determined that none ever would!

"Now the chemist had a friend who was the top surgeon at Charing Cross Hospital. His name was Mr. Lake, it was. He was a most important man and very difficult to see but my chemist friend said he could make an appointment for Ann. So I called the lady doctor and told her we were going to see Mr. Lake and asked her that if Mr. Lake said surgery was not recommended for Ann would she call off her threats?

"She was miffed as all get out but said that if we *did* get an appointment with Mr. Lake and if he *did* say such a thing—and in writing—then she would not bother us any more.

"So Bertha took her to see this great doctor and I paced up and back in front of the hospital like a crazy man. Finally Bertha came out all smiles and waving a piece of paper. She said Mr. Lake had examined the baby and had called in his students to look at Ann's rear end and everyone had been impressed but he agreed—in writing—that 'under no circumstances should the child be operated upon.' I ran all the way back to the lady doctor and, exhausted, waved the paper under her nose. She never forgave me but she never bothered me any more either."

Ann never was operated upon by any doctor "on this earth" and is today a healthy and very attractive wife and mother. Somewhere along the way, she doesn't remember how or when (she thought she was like all the other girls in school) an opening appeared, naturally. It was not placed where the anus normally is but almost side by side with the opening of the urinary canal. She knows that God healed her through the administration of Hoo Fang because after that visit to Mr. Lake, Hoo Fang told the Plumes, "Don't worry about anything, it will all be taken care of."

(Today Ann says that God through Hoo Fang was also responsible for the birth of her son Clint. She had become pregnant twice and lost them each time because she wasn't carrying them in the womb but in the tubes. She and her husband saw all kinds of doctors here in the United States and each one of them wanted to operate on her and give her an anus. Then one night Hoo Fang, through her father in trance, told her and her husband Lee: "If you will go along with me and wait six years, you shall have a little flower." Almost six years to the day she became pregnant and the doctors wanted her to have the child by Caesarean because they were afraid if it came down the double channel it would cause too much pressure on Ann's internal organs and possibly tear them loose. The baby was born normal and healthy and Ann came out of it in perfect condition. The amazed doctors told the proud father that the womb was "heart-shaped.")

When the war was over and the nation had returned to peace, Reverend Plume got his own church and soon had an impressively large and loyal congregation. They would still probably be in England if two of their daughters had not married and moved to the States. Bertha missed her daughters and wanted to keep her family united. "Then, too," she says, "we had been told by so many mediums that Harold should go and set up a church in America. The Americans needed him, we were told. And they said we'd make a good living and get out of the chilly London air."

So they sold everything they had, and bundling up the younger daughters, took a plane for the United

States. Maybe they were ready for the Americans but the Americans weren't ready for them. They had a great deal of difficulty and hardship at first and when Harold finally found a church where he could be the assistant minister it didn't pay enough to make ends meet. Both he and Bertha worked during the week in a hospital-rest home in Zion, Illinois. Worked there and hated it.

Then they decided to come to California and once again packed everyone and everything and made the long trek across the continent to settle in Los Angeles. He was able to get his own church going after a while and started healing people as in England. He found others interested in his work and began to train a few loyal parishioners to help with what he was doing. (Once when a woman came to Bertha and told her that her husband was suffering from prostate trouble, a helper commented that it couldn't be too bad to have that because angels also had prostates. When Bertha asked her what in the world she was talking about, she quoted the first hymn in their songbooks that read, "All hail the power of Jesus' name, let angels prostate fall." Both Bertha and Harold doubled up laughing and explained to her what prostate trouble was. But the helper was indignant. "For heaven sakes," she said, "if that's what it is, what's it doing in the hymnbooks?")

From the smoggy Los Angeles area, the Plumes moved their church to the little town of Redwood City just a few miles south of San Francisco. They had been asked to come there by a church group that needed a minister.

In their new church, a converted store with the words "St. John's First Chapel of Healing" lettered on the door, Hoo Fang's miracles came thick and fast. Letters of thanks fill three large scrapbooks.

"I wish to express my heartfelt gratitude," one woman from Van Nuys, California wrote, "for the healing I have received for a tumor that was located in the female region. Two weeks ago I had a check-up by my doctor and he could not locate the tumor although last October he told me I'd have to have a hysterectomy. Prior to my coming to the Chapel the tumor was, to my touch, about the size of a grapefruit. It had been growing steadily for six years. There was no passing of any material. It just wasn't there anymore."

And a lady who had come to him from Springdale, Arkansas, wrote after returning home:

At the time of your services I could not be sure that any healing at all had taken place. My left leg has been numb for years, growing worse since 1957. The prognosis was wheel chair in 15 to 20 years according to my MD. He was amazed this morning when he found reflex in my ankle and a wee bit in my knee. My wrists have always been very sore and painful. Now they are almost totally recovered. It was indeed a gift from God. Thank you again.

One of his more spectacular cures at that time dealt with a Canadian woman who was in a hospital awaiting an operation for what her doctors termed a "tumor in the stomach." Gangrene had set in and she had overheard the nurses saying that she wasn't expected to live. Call it spirit guidance or whatever, but the day before the operation she happened to read an article in the local newspaper about Reverend Plume and his work. She dressed, walked out of the hospital without saying good-by to anyone, and took the first plane for California. In a few hours she was sitting in Reverend Plume's chapel receiving healing. She only had that one session, for Hoo Fang told her, "That's it." She caught a plane back to Toronto the next day.

Aboard the plane she had the overpowering urge to go to the bathroom and once inside the small compartment she passed a huge black hunk of flesh. Putting it into an airsickness bag, she took it to her doc-

tors. They identified it as a rotting five-month-old
fetus. This was the "tumor" they were going to operate
on. She wrote a long letter to the Plumes.

> Where do I start to thank you? God bless you and
> your wonderful family. I shall send you a picture of
> the growth that I passed and which two medical doctors
> say I couldn't have (1) without unbearable pain and
> (2) the particular way the growth was secured. It was
> supposed to be impossible, at least in these times they
> say and (3) without bleeding to death after. How
> could I add to their disbelief by telling them that I
> carried my heavy luggage out of the airport two hours
> after passing this thing? But these are the facts. To add
> a little humor, I had to declare the growth at customs
> and you can imagine the ramifications.

The star football player at San Jose State College
injured his back. He came to Reverend Plume (after
seven different doctors had examined him and forbidden him to play that season) and his back was put
into place immediately. When the athlete mentioned
that he was going to be fitted for contact lenses that
he could wear while playing, his eyesight was cured.

It was about this time that an angel appeared. Not
the kind with feathers and halo but the Broadway
kind: a backer. A doctor friend of the Plumes had a
patient who was impossible to cure. He asked Harold
if he would look at him. But he warned him in advance that the man was an atheist and didn't believe
in any kind of faith healing. Harold said he wouldn't
tell the man who he was. When the man appeared
and Harold talked to him, he asked, "Can you help
me?" Reverend Plume replied, "Only God can help
you, but I can try and *convince* Him if you wish." He
started working near the man's back. Soon he heard
the voice of Hoo Fang saying, "That's it."

The man was delighted. "What'll I do?" he asked.

"What do you like to do?" Harold asked him. The

man said he liked to play golf. "Well then," replied
the reverend, "play golf like hell and enjoy yourself!"

Sometime later the man appeared again, but not
for a healing this time: to establish Reverend Plume
in a church of his own in Monterey. The Plumes were
overjoyed because both of them liked the Monterey
area and they knew they could make a go of a chapel
there. They were given a vacant store for a church
and a house to live in. The angel paid all the bills ...
except a salary of any kind for the Plumes. The
money went just for rent, utilities, and transportation.
But like everything else that is too good to be true
complications arose and soon the angel pleaded poverty. His businesses were affected by inflation, he
said, and he would have to stop sending them financial help. He suggested they give up the Monterey
area and go back to Redwood City on a full-time basis. By this time, of course, the Plumes had built up a
steady congregation and the idea of abandoning these
people was out of the question. So they've remained
in both places, barely meeting their monthly expenses
and praying that someday a real angel will come
along who won't back off when things get a little
rough for him.

Reverend Plume is saddened by this adventure, for
he has had his heart set on a permanent chapel of his
own for years. (The present one in Monterey is up
over a restaurant in a poorer part of town.) "They
just reminded me down at the Social Security Office
that I'm sixty-five. I said to Bertha, 'My God, I can
hardly believe it. I should be retiring.'"

"Instead of that," spoke up Bertha, "he's doing
twice as much. We had one hundred and fifty-one patients last week! In Redwood City we start on Sunday
evening and give a service at seven-thirty. No
healings. The healing services are on Monday, Tuesday, Wednesday, Thursday, and Friday from one-
thirty till five. Then we have tea and open again and
work from seven in the evening to sometimes one or

two in the morning. And then we come down to Monterey and have the same hectic schedule here, except that I won't let him do any work from Monday to Wednesday. He has to have *some* time off! But there is always somebody who can't wait or who is dying in hospital or who needs to have a funeral preached or a wedding consecrated and off he'll go no matter whether it's his free day or no." She glowered at him and shook her head, but it obviously didn't do any good.

(Bertha didn't tell me and neither did the reverend, but there are times when there isn't enough money left after paying the rent to buy food or clothing for themselves. They never charge for a healing. There is a plate on the office counter and a sign on the wall says: "No charge is made for the healing. A suggested love offering is $10 per person. This is to enable the work to continue." If you want to donate, you do. If you don't, then don't. Often when people have been healed of something that will save them a twenty-five-dollar visit to their doctor or the hundreds of dollars that an operation would cost, they'll walk out and just say thank you. One woman, after being healed of an illness that would have cost almost two thousand dollars in a hospital, promised to send them fifty dollars for their services. The check never came. Another woman, cured instantly, happily wrote out a fat check. The check bounced.)

"I've always visualized a church of my own," he sighs. "One that would be here after I've left this state of consciousness to show people that I've done something. It would be there as a building . . ."

"I don't agree with that!" Bertha interrupted. "What are buildings? You don't have to have a pile of old bricks with your name on it hanging around! David," she turned to me for support, "rule him out. This is one thing we always argue about. I say, what's in a building? What we've got now's beautiful. . . ."

"It's not mine," he said softly.

"Well what difference does it make?"

"I just wish that somewhere there was a little old lady who would hear about me and say 'Reverend Plume, I'll build your church for you. What would you like?' It would be a very humble place. I'm not looking for a temple, just a humble little church where I can work as a channel.'"

"Well," put in Bertha, "I don't know what you're worrying about. The healing you've done all your life is recorded in God's books. The Supreme Being knows what you've done. That should be enough."

"But it isn't," he said quietly and shook his head.

"Reverend Plume," I asked, "if you don't have a building when you pass on will you have felt that you failed?"

He looked at me. "Yes, I would, for I had a vision when I was in Los Angeles of a small church, a round church with seats for one hundred and fifty people, a healing room, an office, and a couple of toilets. That's all I want. I saw that vision and felt I had to accomplish it, for when I have built it I will have accomplished what I should have done."

"But what good is a building," I probed, "if you, the man with the healing power, have passed on? Who will take your place?"

He smiled a broad smile. "The one that Hoo Fang brought into the world. I *know* that he will carry on my work. He already has."

"Already has?" I asked. "You mean Ann's little boy, Clint?"

"Yes. When he was just eighteen months old and Ann was out here visiting he watched me give a man a healing. He saw me place the tissue paper and saw me press my fingers into the body. So a woman came in and sat down on the healing stool and quick as a flash he grabbed a piece of tissue and pushed his little fingers against it. Well, the woman jumped and she said, 'That little baby's got his fingers inside my body!' Wasn't that something?

"Then a few months ago when Ann and Lee came back here to live, Clint visited me again at the chapel. I figured he'd forgotten all about the healing techniques but when a lady came in and said her problem was hearing he asked me, 'Granddad, can I heal her?' I said, 'sure you can.' So he took a tissue paper and put it up against her ear and he wiggled his fingers a bit and then he walked to the back of the chapel and said 'One, two, three, four, five. Can you hear me?' Well, the lady says to me, 'Bless his heart, I can hear every word he said!' Then she complained that she had something wrong with her eyes, so again he put a tissue paper on her eyes and when he was finished he walked to the back of the chapel and said, 'One, two, three, four, five. Can you *see* me?' Well, we both had a laugh about that but she did go out of there seeing and hearing better. He also knows how to close the aura."

"Close the aura?" I asked. "How do you do that?"

"You make your passes over the body, see, from the head all the way down to the ground." He jumped up to show me how it was done, making downward motions with his outstretched fingers. "Never work on a patient and not close them off afterward. People will look at me and say, 'Well what's he waving his hands in the air for?' But I'm not. I'm closing off the aura."

"This is *after* you've gone into their body, right?"

"Well, I'll tell you something surprising. I don't know sometimes when I've gone in or when I haven't. There are times when I'm very conscious of it and other times when I'm not. I really don't know what happens. Hoo Fang told me that he disintegrates my fingers by vibrating them very rapidly. You know if you took this sofa and vibrated it fast enough it would disintegrate. So it's the same with my fingers. And when my fingers, in that fast state, touch another person's body they also feel that vibration and that part of *their* body disintegrates. That's why the energy is allowed to slip right in without a scar and without any blood. It's the darndest thing. Been filmed you know, but," he added, "often all the photographer gets is a blur or a black band across his negative. It's as if Hoo Fang didn't want anybody to take a picture of what's going on."

"And the patient has nothing to do with this?" I asked. "They can be complete skeptics and still receive a healing?"

"No, because it seems to depend upon the state of mind of the person sitting in the chair. Are they sitting there in a state of believing or are they sitting there in a state of doubt? Are they thinking 'I've heard of the work of this man but I don't believe it'? If so, their mind is affecting their whole make-up. If they come in and *doubt* me but *trust* God that's different. Even while they are doubting, if they will say 'God heal me,' then they will be healed. It's not *me* doing this healing, you know. It's not me. It's God. That's who should be getting the praise. That's why some of these cases have been instantaneous healings and I feel the energy flowing and I know they are being healed.

"But there are some who will never be healed. And I've known when there was no possible chance. One lady came to me and I knew there was no hope for her and I took her daughter aside and advised her that her mother didn't have long to live on this earth and one week later she was gone. A few weeks ago a lady came and asked me to go and see her father, who had had a stroke. He was in hospital. I refused to go there because I don't like the vibrations in those places. I can do my best work right in my chapel where I have made the vibrations myself. And in private homes! The vibrations in some of them because of all the family quarrels and carryings on!"

He changed the subject. "When death is inevitable the aura is colorless you know. It's a kind of gray. An aura is nothing more than an electric field of energy with colors that pulsate and change all the time, depending on your state of health or your mental attitude at the moment. I can diagnose with the aura but I don't. This is not allowed by state laws. Science has also got to come to the conclusion that they can diagnose through the aura as well. There should be a violet flash in the aura, that's the color that goes to the heart, and this violet flash, when a person is in good health, is quite brief. Now if you don't see that violet at all, you know that there is something wrong with the heart. But I don't dwell upon defects. People will come in wheel chairs and tell me they can't walk. Well I can see that! But I *know* that with God *nothing* is impossible. That's how I work. I *see* that person walking. I don't see the defect when I work on them. I only see it when they come in. As soon as they are sitting in the chair I see them as completely cured."

"You don't see the organs going back slowly to what they should be?"

"I see them *immediately* cured. They are, as far as I'm concerned in my soul's eye, perfect. Perfect as God made them. God creates them perfect and they *are* perfect. But imperfections do creep in, that I'm aware of. Perhaps something from their mother or their father stayed over but that is not my affair. I'm not their judge.

"As I get farther and farther away from orthodoxy I get farther and farther away from the surgeon's knife. Now that doesn't mean to say I don't believe in surgery. I'd be a fool if I said I didn't. But I don't believe in using it as much as they do here and I'm definitely against exploratory surgery. You know, this nonsense of open up and let's see what's inside."

I told Reverend Plume I agreed with him. I've known several people whom doctors had opened up when they had no idea what was wrong and who died later because of these exploratory operations.

Reverend Plume has no great love for doctors even though he admits that they are necessary many times. Blood transfusions are needed. Insulin shots are necessary. Broken limbs, accidents, and all the other sudden things that happen to people that only doctors can take care of. The doctors in his area have investigated him and the AMA has looked into his practices simply because his cures are so spectacular. He doesn't advertise for clients. He doesn't prescribe medicine. He doesn't diagnose. He is a minister of a church whose basic tenet is that healing is part of God's gift to man. His brushes with "the authorities" have been memorable.

"I once saw this strange mug looking in my chapel here in Monterey and saw him stop two people as they went out, so I said to Bertha, 'Go and tell him if he wants any information to come in and ask me.' But when she went on the street he ducked away and was gone. So pretty soon, there he is back again, peering in the door. Carrying a briefcase, he was, and wearing a raincoat like in one of them mystery movies. So I catch his eye and wave him into the church. Well, he can't do any more than come in after that, so he does. I welcome him to the church and he says to me, 'What kind of healing do you do here?' I said, 'You can call it what you like. You can call it divine healing, faith healing, why do you want to know?' So he said, 'Do you know the healers in Ashland?' So I said no but I told him I do know of them and I also know of the healers in Brazil and the healers in the Philippines and the healers in England and all doing a wonderful job for mankind. So he said, 'Do I suspect that you come from England?' and I said, 'Yes. From a free country.' And I looked him straight in the eye and got on the offensive. I could tell the spirits were guiding me now and I said, 'Which it would do great things in this massive country to place just a little credence on this particular work that I'm doing. There are such a list of can and cannots here, which, to me, borders on dictatorship—the very thing we fought World War Two about.' I'm still looking him in the eye. Now he says, 'Is it true that your daugh-

ters work with you?' and I says, 'Yes, and I'm very
proud of it'; so he says, 'I don't suppose neither you
nor your daughters would tell anybody to bathe their
eyes in cold tea. . . .'

"That was what he was fishing for!" said Bertha.
"Somebody had told him we had suggested bathing
his eyes in cold tea and that is against the law. That's
the same as prescribing medicine!"

"So I said, 'No, sir. There's the church charter and
obviously as the head of the church I know exactly
how far I can go. I know I'm not allowed to
prescribe, I know I'm not allowed to diagnose. I *can*
do both when spirit is with me, but I don't. I'm not licensed, so I don't do it. Without a doubt my wife or
one of my daughters might say to someone that so-
and-so bathed their eyes in cold tea and felt much
better for it, but they would never *advise* anyone to
do it. There is a difference, you know.' So he says,
'Oh. Thank you. That answers my query,' and he
gives me his card: 'Professional Investigator for the
State of California.' How about that? The sneaks!"

Reverend Plume has had some other visitors in his
chapel that he hasn't liked. One was a couple with a
young son that was hyperactive. They had brought
the child and their dog for a healing. (Reverend
Plume has had some amazing results in curing animals.) Well the child wouldn't stay still one minute
and was into the toilets spinning the paper, spraying
the deodorant, and splashing the water. Then he ri-
fled through the hymnbooks, slammed the door, and
finally ran a stick up and down the reverend's new
Venetian blinds. That did it.

"The parents were sitting there so calm and peaceful and never once told the child to sit down and
mind his own affairs. So I exploded. 'Young man, I
only regret that I'm not your father,' I said to him. So
he stuck his tongue out at me! Well they had had him
to all kinds of psychiatrists all over the state and it
hadn't done any good. So I said to the father, 'Do you

know who should be on those couches? You! You're the case, not the child! Where's your leadership for this child? Haven't you got any backbone? You've made me so damn mad I'm going out!' So I went out and into the animal healing room and was on the floor with the dog and he was responding to treatment beautifully when in walks the father. Well, I was furious because he was upsetting all the vibrations. I threw them all out, I did. Father, mother, child, and dog!"

"And I was very annoyed with Harold," put in Bertha, "because he didn't heal the dog. That poor old thing. It wasn't its fault that its master was such a bore."

"The dog will be healed by God someplace else! I just couldn't have that man in there upsetting all the vibrations! That is where I work. It's a healing chapel, for God's sake!"

"And then there was the man who came in and asked one of the girls for the sex powders," put in Bertha.

"That old coot!" Reverend Plume exploded. "The very idea of him! He came waltzing in one day and had the nerve to tell one of my female assistants that he was sixty years old and had picked up with a woman who was forty and wanted my assistant to work on him to perk up his sex organs! So I told him that this was a respectable church of the Lord and if he was sick I'd work on him, but it was no place to play games. He said he'd heard I had a Chinese doctor and that years ago in China there was a brown powder that they used to give a man back his sexual drive and wouldn't I ask my guide for it? 'Get out of here,' I shouted. 'You've insulted my assistant, you've insulted my church, and now you've insulted my angel friend! You can insult me as much as you like, but don't insult God's guardian angels!' And I threw him out. I did. I threw the blighter out!"

Hoo Fang isn't the only guide that works through

Reverend Plume. There is Dr. Emma, who works on skin and skin grafts, a French spirit named Dr. Pierre, who does the heart operations, another Chinese named Dr. Yen, who treats the eyes, an African native who works on animals, and an American Indian who does all the bone settings. Hoo Fang does many of the operations but often calls on one of the others when a specialty is required. Reverend Plume considers Hoo Fang like a head doctor with a staff of medical experts under him.

This collection of specialists has literally performed miracles if the letters and testimonies from hundreds of people are to be believed. I took a random selection of names and addresses and wrote to them asking for written testimony of their healings.

"Recently I underwent an operation for a ruptured hernia," wrote Elizabeth Teixeira of San Carlos, California. "The previous evening, on Sunday, Hoo Fang's helper, George, came through during Reverend Plume's service and informed the congregation that Hoo Fang was at the hospital and would remain with me until after the operation. Knowing of his presence was a tremendous relief, and though I did not have a vision of him when I came out of the anesthetic, I was conscious of hands rubbing my abdomen. I give thanks to God, again, for sending his helpers to care for me."

And from Campbell, California, a Mrs. H.B. wrote:

I heard of Rev. Plume through my doctor in Los Gatos, California. In fact it was this doctor who drove me to Redwood City to see Rev. Plume. I was suffering from an acute attack of bursitis in my hip—every step felt as if a knife was stabbing me. I consulted a Dr. B—— of the Kaiser Permanent Hospital Plan in Santa Clara on Oct. 15, 1969, with severe pain in my right hip and leg all the way down to my toes. Dr. B—— had x-rays taken and diagnosed the condition as bursitis. Then I consulted a Dr. M—— a week later at the same hospital and he too diagnosed the condition as bursitis. He gave me pain pills and also Butazolidin to keep down the inflammation.

I do not have the exact date I saw Rev. Plume but it was about a week after that. I was in a good deal of pain and walking was almost impossible. I was suffering so much.

Rev. Plume worked near my spine and the tissues on the left side of my back. He explained to his workers (his wife and a young lady) that "they" were using red rays for the healing. They conversed about the doctor who was helping (I gathered the doctor was on "the other side").

At any rate, the next morning after the treatment the bursitis was gone and I could walk freely. That was in 1969 and the bursitis has never returned. Thank God.

There are others. A woman with disintegrating hip sockets. A woman who was going blind of some rare disease (so rare that Stanford University wanted her to give them her eyes *before* she died) and who is now driving a car and leading a normal life. There was a dog with bowel cancer. There were heart surgeries, hearing restored, and infections flushed away.

But there are others that the reverend and his helpers can't help. He admits that everyone who comes to him is not cured. He doesn't want anyone to think he is God, with the answers for everything. He calculates that eighty per cent of the people who come to him are healed. The other twenty per cent must be turned over "to God or another healer. For some reason I just can't do it."

One of his most perplexing cases was a boy who was perfectly normal until he reached the age of two. Then he began to forget things. He forgot everything, including how to move his arms and hands, how to talk, and how to walk. Before his mother's eyes, he turned, in a few short months, into a vegetable. They took him to the best doctors in California, who said that while they didn't have a name for the disease what was happening was that the coverings on the endings of his nerve fibers were being destroyed and this destruction stopped the carrying of messages to the brain. The messages were still there—the child was still intelligent—but the messages could not get through. He was a prisoner inside his own body. They gave him two years to live. That was in 1967.

Then the attractive young parents heard of Reverend Plume and came to one of his services. By this time the child had forgotten how to chew and how to have a bowel movement. His eyes were dull and his skin was pallid. To keep him alive, he was being fed through a tube each day at a local hospital.

"After just one treatment with Reverend Plume," his mother told me, "he regained his memory to eat and swallow. Each week we saw another improvement. He had color in his face and his eyes were bright and alert. He knew who I was and he recognized Reverend Plume and Bertha. He got so he could lift up his arms when he wanted me to take him. And he gained weight."

The child became able to communicate directly with his mother through a series of pictures. She would sit him on her lap and put a pencil in his hand. With his mother holding his hand, he was able to draw pictures and designs of what he wished to tell her. She is positive that some special psychic communication developed between them.

Yet suddenly, and for no real reason, just as he was showing marked daily improvement—he died. Reverend Plume, who had kept this child alive for eight years longer than the medical doctors had given him, preached the funeral service.

The reverend is very unhappy with that case. "By all rights that child should have been healed. But he wasn't. I've seen people who deserved it much less walk out of my chapel completely cured. I don't know why God didn't cure him. The only solace we have is that God gave him time enough to get to know his mother and father. He gave them a lot of happiness. He also gave a lot of encouragement to all of us while he was alive. It must be part of God's undisputable plan. It doesn't seem fair but I suppose He has His reasons."

The energetic white-haired little Englishman will continue to work with cases like this one until the day he "passes over." It's his entire life. He has dedicated himself to his fellow man's sufferings. Few of us would do the same.

"You see, David, for so long—so long—I've laid myself open to investigations, comments, vulgar remarks, and it's taught me to become an even chap on an even keel. I've had people tell me straight to my face that I'm a phony. That I'm a kook. I just look at them. I say, 'All right. It's quite all right but look at the end result. Don't look at me because if there is something positive happening at the end result that's enough for me. If there's no end result then I'm a phony.' "

He sighs. "You judge a man by how his works turn out and don't condemn him if his methods are different from yours."

＊　＊　＊　＊

Harold Plume died in his sleep in July, 1976. His one request was to have his ashes returned to England. He never got his "own church."

# Martello's Witchcraft

Leo Louis Martello is a witch in New York City. He has been active in civil rights movements for witches and once staged a "Witch-In" in Central Park. He is an author on witchcraft and a teacher. He is also a practitioner.

"As a member of the Old Religion I place my complete faith and trust in the Goddess. In 1960 I suffered from a slipped disc in my lower back and I was in excruciating pain. It sometimes took me over an hour just to get out of bed. I went to my medical doctor and he took X rays, which revealed the slipped disc. He suggested that I would have to go into the hospital and be 'put in traction.' My intuition guiding me, I said, 'No.'

"I placed my problem on the Horns of our God and prayed to the Goddess of our Sicilian tradition. Our coven performed a healing ritual. That night I slept well. When I awakened the next day the Goddess said, 'Go see Big Joe.' I did. (He ran the Happiness Exchange radio program here for many years and I appeared on it often, doing handwriting analyses for the listeners.) He gave me the name of an old blind black chiropractor. I went to this man three times. He told me that along with his manipulations he practiced faith healing and believed he was a channel for divine or cosmic guidance.

"I went back to my doctor and asked that my back be X-rayed again. It was. To my doctor's astonishment the X rays revealed *no slipped disc.* I've never had a pain again till this day.

P.S. "Healing work is done by our covens regularly though we do not solicit this. There is NEVER any charge for work done in this circle and it is usually done by request.

"Blessed Be."

# V
# Ethel de Loach

The girl was only sixteen years old, yet completely crippled by cerebral palsy. She had been to many doctors and in and out of several clinics. Tests had been taken. Reports had been written. The medical men agreed: hers was a hopeless case. The only one who didn't agree was the girl herself. She was determined to get better.

A mutual friend heard of Ethel de Loach of Morristown, New Jersey, and asked Mrs. de Loach if she thought she could cure the girl. Mrs. de Loach asked that the patient be brought to the friend's home at an appointed day and hour.

"The first time I saw her she was practically dragged across the living room," the New Jersey housewife recalls. "She had no control of her legs; in fact one of them was constantly clamped down to keep it from flying up in the air. Her left arm was turned up against her body and her closed fist was pressed against her breast. She was in terrible physical shape and I asked myself if I really knew what I was doing by accepting such a case. But we got her down on the sofa and I started to work on her. Or rather I should say my guides came and worked on her through me.

"In just one treatment she was able to lower her arm and I wish you could have been there to see the

123

expression on her face as she opened that clenched
fist for the first time in her life. For the first time in
her life she saw what the palm of her hand looked
like! It was beautiful. We all cried a little that afternoon. Since then she has had several treatments and
she now uses both her arms and both her hands, she
has thrown away that leg clamp and walks on her
own power through the aid of crutches. Her appetite
has returned and she chatters all day now. Her
mother told me she never used to say a word. She
even talks in her sleep, trying to make up for lost
time, I guess. But the best part is that she is in love,
and that's important to her. It's one more motivation
to get better. She says that when she can walk without any support at all she's going back to those doctors and those clinics and ask them why with all their
medical schooling, they weren't able to do what Mrs.
de Loach did."

The doctors probably won't have an answer. If
they do come up with one, it will be something like
"gradual remission" or that the girl's illnesses were
psychosomatic even though they have X rays of her
and operated on her, proving that, for them, it had
been physical. They would never give a soft-voiced
mother of four and her ghostly medical men the
credit.

Ethel de Loach is used to not getting any credit
and for a long time she didn't want any. "I tried to
stay out of the limelight," she says. "I didn't want my
neighbors to think I was a kook. I knew that the more
publicity I had and the better known my name became the more I would be scoffed at and doubted. I
don't care any more. The time has come for all workers in metaphysics to come out and stand up for their
beliefs. Parapsychology is now an accredited science
and is being taught in universities across the nation. I
feel that our transition is very near. Not my personal
transition, I don't mean my own physical death, but a

transition for everybody. It will be a transition in our ways of thinking and accepting. People are going to become more real, more considerate of others, and less materialistic. I also feel that the guides who work with me have given me an extra push to bring me into the public eye. And," here she looked steadily at me, "I feel that survival of bodily death is going to be definitely proven and not too far in the future." She paused, letting that remark sink in as we sat in the lounge of a New Jersey hospital where she had just finished working on a medical doctor who was a patient there. "I can tell people that it has been proven to me," she continued, "but just my saying it isn't going to convince anyone. They will have to experience proof in their own lives and this is going to happen soon. It's soon to have to happen because humans think they are here in this dimension and that people in the spirit world are down in hell or up in the sky somewhere but they are really right *here*. Right beside us."

"How can we see this dimension?" I asked.

"We can't all see it but many of us can *feel* it," she replied. "We all know there is electricity in the air. I put out my hand and it is full of electricity. We can't see the electricity but we *know* it's there. Maybe some of us are a little more—I don't want to use the word *advanced* but maybe some of us have learned a little sooner than others how to contact it. I had a talk with astronaut Edgar Mitchell. He is also aware of this energy. He knows it's there. We talked about it. He asked me what I thought it felt like and I said it was a little denser than the air around us. In this field there aren't just the right words and our vocabulary is limited but the best I can come up with is *colloidal*. Almost like particles suspended in nothingness.

"When I do healing it's there. As much of it is there as I need. I just reach out and collect it and I can attract it and direct it to the person I'm working on. It's been there since time began and it's there for all of us to use."

There was a time when Ethel de Loach didn't know about this energy, and to her knowledge, didn't have any guides or healers around her. She grew up in a small town in Louisiana where her father was the local Presbyterian minister. She was the oldest of eight children and when she wasn't taking care of her brothers and sisters, serving in the small church, or cleaning the house, she would be out working in her father's fields or taking care of the family livestock. They kept several hundred acres of strawberries, which helped to make up the difference that church collections lacked.

"It was there that I began to develop my ESP," she says, "not with people but with animals. When my father would tell the farm hands to get the animals ready to send to market or tell them to kill one of them for our table, I *knew* the animal sensed what was going to happen. They knew they were about to die and I knew they knew it. Animals always came to me when they were injured or in pain. I was the only one that could release a dog or a cat from a steel trap. They would snarl and bite at anyone else who tried to free them, but they calmed down when I knelt beside them. People would bring me their sick birds and animals and I'd just hold them and they seemed to get better. Even if it was a wounded wild bird, it would stay calm and unafraid in my hands as if it knew I was helping it. The animals were trying to tell me about healing long before I knew about it myself. I loved my life on the farm, but unfortunately Father couldn't make a go of it and so we moved up to New Jersey, where he got a job as a chemist. Mother was happy because more money was coming in, but I don't think Father was ever really happy once he moved from his parish and his plowed fields."

Young Ethel's dream was to become a nurse, but there just weren't funds available for the four-year course so she took side courses in first aid and nutrition. She worked awhile for the Department of Agriculture, teaching people how to cook food properly and taught a high school course in cooking for maximum nutrition. Then the war came along and crash courses were offered in nursing. With her interest and her background she took the course and graduated with honors. During this time she married, had four children, and was divorced. She doesn't involve her ex-husband in her present-day work.

She didn't want to say anything else about her married life so I asked her about her healing. Her first healing.

"It came as a complete surprise," she said. "People have always told me, as far back as I can remember, that if they were ill when I arrived, they always got better after I walked in. They seemed to be aware of a power that I wasn't. I was always very shy and had a terrific inferiority complex and when they told me this, I thought they were just saying it to be nice. Now I know what they were feeling because people tell me the most incredible things.

"Anyway, my daughter Marie was the first person I healed. She loves to ride horses and one afternoon she and a girl friend were out on a riding academy's trail when a small boy in front of them fell off his horse. Well, Marie dismounted and went to help him. He wasn't hurt, just frightened. It must have been his first time on a horse. He started to get back on the animal but from the wrong side and the horse kicked out. Unfortunately, Marie was standing just behind the horse and she got a terrific blow in her knee. In just a few seconds it swelled up like a basketball. How her friend managed to get her home, I still don't know.

"That was a Sunday and a holiday, so, of course, I couldn't get a doctor to come to the house. We lived way out in the country then and I was desperate. Marie was in terrible pain and sobbing and I knew something had to be done because her knee might be broken.

"Well, I remembered that I had just finished reading a book about Ambrose and Olga Worrall called *Miracle Healers*. I figured that maybe if I placed my hands on Marie's knee, possibly it would calm her down until a doctor could arrive. So I put my hands on her knee and much to my amazement my hands began to move. They skimmed and darted around her knee like a pair of butterflies, hardly touching her at all. I looked at my hands and I knew that I wasn't moving them. It felt as if someone else was making those hands move. I couldn't believe what was happening but I let them go. My daughter was lying on her back and suddenly she shouted, 'Mom! I see the most fantastic colors all around you! It's like a rainbow. The colors keep going up over you as they change.' Well, I knew that she was running a fever and that she had a vivid imagination, so I didn't believe any of the things she was saying, yet my hands continued to move on her. I was startled when just after a few minutes of this, she smiled and said that all the pain had gone. And that wasn't all.

"She told me that she was being taken into a beautiful building with an oval entrance for a door. They were carrying her in and when I asked her who 'they' were, she said they were two people of authority, almost like policemen. She said the walls were a beautiful shade of soft bluish gray but then added that they were not really walls at all, not the way we know walls to be. She saw an enormous number of books all about the room. She couldn't make out any of the titles, but she knew they must be important from their size and their bindings. Then she said, 'A man is coming up to me. I don't know who he is but he looks very kind and he says to me, "You will be all right."' After that she fell asleep and I tried to estimate how long I had been working on her. It couldn't have been more than an hour. She slept all night. There was no pain whatsoever. In the morning the pain was gone and so was most of the swelling, but it was ugly and discolored. I asked her if she wanted me to try it again and she said yes. When I placed my hands on her, they started to move again, much to our amazement. That day all the swelling left and we never did have to call a doctor." Ethel was confused and concerned about what had happened and asked Marie not to mention it to anyone.

A few days later one of Marie's girl friends came hobbling into their house on crutches. She had had a wart removed from the bottom of her foot and even though the doctor had given her pain pills, they were not having any effect. "Oh, Mrs. de Loach," she said. "I just don't know what to do."

Before Ethel could stop her, Marie blurted out: "My mother can heal you. Lie down on the bed." The girl eagerly agreed and Ethel found herself with her second patient in less than a week. She told her that she couldn't guarantee anything, but when she placed her hand on the girl's foot, her hand began to move. The pain went away. When she told the girl she could get up the youngster said, "Mrs. de Loach, please thank the doctors that have been helping me. I can't see them but I can feel them all around me. There is a beautiful blue light all around me. I feel so peaceful here. Please thank the doctors for me."

A few weeks later the slightly built, reddish-haired woman with the green eyes went to hear the authors of the very book that had inspired her to attempt a treatment on her daughter. "The Worralls were having a meeting at the Lexington Church in New York City and I arrived late. As I walked down the aisle toward a vacant seat in the front row I could feel Ambrose Worrall's gaze on me. It was more than just a glance at someone who was interrupting his lecture, it was a sudden psychic force that almost knocked me down. Something very powerful traveled between us and as I looked up at him, I saw his fantastic aura. It was bright and multicolored. When I sat down, I looked at him again and had one of the most amazing sights of my life. I saw a class in healing behind him. The gentleman, in spirit, that was leading the class wore a natty dark suit, a white shirt, and a bow tie. He had taken great pains with his appearance, yet one little lock of hair had escaped and fallen over his forehead. I couldn't believe that I was seeing a spirit who had problems keeping his hair combed, but there he was standing right behind Mr. Worrall and instructing a class of about a dozen other spirits in the art of healing. I could hear his voice as easily as I heard Mr. Worrall's. I was amazed then but take these things for granted now. Often people will tell me they see a class in healing when I am giving lectures. It's not the same professor with the cowlick but others who are, more often than not, Orientals."

She looked at me, unsure whether I was believing her or not. She paused and then said: "I know that you've talked with other healers all across the country so that when I tell you about things that have happened you know I don't have to embroider them." I nodded in agreement. She relaxed once more, needing to know that I didn't consider her a "kook." "I don't have to exaggerate, you know that. In fact, I soft pedal it, if anything, because it sounds so incredible. If I told it like it really was, most people would think I'd flipped. I'm not trying to fool or impress anyone."

"You don't have to," I assured her, "your record speaks for itself."

And it does.

Take the case of the attractive overweight lady who wrote asking for an appointment because her gynecologist had found two lumps in her left breast. The doctor wanted her to have immediate surgery. She refused. She wanted to have Ethel de Loach work on her first. Mrs. de Loach remembers that the lady had more than just a growth in her breast. She had ulcerated legs, which had to be bandaged; she had only one kidney as the other had been removed by surgery; she had bleeding hemorrhoids; only thirty-three percent hearing, and poor eyesight because of a corneal transplant for a cataract. Ethel, amazed that a woman with all these ailments could still be so cheerful, gave her a healing but cautioned her that the results might be slow in appearing. A week later her doctor's examination showed the lumps still in her breast but she steadfastly refused to be operated on.

Twenty-nine days from her healing treatment she wrote that her breast felt soft where it had been hard, her hearing had improved somewhat, and her legs had stopped hurting completely. She came for another treatment and Mrs. de Loach was amazed at her weight loss and her healthy appearance. Then she went to see her doctor after a six weeks' absence.

"He wasn't pleased with me," she wrote. "I told him I felt fine but he said I'd have to have a complete examination. He kept examining my breasts and he had a funny expression on his face but he didn't say anything. He kept asking me about this and that—not mentioning the breast, so finally I told him I was anxious to hear about those two lumps. He said, 'Oh, don't worry about them any more. They're so tiny, you don't have to go to the hospital.' I was so happy that you healed me—that I told him. He blew his top! He said the lumps simply dissolved. Thank you for healing me. Thank you and God bless you."

After another month had passed, her legs cleared up completely and her eyes were tested at 20/20 vision.

Or take another case.

A man phoned Ethel one morning pleading and almost sobbing in desperation. "Will you please help my wife? She is desperately ill—she is my whole life—I've got two daughters—they're all I have—I must get help for her. She had a major operation the day before yesterday. It took almost all day and she can't even whisper my name. Will you please come? I'll do anything, I beg you, please come!"

Ethel took the name of the patient and asked where she was. She was in one of the nation's top research hospitals. She told the husband to make all the arrangements and to be sure and tell the wife that she would be there at two-thirty the next afternoon.

"As we drew the curtains around her bed," Ethel recalls, "I asked him to stand at one side and to try to keep anybody else out. I looked at his wife, swathed in bandages and hooked up to tubes and medical equipment, and wondered how much I could help her. I took her hand and she clung weakly to me. I just said, 'Have faith. The most wonderful doctors are here to help you. In just a moment they will diagnose and get to work immediately.'"

Ethel was able to work for fifteen minutes without interruptions when suddenly a doctor on the hospital staff came in through the closed curtains. He stared at Ethel and then quietly asked if he could have a few minutes with the patient. Ethel stepped out of the curtains, the doctor did whatever routine work he had to do, and turning to Ethel, he said, "You may have her back now." Ethel worked for another half hour. The woman fell asleep, her face serene.

The next day the husband was again on the phone. This time he was exuberant. And almost incoherent. "Mrs. de Loach, do you believe in miracles? There is a God! The doctor and nurses can't believe what happened. My wife got out of bed and walked down the hall. She wants her radio and her cosmetics. The doctor says the stitches look ready to come out and her wound is much smaller. Oh, I don't have words to thank you." He paused and there was a moment of silence. Then—"Mrs. de Loach—*who are you?*"

Others have been asking that same question, but none as studiously as Mr. E. Douglas Dean, a tall broad-shouldered man with a soft voice and a sense of humor who has been looking into "what makes Ethel tick." He is qualified. Mr. Dean teaches computer programming and statistics at the Newark College of Engineering. While he was president of the Parapsychological Association, he succeeded in affiliating his organization with the American Association for the Advancement of Science. That one step legally took parapsychology and all its ramifications (ESP, healing, communication with plants, etc.) out of the fortunetelling parlors and gave it scientific respectability. The world of the occult should erect a statue to the man.

Mr. Dean has been researching ESP by using such medical instruments as the EEG and the plethysmograph for almost fifteen years. He is founder and president of the New Jersey Society of Parapsychology where his number-one research material is a lady named Ethel de Loach. He is very impressed with the results he has obtained with Ethel by the Kirlian photography method. This is the means of capturing the electrical charges emanating from a healer's finger tips on film. The technique (so expertly reported to U.S. readers by Shelia Ostrander and Lynn Schroeder in their now-classic *Psychic Discoveries Behind the Iron Curtain)* was invented by Semyon D. Kirlian, a Russian, from a small town near the Black Sea. Its idea is quite simple even though the results are astounding. A healer goes into a photographic darkroom and places his fingers flat on the emulsion side of a roll or sheet of unexposed film. This sits on a copper plate insulated by plastic and varnish. Then forty thousand volts shoot across the copper in square wave pulses of frequency up to fifty thousand cycles a second. "Instead of getting electrocuted, you get perfect photographs of the aura energy in the healer's fingers when the film is developed," says Professor Dean.

These pictures show extraordinary colors and sunlike bursts of energy around the silhouette of a healer's fingers and hands. Mr. Dean has noted that the impulses are strongest when a healer is actually working on a patient. He has also captured the increase in energy *into* the patient *from* the healer by photographing the patient's emanations before and after a healing treatment. It seems that the energy that comes from the healer is absorbed into the energy field of the person being healed. (Dr. Thelma Moss of U.C.L.A. has also shown that sometimes a healer can drain off the energy of a patient, leaving him in worse physical shape than he was before the treatment. These people are called "vampire healers" by psychics and others in the metaphysical field of study.)

In May of 1972 Mr. Dean tested the equipment on Mrs. de Loach for the first time. "We tried first with her left midfinger while she was at rest, and then when she thought of healing. The latter show much bigger energy emanations than when at rest. Then we tried color shots, and Ethel gave the most intensely interesting orange flare shot appearing about a half inch away from the inside of the finger. We have found that her nails give flares and emanations too. In the color shots we got blue and white emanations when she was at rest. I have another color slide that was taken when Ethel was actually healing a wen on the right arm of the patient. The at-rest colors are on her finger tips, but very strong orange flares are further in toward her hand. The orange flares are perhaps a centimeter away from the skin of her second knuckle. The wen was gone the next day. With Kirlian photography," states Mr. Dean, "the evidence for 'psychic' healing gets stronger and stronger every day."

Ethel is not overly concerned with the scientific reasons behind her healings. What concerns her most is that the healings are accomplished and that she has been chosen the "channel" through which these energies are directed.

"Do you know what those spirits made me do in the beginning?" she asked. "Yoga! Everything happens to me! I didn't look for any of this but when they decided to make me start doing these things they felt I had to be in better physical shape. I was sitting in my dining room one night, looking out of the window at the clouds and the moon and feeling sorry for myself because I was all alone, when all of a sudden I began to move in my chair. There were movements and more movements and I wasn't doing it. After a while I got to enjoy it and sat fascinated as they moved my arms and legs all around me in all sorts of strange but comfortable twists. Then they made me stand up and exercise and I knew they were putting my body through various yoga positions.

"The dancing started a short time later. One night about midnight I was all alone in the house and I turned on the radio to get some pleasant music and when it came on I thought it was so beautiful that I started to dance. I danced around the living room and down the hall and into another room thoroughly enjoying myself—when suddenly I knew that I had a partner! An incredible invisible partner! Oh, how we danced! We rhumbaed, we tangoed, everything! The music went on for two or three hours. If someone had come in they would have carried me off to the loony bin, but I love to dance and they still come and dance with me from time to time. What they were really doing, with both the yoga and the dancing, was to get me into condition for the type of fast healing I do."

I was curious. "Does your healing depend upon the energy force around you or the force inside you? Is it dependent upon the spirits working with you? Could you do it without the force and could you do it without the spirits?"

"In my experience," she replied, "there are many ways to heal. And I think that this energy—I don't know if that's the right word but that's all we have right now unfortunately—can be directed in so many ways. It can be directed by my touching my hand over you. It could be directed to you even by a glance. You could have a wound on your leg, and this has happened many times, I won't touch it, I'll just stare at it. There will be some energy going from my eyes and I will notice what I call 'the healing light.' It's like a faint beam of sunlight in an irregular pattern moving around the wound. As this light moves, somehow in my vision I see the wound closing and healing and new skin taking over. Usually by the next day the wound is healed, no matter how bad it was."

"But do these wounds being healed have anything to do with spirit?" I insisted.

"No matter what kind of healing I do I have these wonderful people in spirit with me and they direct the use of this energy that you have seen in Professor Dean's photographs. I've been told that there are over sixty persons who work with me from the spirit side and they help me with all kinds of healing. Everything from the setting of bones, to labor pains, to eye problems, to cancers, to emotional troubles. You name it and they'll send an expert in to heal it. There is a fantastic hypnotist who works with me. Three passes of my hand over a person and they will be completely out, and I've never studied hypnosis.

"I have wonderful guides and they laugh with me and we have a lot of fun, but they feel that healing is a serious business. When they are working they are very serious but when they lift out a cancer, for example, they become joyous. I've had people come to me with terminal cases or when their doctors had told them that they hadn't another moment to waste before having an operation, and *my* doctors would take just about fifteen minutes to lift out the cancer. It would vanish and I'd hear them laughing. Often they will almost shout at me, 'It's out! It's out!' "

"Do you know who these guides are?" I asked. "Are they entities or are they nonentities? Have they lived before? Have they been doctors? Have they been friends of yours in past lives?"

"There is a great variety of them. Many of them are Oriental, some are Western. There are no American Indians that I know of. I have been told that many of them are of the Shu-Ming dynasty. Much of the treatment that people receive through me are methods that were used in that fifteenth-century dynasty.

"There are many that work with me and they know I have to have variety in my life. I wouldn't be happy tied down to just one doctor the way that George Chapman in England, for instance, works with his Dr. Lang day after day. I met George Chapman and Dr. Lang both when I was over there. They operated on my eyes and it was successful. I think he's just fantastic, but I'm entirely different. I've got to have lots of people—or in this case spirits—around me. One of them, I'm pretty sure, is Mesmer. I've felt him many times because the type of treatments he used to give are done through my hands. People have seen Sister Kenney working through me as well."

One of the things that surprised me was that patients swear up and down they are being stuck with acupuncture needles during some of her healings. Often the marks remain on the skin where the phantom needles have been inserted. These operations have been witnessed and corroborated by Japan's acupuncturists and doctors who have studied acupuncture in Japan. Ethel herself has never studied this ancient art. When famed British clairvoyant Malcolm Bessent visited the United States, he spent several days with Ethel at her New Jersey home. (He had been invited by the Maimonides Dream Laboratory to pick up objects clairvoyantly that they would send while he was sleeping. They projected ten items to him mentally and while asleep he picked up eight. He was upset that he didn't get all ten.) One evening Ethel gave a party to introduce Mr. Bessent into local metaphysical circles and a guest complained of sharp pains in her kidneys. She looked as if she was going to faint. Mr. Bessent suggested that Ethel do something for her. They stretched the girl onto the sofa and as the operation began, the psychic Mr. Bessent saw a strange scene.

He said that behind the sofa, on the opposite side of where Ethel was standing, appeared an old Oriental man with a Fu Manchu moustache and a little red cap on his head. On both sides of Ethel stood two younger Oriental men. One was carrying a handful of acupuncture needles and the other would take a needle from him and insert it into the girl's body as Ethel passed her hand rapidly over the patient. He said that some of the needles were twirled and manipulated. Just before Ethel finished, the two younger men, guided all the while by the older one, removed the needles and then disappeared. The patient remarked that she felt a great deal better but did complain of needlelike pressures. It was only then that Bessent told her and Ethel what he had seen.

"I didn't tell her what was going on as I was working," Ethel says. "I never say anything while I'm operating. I don't want to put the idea of needles or anything else into their minds. If afterward they tell me they've felt needles okay, but I'm not going to give them the suggestion. My eyes are almost always closed, especially if it's a serious condition because I feel it is absolutely vital that I listen to the guidance and it has to be exactly right. As you know, in acupuncture some of the points are only a tenth of an inch apart and if I move my hand deliberately—under my own free will—some of those psychic needles could go into the wrong place. I am extremely careful to let them control my every movement."

She laughed. "My guides are so clever, they have very subtle ways to make people aware of their presence. I remember a girl who was in one of my classes. Her mother was always running to the doctor with all kinds of female problems, but she refused to listen when her daughter told her my doctors could cure her. But the girl insisted and finally, just to shut her daughter up more than anything else, she came to see me. I managed to convince the woman to get onto the bed, to remove her shoes and to relax. She did all this with great misgivings. The guides went to work and operated on her, using acupuncture and clearing up a great many of her nagging health problems. But they did something that I knew she couldn't possibly miss. And she didn't. On the way home in the car she turned to her daughter and said quite indignantly: 'What I want to know is where did she get that long needle she stuck through my foot?'"

Even though a needle mark can show up on the physical body, Mrs. de Loach insists that all her operations are on the etheric or auric body rather than the physical. "Any psychic operation is done on the etheric body," she said. "I've heard that the Philippine healers operate on the etheric but the effects can be seen on the physical. You might feel a slight discomfort, but the actual work is being done on the etheric. My hands do touch the patient sometimes, of course, but most of the time they are above his body in the laying-on-of-hands tradition."

"Getting back to the knowledge that the cancer is being lifted out, do you actually see it being removed or do you take their word for it?" I asked.

"I *sense* it has been lifted out," she said after a moment's thought. "The patient senses it has been lifted, too. Somehow I have a *knowing* that it is being lifted out, just as I have a knowing that very instant the healing has taken place."

"And when that 'knowing' comes do you stop your work?"

"Not always. You see I am not the one who decides to stop. When it is time, the power is released from my hands and they cease moving. You must understand that I am just an instrument. These people do the engineering. They control the mechanics and have complete control over what happens. They make the decisions as to which of them will work through me on each particular patient. Very often more than one will be there with me. People have told me that they felt an extra pair of hands on them. If I should be at their feet, for example, they might feel another pair of hands on their shoulders. They have also assigned certain spirits to me as protectors to make sure that no destructive or negative energies can get through to me. They have spoken strange words to me during the operations and I've had to look them up in medical dictionaries to understand what they are talking about. Sometimes when they want me to know the exact nature of an illness they will tell me to find a certain book and open it to a certain page. And there, believe it or not, will be a detailed description of what is ailing the patient.

"Many of my patients have seen these doctors with me and so have several clairvoyants who've witnessed the operations. They've seen the entire bodies, not just the hands or the eyes. Once in Chicago a clairvoyant described the people he saw working with me and later in New York another medium described the very same people. I'm still a doubting Thomas. I need this kind of verification."

"Are you tired after a healing?"

"I used to get quite exhausted until I learned more about getting the energy back quicker and as I learn more my guides are becoming more considerate of me. They seem to have added more people around me to give me a booster shot of energy at times. I can feel this energy surge through me. If I have a patient that is in very bad condition, I can always feel the added power the guides have sent into me."

"Have you ever had a case you could not heal?" I asked.

"I have had several people who have come to me who haven't really wanted to be cured and there was no way my guides would work on them. A number of people wanted, subconsciously, to keep their illnesses for various reasons. You can't cure people like that.

"One type of illness I prefer not to treat is mental illness. I have cured some people, but they require a tremendous amount of attention. They have to be seen once or twice a day and I am physically unable to do that. We don't have a center or any place where these people could come and spend some time. I have also done a number of obsession cases, but they are really very hard on me. Here again, even though I've exorcised people, sometimes at incredible physical expense to myself, I've known that they would allow this to return to them.

"I think the majority of people in mental hospitals are possessed. I worked with retarded children for many years and I feel that these children are very vulnerable to possession. Entities who are of low mentality and are wandering around with nothing better to do will see a child with a lower mentality than theirs and it will become a sitting duck for possession. It's a field that needs a lot of exploring. Unfortunately, there are not enough qualified people around to do it."

"Speaking of 'qualified people,'" I said, "what do you think about medical doctors giving exploratory operations?"

This is where psychic healing, if you want to call it that, can be of tremendous help," she stated. "If you are able to diagnose psychically, then you can tell a doctor what is wrong with a patient and many times avoid an exploratory operation. The law says I am not allowed to diagnose, but I am *able* to diagnose. I am also not allowed to prescribe medicine and I don't. My system of diagnosing is the oriental one. A patient comes to me and I look at him and take in his eyes, the color of his skin, his breathing, and his aura colors. Especially the aura colors. I try to turn this off when I am out socially, but if I see an illness and I feel that person should know that something is internally wrong with him, I'll tell him. I try not to do it often, but it does come creeping in sometimes. I've been places with groups of people and I'll see someone across a room and I know I can help that person so I'll go over and start a conversation and while I'm talking I'll start sending healing into him and he'll say, 'You know, since talking to you I feel so much better!'"

"Do you have to be with a person to heal? Or isn't distance important?"

"I have healed over great distances. I know I have because people have written me or told me over the phone that a healing was accomplished. For instance, someone would call me and tell me they had a brother-in-law who was in such and such a hospital in such and such a town and would I heal him. All I need to know is the name of the patient and sometimes his room number. Then I mentally picture this man getting up from bed. I picture him with the color returning to his face and his breathing normal. Whatever I do only takes a minute. I believe that healing of this kind starts the moment help was asked."

"The *moment* help was asked?" I repeated.

"The moment that the woman called asking for help for her brother-in-law the healing began. As she was asking I was mentally tuning in with her and sending healing to the person."

I was anxious to get her definition of faith healing before our interview ended that afternoon. She had given me three hours of her valuable time and I knew she was anxious to get back to her "normal" (if you could call it that) business.

"There are supposed to be all these different types of healing," she said. "Psychic healing, spiritual healing, and faith healing. They all work with different people at different times but I don't consider myself a 'faith healer.' Yes, I have faith in my own abilities and faith in the marvelous doctors who work through me, but I don't put my healings on a religious level. I don't pray with my patients and don't ask them to pray, either. Sometimes they feel better if they say a short prayer, but I leave that up to the individual. There is no ritual with me, no music, candles, or incense. If a person is Jewish or Catholic or Buddhist, my type of healing will not conflict with his religious beliefs."

She rose to go and I turned off the tape recorder. As she was getting into her coat (snow was falling outside in the cluttered New Jersey street), she started talking about death. I quickly switched the recorder back on.

". . . even dying is a kind of healing. My healing, seems to do wonderful things for those that are dying. I was once invited to a hospital in New York by the sister of a woman who the doctors had said had only a week to live. There was only one way to describe her and that was as a skeleton with skin on. It was terminal cancer and she was completely eaten away. The doctors had her heavily sedated, but I had asked the sister to hold off the drugs until after I had worked on her. I always do that because it's very difficult to work on a person whose system is filled with drugs. She was so wasted but my wonderful guides went to work on her and when I finished, she seemed to have more color in her face. She even opened her eyes and spoke a few words with me. And I started to cry. I don't know why. They weren't tears of sadness or of joy, but just strange tears that seemed to come from very deep inside me. All the comfort I could give her sister was that she would feel no more pain. I could not promise her a prolonged life or even a cure.

"The beautiful thing was that she didn't have any more pain. A day or two later she insisted on getting out of bed and sitting in a chair. They didn't have to give her any more drugs. She told her sister that she knew she was going to die but that she wasn't afraid.

In fact, she was looking forward to the experience and felt so good about it that she felt like dancing. The number-one fear of everyone is death. This type of healing can erase that fear and make their passing so much easier."

It was a month later that I saw Ethel de Loach again. She had invited me to Morristown to sit in on one of her healing classes. I was curious to see how she "taught" healing. Obviously, *she* had never taken such a course and I wondered how much a neophyte could do on his own without spirit guides and doctors having chosen him first.

We had dinner in a Chinese restaurant and were joined by Marie, her very beautiful and very psychic twenty-year-old daughter. Ethel explained that she feels everyone can heal to a certain degree and just because you don't feel that you have been singled out the way she was is no reason to think you don't have any healing ability. "Healing is a sense that has to be developed," she remarked over her won ton soup. "It's like learning to play the piano or any of the other natural talents we all have within us. Granted some of us will always play chopsticks while a few others will become concert stars, but we all can play the piano in some way or other if we set our minds to it. Learning to heal is the same type of development.

"Anyone can become a channel for this. I'm not an exception, but there is one important rule: you must not be afraid to try. The people on the spirit plane want even more than you do to work with you. Once you realize and accept the fact that they really and truly are studying and trying to demonstrate their knowledge through you, then you can relax and let them take over. I've had some that have been working with me for ten years. I haven't been healing for ten years but they've been *with* me and studying the best way to work *through* me. We all have people assigned to us to learn our individual ways and to find out what we are capable of. Once you accept this and believe this, then you'll have the gift of healing much more quickly. I tell my class to sit down and meditate and to just *believe* that they have these guides with them. I tell them to talk to them just as easily as I'm talking to you now. You must tune yourself in like a radio and if you find the stations are not coming in very well, then fiddle with the dial until you get them loud and clear. You are a radio set for the other side and you have control of the buttons. You can tune yourself in to the universe and pick up universal knowledge and wisdom. All you have to do is *believe* you can do it."

Marie smiled at me and said, "You know, I think that even that horse that kicked me was part of the guides' master plan for my mother. If I had not been so seriously hurt, she would never have had the courage to try her healing ability. It was a painful way for them to bring the word to her but, looking back, I'm glad it happened."

We drove to the Unitarian Fellowship building and as we entered the old brick edifice Ethel told me that she wasn't happy with the vibrations there and that she surrounded herself with white light each time she had to conduct a class in there. The room where her students were waiting was a large area with a blackboard and several movable desks. There were two bare neon tubes in the ceiling and a couple of bare bulbs on a far wall. On a bulletin board were some childish drawings (with shiny stars and the word GOOD written on them) left over from a previous grade school class.

It was a Wednesday night (her class in healing is once a week) and there were twenty-three people there, all of them adults, ranging from the early twenties to late sixties. The majority were women. The first order of business was to tell of any unusual healing experience that had occurred since last week's meeting. The students sat in chairs around the wall. They would have formed a circle if the room had been square instead of long and narrow. Ethel went from person to person and each of them shook his head. Then an attractive girl named Julie spoke up.

"My husband had a third-degree burn on his arm," she said, "and it was very bad. I could see raw meat. I was concerned about trying to heal it because I knew my hands would add more heat. But I worked on it anyway and now it's covered over and the blisters have gone. It's only been three days since I worked on it but it has dried completely."

An older woman was the next one to have a story. "My girl friend's mother had gone to a chiropractor during the week to get rid of this terrible pressure in her hip. She called me on Sunday and said 'Mae, I know you are taking healing classes. Could you do something for my mother?' I told her to call me back in an hour. So I sat down and meditated and went into a level and sent her healing. Well, an hour later she called me and said, 'My God, Mae, it went away!' And her mother's pain hasn't returned since."

Ethel explained to the class that Mae has a special system all her own for absent healing. If a person has a problem in the head, she takes a wig stand and imagines that it is the person's head. When someone has trouble with his lungs, Mae gets out something that works like an accordion and by pushing and pulling on it, she imagines she is healing the lungs. Once a person needed help with his legs and Mae went to work on a table leg. "If there are twenty-five people in a room and they are all healers," said Ethel, "there will be twenty-five different methods of healing."

Georgia, another middle-aged lady, had a story to tell. "I asked for healing to be sent to a friend of mine named Lois. She was waiting in a darkened room. She and I have been tuned in together for a long time. She waited and meditated and said that she got a burning sensation in her chest and then she got very cold and stayed cold for about an hour. She hasn't had another attack since then. But the funny part is that she said she could see my face as I was concentrating and she said I was trying so hard that I looked mad."

A young woman from New York City spoke up when the others had finished. "I just wish to thank you and the class because I gave Kathy Jean McArthur's name last week for a healing and on Thursday, the day after the class prayed for her, she was much better than she had been for months. Her mother called me and told me she had wonderful news. Kathy was eating like a horse, had new energy and for the first time she had the will to continue fighting. Her mother was crying she was so happy."

Ethel's lecture that evening was on nutrition and the necessity for the healer to be in as good a physical and mental condition as possible. "If you are not feeling well yourself and you try to heal someone, you pull down your own health by sending energy into the other person. If you have a disease and you are treating someone who is worse off than you, you could, without meaning to, pass on your disease to that person because they are in a vulnerable weakened state. Or, on the other hand, you could possibly take on the illness of the other person because of your own weakened condition. It is very important then that before you heal you examine your own state of health first."

She spoke of the proper rest and exercise needed and also the importance of making sure the food future healers ate was not contaminated with chemicals and pesticides. Ethel admits to being "a nut" on the subject of nutrition and organic food.

A student asked her how she got her energy back after a healing, for the student was usually exhausted for several minutes after she had worked on a patient.

"When I've finished, and depending on the amount of energy I've sent them," Mrs. de Loach said, "I feel very hungry. And also very thirsty. It seems that this energy uses a lot of the moisture in your system. Once someone saw clouds of vapor coming from my back as I was healing a person who was desperately ill. I was wringing wet and I'm not a person who perspires even in the summertime."

She also cautioned her class about healing one person after another until exhaustion sets in. She said that even though they would feel deep concern for all those waiting in line that the healer also had to be concerned for his own strength and must have a cutoff period. If not, he would get so run down that he wouldn't be able to heal anyone. She said that once after a strenuous all-day session at New York's Commodore Hotel she was so drained that she spent the entire next day in bed.

Just a few minutes before 9 P.M. a student pointed to her watch. "It's now time for the prayer healing circle," Ethel said. "This is when a student gives the name of the person he wants healed and asks the united power of the class to go and heal that person. Most of the people you will hear mentioned you won't know and you will never see. If you know someone who is lying ill right now in a hospital you can envision this person and see him as you want him to be. In perfect health, up from the bed, breathing normally, and with full color in his face. You see what you want to happen," she said, looking at me as if to explain more fully, "and this makes it happen. We will start with the girl beside me and go around the circle, then we will have a few minutes of silence while we send healing to those who have been mentioned." She nodded and the girl began.

"My mother Joanna, who is in Germany and is suffering from a stroke," she said softly. "Kathy Jean again, please," said the girl who had reported earlier. "Jenny, she's in New York City with cancer," said another. "Mark." "Jane." "Sandy, he has a tumor behind his eye." "Gail, she's had a stroke." "Jim Brown in New York, who has trouble with his foot." "My friend

Jan." "Joe Hirsh." "Helen." "My sister Stephanie in Iceland who needs help for her eyes." "Rose Ann, who is ill and needs to take tests for open heart surgery. I hope she doesn't need it." "Adele Ross in New York." "Al, he's had surgery and there's a blood clot in his knee." "My mother." "A little boy on my block named Johnny. I don't know his last name but he's in the hospital." And so on until the circle reached Ethel again.

Then came the silence. It started out just as ordinary silence. There were no voices, just soft breathing. Then the movement started. It came slowly from the right and moved to the left. Then it came again, this time stronger. Soon it was like a current of electricity running around and around and around the bodies of those of us in the room. It felt like it was from the solar plexus level and rose up over our heads. I wanted to open my eyes and see if I could detect any movement in the air but the feeling of power, and yet of peace was so satisfying I didn't want to break it by trying to prove it tangible. It lasted for almost five minutes, building up and rising up until the room seemed filled with this amazing energy. When Ethel called time there were sighs of contentment, several murmurings about the "power really being strong that night," and general satisfaction over the fact that they had been of help to those who were unable to help themselves.

Ethel called the class back to order and resumed her lecture on nutrition but one man kept interrupting. He didn't mean to do it, it was just that he had this persistent cough and every five minutes or so he would start to wheeze so badly that he had almost to run from the room to keep from disturbing the others even more. Outside, in the corridor, we could hear him coughing.

Finally Ethel looked at him and said: "I usually don't do this in a class, but would you want a healing?" He readily agreed and a thin plywood table was brought in and placed in the center of the room. His bulk made the table sag and so several of the movable desks were propped under it but it still made a cracking sound when he clambered onto it.

He lay with his stomach up and pointed out where the pains in his neck and chest were. Ethel stood over him, squinting and studying his body through half-closed eyes. "Turn over," she said.

"But the pains are on *this* side," he insisted.

"I don't care where you *think* they are," she answered. "I get that you are to turn over so the work may be done on your back."

Like a beached whale he flopped over and tried to get comfortable on the hard table. Ethel pulled off his shoes and then removed her own shoes. She asked if anyone there knew why she was doing this. The guesses were that she wanted to be closer to the earth element or that it helped with the electrical movement or just that her feet hurt. She shook her head. "I remove my shoes," she said, "because I feel in awe of the forces working around me. It's the only way I know to show my humility before them."

Then she closed her eyes and stood silently beside the table for almost a full minute. The class sat without moving a muscle, all eyes on her.

A soft smile came to her face and she began to sway slightly. It was a gentle swaying and soon her hands were moving in the air near her chest. The hands glided gracefully, finger tips seeming to sample the air around them. In spite of her green knit slacks, yellow beaded sweater, reddish hair, and eyeglasses she looked somehow oriental. All I could think of was a very modest geisha. While she claims that she does not go into trance but knows she is "highly vibrated and on another plane" she had all the aspects of trance as she scanned the body on the table, scowled at what she saw through her closed eyes, and moved in quickly.

Her hands went to his neck and the fingers darted

lightly over the skin. I saw what looked like puffs of
light coming from them. Others noticed it too. Then
she began to run her fingers down his spine as if she
were playing a piano. The playing was rapid and
silent, going down his back, over his head, down his
legs, across his behind, never quite getting down to
his feet, and then down both arms. As one hand
would play the psychic keyboard that only she was
hearing, the other hand would be poised in the air
like a bird stopped in flight. Then, quickly, that hand
would dart down toward the body and the other
hand would lift and hover silently in the air.

Then she scowled, withdrew her hands, and peered
at his neck through her closed eyes. She scowled
again and tilted her head as if she was listening to
someone speaking. She nodded her head in agreement and the fluttering hands darted back toward the
body. This time they made little stabbing gestures
and, I was sure, were placing psychic acupuncture
needles all down his spine. That done, she stepped
back, saw something she didn't want in his aura,
reached in a quick hand, drew that something out
and threw it on the floor. Then she peered again and
seemed pleased that it had been removed.

Her hands flew again, playing that phantom keyboard, pulling out the invisible needles. One by one
they were removed and placed in the hands of someone who waited unseen beside her.

This done, she turned toward me (I was standing a
few feet away against a wall), opened her eyes
briefly, bowed, smiled, and resumed her hand fluttering.

Then she was finished. The hands fell down at her
sides, white and lifeless. She began to breathe deeply.
Her smile faded. Her eyes fluttered and her body
twisted as if to shake itself from some sort of harness.
She moved her shoulder blades and reached up to
massage her back. Then she shook suddenly and

opened her eyes. Everyone in the room relaxed with her.

Especially the man on the table. "Okay," she said, slapping him on the fanny, "you can get up now." The class laughed with the released tension but the body didn't stir. "He's asleep," someone said, and the class laughed again.

"Hey, you!" Ethel prodded. "Time to get up. The operation's over."

He stirred his arms and managed to swing himself into a sitting position. "Wow!" was all he could say. "Wow!"

He returned to his seat and Ethel went back to her lecture. She spoke for about a half hour and there were questions for at least another half hour, yet I noticed that *not once* did the man who had been worked on have to leave the room. Not once did he cough or make those strangling noises that had come at five-minute intervals before she had given him a healing.

After the class broke up I asked him what he felt. "It was strange," he laughed, "but there was this peacefulness. My body would tingle at times and sometimes I thought I heard music. Like a piano. The tickling in my throat went away. The heaviness in my chest went away. I'm breathing much freer now. I didn't feel any acupuncture needles but *something* made my body tingle. Anyway, who cares what I felt then. The important thing is that I feel one hundred per cent better now."

# The Swami and Peter Max

Famed New York pop artist Peter Max had invited the Indian sage swami Satchidananda to be a guest in his apartment. He asked groups of young people to come and hear the bearded yogi and eventually helped to set up an American-based *ashram* for him.

One day his young son Adam came down with a high fever. He couldn't sleep and refused to eat anything. Several doctors tried everything they knew but the fever refused to recede. He asked the swami to see what he could do.

The Indian took an ordinary glass of tap water and, holding it to his lips he chanted softly over it. Neither Peter nor his wife Liz understood the words. "Take a few drops of this water on a spoon and give it to Adam," he told them.

Carefully they opened their son's mouth and put some of the water on his tongue. He swallowed it. Very soon afterward he began to cry. He was hungry and tired. The fever had passed and he was well once more.

# VI
# The Fullers

"Can God Fill Teeth?" the small announcement in the local paper asked. For those who had never heard of Brother Willard Fuller and his "dental ministry" it was just another ad, but for those who knew of this man and knew of his work it was an invitation to a miracle.

The people came into the small church in Carmel, California, respectfully, yet bursting with excitement. They wanted their miracle.

A piano played up front and the crowd settled into the pews. It was a normal-looking church gathering. Mostly whites, a scattering of blacks, and a few Mexican-Americans. They were not well dressed or poorly dressed, just dressed like an average middle-class congregation. Except that they weren't a congregation. Few of them were members of that particular church. Few of them were even members of *any* church. They were mostly Protestants, but there were a few Catholics, a couple of Jews, and a group of Hippies who preferred Buddha to Christ. They were united under one roof to hear a "fantastic" man preach. They were going to listen to this man, he was going to touch them and all their dental troubles would be over.

The local minister came onto the platform behind the pulpit. He was followed by a man and a woman.

The man was tall, big-boned, and well dressed. He had snow-white hair and wore a pair of horn-rimmed glasses, which accentuated the masculinity of his face. The woman was lovely, with flowing shoulder-length dark brown hair. She wore a burgundy gown simply cut and neatly buttoned at her wrists and neck. She wore no jewelry except a wedding ring. There seemed to be a special radiance coming from her round, high-cheekboned face. She smiled and others caught her exuberance and smiled in return.

The minister introduced the couple as Brother Willard and Sister Amelia Fuller. He told something of their background and something of their past healings. It was a short speech because the service would probably go on until way after midnight and it was almost eight-thirty. Sister Amelia rose and walked toward the pulpit. She had a songbook in her hand and asked the congregation to turn to a certain page. The piano player began the introduction and sister Amelia began to sing. Others joined in but her sweet, high voice could be heard above them all. The congregation was singing words but Sister Amelia was singing praise to God. She moved quickly across the platform, commanding her exuberance to seek out the laggers and to stimulate the timid to raise their voices to the Lord. Her infectious energy was like wildfire across the small church and when the song was over she laughed and said, "Thank you, Lord. Oh, thank you!" Then she called out another page number and this time the eager congregation jumped in with her. She directed their voices, their rhythm, and their spirit and soon everyone was singing loudly with beaming faces and contagious enthusiasm. The last notes vibrated around the room and Sister Amelia grinned. "That was beautiful," she exclaimed. "Just beautiful! It makes me want to shout with joy when I hear so many voices praising the Lord!" A murmur of self-satisfaction rippled across the congregation. They were also pleased—surprised yes—but also pleased at how they had sung the hymns.

Then it was Brother Fuller's turn. He stepped slowly to the altar and began to address the group. His voice was deep, his enunciation clear with just the slightest trace of a southern accent. He told them of the Lord's power. He told them of the faith needed and the blessings granted.

He spoke for almost fifteen minutes and when he was finished, someone (obviously unaccustomed to attending church) applauded. The pianist began to play and while Sister Amelia sang, the regular minister asked for an offering to be collected.

Brother Fuller rose and walked back to the pulpit. He stood there for a few seconds in silence, his eyes closed. Then he announced in his deepest voice, "The power of the Lord is upon me tonight. All those with dental problems please stand and form a line. Be prepared to receive the blessing of the Lord."

At this, almost everyone in the church rose to their feet and hurried into the aisle. Those closest to the pulpit formed a line across the front. Others formed a line that went back up both aisles.

Brother Fuller prayed again, asking that those with needs be healed. Then he stepped down from the platform and walked to the first person, a woman at the head of the line. Placing his large hands on both sides of her face, he commanded: "In the name of Jesus be thou every whit whole!" He removed his hands and added, "Thank you, Jesus. Thank you, Father." Then he moved to the next person, placed his hands on the man's face, and repeated, "In the name of Jesus be thou every whit whole!"

Down the line he went, one at a time, stopping to lay his hands and asking for a healing on each person. The longer he took, the faster he spoke and his hands seemed to have a life all of their own as they moved down the line and up the aisle.

When he had finished he looked exhausted, but instead of sitting down he went back to the first woman he had touched. With a dental mirror and a flashlight in his hands he asked her to open her mouth. She did. "Do you have any gold fillings?" he asked her, shining the light around her teeth. She shook her head "no." "Well, you do now," he said softly. "Three of them," and he handed her the specially constructed dental mirror so she could look for herself. She let out a gasp. "I do have gold fillings now!" she exclaimed aloud, and she pointed to them as others broke ranks to see for themselves.

But Brother Fuller had moved down the line. Three, four, five people and none of them with anything different in their teeth. Then a woman shouted. She clutched her face and broke into a sweat. One could see her jaw turn a crimson red. She put her hands to her mouth and then took them away again. Brother Fuller moved over to her. "In the back," she muttered as he probed with his mirror and flashlight, "that broken tooth next to the one with the cavity."

"I don't see any broken tooth," he said laughingly. "And I don't see any cavity either."

"You're kidding!" she screamed. "The back tooth was broken and the one beside it needed a filling. You mean they've both been repaired?"

Brother Fuller handed her the mirror while a half dozen others peered into her mouth. "I don't believe it," she said.

"Why not?" Brother Fuller asked her. "Didn't you come here tonight for this? Didn't you have the faith that the Lord would heal you?"

"I don't know what I thought when I came here," she said, trying to speak as others kept looking down her throat. "I believe in Jesus, but I didn't really believe He would heal me."

"Praise the Lord," said Sister Amelia. "She believed in Jesus but not in His powers. Now you know that He is with us and can do anything He wants to, don't you?" The woman, still stunned at what had happened, began to cry. "Yes," she said. "I believe now. Oh, I believe in Jesus now!"

Then one by one people standing in different parts of the room began to feel strange sensations in their mouths. They called out to their friends, the friends searched their mouths and ran their fingers over gums. While some waited for their healing to take place, they looked at the healings taking place in others. There were cries of "I don't believe it," cries of "Look, the filling is changing color!" Cries of "Did you see that?" and cries of "Over here! Her teeth are getting whiter!"

A dentist's assistant sat by herself with her small son. She had come that night to report to her boss what a fraud this itinerant evangelist was. Her son had a front tooth that was crooked. Her boss had been unable to fix it. She wanted a healing, yet her better judgment told her it was impossible. When it came time to stand up and be touched she sat perfectly still. She had no intention of making a fool of herself in public. Many people there knew the dentist she worked for. Then her son began to complain of a burning sensation. He grabbed his mouth and looked wide-eyed at his mother. Then he took his hand away and pointed. She looked. His "dog fang" tooth was moving! It was slowly turning and positioning itself into line with the other teeth. She screamed and others came running to verify what was happening. The boy proudly showed everyone where "God touched me" while his mother sat there wondering what had happened, because she hadn't permitted Brother Fuller (let alone God) to place his hands on her son.

This happened in Carmel, California, but scenes like it have been happening in hundreds of towns in almost every state since 1960. Teeth have been filled, gums have been healed, new teeth have grown in, fillings have turned to gold, pyorrhea has been checked, and loose plates have suddenly fit.

I wondered who this man was, this healer with the

unique talent for dental work. I had seen a perfect set
of white teeth with gold fillings in the mouth of a
woman in Chicago who told me that Brother Fuller
had touched her. I met a young man who had lost
four teeth in an automobile accident. He had X rays
to prove it. Yet once touched by Brother Fuller those
teeth had grown back instantly. I know a man, well
into his sixties, who can no longer wear his false
teeth. Brother Fuller touched him and new teeth are
starting to come in.

I figured that a man who can heal teeth must be a
millionaire. While only a few of us have cancers, tumors, broken legs or internal problems, almost all of
us have dental problems. I figured that the man must
have an organization à la Billy Graham to front for
him and to keep him from the mobs which must constantly besiege him. I figured he would be impossible
to interview because of secretarial red tape à la Kathryn Kuhlman or else be so very busy à la Oral Roberts that it would take me six months just to get an
appointment. I figured all these things—and I figured
wrong.

Just one week after writing to his post office box
address in Jacksonville, Florida, I received a letter
from Mrs. Fuller. She had typed it herself and it was
two pages long. Instead of getting the brush-off or an
appointment in half a year's time, she said I could see
them on the day I had suggested. Brother Fuller
could give me three full evenings, if I so desired, but
"alas, we have no services for you to attend," she
wrote. "A lack of funds caused us to decide to stop
the tours until we could either have a better system
of keeping the ministry available cross-country or decide to retire completely."

Delighted they could see me but puzzled by their
lack of funds and concerned that they were considering retirement, I confirmed the interview and flew to
Jacksonville.

I'll admit that I was a bit wary of interviewing

these two people because they were to be the only really *religious* healers in this book. By "religious" I mean they were the only ones with an active campaign of preaching in a church, healing, and going on to another church. With the exception of Reverend Plume, the others in this book were "religious" in the fact that they became ministers to avoid the law or else held sessions in their homes that were more for healing than praising the name of God. Then, too, I had just seen the movie *Marjoe* and the bad taste of his deceitful actions as a Pentecostal minister had left a bad taste in my mouth. I didn't want another "Marjoe" in my book.

I'm happy to say I didn't get one.

Brother fuller met me at my downtown hotel and drove me across the bridge to his section of Jacksonville. They live in a modern apartment complex which is constructed like a series of two-story houses. The area is quiet and upper middle class.

The living room was decorated with modern furniture supplied by the building. A few personal mementos were scattered on tables or on wall shelves. A grandfather clock chimed every quarter hour. Amelia Fuller came out of the room they use as an office, looking radiant and apologizing for the ruckus her dog made when I came in the front door. He had stopped barking now, and she sat beside me on the sofa as I got my tape recorder plugged in and fumbled through the first questions. Right from the start it was Sister Amelia who answered every time I asked a question. Her husband prefers that she take over at interviews or in business deals or in itinerary planning. Her bounce and excitement with everything are a perfect counter-balance to his calmness and matter-of-factness.

I began by telling them that of all the healers I'd interviewed so far their religion was more in evidence than any of the others.

Sister Amelia set me straight on that. "You must

understand that Brother Fuller's ministry is unique as against regular Pentecostal ministry, or ministries like Kathryn Kuhlman's or Billy Graham's. Those evangelists have financial machines behind them or large structural organizations. Ours is more of a personal relation with the people, with no big money nor big board of directors to guide us. It's more personal." Her dark eyes flashed and she tossed her brown hair. "I'm reading a mystery story right now in which the heroine is a Japanese girl but also black. Her father was a black American soldier. She is Japanese, yet because of her inborn differences she is not accepted by either the Japanese or the Blacks. I bring this up because Brother Fuller's position is not strictly Pentecostal nor strictly metaphysical. Nor is he a universal ambiguity, but rather a solid rock in Jesus while penetrating into the deeper things of the metaphysical world. Therefore, he can't have an environment that is strictly Pentecostal or strictly psychic. He has to straddle both at the same time."

"Well then, where does your greatest acceptance come from?" I asked. "Do you work more with people in the religious field or with people in the metaphysical field?"

"Both," he replied. "We work well with all people."

"The only problems we've ever had," Sister Amelia said, "were with ministers who are dyed in the wool of one persuasion or another and who find fault with anyone who doesn't teach their particular brand of religion. They are upset when Brother Fuller prays for a person and a miracle occurs and that person happens to be a so-called 'unsaved' person like a Jew or a spiritualist or a psychic or a nonbeliever. But *people* in any environment love his ministry. We never have any problem with *people* because our ministry is basically the reality of God and the love of Jesus. We teach that the three-fold man—spirit, soul, and body—exists and that we can all use spiritual power to better our lives. And we also teach people to worship God. That's the platform."

"You wrote in your letter that you've stopped your tours. Why? Isn't there an interest?"

"Oh, there's an interest," she replied quickly, "but neither of us are business people. We have to do everything by ourselves. After a while it becomes discouraging."

"From lack of places to go?" I asked.

"From lack of funds," she said. "For many years Brother Fuller and I traveled only in the church environment and Brother Fuller was known as an evangelist, meaning that he would come to a new town, preach in a local church for a week or two, and then move on to another town. This became unsatisfactory to us because the Pentecostal environment was too limited. So he moved into town halls and public meeting places, but we were still always traveling."

"And that takes money," I said.

She smiled and nodded her head, looking at him and then back to me. "The world doesn't know this because we've never made it a point to tell anyone, but all these years we've lived off whatever donations or love offerings were given to us. We don't charge for a healing, don't sell tickets at the door, and ask only for a free-will offering. If a person doesn't have a dime in his pocket, we minister to him just the same. Even if they've received a dozen gold fillings. We are doing the Lord's work and He always provides the basic necessities. Brother Fuller would preach in a town and sometimes we barely had money to pay our hotel bill. Whenever we did get a little extra ahead, we would go off someplace like a remote area in Georgia, or an Indian reservation in New Mexico, or a ghetto in Philadelphia and minister to the poor. They need so much work yet they can't afford to pay us. So all our money would go out in daily expenses and nothing would be coming in. Finally we closed a revival meeting here in Jacksonville and just stayed on. We rented a house and then this small apartment. This is where we will stay until we can get things put together again."

Like every woman, Amelia Fuller wants a place to call home. It's been a long time since she could unpack her own set of dishes or worry about a potted plant. Hotel and motel rooms, after a while, get depressing. Staying in other ministers' homes only made her want a home of her own even more. Her feminine good sense decided to try and put down a root or two in Jacksonville.

Amelia Fuller wasn't always a preacher's wife. She was born in Texas of a German mother and a Mexican father who was a representative of the Guatemalan government in the United States. She was raised a Methodist but admits to not having too much interest in religion. She got a Bachelor of Science degree in education from Trinity University in San Antonio and did postgraduate work in psychology, biology, and sociology. For eight years she taught a class of first-grade children and pioneered some Head-Start activities for preschoolers. During that time she married, had a son, and was divorced. She doesn't want to talk about that first marriage, but she loves to talk about her second.

"I met Brother Fuller at a revivalist meeting in San Antonio," she says, "and while I was interested in the message he preached, I wasn't especially interested in the man. I had obtained a divorce and was content with my life. I started going to meditation groups and studying ESP and then one night I had an experience that still sends shivers down my spine.

"I was lying in bed, ready to sleep, and saying a prayer for God to bless my son and to look after him. I'd joined a group that showed me the power of prayer and I wanted my boy to get better grades in school. Well, all of a sudden there was this strange tingling sensation in my toes. It was like a thousand little pinpricks and it worked its way up my body in a series of waves. It was the most unusual sensation I ever had and it was thrilling! Soon my entire body was vibrating with these little stabs of energy and as they came up over my face I said aloud, "Thank you, Father! Oh, thank you, Father!'"

Then she began to communicate with God, she claims. It wasn't an audible conversation but a series of statements, questions, and answers that came from deep within her mind. She wasn't asleep, she wasn't dreaming. It was as real to her as if she had been in face-to-face conversation with someone. She is positive this someone was the Creator.

"The next day I was in an office and I said to a perfectly strange man, 'Sir, about an hour ago someone bumped into your parked car, dented your fender, came into the building with his name, address, and name of his insurance company, and gave it to you. Isn't that correct?' The startled man agreed that it was. Then I looked at a woman friend of mine and told her the exact number of her Social Security card. She had to take it out to verify the number for herself. Another friend of mine gave me a difficult mathematics problem to solve. Now arithmetic has *never* been one of my favorite subjects, but I gave her the answer to this complicated problem in an instant.

"I believe that the clairvoyance, the precognition and the highly developed ESP sense I have came as a direct result of that visitation from the Father. ESP is a natural ability that we can all develop but mine came immediately to me. I have developed these things so they can be of significant help to people. Although I do get things like what color car you drive or how many times you've been married or what your real name is or any of this sort of thing, but rather information that would answer someone's need. If a person has a problem, I get an insight on how to solve it, or if they want to know how they got into such a situation I get psychic help to tell them the cause. Many times I can see into the future for them and help them on the right path to their endeavors."

Her psychic abilities helped her when it came time to remarry. A full twelve months had passed since Brother Fuller had been in San Antonio and she decided to go to the revival again that year. A few weeks earlier she had, during meditation, resolved that if she ever married again it would be to a man who was doing God's work and a man who would want her to help in that work. A voice from inside told her that when the right man came along, he would say, "the Lord has put us together."

After Brother Fuller finished speaking that night she reintroduced herself and told him of some of the things that had been happening to her as well as her meditation classes and her work with mentally retarded and non-English-speaking children. He invited her out to supper. They went out several times during that week and then one night he told her that while he had previously been married and had fought the idea of remarrying, he was sure that she would fit in perfectly with the work he was doing. "I feel," he said, "that the Lord has put us together." That was all the convincing she needed. They were married soon afterward. This was in 1963.

Brother Fuller's own life is as diverse as his wife's. He was born in Grant Parish, Louisiana, in 1915. It's a small, predominantly Baptist town and young Willard attended the Baptist services regularly. When he was fourteen he felt the urge to be a minister and stated his willingness at the altar of a sawdust revival session, but he didn't do anything about it. Again, at seventeen, he felt "the call" but he stammered so badly he was ashamed to talk in front of any group. Once more he ignored the call. He went on to college, got a Bachelor of Arts degree in Business Administration and a degree in Electrical Engineering. He went into the Army and came out a master sergeant. His stuttering had stopped.

He returned to his home town and while he still felt the pull of the ministry he was preparing for a career in engineering. One night a traveling evangelist came to his home church and he attended the service. The sermon that night was "Go Preach." Willard thought it was a message for him, but he chose to ignore it. The next night he returned to the church and the evangelist had an announcement to make. "I had planned to speak tonight on another subject, but the leadership of the Holy Spirit has impressed me to continue with the subject 'Go Preach.'" This time the thirty-year-old Willard *knew* the message was for him and later, kneeling in front of the pastor and the evangelist, he dedicated his life to the Lord.

In 1946 he entered the Southern Baptist Theological Seminary in New Orleans and received his degree in Theology. He soon was preaching in Baptist churches. His easygoing manner coupled with his six-foot-four frame and two hundred and twenty-five pounds make memorable impressions on the various congregations. He began to hold revival meetings of his own.

At a religious camp meeting in 1958 he felt the urge to get up from his seat and walk to an isolated place outside the campgrounds. As he waited a stranger came up to him, reached out, touched his hand, and gave the young minister a message. "He told me," Brother Fuller recalls, "that I would be used as a funnel through which God would pour blessings on His people. I knew it was a message from the mind of God delivered by the voice of this stranger."

He began to look carefully at the strict Baptist set of rules he was forced to abide by and dropped out of the church to become a Pentecostalist. Once at the private home of nondenominational Christians he began to speak in a strange language. "Through no will of my own I was speaking in an unknown tongue. I couldn't stop. I went on in delirious praise and it was an evidence to me of a spiritual touch. It was more profound and caught hold of me more deeply than any other feeling I'd ever had in the spiritual realm before."

Three nights later he was alone and on his knees, asking the Lord really to use him. "At that moment I had the richest contact of His spirit that I ever had or ever dreamed of having. It was a distinct voice from outside my body. It said, 'I have given you the gift of miracles, the gift of healing, and the discerning of spirit. You shall lay hands on people in the name of Jesus and I shall heal them.'"

The healings began at his very next service. "I would teach spiritual truths and ask those who needed healing to come forward. A majority of the healings were instantaneous. I saw external cancers just dry up and fall off. I saw goiters disappear right in front of my eyes. I saw people that had been eating milk toast for years because of stomach ulcers suddenly begin to eat bacon and eggs and onions and all sorts of food. I saw horrible warts and growths just disappear. The powers of the Lord were vividly shown through me."

Then he heard of an evangelist named A. C. McKaig, who was supposed to have the power to fill teeth. "I was anxious to meet this man, so I traveled one hundred miles one way to where he was holding his services." He introduced himself to the healer and watched as members of the congregation stood in line and had their cavities filled

Near the end of the service McKaig announced that he was going to lay his hands on the visiting preacher and say a prayer for his ministry, but when he placed his hands on Willard's head, he suddenly began to speak in prophecy. "Think it not strange, my son," the voice said, "that I do these things through my servant, for all of the things that thou hast seen me do through him I shall do through thee, and

greater things I shall do through thee than thou hast
seen me do through him."

Willard Fuller felt a power sear through him and
he passed out. Since that day in March 1960, he has
been able to "pray in the name of Jesus and see teeth
filled by the power of God."

Some of the letters he has on file:

"I watched you pray for the many people who stood
in line in Immanuel Temple," wrote Reverend A. E. Lee,
the pastor of that Los Angeles church. "They were people I had known for years, many of them members of
my church. Yes, I saw gold, silver and porcelain fill teeth
right before us. I saw black decayed spots change and
become beautifully white. Holes in teeth completely
disappeared. One child, not in line and not even prayed
for, suddenly had a cavity filled with silver.

"To me it was and is the most amazing thing I have
ever witnessed during a lifetime of ministry."

A Mrs. Ruddick from Pueblo, Colorado, wrote:

After prayer for those in the healing line, I looked into
the mouths of several people. I saw gold fillings. Dentures were tightened. Sore gums (pyorrhea, etc.) were
healed.

I saw a cavity on a five-year-old boy being filled with
a white material moving with a slow, circular motion. I
kept saying to myself, "What am I seeing?" I was on the
borderline of doubt. This is hard to explain at this time.

There is a little deaf boy, aged 9, in my neighborhood
who has a great fear of dentists. I wanted very badly to
have this boy healed because of his handicap and also
his fear. (I, myself, have a little deaf girl.) I told his
parents what I had seen at the Revival, and asked them
if they would mind me taking him for dental needs as
he had two large cavities in his lower jaw. (I saw them.)
They agreed but were skeptical.

Reverend Fuller asked those with dental needs to
come forward. I noticed he stressed the two words
"believe" and "faith." He prayed for them. It seemed

his whole being was for those in need. The little deaf boy's brother, who was standing next to him, received a filling. But why did not the deaf boy, who was in such need?

We came home. I sat with the parents and checked off and on into his mouth. I then looked at the clock. It was 11:10 P.M. I asked the little deaf child to let me see, as it was late. Myself, his mother and father looked into his mouth. His teeth were being filled slowly with a circular movement and a white material was being molded into the cavity as we watched. I was so excited I was speechless. My God! It's happening. There is still some decay which I know will be completely taken care of. This morning I checked again and a little more filling has been added.

My own daughter, aged 9, had a filling placed. Thank goodness, it saved me a dental bill.

## A Mrs. Mercer wrote from Moorpark, California:

On the night of June 20th you laid hands on my daughter, Connie Sue Mercer. In an instant the Lord uncrossed her front teeth that had grown in crooked at the age of six. She is now ten years old.

I know that we could never afford to have them fixed as we have seven children. I am so happy to have it happen to my child; my small children are learning what God can do if they have faith and trust in Him.

Thank the Lord He put wonderful ministers on earth like you.

## From Louisville, Kentucky, Miss Vivian Williams wrote:

God wonderfully filled two of my teeth after Brother Fuller prayed for dental work. One filling is of porcelain and the other of silver.

A lady who wishes to be listed only as B.J.A. wrote from Springfield Ohio:

I was watching my mother receive some dental healings when I felt strange in my own mouth. I went to
my chair and sat down and looked in my compact
mirror. I saw my badly crooked bottom teeth just *move
steadily until they were straight*. I had never been to a
dentist and had not been prayed for. Everyone knew
that I had badly protruding teeth.

From Jacksonville, Mrs. Jo Ann Zeiger wrote a full
page humorous letter on how she felt about the Fullers and their ministry:

Son-In-Love is beginning to feel like a small amphi-
theatre what with half the county crawling in and out
of his mouth to look and marvel. Do you realize that
thanks to God and the Fullers you have provided us all
with table conversation for the rest of our lives??? The
kind which causes forks to freeze in mid-air and jaws
to sag down to the belt buckle?
But most of all and a thousand times more important,
you showed us God's miraculous love made visible. What
language, dialect or lexicon holds the proper words to
properly thank God and the Fullers for that?

Newspaper reporters are a notoriously skeptical lot
and usually treat "faith healers" with disdain or ridi-
cule. Bill Middleton, of the Jacksonville, Florida,
*Times-Union*, attended a service of the Fullers' and
published what he saw on October 2, 1971. He described the meeting and the laying on of hands:

For many minutes the church was relatively quiet as
Rev. Fuller examined dentures and gums, and the
congregation "waited."
Then there were murmurs, then exclamations of surprise. Soon there were open mouths of astonishment as
well as open mouths that had been "healed."
One woman said that the stains on her teeth appeared to be lighter. Another said that her dentures were
loose but she could feel them tightening.
There was Amanda Smith, who stood in the church

aisle. She had a radiant smile as she explained that her two front teeth had been crooked. "Now they're straightened," she said. They looked straight enough. "It scared me at first," she said. "I could feel a tingling in my mouth."

Others said they also felt tinglings. Some said they felt a numbness.

A cluster of the curious was around Ann Bolling Jones, who was shaking her head in disbelief but belief. "It's been a whole change," she said. "All of my fillings were dark. Now, they're bright. And a crooked tooth that I have is definitely moving."

Linda Barnes: "I had an old silver filling. Now I have a new one."

Jess Neely: "One filling is turning to gold. It's a miracle."

Duane Kimbriel, age 9: "My gums overlapped my teeth. Now they don't." He opened his mouth. Everything appeared normal.

But what perhaps brought on the most excitement were the cases when a "filling" could be "seen" coming into the mouth.

It was noted that never did Rev. Fuller even suggest that a person had been healed. He let them say what was wrong, and what they thought had happened. If a person indicated that a change had taken place, Rev. Fuller took no credit. He thanked the Lord.


The reporter later phoned several Jacksonville ministers asking them what they thought of what he had seen that night. None of them wanted to have their names mentioned in the paper but gave comments.

"In substance, they said, 'If you believe in the Bible, and if you believe in the miracles in the Bible, is this any different?'"

I closed the lid on the box of clippings and letters and said, "Brother Fuller, when you think that nine out of every ten Americans need something done to their mouths, you would think you had built the better mousetrap. You're the only one I know who is doing this. Are there others?"

"Yes, there are several," he admitted, "but none with the number of results that we have had."

"Many people have prayed or been in contact with spiritual energy that has resulted in dental healing," his wife added, "but in Brother Fuller's ministry there are as many as seventeen hundred people a year testifying to dental healings, and twice that many claim that other physical needs have been met. Since the traveling ministry has been curtailed, we now have a heavy mail ministry. We received a letter from a lady in Sweden who said that she had a cavity in her tooth and would we pray for it. So Brother Fuller prayed and we received another letter saying that a gold filling had appeared."

"When you say you pray for someone," I asked, "do you really pray or do you file it away in the back of your mind and let your subconscious do it?"

"I physically pray for the person," he replied. "If I'm in their presence, I lay my hands on them. If a letter arrives, I touch it and pray at that moment. Sometimes we set up a particular hour and the person knows I will pray for them at that time."

"Is it always the same prayer?"

He nodded. "I always say, 'In the name of Jesus be thou every whit whole.' "

"And then he says, 'Thank you, Father' or 'Thank you, Jesus,' " his wife added.

"You don't go into any more detail explaining who these people are or where they live?" I asked.

They both laughed. "I always assume that God knows more about them than I do," he said.

Mrs. Fuller pointed out that before, during, and after her husband prays, supernatural manifestations often occur. "People will receive sensations in the mouth or a visible sign in the air of some strange substance. Long after he has done something some strange matter can be seen. Which means that there is a spiritual energy that creates a response when contact is made, either physically or mentally."

"If you had to describe this in words," I asked him, "how would you do it?"

"The power of God," he said simply.

"But is there *another* way to describe it?" I insisted.

"No. The power of God," he repeated.

"Energy," Mrs. Fuller said. "Everything is energy, but this is energy from the very highest source. It is energy in its purest form."

"But does this energy come through your guardian angels or . . . ?"

"We go straight to God," he said.

"God is only three letters," Sister Amelia added. "G . . . O . . . D. But wherever the highest heartbeat of divinity is or wherever all creation begins to flow, that is where Brother Fuller goes. We are both of the opinion that this *source* is capable of making an intimate communication on a personal basis and that is the source he taps."

"But what about people who say they operate with the power of a spirit guide?" I asked.

"That's what they do."

"Yet their Chinese doctor is *not* the Godhead," I insisted.

"No," she answered, "but there are spirits on the other side who are ready to help us mortals. I've seen them. Sometimes we get information from spirits on the other side. That's not the source of *his* power, you must remember."

Brother Fuller laughed. "At one time someone suggested that I get an entity to help me out in my healings. My question was which entity should I get? Who is higher than God?"

"Well then, if this power *is* from the Divine Source," I questioned, "and is so all powerful, why then isn't everyone who comes to you and believes in your powers healed?"

"I'll give you a truthful answer," he said. "I don't know."

"I'd like to add something to that," said Mrs. Fuller. "Show us the healer who heals everyone he touches. Let's suppose that there are a hundred people in line for a healing and Brother Fuller touches them. Well, seventy-five will be healed."

"That's quite a percentage," I admitted.

"We've had dentists follow us and stand beside us and look into the mouths of those being healed," she continued. "That's the way it's always been with him. The majority of the people who come to him receive something. We've had physical healings that everyone could see with the naked eye. I remember that woman who came to us that couldn't control her eyelids. One touch from Brother Fuller and she was healed. And how about that man who was brought in to you with a torso brace?" Brother Fuller nodded that he remembered. "Two men had to carry this ill person into the church. He couldn't move. He was scheduled for an operation the very next day. Well he was healed in an *instant*. He took off the brace and walked out."

"It could have been faked," I suggested, playing the devil's advocate.

"It wasn't," she laughed; "we have too many people trying to catch us in something like that. Some people would love to see our hides on the fence. If this had been a fake it would have been in all the papers the next day, but being as it was a real miracle of God, nobody paid any attention to it.

"Once a man wrote a book about healers and devoted a few paragraphs to Brother Fuller. He never came to interview us personally like you are doing, but he talked to me over the phone. Well, he condemned Brother Fuller as a fake. He based this premise on the story of one woman, the only woman he could find in his area who had been to see Brother Fuller. She told him she had gone to a service and had a cavity and when she looked in her mouth there was a substance in that tooth. She went to the dentist and he told her it was just a temporary filling. So the woman assumed that Brother Fuller had slipped that into her tooth." She laughed and gave her husband an affectionate look. "Why, I'd be excited over that, if it were true! To think that my husband had that sleight of hand? I love magic and being married to a man who was a sleight of hand magician would thrill me to death." She laughed again. "Now it wasn't more than a few weeks later that a similar case occurred. A woman received something soft in her tooth. It began to harden and she picked it out and threw it *away!* Well, it grew right back in there again and turned to solid porcelain."

"We don't know in what form this energy is going to manifest," Brother Fulller said. "We can't tell in advance which way the energy will take."

"One writer even said that Brother Fuller had false teeth! Imagine that!" and she was becoming indignant. "He has all his own teeth! My teeth are much better since I married Brother Fuller. Not that I don't need dental care occasionally, but it's been six years since I've been in a dentist's chair." (Her teeth looked perfect, even and white to me. So did his.)

"We had a young man from Oregon write to us a few weeks ago," Brother Fuller said, "asking if we recalled someone at one of our meetings who was running around with a pad and pencil and taking down the names of those who had been healed. He said that he didn't believe in what we were doing and was going to write an article proving we were frauds. He waited a couple of weeks and visited each of the people who had had work done. He wanted to see them in the quiet of their own homes and after all the excitement of the religious service had passed. Well, he said he had to tell me that all those people still had their fillings and that what we were doing was really true."

Sister Amelia changed the subject. "There is a key to this healing that I have worked out in my mind and I don't know whether I've even talked about it with you, Brother Fuller. To me, looking back on all the years I've shared with you in the ministry, wherever we went we always had people very impressed with our worship service before the healing. It seems to me, now that I have time to think about it, that one of the reasons why so many received healing is that we were able to get a conglomeration of people of all persuasions in an atmosphere of the mood of the Holy Spirit on them. Whereas in a strict church atmosphere, there is a restraining. For instance, what is a Catholic going to do in an Assembly of God church? Or a Buddhist, if he's over here, in a Pentecostal church? Or a spiritualist if she has to put up with all the loud shrieking that goes on in some Pentecostal churches? But when *we* have the worship service it's completely our own. There are no traces of the religious environment that we happen to be presented in. Do you understand what I'm getting at?" Her husband nodded his head that he did. "People like to feel free of other people's dogmas; therefore, at our services the majority of them will open up, ready to receive spiritual energy. Their 'faith' doesn't matter."

"All under one roof worshiping together," said Brother Fuller.

"Yes," she replied, "and I think that's why things happen. The spiritualists want to attribute everything to spirits on the other side. A Science of Mind or a Unitarian or a Jew all have their own concept of what God *is* and we get them unified in a worship service where no lines are drawn. We present something that's real without offending their beliefs."

"Okay," I said, "but you've told me this energy has happened in private homes and even through the mail; then the *service* is not that important to the whole thing."

"Completely wrong," she said quickly. "The amount of healing outside a church service is much less because the anointing is not as strong. When Brother

Fuller is in front of a great many people, an anointing comes on him for the strict purpose of blessing the people."

I turned to him. "Then you use the energy of a large number of people to effect your healings," I said.

"No," he replied. "A large crowd tires me out. My energy comes directly from God."

"Could you work in a clinic," I asked, "taking clients every half hour or so the way some healers do?"

"No," he said again. "There would be no emphasis on the spirit in a clinic like that. The basic motivation for this energy is the spirit."

Sister Amelia had been frowning, now she turned to her husband and asked, "I have a question, okay? I've always been curious to ask you what happened that afternoon in Saratoga, California. You didn't have a crowd of people and there really wasn't a spiritual atmosphere." She turned back to me. "It was the darndest healing!" she said. "I was in a room with seven or eight ladies and we were talking social talk when Brother Fuller came in. He didn't do a thing but smile sweetly because he wanted to get me out of there as fast as he could, and each of those ladies asked him for a little blessing." She was talking to her husband now. "You laid hands on them and you had that *amazing* healing with that woman who had that tremendously burned hand. Was it prayer, faith, or the gift of healing?"

"I think it was the gift," he said after a few seconds' pause.

"The bandage *flew* off that woman's hand! She had it secured with adhesive tape and it came flying off her hand. She had a third-degree burn from the night before and it was healed! God healed her. Whammo!"

"There is no pattern," he said softly.

"No, but there's an authority," she replied quickly.

"God has the authority to do anything He pleases,"

Brother Fuller said, and started telling me about a healing that took place in a black section of Brooklyn. It was in an all-Negro church on Ralph Street. He and Sister Amelia were the only whites there. They had been conducting a two-week revival service and while many healings had taken place the collection basket never yielded more than a few dollars each night. "There was a nineteen-year-old black boy there who had terribly rotted teeth and he was also mentally unbalanced. You could tell that just by looking at him. He would walk thirty-seven blocks from where he lived to reach the church and when he couldn't find someone to drive him home, he'd sleep there overnight.

"Well, one session, toward the end of the second week, he came up to me just before the prayers and the healing were to take place. He had never said anything to me before, just sat and watched. But that night he said, 'Brother Fuller, I want you to pray and ask God to fill my teeth. You see, I'm dumb. I know I'm stupid. My brothers and sisters say I'm stupid. My father calls me stupid and pushes me out of the way. Could you have God show my parents and brothers and sisters that I'm not as stupid as they think I am? If God fills my teeth then they will know that *somebody* likes me."

"Well, this was all mumbled in his halting way and by the time he had finished, everyone had tears in their eyes and Sister Fuller was crying so she couldn't help with anything.

"But I touched the boy on both sides of his face and prayed to God to make him whole. There was a silence in the tiny, overheated room and we all waited for a miracle. We all wanted a miracle.

"I asked him to open his mouth and his teeth were just as rotten as they had been before. I didn't understand why God had not heard his plea. Others in the room sighed with disappointment and my wife was now crying harder.

"Then it happened. It was the most audible healing that has ever taken place through me. One by one the fillings came in, popping like kernels of fresh popcorn. They exploded and fillled out until he had a complete set of brand-new white teeth, the most beautiful white teeth he had ever seen in his life. We were all terribly pleased and thanked God with all our hearts.

"The next night he was back. But this time he was a different person. 'I came back and I am *somebody* now,' he told me. 'When I got home and Momma and Daddy saw those new teeth they didn't slap me around. They didn't call me stupid. My sister told all of them that they had better not hit me any more because I was somebody special. She said, 'God's got His hand on him.'"

I agreed it was a moving story, but I was curious as to what *he* saw when he looked into other people's mouths after a healing.

"I have a flashlight and ask them to open up. Then I'll see a cavity and in the bottom of that cavity there's a round silver spot. It's about the size of a pinhead and it glistens. It looks solid. Then it begins to expand and in three or four seconds it fills the entire cavity. Other times it goes so slowly that it takes two or three weeks to fill up."

"How about the dark cavities that turn white?" his wife prompted.

"A person will have a cavity that is a deterioration and it's all black. Then we look and it's all white inside, all cleaned out and nice and white. The cavity gets smaller and smaller until there's nothing left. There have been two cases so far where people have observed a golden vapor in the air in front of a person's mouth before a gold filling has appeared.

"The congregation can get pretty excited with something like that. There I am with a flashlight and I'm looking in a person's mouth and it's pretty hard to keep others from looking over my shoulder. We see white porcelain. We see silver and gold quite a bit.

We see new teeth grow in. We've had crooked teeth straighten up and loose plates tighten.

"Sometimes we will watch as a silver filling changes to gold right in front of our eyes. My wife gets so excited! We've had people with those composition fillings that dentists used during the Second World War when silver was hard to get and they have turned into brilliant gold right in front of our eyes."

I told him that a man in Carmel described seeing "an invisible hand squeezing an invisible tube and watching a white paste come out of nowhere, enter a cavity, fill it, and smooth itself over."

"This is true," Mrs. Fuller said. "We've seen that many times."

"When these fillings are analyzed," I asked, "are they really gold and silver?"

"Those who have had scrapings from these fillings studied by professional men all report that even though it looks like gold or silver, it is a metal unlike anything known by science today."

I admitted that was pretty mind-blowing, but wondered why, afterward, if I believed the stories of psychic dentistry, I found it strange that the metals were not of this world as well.

"Why does God have to fill teeth?" I asked. "Why is there a need for the *physical* here? Why doesn't He just implant new ideas in the mind rather than new metals in cavities?"

"It's to awaken in the individual the fact that God *is* and that God's power is available and we can all use it," he answered.

"Yes," Sister Amelia said excitedly, "but please recall that in the midst of enlightenment there are still those who are not enlightened. There were four suicide attempts in Seattle, Washington, and they were determined to kill themselves until they saw God fill teeth. This demonstration of the power *completely* changed their minds."

"Do you think this is why Jesus healed?"

"No," Brother Fuller replied. "I think Jesus healed primarily because He had a compassion for the person He healed. He was establishing a precedent for what we are doing today. He said, 'As I have done, so shall ye do.'"

"Which leads up to another point we've never mentioned," said Mrs. Fuller. "We do not believe that Jesus' healings through us or anyone else *primarily* occur to bless that person or get him healed. Many of them are a *sign* to the world. That this is possible. That there is really this power available. We are convinced of this because we've seen too many precious people with great faith but with a great affliction never get healed. And some hostile non-believer will come along, who has a faith even smaller than the grain of mustard seed, and he'll get a healing in an instant. The skeptic needs the proof. The other person already *knows*."

"We had a lady who received a filling of a cavity but it was just half a filling," said Brother Fuller. "Just half of it was filled. The other half was empty and we couldn't figure out what had gone wrong. But she was so excited about it that she made a beeline home to show her husband. She said that he sat her in a chair and lit a flashlight to give it a good close scrutiny and as he was watching it very closely it finished filling up.

"We knew why then. That man came and told me that 'if my wife had come home with her cavity filled to the top I would have said that she had gone to the dentist instead of going to church.' He didn't trust his own wife to tell him the truth about God's powers. But *seeing* it changed his whole life."

"He accepted the Lord," said Sister Amelia. "Most people don't come to us for the Lord. They come for the miracle. The main thing for us is that they receive miracles and at the same time see that the Lord is real.

"We are doing what we can as we are able to help alleviate human suffering. We minister in homes for the aged. We are endeavoring to help young people, those who need help getting to their feet again. We instruct them in the deeper truths so that they can build a lasting, solid foundation for the inner man. Brother Fuller continues to pray for those in need. And I give lectures on extra-sensory perception from time to time. I also counsel people who come to me for psychic help." (A gifted psychic in her own right, Sister Amelia told me of several of her psychic experiences. She is expert at psychometry, prophecy, and ESP. Several of her predictions have been carried out right to the letter.)

"Brother Fuller and I hold simple worship services at our little House of Prayer. We try to inspire people to live the radiant, victorious life, the life God intended us to live, fully, joyously."

They were about to go off to a church service and as I packed my paraphernalia I asked a question that had been bugging me all night. "Do you always address each other as 'brother' and 'sister'?"

They laughed. "Always," they said in unison. "Sometimes I call him Poppa," Mrs. Fuller admitted.

"Never *Reverend?*"

"Good heavens no!" she exclaimed. "He is always Brother Fuller, *never* Reverend Fuller. And it's never 'reverend' anybody else either. God is the only revered person."

She put her arm through mine as we headed toward the door. "I don't mind your being my 'brother,' but I'm going to *worship* God."

# The Korean Soldier

The patrol was somewhere near the border of Cambodia. They were mostly Koreans. The medic was a young American. They had been warned to look out for sharp stakes that the Viet Cong had planted everywhere in the area. The stakes were made of metal with jagged edges coated with disease germs. Many soldiers had stepped on them and died.

The young medic was walking ahead of the group when he heard a cry of pain. Turning, he saw one of the Korean soldiers pulling at his right leg. To his horror, he saw that a stake had entered the Korean's foot through his heavy army boots, had gone up the foot and out above the ankle. The Korean dropped to the ground.

The American stood stock still for a few seconds, shock written on his face as he tried to think what help he could be with only a first aid kit. The blood was spurting "like someone cleaning a fountain pen". An artery had been severed. He ran to the Korean, who was now seated on the ground in a lotus position. The American knelt down beside him and offered assistance, but the Korean shook his head. He had placed his fingers an inch or so above the jagged wound near his ankle. He pressed tightly and closed his eyes.

The medic could see the torn muscle and even a

piece of the bone as he looked through the ragged patch where the skin had been ripped away. "But as I looked," he later told his commanding officer, "a scab formed rapidly over the wound. Then just as rapidly it fell off leaving a patch of pink fresh skin underneath. The whole process couldn't have taken longer than three minutes."

A helicopter landed and took the Korean to base hospital. When he arrived there was no opening in his ankle or on his foot. An X ray showed that the artery had a thick band around it where it had been torn, almost like a ring a plumber would put on a broken pipe. The following day another X ray showed the ring was gone.

And so was the Korean. He walked out of the hospital and never came back.

The medic was asked to write "something else" on his report because such a statement would only cause trouble for him with the higher-ups. The men in the hospital pretended they had never seen any X rays. The young American, fascinated, started making inquiries about the Korean.

Other Koreans in the camp couldn't (or wouldn't) tell him much. The injured man was older than all of them, about forty, had come from a small village, and was unmarried. That, they knew. Oh yes, one other thing that might be important to the case: he was also a Buddhist priest.

# VII
# Bob Hoffman

Dear Mr. St. Clair:

I'm glad to hear about your book and I'm excited about you including Bob Hoffman in it.

My problem was not as big as I suppose a lot of peoples' are, but I think that's what the majority of people in this world experience. Anybody who knew me before going through therapy would have said, "He's a very nice, healthy, good-looking guy with everything going for him." Yet, inside me was a discontentedness, a turmoil that I never allowed to show. Most people would either say this was normal or else they wouldn't have acknowledged that it existed.

Bob took care of this for me but not until I had, on my own, tried yoga, cosmic consciousness, prayer, the Bible, etc. My life now is simply beautiful. I understand people and their problems and more important, I totally know myself. I don't say I still haven't things to work out because life's course is full of changes. But now I am happy, content. My nervously chewed-off fingernails are grown out and I can love—the most important thing in the world. Life is just great for me.

Sincerely,
Eric.

That was one of the letters that I received from former patients of the psychic-psychiatrist Bob Hoffman of Oakland, California. He is a healer of the mind rather than the body. He uses no incense, prayers, or spiritual ritual. He is blunt, self-assured, and direct. He claims to be able to do in just twelve weeks what other psychiatrists do in five years. He and his spirit friend, Dr. Fischer.

Perhaps the best word to describe Bob Hoffman is "formidable." He comes on strong; he is absolutely certain that he is doing the right thing and takes a back seat to no one. He has been cursed, accused of charlatanism, and of being on an ego trip. It doesn't bother him. "How can anyone condemn me who doesn't understand what I do?" he asks. "There's no condemnation with understanding. What I do is easy to understand. I make a person love himself because without self-love, he can't possibly love anyone else."

Bob Hoffman considers himself "a salesman of love" much the same way his father was a peddler of junk in Buffalo, New York. His parents came as immigrants to the United States from Russia. Bob, the fifth of six children, was born in 1922. He doesn't say too much about his parents except that they were very poor and his father was in a constant struggle to survive. Drafted into the army, he decided to settle in California after the war was over and, remembering his parents' lack of money, he began to think only of acquiring some for himself. He opened a tailor shop in Oakland and soon opened another. In a few years' time he had four shops, not just ordinary, dimly lit little places but fancy establishments, and the name Bob Hoffman Custom Tailor and Shirtmaker was known (and respected) in the Oakland-San Francisco area. He married and had a son. He lived well and was invited to the best parties. He had no reason to believe that he would ever be anything else than a successful merchant. Never for an instant did he suspect he would become a psychic-therapist communicating with a deceased psychiatrist.

Unlike almost every other healer-medium, Bob never had a psychic experience when he was a child. He hadn't had any and didn't know anyone who had.

He was not interested in the subject, didn't read about it, and didn't think about it. Talking to the dead was as far from his mind as flying to the moon.

Until that afternoon in Las Vegas.

"In 1952 I was in Las Vegas with my wife. We had checked into a hotel and were awaiting the arrival of my brother Harry. He was supposed to drive in from Los Angeles that day. It was a Sunday morning and I heard my brother call my name. I said to my wife, 'They're here,' and went to open the door. There was no brother Harry. I asked my wife, 'Didn't you hear Harry call me?' She said she heard no one. I'll be damned, I thought, and the phone rang. It was my sister. 'Fly home immediately,' she told me. 'Harry is dying of a cerebral hemorrhage.' All the way back I wondered about hearing his voice. He died and I put the whole thing down to coincidence.

"Nine months later my mother passed away, also with a cerebral hemorrhage, and I was the one everyone in the family fell on. I was the rock. I had to make all the funeral arrangements and all the decisions. I was real strong and it was great. Then several months later I began to fall apart and question this whole idea of death and what it was all about. I began to have doubts about continuing my own earthly struggle. I wondered whether it was worth all the fuss.

"I was a pretty unhappy young man. I was trying to raise a family and manage my shops, and when I expressed my doubts to one of my customers, he suggested I go over to Golden Gate Spiritualist Church in San Francisco and see Reverend Becker. Well, I didn't want any of that spooky stuff and didn't intend to get involved with a bunch of Holy Rollers, but he told me it was a legitimate place where you go in and write a little note and seal it in an envelope and then sit and wait for the medium to answer your message. When he told me that the medium would be blindfolded and would give me my initials, I told him it sounded like a magician's trick, but he assured me it was on the level. He said the medium would bring back the spirits of my mother and father and I could talk to them. But I said, 'Oh, cut your kidding! When you're dead, you're dead!' But you know how human beings are. Curiosity gets the better of our natures, and so one day without anyone knowing where I was going or what I was going to do I went to that church. The place was jammed with at least two hundred people. I didn't know a soul there. I wrote a note that said, 'May I have a message, please?' And signed it B.H. That's all it said. I watched my envelope in that basket with the other two hundred envelopes all during the so-called religious ceremony. For some reason my envelope was the fourth one the medium picked up. She called my initials and I replied. Well, when she started to describe my mother, it blew my brain because she described her perfectly and said that she had suffered from migraine headaches and had died of a cerebral hemorrhage. Then she said that a brother named Harry was standing next to me and she described him perfectly too! It really blew my brain! I went out of there wondering what it was all about but I didn't bother to look into it any deeper. I guess I was just halfway glad that maybe there is something after death and I forgot about it."

He couldn't have dismissed it completely from his mind for ten years later the mother of a very close friend died and in his efforts to cheer him up, he said that a medium had told him there was no death and if he was interested he would go to a Spiritualist church and try to get a message from his friend's mother. "I really didn't believe it," he recalls. "I was just trying to cheer up a buddy. What else do you say?"

He went to a small church near one of his Oakland shops and after the ritual had been disposed of he saw "ordinary people standing on a platform giving messages from the spirit world." His friend's mother didn't come through that night—his own mother did. And once again "it blew my brain."

What followed next would be out of character for anyone else but Bob Hoffman, a man who is incredibly practical and who can't stand not knowing what something is all about. He, this Jewish materialistic merchant, asked the minister to teach him how to communicate with the dead.

He was given the name of Reverend Rose Strongin, made an appointment and went to see her. He sat on a hard-backed chair, fascinated, listening to this woman from seven-thirty in the evening until one-thirty in the morning. She told him about ESP, spirit communication, trumpet voices, séances, automatic writing, and all the rest. Even though he couldn't accept her spiritual philosophies, he began to study with her. The course lasted six full months.

"What I was doing was learning how to develop my natural sensory perception. NSP, not ESP. I don't believe in ESP. The 'E' stands for 'extra' and there is nothing 'extra' about it. Extra means something unusual, and that's nonsense. We've all got it and we can all learn to put it into practice."

He tried his new knowledge on his friends and they just laughed at him and called him a kook. This was, after all, before psychic studies became the "in" thing. "They would laugh at me," he says, "but they had to admit that everything I told them was true. That would kind of bug them."

While he was calling his shots with amazing accuracy, he still didn't know what he was doing. He still didn't believe he was talking to spirits or reading friends' minds. And at the same time he was throwing out all the ritual and dogma that his teacher insisted had to accompany these feats.

"She said you couldn't sit cross-legged or cross your arms because the spirit couldn't get through. Well, one day I crossed my arms and crossed my legs and it

worked just as well. You had to turn down the lights,
I was told. I'd leave them on and the messages would
still come. These were all just man-made dogmas to
be thrown away. And I threw them. Years ago I had
had it with all the man-made dogmas, doctrines, and
rituals."

In spite of the rituals, he joined a local church and
began to give public readings. His messages were always a little more from left field than the other mediums because he would spare no punches when
thoughts came to him. One night he told a married
woman how her boy friend (now in spirit) used to
make love to her in the kitchen. He gave a list of seventeen different things that the woman swore could
only have come from her dead lover. But Hoffman
still wasn't sure the messages were from the dead.

He was told by other mediums that his spirit guide
was a psychiatrist named Dr. Turk. He laughed at
that. "I didn't know anything about psychiatry. I was
a tailor. Why didn't the spirit world assign me a master tailor as my guide?"

Still the skeptic, a week after the seventeen-point
message from the lover, Bob and his wife prepared to
go out to dinner. He didn't know the host and hostess. They were friends of his wife's and as he took a
shower, he told his mind that if there was anything at
all to this business then he wanted to know what
would happen at the dinner that night.

The first picture he received was of a square house.
Then a Spanish church with old tiles. Then he saw a
door opening and a five-year-old blond child smiling
up at him. He entered the house (in his mind) and
looked to his left. There were two magnificently
carved Queen Anne chairs. Then he was taken down a
flight of steps and into a room with several small tables. He saw a woman's hand with a huge topaz ring.
Then he saw a flaming dish being taken from a table.
(He was pleased with that because he loves flaming
desserts.) The last image was of a Spanish dancer's

black, wide-brimmed hat, the kind with tassels on it. He made a list, put it in his pocket, and drove to the dinner, positive it was all nonsense.

"We got to the house and sure enough, it was square. But so what? Lots of houses in Oakland are square. Then I turned around and across the street was the Spanish-style Catholic church. The door opens and there's that little girl. I said, 'Uh-oh.' Then I look in the living room and there are those two chairs and I say, 'Oh, wow!' And down we go into the rumpus room, which is filled with card tables. By this time I'm beginning to shake. I'm looking at thirty-eight people there and I'm looking at all the women's hands for the topaz ring. No dice. No topaz ring. My wife and I are seated at a card table where there are two people missing. Ten minutes later in comes a doctor and his wife. They were late because he had a last-minute call. She sat beside me and there was that big topaz ring! I thought, 'Great, I can hardly wait for dessert!' But dessert comes and it's ice cream. So there, I said to myself; it was just a long string of co-incidences. With that I was ready to forget the whole thing when suddenly the straw centerpiece on one of the tables burst into flames and there was my host holding the flaming centerpiece in his hands before he threw it into the fireplace. So now I had to find that Spanish dancer's hat. I looked everywhere after dinner, but it wasn't to be found. I just knew it had to be there so I went up to one of the guests and started working the conversation around to that hat. I told her I'd been to Mexico and I liked it very much and there was a dancer there that had a black hat with tassels. I admired the hat, I said. Her face lit up. 'Do you like those hats? So do I. I wanted to buy one today in a shop but they wanted so much money for it that I refused to bring it home.' So there was the hat. In the mind of one of the guests. I knew that I had stumbled onto something and I demanded to know what it was."

The next day he went into the special room he had constructed in one of his shops for his readings and meditations and asked to speak to his guide, Dr. Turk. "Okay, I got to know. I'm not going to do this anymore unless I have a logical explanation of what I'm doing. It doesn't make sense. People have been writing books about this and scientists are experimenting with this but still nobody has the answers. When I read someone's mind, is that *me* or am I tuning into the spirit world or what? I'm supposed to be your medium and you'd better tell me."

The answer he received began with a question. "Where is the mind, Bob?" Bob pointed to his head. "No, it isn't. There is no physical mind. That's a scientific terminology given to something that science knows nothing about. There is no mind. There is a brain. Science has proven we can mentally communicate with a living person. That means something nonphysical is in communication with something nonphysical belonging to another being and coming back to your body and relaying the messages across your brain to visually see it in your 'mind's eye.' Doesn't it make sense then, Bob, that if you can mentally communicate telepathically with a living person and since the mind isn't physical, why then can you not mentally telepathically communicate with someone who has no body?"

To Bob Hoffman that made sense and he's subscribed to it as fact ever since. "From that point onward I knew I was mentally communicating with the minds of the dead. This concept that came to me in answer to my frustration not only makes good sense but there is a knowingness that comes with this work. When your vibrations are right and you know that you know that you know. I know that I know that I know that the nonphysical mind can communicate with those who have bodies and those who don't have bodies. I haven't looked for corroboration from others in this field because I do not involve myself with the so-called professional psychics. I don't have the time and I'm not interested in their theories. I've got to discover for myself. I read a few books earlier. I don't read them now. I've found everything they tell me quite to the contrary. There really is no conscious mind or subconscious mind. What happens when I am talking and I move my hand? According to my knowledge, the thing that moves this hand, makes my heart beat, keeps my intestinal juices flowing—keeps me alive—is my psyche. My soul. My spirit. My electromagnetic force field. To put it into one semantic term, the spirit of me. The eternal part of me. And that works on its own. It doesn't require the brain to operate it. It tells the brain what to do. The brain is the computer, the mind is the computer card. It goes into the brain and the brain reacts accordingly. We use various mind trips in our therapy to prove this. The problems that we have on our earth plane come from the fact that our minds are sullied. We have proven that if the mind is cleaned of the negativity and returns to the free will that God gave it then the brain can be recomputerized to react positively. This is the basis of what I do. I'm a mind cleaner, not a brainwasher."

He began giving more and more readings and noticed that he was touching on health matters as well. One woman, because of what he "saw" in her body, had a doctor's checkup and an unknown malignant cancer was removed. He dropped out of all church activity, determined to find the answers for himself.

One of his father-in-law's friends, at this time, was an elderly and respected psychiatrist named Dr. Sigfried Fischer. Bob and Dr. Fischer used to have long talks about the possibilities of spirit contact and how spirit could influence human life. Bob was on the spirits' side; Dr. Fischer refused to believe in it. The doctor had a good practice but wasn't especially pleased with the results he had been getting with his patients. He wanted to make a break-through into new techniques but he was positive the spirit world had nothing to offer in this line. He jokingly agreed that whichever of the two died first would try to make contact with the other from the spirit world. Dr. Fischer died and Bob forgot their agreement.

One day a married couple came for a reading and Bob heard himself tell them that the husband wasn't showing enough affection to his wife. Immediately she jumped up and pointed an accusing finger at her spouse. "You see," she shouted, "I told you! I told you!"

Then Bob got angry with his spirit guide and silently demanded that he have some explanation to give the husband for this blatant remark. "I have no right to play God," he told Dr. Turk. "If you're going to say something like that you'd damn well better tell me why. I want constructive criticism, not destructive."

Immediately he saw a brand-new scene. It was the husband when he was a little boy. He saw him in the back yard of a farmhouse and he saw a woman coming out of the house calling the small boy to dinner. The child laughed and ran from his mother and hid behind a huge tree. She chased after him, laughing and trying to catch him. Each time she would grab for him he would get away. They were both laughing. Finally she got exasperated and when she caught him, she turned him around and gave him a severe spanking. "And since that moment," Dr. Turk explained, "he never trusted her love. All during his lifetime she loved him and then chastised him. Up and down. A seesaw. Does Mommy love me or doesn't she love me, and he couldn't trust a woman's love. He had never really trusted any woman in his life."

Bob told the man what he had seen and heard and the husband was dumbfounded. He said he remembered the incident perfectly. "Mr. Hoffman, I've been seeing a psychiatrist for two years and that scene never came out. It all fits together now. That scene makes me understand many things." He held out his hand. "You should be my psychiatrist," he said.

Bob just laughed and told him he was only a part-time medium and didn't know the first thing about psychiatry. But he was grateful that he had been able to help him.

A few nights later he awoke with an uneasy feeling that he wasn't alone. There at the foot of his bed stood Dr. Sigfried Fischer. Bob thought he was dreaming and mumbled at the image to go away.

"Just a moment, I want to talk to you," said the ghost of Dr. Fischer.

"Aw, come on," replied Bob. "I want to get some sleep. Anyway, you don't believe in this stuff."

"Bob," insisted the visitor, "you know I exist. You know I'm in spirit so let me talk to you."

Bob sat up and paid attention. It was to be the most important conversation of his life. Dr. Fischer told him that psychiatry was not succeeding on the earth plane, that doctors were spending much too long delving into a patient's mind dredging up useless information that had no bearing on a solution to their problems. This approach did nothing but pile up debris that had to be painfully and expensively sorted out and quite often obscured the real reason for a client's neurosis. He mentioned the husband and the beating he received from his mother. "He's been in treatment for two years, yet you were able in one sitting to come to the crux of his problem. That wasn't just a lucky guess, Bob. It is part of what I've been working on over here."

"What do you want from me?" Bob asked.

"You know that when I was on the earth plane I was searching and never found what I was looking for. It was part of my Karma; I understand that now. But here I am on this side and I have new sources of information. I also have you, a medium, as a friend. I can feed you this knowledge and together we can create a better system. I can show you how to help people."

"But I'm just a tailor," Bob protested. "I can't help anybody. Who will listen to me?"

"Don't worry," he said, "the doors will open."

"Yeah," Bob replied. "I've heard that time-worn cliché before."

"We have a rapport and we can communicate," he answered. "Won't you at least try it?"

"On one condition," Bob replied. "I've got my problems, too, you know. I'm mortal with all the mortal hang-ups. Solve my problems with your method and I'll go along with you."

Bob Hoffman is deliberately vague on what happened after that other than that Dr. Fischer took him through the rudiments of what he first called psychic therapy and is now known as the Fischer-Hoffman Process or a spiritual alternative to therapy. Whatever it was took about five hours and "suddenly I had everything together. Answers that I had been searching for were there. Situations that I didn't know how to solve were explained. It all happened very quickly but I *knew* I had been helped. I *knew* that in those five hours I had passed the equivalent of five years on a psychoanalyst's couch.

"This method works. Together, Dr. Fischer and I, with validation and support from an increasing number of mental health professionals, have developed it, refined it, expanded upon it, and perfected it."

He began holding group sessions in his home, working on the method and watching its results. He spoke to groups of doctors and psychiatrists in the San Francisco area and a few of them started sending him their problem patients. Not that they had the faith that Hoffman could cure them but they wanted to show him up as a fraud. It didn't work that way.

"A psychiatrist sent me a woman whom he had been treating for many years and was about to commit to a local mental hospital. She couldn't sleep at night because she saw ugly faces and would hear ugly voices. Well, I worked with her and taught her how to close off the channels that were bringing those disagreeable things into her physical plane. She hasn't taken a sleeping pill since.

"A twelve-year-old boy, who had been urinating into his bed every night, was sent to me. I looked at the kid but there was nothing I could do until Dr. Fischer gave me the information. You see, if I personally interpret a thing I may make an error. Jeane Dixon says in one of her books, 'It isn't what I see that is wrong, it's how I interpret it.' Anyway, I look at this kid and then Dr. Fischer gives me the answer. 'Hey,' I said, 'you're afraid of the dark.' 'Yeah,' he says. 'And you see all kinds of monsters, don't you?' And he says, 'Yeah, I sure do.' 'Would you like to get rid of them?' He says, 'Can you get rid of them?' 'Sure I can get rid of 'em.' We used our method; he got rid of the monsters; he hasn't urinated in his bed since."

The doctors began sending more and more patients to him and soon he found himself working six days a week at his stores, six nights a week with clients, and it was just too much. In 1968 he decided to take a leave of absence from his main shop, put his manager in complete charge, and open a small suite of consulting rooms. He thought it would just be for four months. "Well, today I'm treating not only the patients these doctors sent me, but the great-great-great-grand referrals of original clients. I sold my stores, I built myself a mountaintop retreat, and I got a divorce. My entire life is dedicated to this psychic-therapy now."

His life is also dedicated to the dozens of groups he lectures to every year, the radio and television appearances, and the reporters and writers who come asking for interviews. He has written a book on the method: *Getting Divorced From Mother and Dad, The*

*Discoveries of the Fischer-Hoffman Process*, published by E. P. Dutton.

"People always ask me how I accomplish the miracle of mental healing with only a three-hour weekly visit over a little more than a month's time. I *don't* create a miracle in such a short length of time. I bring people to a realization of what their problems are. This method of psychic-therapy is so basically simple that it amazes me it hasn't been discovered before. And I didn't discover it—it was sent to me. I take no credit for any of this. I knew nothing. I never read a book on psychology or psychiatry and I refuse to read one today."

The basic problem we all have, according to the Fischer-Hoffman method, is that very few of us love ourselves.

"Ask yourself how much you totally love yourself. If anybody loves themselves totally they're pretty lucky. Ninety-eight percent of the people in this world have problems and if you are part of the remaining two per cent you're also abnormal because you're outside the norm. In this therapy we find that the greatest problem is the feeling of desolation, loneliness, or unworthiness. A feeling of not being loved. A feeling that there is nothing in ourselves that is worthy of being loved.

"People don't love themselves because they weren't made to feel loved by their parents.

"We tell our clients to go home and make a list of all the things they disliked in their mothers and fathers. To write down all their negative traits and after they've done that to look at the list and ask themselves truthfully how many of those same traits they also have. It blows their brains because they find themselves overwhelmingly, negatively, exactly like Momma and Poppa or a combination of both.

"The world's most crippling force power is this thing called 'negative love.' God forbid it should be all positive. If you're not negative, you can't buy

Mommy's love. 'See, Mommy, I'm really not any better than you are. Now will you love me?' And that's called negative love. God forbid that Daddy should have an opposite trait so the child rebels against the negative love and wants a positive link to Daddy. Then he's torn in conflict between relating to both Mommy and Daddy at the same time. The theory is negative love. That's what we have to eliminate through mind cleansing.

"But how can you change a life pattern that was created in a child—programmed into a child—during his first thirteen years? Dr. Fischer did it for me one night, but then I was blessed. It takes me thirty-six group hours to do it, then it's up to the individual to continue."

When a client leaves the first session he is told to go home and write his own emotional autobiography of what takes place during the session. Often he leaves out important items that cut too deeply into his emotions or else he colors what took place to his advantage. Hoffman uses this as a guide in the next session, reading it like a road map of self-imposed detours and blocks. At the end of this session the client has a correct version of that preliminary session. This autobiography continues until the therapy is over and the client has a completely written report on what he really is inside and what really took place up until the age of thirteen.

"You may be intellectually, spiritually, and physically your present age, but many of us remain emotionally crippled at the age of thirteen. I'm not God, I can't change those thirteen years, but I've got news for you. Forgive me if I use an expression like 'crap.' Negative crap—what happens to it? What happens to human feces and horse manure while it decomposes and decays? It becomes something positive. It becomes recycled and becomes fertilizer. It makes things grow. So we take the negative crap out of the childhood of an individual and turn it into self-love and self-actualization.

"I no longer do psychic readings. Instead I teach the clients to psychically discover how they've related emotionally to their mother. I prosecute the mother in that session. I really pull her apart. I make the client see the real woman behind the apron and the gray hair and the smile. I turn her into a naked monster. I nail her to the cross, I accuse her of everything she's done to cripple that person emotionally. I've treated people who were sixty or seventy years old, still searching for Mommy and Daddy's love and angry because they never felt loved as a child. They've carried this search into their adult lives and can't relate to their husbands and wives.

"God forbid a husband should relate in love to his wife! That would be outdoing his mother, whom he couldn't relate to in love. Unless he can relate first to his mother in love, he can't relate to his wife. So, therefore, he's got to destroy his marriage with arguments or have other problems because until he is freely and lovingly divorced from his Mommy he can't be himself. Until you are yourself, until your thirteen-year-old emotional self grows up to your present age and joins you physically, spiritually, intellectually, and emotionally as one entity—and grows from year to year that way—you are in conflict *three* ways: between Mommy and Daddy and trying to be yourself.

"Okay, we nailed Mommy to the cross that first week. In the following week I say that while all of this is true, you are not overtly guilty for being you. You were negatively programmed. Now let's see what kind of a childhood *Mommy* had. And then we read her childhood. It's usually about ninety per cent accurate. You now find compassion for your mother. What does compassion mean? People say it means to be sorry. Hell, no! Compassion means sorrow for a person's plight, with a strong desire to alleviate the cause or remove its pain. If I can get you involved in compassion for your mother after you've seen that her life not only wasn't any better than your own but that she has lived twice as long, then you will have more compassion for her suffering.

"Then we go to the father. We nail him to the cross. We point out everything he did to hurt the client as a child.

"There are many causes, many reasons—no set pattern for any therapy. Nailing the father to the cross, the following week we absolve him just like we did the mother. We see the little boy he was, to become the man he was, to relate in the marriage as he did, to become the father he did that caused such an effect on the client. If a child happened to be raised by a grandparent or in an orphanage we look at those adults in the same way we looked at the parents. There's no such thing as a set reason why people behave as they do, but the main reason is that they don't feel they can make friends easily because they'd rather reject before they are rejected.

"Then there's the last session called closure. It's a mind trip, but then everything's on your mind, isn't it? If I could take a vacuum cleaner and draw out all the dirt in your mind, all the things that bug you, your mind would be cleaned. Well, thanks to Dr. Fischer, we have trips that clean the mind so that the individual learns how to love himself and love his parents in spite of whatever the parents put on him. He learns to accept, forgive, and find compassion.

"We teach people how to love. That's the primary object of the Fischer-Hoffman method. Unless you love yourself it's impossible to love anyone else. Oh, you can act out the actor's part that you see on the screen and think, 'I'll go home and make love to my wife like that,' so you go home and make love that way but all you're really doing is putting on another act. Most people seem to think they are giving love. Some people find it very hard to realize they don't give love at all. If they do give, they give selfishly—to get. To take. To fill their empty emotional cup. 'See, if I'm good in love then you're going to love me.' When they accept that they can give love with no thought of return or reward for themselves, then it comes back like bread cast upon the waters. If you love yourself, then you can love and understand everyone. You don't have to understand a person's problems, just understand that they've *got* problems. Understand them, but don't condemn them."

Bob Hoffman's relationship with Dr. Fischer is that of spiritual guide. He talks regularly to the spirit and will occasionally halt his conversations or thoughts to get a message or an impression from the spirit world. He claims that Dr. Fischer has never let him down in providing any information he's asked for and that the entity is always there when a client is having a consultation. Bob does not have to say any prayers, put on any special music or sit meditating in the dark for Dr. Fischer to come through. "He's just always here when I need him."

There are dozens of letters in his file thanking him and Dr. Fischer for their psychic healings. One at random from a thirty-seven-year-old businessman:

I'd like to add an overall review of my feelings and impressions of our sessions. My first thought is that if I had a choice of doing it over again without *any doubt* or reservation I'd do it again. In material terms, in regard to time and money it was the best and cheapest investment I could ever have made. You removed a thirty year old tumor deeply embedded in solid ego rock. In spiritual terms I've been given a new pair of shoes to wear on my long journey into the infinite. In the past I was never able to walk very far for any length of time but now the paths will be smoother for me to follow and I can proceed at a faster pace. I guess in looking back and reflecting, all children regard their parents as so-called perfect, God-like beings incapable of making any mistakes as far as their children are concerned. I can easily see the resentments built up against parents emotionally as they disappoint the young child. As one grows up and learns about the so-called beautiful people, happy marriages, wealth, etc., it's very easy to create a very deep resentment against parents who are the exact opposite to the ideas and ideals being taught by society, movies, television, advertising, and radio. During my childhood I thought my home life was nearer to hell on earth rather than the heaven on earth that everyone strives for. I got out of the house at age 20 via the U. S. Army but that house never got out of me. I've been carrying it on my back all these years. But now, for the first time I can see my parents not as Mom and Dad but two human beings who had a very troubled childhood of their own which resulted in family turmoil due to *their* inability to resolve each others' problems. It's funny now to think that my parents are also human beings with childhood problems of their own. The fact that Dad went to his grave without my loving him fills me with great mourning. I want to meditate and send my living spirit to him to tell him that at last now I finally understand and love him very dearly with all my heart. At least Mom is still here and I've been rethinking a lot in order to give her my true love. I have a lot of re-structuring and re-balancing to do, and it may take time, but I know I'll do it.

Bob no longer gives private sessions, or does psychic readings. His 60-hour work week is spent at his Quadrinity Center in San Francisco, a non-profit corporation. There groups of people learn self-love, self-acceptance and self-esteem. The Center trains others to teach the remarkable method that was given to Bob from the spirit world.

# The Baby and Jean Coleman

Jean Coleman, an American Indian, is a registered nurse who lives in San Jose, California. She told me the following story and I asked her to put it in writing.

"While employed by a large hospital in town, I had a most unusual experience. There was a policy in the hospital, that if there was a surplus of nurses on one floor while another floor was understaffed, we were transferred to that floor for better patient coverage. That morning the pediatric floor needed another nurse and as it was my turn, I went, but I didn't like it. I always became so concerned when I had to work the children's ward because they were so small and often in such pain.

"I was doing some charting when I heard a baby crying. It was a high-pitched wail and very distressed. I knew I had to check. I went into the ward and there was a two-month-old baby in the croup tent. Above the crib there was a sort of floating, a cocoon of mist, and the body of the baby. I was shocked to say the least and more than a little frightened. I didn't know what to do. The nursing books had never mentioned that one. I seemed to be in a daze. I was almost unaware of the words that came from me: 'Come down from there and get back into this body right now!'

"I unzipped the croup tent and took the baby in my arms. It was blue and mottled and gasping for breath. All my training had told me that a baby is best left in the tent no matter what the problem is but I sat in the rocking chair and held her. As I held her, I felt what I can only describe as an electrical current coming from somewhere, and through my arms to the baby. The current came in waves, ascending and descending. I held her for what seemed a long time. Her skin became much clearer and she slept. Her breathing was normal. The mist above the crib was gone. I hadn't seen it disappear.

"I put the baby back in the crib, zipped up the tent, walked out of the room, went into the nurses' bathroom, locked the door, and shook and sobbed. Whether it was the enormity of what had happened or the release of tension or what, I don't know. After I had composed myself I went to the desk and looked at the baby's chart. The prognosis: poor.

"Two days later I asked the regular nurse on the floor about the baby. She said she had been sent home and in good condition."

# VIII
## Dorothy Vurnovas

News of Dorothy Vurnovas' talents as a healer reached me only after I had gotten to know her as a trance medium. In those days she was in contact with the spirits of recently departed children, naming names and trying to make contact with others on the spirit plane who would take notice and help these little lost souls.

Then, when I announced that I was going to do this book, letters from all over the West Coast came cascading onto me telling of the healings they had received from Dottie's hands ... or over the phone ... or via prayers ... or through her astral visits. Naturally, I wanted to see her again.

At that time she lived in a medium-sized mobile home in San Jose, California. The trailer was neatly furnished and ample enough for her and her husband Chris. She did most of her healings, readings, and counseling during the day while he was working at a sheet metal mill. That way when he came home she was Dottie the wife and not Dorothy the mystic. One night a week, Friday, Chris took his folding chair and a magazine and went out behind the trailer to wait until her weekly healing session was over. It's not that he didn't believe in it, but the living room held only so many people.

Dottie is a remarkable little creature. She reminds me of one of the munchkins in *The Wizard of Oz*. She stands just four foot seven inches tall, is round in both face and body, and has a small but powerful voice. She dresses casually, is unpretentious, and there is nothing about her that would give one the idea that she had any special link with the "powers." Not until you look into her brown eyes, that is, and then you see the energy, the strength, and the knowledge. They are eyes of a person who has experienced much and who has learned by it.

When I arrived at her trailer, tape recorder in hand, I didn't expect to find three other ladies with her. At first I was annoyed because I wanted to talk to Dottie alone; then I was very pleased for these three women had all been healed of one ailment or another by Dottie and assisted at her Friday-night healing sessions. The conversation got away from healing several times, but Dottie always brought it back. I could see, as I watched and listened, that the little lady was a born leader. She knew just how far to allow her friends to go. Then she would bring them back with the nudge of a velvet glove. No wonder they look up to her and respect her.

Donna Stabnau, a dynamic talkative woman, started the conversation by telling me how Dottie disappeared one night right in the middle of a healing session. "I was looking at her, really concentrating on what she was doing, and her face began to fade in and fade out. Once an oriental face appeared. Then the whole body went. It was quite frightening because her whole body just went blank. I couldn't see her any more, at all. I could see the chair and it was empty. There was nothing. Not a mist, nothing. She was gone."

"I'll agree to that," spoke up Sarah Swift, a small, middle-aged lady with an English accent. "Two weeks ago at a Friday-night session, I was in the corner across from Dorothy and she said to me: 'What are ya starin' at?' 'At you,' I said. 'You've gone!' "

I turned to Dottie, already perplexed, and the interview had just begun.

"When this happens," she said calmly (considering the subject under discussion), "I feel I've gone. I feel I've arrived at a higher plane. I'm aware that I'm not sitting in the chair. It's a kind of astral projection where I take my body with me. I go up to the higher planes to bring energy down to the earth's surface for the healings."

"Well, why is it necessary to disintegrate your body at the same time?"

"It just happens," she laughed. "I give the healings from the physical so I imagine my physical being is being recharged at the same time I'm given the energies. Sometimes I get so recharged that I have to do something to discharge myself before I can sleep that night."

"After you've had a healing service," I asked, "do you feel exhausted and let down?"

"On the contrary, I feel really lifted. I feel light. You know, sometimes I come in here, my head aching so bad I can't stand it, and then I start to feel beautiful. Other times the vibrations in here are so high that I think my head is about to burst, but always after the healings I feel great. I don't feel drained, just relaxed and at ease."

Dottie began these Friday-night healing sessions in April, 1969. Almost from the beginning they were packed with friends and strangers wanting a cure. People drove for miles to attend and the living room overflowed. Because of the large Mexican population in the San Jose area, several of the cures have had to be translated into Spanish.

The sessions were really quite simple. Dottie and her regular group of four auxiliary healers sat in silence for a few minutes. Then one said a prayer asking that the power be brought into the room. Then one by one those who had come for a healing were brought into the center of the group. Sometimes the laying on of hands was used. Other times only thought vibrations were sent. Quite often those who were merely standing on the sidelines got healed as the energy built up and seeped into the far corners of the trailer living room.

An important part of each session was the energy directed to a glass bowl that sat on the coffee table in the room. In it were names of people all over the world who had asked for an absent healing. Their names were kept in there until the healings were complete (Dottie sent healing into the bowl daily by herself) and then removed to allow others to have a chance.

The sessions lasted an hour or two or until Dottie felt that there was nothing more to do. Then another prayer was said and it was over until next week.

There was no charge at these sessions, not even for the coffee and doughnuts that were served. Dottie doesn't feel right in charging for a gift she has received from God.

Often an emergency will come up and Dottie will hear of someone needing instant prayer healing. She'll get on the phone and call others until a chain has been formed around the country. Then at the agreed-upon time they will sit down and send healing to that particular individual.

A man in San Jose wrote to tell me of such an experience:

My wife's sister and brother-in-law live in Texas. They are both in their early seventies. They are so close to my wife that when she heard Sam was to have surgery on the colon and that the doctors only gave him a thirty per cent chance of survival, she immediately flew to Texas. But before she did she called Dorothy Vurnovas and asked her to pray. Sam has a heart condition, very high blood pressure and several other complications. Mrs. Vurnovas' group began praying immediately. Sam survived the surgery against those impossible odds and his doctors were amazed. The colon, however, had been cancerous and Sam began slipping. My wife called Mrs. Vurnovas from Sam's room and long distance over the telephone a healing took place. Sam rallied, was home two weeks later, and has never had a relapse.

For some reason, Dottie's power can be transmitted even over the phone. In September 1973 I was visiting my parents' home in Warren, Ohio, when a friend, Delores Mook, showed me her red and swollen skin. It was an allergy, her doctors claimed, and they said she would have it all her life. It was a reoccurring illness that would become so intense that she could neither work nor sleep and then her doctors would put her in the hospital and fill her full of serums and pills. She was almost in tears at the thought of having to commit herself to the hospital again. I gave her Dottie's phone number and asked her to call. She phoned that night, and I saw Delores the next day. The rash was gone. The swelling was down, the itching had stopped; and the hospital appointment had been cancelled.

I received a letter from a woman in San Jose who wrote: "Last March when I was very sick with pneumonia, I spoke to Dorothy Vurnovas on the phone and immediately my chest began to feel better. Two days later when I went to see my doctor she said he was amazed at how much better I was. He said he couldn't believe the recovery I had made. A week later I was back to my old normal self with no scars on my lungs. I am very glad to know this remarkable woman."

Donna Stabnau once was on the phone to Dottie telling her about a co-worker in her office who had been complaining for a week that he couldn't turn his head because of terrible neck pains. Dottie asked her to put the man—a stranger—on the line. "Dottie start-

ed talking to him and while I watched I could see
water running down his face and off his arms, he was
perspiring so. He was feeling the power, taking it into
his body. When he hung up he looked at me and
shook his head. And he could shake it, and twist it as
well. The pain went away and never came back."

Dottie volunteered an explanation. "A lot of people
call it psychic healing, but I came up with a new
name. I call it telepathic healing. What I do when I
am giving an absent healing is to get into the cells
and telepathically command that the Christ-con-
sciousness or God-consciousness in these cells burst
forth and release their miraculous healing powers. So
they can heal themselves. As I do this I am telepathically directing this power so that they will divide
and multiply and take over the sick cells. And this is
the way the healings come forth.

"Each healing, however, is different, depending on
what has to be done and to whom. My friends from
above will say, 'This time do so-and-so. This time
don't use the white light. Use the blue light on this
man.' Sometimes I go through a lot of rigamarole. I
got a letter from a man in Paris, France, who had
varicose veins. While I was directing and trying to
make the veins come up center to close the little
knobs that were ruptured, something said, 'Now write
his name and the disease on a piece of paper, burn it,
and take it out and let it go to the four winds.' So I
took it out onto the railroad tracks and let the ashes
blow away. I don't know *why* they asked me to do
this, I just did it."

I wanted to get back to the stranger on the telephone. "What did you do to the man in Donna's office?"

"When he came on the phone he said he had this
neck thing, so I started by getting behind him physically and placed my hands on his neck and started
massaging the muscles to relieve the pain. After that
I just directed a heat force."

"Now all this time you were in conversation with him?"

"No, I just said be quiet a minute and let me know when you start feeling a warmth."

"And then when the heat was on him," Donna cut in, "you could see the water running off his face. It was pouring right off his forehead. I know she does just beautiful things because I've had them happen to me. I'd been under a doctor's care for over two years with a terribly bad colon. If I would get upset or excited the pain would be so bad that I would pass out right on the floor, go out like a light. Or if I ate anything that was highly seasoned—anything—the same thing would happen. I would have so much pain that I thought I was dying. The doctors checked and gave me all kinds of tests; and finally they hooked me up to a television set and put some tubes into my rectum and they said they 'thought' they knew what it was. They talked about an operation.

"So I mentioned this to Dottie when we were having our healing circle and she said, 'Okay, lie down on the floor, Donna.' So I got down on the floor and she put her hands very lightly on the spot that was irritated and I could feel pressure going down my side and into my stomach just like someone was in there working on it. I could feel it. I could feel something happening in there, and I knew she hadn't moved her hands or anything. They were just laying lightly there and she wasn't putting any pressure on my stomach. And the following week I came back and got on the floor again and I could feel it draining. And then there was this terrible smell, this odor. I was completely clothed but everyone in the room could smell this odor. And that was it. I never took any more medication after that. The burning sensations never returned. After two years of suffering I was well in just two weeks of Dottie's power."

"And after that treatment," put in Dottie, "she went

out and had a sandwich made of that spicy Polish sausage and some green peppers . . ."

"I wanted to see if I was really cured . . ."

"And then she ate about a pound of cherries . . ."

"I can eat anything now. I can get upset, I can scream at my boss, I can bawl out my kids, I can do everything without having to worry about passing out. It was the most perfect healing I've ever had."

I needed more details. "Dottie," I said, "what do you think your hand did when it cured Donna. She said she didn't see it go into her body and it didn't cut a gash into it the way some healers do. So what *physically* did happen?"

"As much as I can recall, I put my hand on her right side, near the appendix. As I held it there I concentrated on the healthy cells taking over the infected cells and putting white light in there as they did it. My full concentration was just on that. The only thing I could physically see was as the healthy cells started taking over they pushed out the essence of the decayed, rotted cells. So that's where that putrid smell came from."

"Does your hand feel hot when you heal?"

Donna answered for her. "Does it! Sometimes it gets so hot you can hardly stand it! When she puts her hand on you you feel like you're on fire. It's a terrific heat but it doesn't burn you. She left her handprint on Sarah one time."

Sarah nodded in complete agreement. "I had a bad back and everytime I would get just the wee bit of a chill I'd have to lie flat on me back. When Dorothy came and put her hands on me back a light flashed up into me head. Nearly knocked the top of me head off. I've not had a pain in there since. And when she decided she was going to cure my asthma she put her hand on my chest and the burn was there for all to see."

"You could see Dottie's fingerprints on her chest," Donna added. "When Sarah came in here she was wheezing something terrible, but when she went out she was breathing normally again."

"Now I'm looking for a job," the little English-woman piped up. "I feel good enough to work and I'm going to get work."

The first time Sarah met Dorothy, Sarah was suffering from neuralgia in her face. Dottie didn't know if Sarah believed in psychic healings or not. "Well, Sarah, do you believe that God can heal you?" she asked. When Sarah said, "Yes," Dottie asked her if she believed in the laying on of hands. Again Sarah said, "Yes."

"So she started working on me," added Sarah excitedly, "and I could feel this power racing through me body and I began shouting to the others around me, 'What's she doin' to me? What's she doin' to me?' and then the pains were gone. All of them. Just gone. I was so shocked you know because it happened so fast."

Now Donna was excited and bursting to tell me something. "When we would come here with something wrong with us she'd put us in a circle and then go over our bodies with her hands and you could see the light coming out of the end of her fingers! One day I was standing there and she stops and she points and pinches my stomach and says, 'It's drawing here, Donna,' and I had forgotten all about it. I had a big cyst there and I'd been to the doctor for it and he said he'd have to cut it out and he put a piece of tape over it. So a couple days after she gave me this healing I took off the tape and the cyst, about the size of a pea, came right off with the tape. Now she didn't know I had it. I didn't tell her but she found it when she was going over me. She did the same thing once when an earring had infected my ear lobe. She told me it was hurting me."

"But that was easy to tell," I said, "all she had to do was look at your ear."

"Yes, but I was wearing a wig that day and my

ears were covered." And she stared at me in triumph.

"I tell them to remember the spots I've pointed out," Dottie said coming to my rescue, "because when I have a dozen people here I can't concentrate on the force and remember all the places myself. Maybe I'm just lazy."

"So each person that comes to you gets this psychic once-over before you heal? Right?"

"Wrong," and everyone laughed. "I started out that way, but I don't do it that way any more. Now they tell me what is wrong and I make a polonium tube and work with that."

"A *what* tube?"

"A polonium tube. They taught me how to make it. They," she quickly added, "are my teachers upstairs. They showed me how to take pure light and form it into a tube that would channel the energy any place I willed it. Like a laser beam but invisible. You know."

I shook my head in the affirmative, not really knowing what she meant.

"And I take this beam of light and focus it on a spot in a person's body and the energy goes to work on the decayed and dead cells, replacing them with new cells full of healing life. They've told me that this polonium tube is going to be an important healing device in the future. So far very few people have it."

"So 'they' want you to work only with this tube now. Right?"

"Wrong." And again there was laughter. "It all depends on the case I'm working on. Each case needs a somewhat different handling."

"Don't try to put Dottie into a category," spoke up an attractive brunette named Carol (who'd been silent so far). "It can't be done. She is a *very* unique personality."

I admitted that I was beginning to see that.

Donna again wanted the floor. "Tell them about Louise, Dottie." Before Dottie could say anything,

Donna proceeded to tell the story. "She went into the hospital for a hysterectomy and the doctor was amazed how quickly she was checked out again. She went home two days early. The doctor told her it was a miracle. I wish she had told him Dottie had been sending her absent healing."

"Well, look at me daughter," spoke up Sarah. "With pneumonia. It only took three days and she was out of the hospital and feeling chipper."

"Three days to get over pneumonia?" I questioned, remembering a grandmother of mine who had spent weeks in the hospital for the same thing.

"Just three days," Sarah stated emphatically. "And her doctor says, 'I gotta look at those X rays again,' and she says, 'No, don't bother,' and he says, 'Why not?' and she says, 'I had a friend of mine workin' on me,' so he says, 'What do you believe?' and she says, 'The power of God and all the healing prayers.' And he said, 'Well, go ahead then.' So he agreed with her, he did."

Once more Donna was trying to catch Dottie's eye. "Tell him about the little baby with the hole in his . . ."

Dottie moved in quickly. "It was a little boy. His mother and father lived in the park here. The father had gotten a partial healing from me earlier. He was in a local veterans hospital for a mental thing and having a horrible time, so I magnetized a handkerchief for him and his wife took it to him. When he went to do his therapy thing, which he hated, he began to get nervous and shaky and he took out that handkerchief that had been magnetized and wiped his face and immediately he became calm as anything. About a week after that he was able to come home for weekends and it was just about a couple of months after that that he was able to come home permanently. So they had this baby . . ."

"Wait a minute," I interrupted. Things were going

much too fast for me. "What did you do to that hand-kerchief?"

"I magnetized it," she said. "I held it in my hands, thought about the man in the hospital, and concentrated all my energies into the cloth. Then, when his wife gave it to him, the energies—that were meant for him—were released and he got the full benefit of them. It's a wonderful way to reach someone when you can't do it physically and in his case not even mentally. Do you understand?"

I nodded my head in the affirmative. In Brazil I had seen them magnetize glasses of water, which the patient drank and felt better afterward, but this was the first time I had ever heard of a magnetized hand-kerchief. (Later I recalled that here in the United States several Pentecostal ministers sell "healing cloths" or amulets that are supposed to carry their healing vibrations. I also interviewed Marcel Volgel of San Jose when I was doing a segment for the television show "You Asked for It." He was experimenting with sending healing vibrations into the leaves of potted plants and then placing the plants near a patient's bed in the hopes that the energies held by the leaves would be given off into the atmosphere of the hospital room. It was basically the same thing Dottie was doing but Mr. Volgel was an IBM scientist and Dottie was just . . . well, . . . Dottie.)

"Anyway, this little boy was brought here by his parents and they told me something was wrong with one of his feet. They didn't tell me *what* was wrong nor did they take off his little booties so I could see his feet. Well, he was always up on the toes of one foot. He couldn't seem to put it on the floor. The other foot would go flat but not this one. So I started concentrating to see into the body to figure out what was causing this. Suddenly I looked at his parents and I said that he had brought this problem with him from his past life. He had been in World War One and he had had a hole shot in his foot."

"And the boy still had his booties on," put in Donna. "Dottie didn't see the foot."

Dottie nodded and continued. "He got shot on the side of his foot just below the ankle and they put a cast on it and as he was walking around in this cast he got blown up. He was killed. Now he was back in *this* life with a remembrance of that hole in his foot but not the rest of the horrible things he saw in the war."

"And the father looked at her . . ." started Donna.

"And the father looked at me," said Dottie, "and told me, 'Do you know when he was born there was a hole in that foot that looked just like a bullet hole?' And they took off his bootie and showed me the place just below the ankle, and you could almost put your finger in there.

"Well, I gave him a treatment and told them to come a week later because we were going to build up the bones and cartilage in there. And I also told them to get him a pair of hard-soled shoes, the kind that come up onto the ankle. So I was working on him mentally one day and I kept seeing a pair of white baby shoes. It was as if the color white was important too. When his mother brought him back she said, 'Do you know I tried to get black shoes or brown shoes but all I could get was white ones.' And then he was able to walk. A few months after that Sarah came over and asked me to guess what the child was doing. She said they were having a block party and he was out there dancing for everybody. He's perfect on his feet and there was no operation needed."

"I have a question," I said quickly, before another story hit me. "This healing is very good for things that have happened in past lives or conditions of birth or interior ailments. Right?" There was a general chorus of agreement. "Suppose there was an automobile accident and they brought a man in here who was cut up and bleeding and had a fractured leg. Would you be able to stop the bleeding and heal the leg?"

They all looked at Dottie. She thought for a moment. "I suppose so," she finally said. "I've never been called in on a situation like that, but I think I could do it. I have stopped hemorrhaging, so I suppose I could stop another kind of blood flow."

It was Donna's turn again. "I *have* to tell you about the two boys who were in the automobile accident."

"Of course they weren't here physically," cautioned Dottie.

"No, they were taken to a hospital. They didn't see Dottie personally. A truck had rolled onto one boy and he was literally crushed. And he was in a coma. For one solid week he didn't come out of that coma. And they wanted to put him in a body cast, but they couldn't because of the coma. As soon as I heard about it I called Dottie and had her go to work on him and ten minutes after she started work—just ten minutes after—he came out of the coma and recognized his sister and spoke to her. Then he went back into that coma. I don't think he was bleeding internally. I didn't hear about that. But he went home without having a cast put on his body."

"And he was crushed by a truck?" I asked incredulously, even though at this point nothing should have seemed incredulous to me.

"Yes. He had three broken vertebrae and other internal injuries plus a concussion. He was really in bad shape. They couldn't believe it when he went home so soon. The other boy in the accident had a broken shoulder bone and a concussion plus some bad bruises on his face. They were going to operate on the shoulder, go in there and break it because something was wrong, and then Dottie worked on his shoulder. They never did have to operate. It healed beautifully."

I looked at Dottie and then asked what I considered a "loaded' question. "Reverend Vurnovas, [she is an ordained minister], does a person have to believe in God or Jesus to be healed?"

Her answer was immediate. "I don't think so. I had an incident a few months ago that pointed this out. I was in a supermarket and this woman had her cart full of groceries and she rolled it over the foot of one of her small children. The boy's toe started to bleed and he was screaming and yelling. So I went over and took hold of his toes and said, 'Oh, goodness, that doesn't hurt as bad as that. You don't have to cry,' and I said to his mother, 'Don't you have a hanky to wipe off that blood that's scaring him?' So she wiped it off and while more blood was coming I took hold of the toe and started working on it, all the time talking in soothing tones to the child. It quit bleeding, the swelling went down, and even the bruise went away. He looked at me and said, 'Thank you, lady, for touching my toe.' We never mentioned God or Jesus. Their names never came into the conversation."

"Then let me rephrase the question," I said. "Could you heal if *you* did not believe in God or Jesus?"

"No."

"Why?"

"Because God does it. He is only using us as instruments. It's God's work and God's power that is doing it. We have to have faith in Him to heal someone. Every once in a while somebody will say, 'Dottie, I don't know how I would have survived if it wasn't for you,' and I tell them, 'Don't thank me, thank God.'"

I decided on another course. "Dottie, do you think that the majority of people who are in mental institutions are really possessed by outside spirits and wouldn't need to be there if someone would exorcise those spirits?"

"I don't know if *everyone* in mental hospitals is possessed, but I do know a great many of them are. Of course the psychiatrists and psychologists don't look for entities; they try to find little wires that have come unglued or little screws that have come loose.

Carol here had a case where a girl was about to be committed to a mental institution. Tell him about it, dear."

Carol crossed her shapely legs and began.

"A young married woman came to me and said she was hearing voices. She was going to a psychologist and he couldn't explain it. Apparently her psychic centers had opened up and she was unaware of it. She asked for instruction on how to rid herself of those voices and then made an appointment to come and see me. I went through a ritual that must have lasted about twenty minutes and I took the entity out and over to the other side."

"A ritual?" I asked, extremely curious now. "The same thing as exorcism?"

"I guess you could call it that. I went up onto the higher plane, only mentally, of course. Dottie taught me how to do it, and I made contact with the entity that was bothering her. I could actually communicate with him. He had been an uneducated man before he died and a plumber and about thirty-two years old. I asked him if he wouldn't like to leave the earth plane and go to a higher plane where he would be taught all the things he needed to know for progression. So he asked me if the higher plane would teach him how to cheat at cards without anyone being the wiser. That had always been his dream while on earth. I told him no, but that there were other more important things for him to learn. I showed him a yellow disk and had him concentrate on it. I concentrated at the same time and this concentration took both of us to the astral plane. I left him there and came back by myself. Of course all this was mental, David; as far as the girl was concerned I hadn't moved an inch."

"So what happened?"

"Well, when I came back the voices were gone. She had had physical manifestations as well. He had been pounding on her body and these aches also vanished. She called me a few weeks later and told me this en-

tity had never returned. But"—and Carol laughed—
"the man was really a character. When I took him on
to the other plane I asked him if he wasn't happy
leaving that lady he was bothering all the time. He
said, 'Yeh. She was a dumb broad!' "

So apparently, I concluded, spirits could be both a
help and a hindrance.

"They help me all the time," put in Donna. "They
showed me how to find an apartment when I needed
one so desperately. If I lose something, they tell me
where it is. I just say, 'Why don't you help me?' and
they help me. Even when I go with Dottie to Las
Vegas they point out the right slot machines."

Dottie laughed. "And when she goes with me she
really needs the spirits there to find me among those
slot machines. I have to stand on my tiptoes to put
the money in them."

I pretended I was shocked. "But aren't you *Reverend* Vurnovas? How does a *reverend* explain playing
the slots?"

"When I want to be very physical and material and
get away from the psychic level, I go to Las Vegas. It
helps me keep in balance with the rest of the world. I
can't always be up on cloud nine, you know. It's a
means of recreation. It's the one thing I like to do. I
don't drink. Some people, when I tell them I've been
to Vegas, will say, 'Oh, that's a sin.' Well, maybe
that's a sin to them, but it isn't to me. I get so high on
this spiritual level that I have to do something to
bring me down again. And we all have to have the
negative and the positive in us to make the whole.
You can't be all positive or all negative all the time or
else you'd explode."

"Her cigarettes and her slot machines don't do anything to negate her powers," spoke up Sarah. "I know
what I'm talkin' about, I do. In 1968 I went over to
England and it was to be a happy affair, but I had
seven terrible disappointments, one right after the
other. So I was in this old castle place that had been

turned into a hotel, and I was feelin' so out of sorts with everything and everyone that I decided to end it all right then and there. I resolved to jump out of the window and kill myself, I did. So before I jumped I said a mental good-by to Dottie. She was way over in California and I was in Sheffield, Yorkshire, and I thought about her dear face that I'd never see again and I said, 'Good-by, Dottie.'

"Well, all of a sudden here comes Dottie's voice boomin' out to me. 'Don't you dare!' it said. 'You sit there! You sit right there and calm yourself. The very idea! You're not goin' to throw yourself through any window! You just sit there and wait till I get there to be beside you.' So I sat there and I waited and I waited and finally calmed down and saw that me killin' myself wouldn't have no bearings on the issues and so I went to sleep and forgot the idea.

"When I got back to San Jose, I resolved that I wasn't going to say anything to Dottie about it. I didn't want my troubles on her back, the poor thing. But as soon as I saw her she said, 'You called me in the middle of the night from England, you know,' and I said, 'I did?' And she said, 'Yes, you called me psychically.' And she told me every solitary word that had been said. Of course, I couldn't say no because it was all true."

"When I got this mental phone call," Dottie explained, "I said, 'if you want me to start working on you, hang up the phone and concentrate on what I'm doing for you.' The phone went dead and so I started on her right away."

"She saved my life, too," put in Carol, "but this time the phone was a real one."

"How'd I do that?" Dottie asked.

"The time with my stomach, remember?" Dottie smiled and Carol continued. "Dottie did telepathic surgery on me. She traveled to me in her mental body while we were talking on the phone. I had a spinal cord injury and the chiropractor insisted that I had disc trouble. It's a very painful thing and there's no cure for it, etc. etc. When I first asked Dottie about it, she said she thought it was a pinched nerve, but I didn't ask her to do anything, so she didn't. I told my doctor that I had had a very bad fall and apparently that's when the injury started. He measured my arm. My left side was becoming paralyzed. I took all kinds of tests. He told me, 'I'm sorry, you have disc trouble,' and I said, 'No, I haven't. It's a pinched nerve.' So he decided to take X rays. He came out with the developed plates shaking his head. He couldn't find any disc problems so he 'guessed' it must be a pinched nerve. That's what I'd told him! So he explained to me where he thought it was and gave me a treatment, but it didn't seem to help. So when I got home I called Dottie and told her the general area of the nerve and she told me to be quiet. She told me later that she was right in the room with me and she was operating."

"What I did was to open the spinal column, reach in and straighten out the pinched nerve," Dottie explained. "The nerve was in a 'V' shape where it had been pinched. I massaged it until it sprung back to its normal shape. There was one strand of the nerve that was caught, and I had to pinch it to dissolve it so it would break loose from where it was jammed."

"I never had any more trouble with it after that," Carol added.

"But what about your stomach?" I insisted.

"Oh, yes. Well, I'm supposedly ulcer-prone and the doctors were treating me for one a few years ago, so when I called Dottie, she said that the adrenal glands were overworked and were shriveling up. So she concentrated and projected a light through both glands. I could feel it! I could feel this heat striking me from behind. I could feel it going through the back on the left side but only halfway through on the right. She told me that the left one was okay and they were working on the right one. Whatever they did, they got the hormones to excrete again and my glands are in fine shape now.

"While they were doing that, she was so quiet and I could feel something going on in my stomach. I said, 'Dottie, what are they doing now?' and she said, 'Oh, just ripping out your stomach.' I wanted to know why and it seems that they thought I needed a new one."

"I guess they figured that while they were in there they might as well take care of other things as well," I said.

"They ripped the whole thing out. I felt awfully uncomfortable in there. Then I could feel something like mesh touching the walls of my new stomach. Dottie said it was the lining and it looked to her like chicken wire being pushed into clay. And I could feel it. There was no hurt to it, but I could feel this sensation of something going on in there."

"You can feel it happening," Dottie said, "but there's no pain when they work."

While Carol had been telling of her stomach, the door opened and a tall blonde in her mid-forties came in carrying a bouquet of bright red roses. When Carol finished, Dottie introduced the newcomer to me as Virginia Smith. "Virginia is not specifically into physical healing. She's gone on to other fields the way Carol has. They were both once my students."

I looked at Virginia. "What do you do?" I asked.

"What *do* I do?" she laughed, and it was a soft, warm laugh. "I work on the soul level with different vibrations helping people find and solve their problems. I work mostly with mental patients as well as doctors and psychiatrists. Also a number of ministers come to me."

"What do they want to know when they first come?" I asked.

"Well, they all want to see if I can spot what's wrong with them. They're either hung up too much on dogmatic religion or, like the doctors, too hung up on material things and they come for spiritual help. The materialists need this help to balance themselves, to get up off the earth level."

"Are you helping doctors to accept the kind of healing that Dorothy is doing?"

"Yes, and I'm teaching them to do it, too, so they can work it on their own patients."

"I'm proud of my student!" Dottie almost shouted.

"Once a doctor sent me a patient from a mental hospital. It was the first time they had ever permitted him to leave. Now he is allowed out on weekends and holidays. He went into Mendocino Hospital a real mess. He was an alcoholic and had had a nervous breakdown. He's doing just great now. The doctors told me I've done wonders but, you know, I never know what I'm going to do before I do it. I just react to individual situations and vibrations and let go."

"Do you go into trance?" I asked.

"No, not even a light one. It isn't necessary. If I can get the needed soul information without jeopardizing myself then it's much better. The information just *comes* to me. I don't have to force myself once I've prepared to receive it. After all, *they* know how much I need to work with."

I had heard of this mysterious "they" all afternoon. I decided it was time I found out who "they" were. "Dottie, who are 'they'? Have "they" lived before? Do they have names like Dr. Jones or Professor Ching? Are they German doctors or Chinese philosophers, or what?"

"They . . ." she began. "When you reach a certain level names are no longer a necessity. You see, names are given to us for our own ego, so that we can say Dr. So-and-So is working on them. In other words, to push our own selves aside and say I'm not doing this, Dr. Fu Manchu is doing it. See? After I received the polonium tube I was told there were seven masters of healing and Christ made the eighth for the Octave of Masters. And I was given their names. This was when

I was first starting. They said that whenever I began my healing sessions or any private healing to call on them. And, in the beginning, I used to call them, one by one and by name, so they would all be there to help. But after a while it seemed as though they left me. They said, from now on you don't need to call us by name, just *think* the seven masters of healing and we shall be there. That's why I don't give them names today. They are all here any time I'm working or when anyone is here for a healing. So I just say, 'they.'"

Coffee and doughnuts were passed around at this point and the conversation slipped away from healing and the masters into girl talk. Someone looked at her watch and realized that we had been there almost four hours, and husbands would soon start arriving home expecting their dinners. Women's liberation has not yet hit the psychic world. I said good-by to these amazing women and thanked them for helping me. I was sincerely glad they had been there for the interview.

As I got my paraphernalia in order, Dottie asked me if I would like to stay for supper. She was making her husband's favorite spaghetti. Not especially looking forward to dining by myself in a local restaurant and being a great fan of spaghetti in any form, I accepted the invitation.

The spaghetti was delicious and Chris turned out to be an intelligent man with a sense of humor and a great capacity for understanding and self-analysis. His work in the local sheet metal mill kept his mind free to think on other, more elevated subjects while his salary took care of all the necessary expenses. Dottie, I was surprised to hear, earns very little from her work. When someone does give her something for her healing it's almost always a pittance in comparison with what they would have paid a doctor, an anesthetist, and a hospital, and even though she charges a flat fee for her past-life readings, they are not as much in demand as her healings are.

I've always been intrigued with past-life readings, constantly on the lookout for someone who could tell me what I had been in previous lifetimes. I've had several readings and they all differ. One remarkable woman (remarkable for the money she charged and the gall with which she charged it) had me on several planets previous to coming to this earth where I was (naturally) in Atlantis, Egypt, and Greece. She said that as a writer on psychic matters, I had reached a "higher plane" of being. I asked Dottie if it was possible for someone to reincarnate and not progress as a human soul.

"I think so," she said, as she wiped and put away the dishes, "because many souls are satisfied at being right where they were. They were happy at that level, and they want to stay there. When I was doing trance work, one of my child guides told about this little old lady who thought that heaven was sitting in a rocking chair and knitting. So for years after she passed on all she did was sit there and rock and knit and knit and rock. Then all of a sudden she said, 'There must be more to heaven than this,' and she got out of her rut and started to progress. There are others who are overly anxious to get back into a body and they'll reincarnate too soon. The Rosicrucians claim that the average time between incarnations is 144 years, so figure that a life on earth is about 65 years, what are we doing with those other 79 years while we are waiting to reincarnate? We are either growing, helping other people, or just content where we are. You see, and this is often forgotten by so many people," she said, waving a coffee cup for emphasis, "the soul has a personality and it's the *personality* that grows and evolves, *not* the soul. The *soul* is already perfect."

I asked if our personalities changed from one life to another.

"Yes, but not radically. We'll bring back the good things because we've experienced the bad and overcome it. I had one man who came for a reading and he had been a wrestler in the last five lives. In this life he was a physical fitness nut. He came to me complaining that life was a bore. I showed him how long he's been in the same old rut—and five lifetimes is a lot of rut—and he changed his life style and is happier today because of it.

"When I give a past-life reading I sit in a chair and concentrate on the person in front of me and as I look at them I'll slip into the subconscious or the third-eye area and then let it tell me what it wants the person to know consciously. While I've found that all of us have past lives I've not found anybody that's in their *last* life."

Chris said that one of the biggest complaints he's heard about past-life readings is that everyone who gets a reading has always been a queen or a princess or a great personality. Dottie was quick to defend her abilities.

"They don't get that stuff from me," she said emphatically. "When they come to me, they find out that they're very ordinary people. Outside of one person, I've never come across anybody that was famous or of royal blood."

"Do you believe that you and Chris were together in a past life?"

"Nope. Chris and I are new experiences for each other," and she shot him a glowing look. "In this lifetime he needed me and I needed him and that's why we were brought together. There are so many people who *think* that in reincarnation everybody you know and everybody you like has been a past-life association, but I disagree. I think that as we unfold and grow, we drop these old ties. If husbands and wives keep coming back together lifetime after lifetime, then there is something they are not doing right. The soul personality has to learn and grow until it knows

all things and can do all things. We have to be as
Christ-like as can be so we can go on to the other
side and help the next guy. Not just come back here
and say, 'I've got this debt to pay,' or, 'I love that person and I wanna be with that person for eternity,' so
they start making Karma for themselves."

"Dottie," I said, "you've been married three times
previously and Chris is your fourth husband. Do you
think when you pass on you're eventually going to be
with one of your four husbands?"

"If I were to see them on the other side I would
probably feel about them just as I do at this moment.
It was nice knowing them, I learned a great deal
from them, but no thanks, I don't want them around
anymore!"

Four-foot-seven-inch Dorothy Vurnovas was born
Dorothy Jopes, in Chicago. Her parents were from
the South but moved North to better employment.
Her father died when she was four years old and life
became difficult for her young mother trying to raise
four children all alone in the depression years. The
woman would go out to work and come home exhausted and with splitting headaches. Dottie would get a
dishcloth and hold it to her mother's forehead and,
rubbing it, she would say, "Mommy, God's going to
make it well." The headaches would go away. Those
were her first healings.

Her mother's financial situation forced her to put
Dorothy and her brothers and sister into foster homes
around the city, Dottie was loved in some and mis-
treated in others but always managed to remain
cheerful, waiting for the day when her mother would
be able to reunite the family. That day never came.

When she was about nineteen years old she made
friends with a schoolteacher who was also a Christian
Science practitioner. One day, alone in the teacher's
home, the telephone rang. It was a woman who was
having an asthma attack. "She couldn't breathe and
she gasped that she needed help. Well, I told her that

Phoebe wasn't home just then but the woman said, 'Then you help me. Somebody has to help me!' So, I said to myself, that if Phoebe could do it, I guess I could do it, too, and I started giving a Christian Science healing over the phone. She started breathing and thanked me very much and hung up. So that was the first time I was *aware* that I could do those things. It was my affirmation."

"Can you cure everybody of anything?" I asked.

"Oh no. There are many things I am unable to cure. I don't claim to be infallible. Leave that to the Pope! Some people can't be cured because of a Karmic debt and others just don't want to be cured even though they say they do. Many people make illness into a law of their subconscious. So naturally it manifests itself in their physical body. These are the people that many times don't get healed.

"You know, there is disease and *dis*-ease. *Dis*-ease, which is an uneasiness of the body no matter what, can be healed. A real disease is a thing that the body or the soul has chosen as a way out of this world and it will not be healed."

"Is it God's will that a person has an illness?" I asked.

"No, God has nothing to do with it. If we were to sit in judgment before the masters and before God and would be asked to *judge* ourselves, we would be much harsher on ourselves than what God would be upon us. What is sin? How many people actually commit what the masters would call a God sin? Not very many. But we make laws for ourselves and when we break our own laws we're committing a sin."

"You mean when Dottie breaks Dottie's law?"

"That's right, because then I feel guilty 'cause I've committed a sin unto myself."

"Well, then," I persisted, "if there is a human law and there is God's law, how do you know when you're operating in God's law and not in your own human law?"

"Think. That's what you do. Think. What *are* God's laws? Most people try to live according to the Ten Commandments. And, they say, if you break one you're committing a sin. There are lots of things that people say are sins and really aren't. Where does it say in the Ten Commandments that you shouldn't be a drunkard? Or where does it say in those Ten Commandments that you should be positive all the time? Or any number of other things. Most times you are breaking man's laws and because you are breaking those laws you have a guilty feeling toward mankind. But you shouldn't have this guilt toward God."

"Then that's where Karma is," I put in, "not in God's law but in man's law."

"Your Karma must be according to your own law," she answered. "Because you know that something is wrong for *you*. So whenever you are doing anything that you *feel* is wrong, then you're really going against your own nature and lousing up your own Karma again."

Chris added, "It's not going against God's nature but going against human nature."

"I like to say," Dottie continued, "that to master the personality of the soul you've got to master your earthly self. Your higher self is already mastered. Your soul is already perfect. You have to master your physical body and discipline it, so it can be attuned to all things."

A short while later I got up to leave and glanced at the bouquet of red roses that Virginia had brought over earlier that afternoon.

"Just look at those poor flowers," Dottie sighed. "I tell people not to bring me flowers or plants because they just die in here. At first I thought it was negativity but I learned later that the vibrations were just too high in this trailer. The vibes are so strong that they force a plant or cut flowers to mature at a much faster rate than they would in most other places. They don't just die, they age rapidly and then die."

I picked one of the flowers up in my hand. The dark and wilted leaves fell into my palm. They looked as if they had been in that vase for a month rather than just a few hours.

"Those vibrations are what heals," said Dottie. "The God-consciousness is within and we can all reach into it and radiate it out to others. The first step toward it is knowing what it is. The second step is *knowing* you can do it. It's there, just waiting to be tapped. How I wish more people would reach for it. What a better world this would be."

\* \* \* \*

Dottie and Chris have moved from their San Jose trailer into a small house "in a valley of terrific vibrations" at Sun Valley, Nevada. "I still do my healings and I still have my groups, but I also make more time for Chris!"

# Merry Harris' Dog

Merry Baxter Harris is a psychic and medium who lives in Calexico, California. She is constantly studying and learning. She wrote me the following:

"I don't fancy myself to be a healer, but when my dog's foot was run over by a car, I tried the Rosicrucian method (I am an adept in this order) on him. He hadn't been able to put his foot down—but after just one treatment, he was able to walk without even limping. This amazed me, for while I *wanted* the treatment to work I didn't really think that I could transmit enough psychic power to *make* it work.

"I really believe that psychic energy is not half as effective in healing as the transmission of *love*. I love that little mongrel—and I'm sure it was *love* that I transmitted to him."

# IX
# Reverend William Brown

I'll admit I was more than a little apprehensive when I arrived in the small southern town. The man I had come such a long way to see was known as being severe and businesslike. His reputation as a healer was one of the best but he also had a reputation for telling people what he thought of them and their ideas. Many people had flatly stated, all across the nation, that this man would never see me. He hated publicity and refused to talk about himself or his work. He had been written up once in a national magazine and the deluge of correspondence, phone calls, and clients hammering at his door was more than he could bear. From that unsolicited article on, he had refused all interviews.

I had written to him from Los Angeles asking for an appointment and frankly didn't expect to get one. The other healers had replied quickly, some even telephoned confirming the dates I wished to see them. But the reply from this man was the last to arrive. I opened it, positive I had been turned down, to be pleasantly surprised by the first paragraph. "How are you? We pray that this shall find you well in spirit and health. Received your letter in good season and thank you very much for it."

The second paragraph confirmed the dates I wished to interview him but the third paragraph cautioned me: "Heretofore, I have put down any attempts to write anything concerning our work, if I had any personal knowledge of it, for the simple reason that we have not, nor do we now, seek any publicity concerning our work. We prefer to go about our affairs quietly and with as much dignity as possible divested of any so-called 'fanfare.' I am consenting to an interview for the very first time because I believe that you are sincere of purpose, and that it could possibly be of some help to the many who seek for truth."

The fourth paragraph was short but explicit. It was written in red capital letters and underlined. "However, there is one condition and that is I DO NOT WANT OUR ADDRESS PUBLISHED!"

Then he summed himself up for me, so that I wouldn't have any false ideas when I did arrive. "I do not and shall not promise or guarantee anyone anything for any reason because I do not know what course of action these physicians shall pursue with any of the cases presented even though it may leave much to be desired in resolving the problem, or problems. I do not make any claims in any fashion, shape or form either expressed or implied. If there are any claims made, they are made by those who have been helped with their problem, or problems, as the case may have been."

The only way to get to this town, except by private car, is to fly into a large city some sixty-seven miles away and take the Greyhound Bus. The bus passes through there twice a day on its way to other places. The trip from the large city to this small town takes almost three hours.

I used those three hours to say a few silent prayers to the spirit world asking for co-operation from this man and also to figure a "plan of attack" where I would overwhelm him with charm to prove to him how important he was to this book. I had made a reservation at the local motel and wasn't to see him until the next day. Good, I thought, that gives me the entire evening to get psychologically prepared.

He was waiting for me at the bus stop.

He came out from the shade of two battered gas pumps, walked across an oil-stained cement parking area, and put out his hand. He smiled. He welcomed me to his town. I was disarmed. Completely. All my plans for attack and counterattack dissolved. The man was a human being, not an ogre. He was warm and friendly, not cold and standoffish. With all my preconceived illusions shattered I let him drive me to the motel where we had an excellent dinner together and got to know each other.

That night, alone in the motel room with Johnny Carson being clever from a box on the wall, I smiled with contentment. And I thanked the spirits for making the Reverend William C. Brown a decent guy after all.

The Reverend Brown doesn't like to talk about himself, so the next day when he picked me up and took me to his home, he talked about the town, its rather psychic history and about the people living there now. "Nobody here knows what I do," he said in a slow voice with just the touch of a drawl. "I'm just a minister without a church to them. I wouldn't ask them to accept what goes on at my place and I have no desire to enter into a discussion with the local people about our work. Almost all of my patients come from other cities. That's the way I want it to be. I'm active in local affairs and know everybody here. I like this place. It's been good to me. It's a kind of haven for the work that is done through me. I don't want to make waves. Let the others in your book make them. I've had it all. Waves could only interfere with what I have to do."

The Reverend Brown is a natty dresser. His sport shirts are right in style as are his trousers and shoes. He sometimes wears a neat hat over his white hair and a pair of sunglasses over his blue eyes. He can be

stern, but he also has a sense of humor. Once he
relaxes with a person he will laugh and crack a few
jokes. The night before, at dinner, he had told the
waitress a joke that made her laugh out loud and
caused the other diners to look up in surprise.

His home is in the better part of town, separated
from the street by a wide green lawn. It is a one-story
building painted white with a large picture window
in the living room. It looks like all the other houses
on the block. Just the way Bill and his wife Nancy
want it to look.

Nancy was not feeling well that morning and after
a brief introduction she went into her room to lie
down. Another person was at the house, a young man
named Chuck. He had come all the way from Charlotte, North Carolina, to be operated on. Surgery was
slated in two days' time. He had had an operation
with human, or physical, doctors a few months previously but he was feeling worse instead of better and
he hoped that Bill Brown's staff of nonphysical doctors could help him.

It wasn't the first time Chuck had been there. He
had had heart surgery with Reverend Bill a few years
before and had been completely cured. He had the
before and after laboratory analysis to prove it.

"Once, when I was living in New York State,"
Chuck told me, "I drove three women down here to
be operated on. One of them was a registered nurse
in a major New York hospital. The operation on her
heart would have taken eight hours to do where she
worked, but Dr. Murphy and the others here did it
all in eighteen minutes. No physical doctor has found
anything wrong with her heart since that time."

Chuck is also a registered nurse (as well as now
being a minister of the gospel) and has been around
doctors and hospitals most of his life. I asked him if
he found a growing acceptance to the kind of surgery
that Reverend Bill does.

"Many doctors that I have talked with, without

them knowing that I was interested in this type of thing, will turn to this form of healing before they will submit to any form of physical surgery on themselves. I knew a woman in Virginia who came to Reverend Brown and had surgery on her spine. A few years later, a medical doctor asked her about it. When she asked him how he knew about the spirit operation, he said he could see the scars. He admitted to being a psychic and that the scars were invisible to most other people."

I wondered what physical sensations people felt when they were being opened up by Reverend Brown's nonphysical doctors and asked Chuck to describe what he had felt.

"When Dr. Murphy or Dr. Chandler is working on you, you are wide awake. They ask you to lie still but to breathe normally. You can feel the instruments moving and the incision being made. When you're lying in bed for the rest period afterward, as the etheric body enters back into the physical body, you feel all the sensations that you would with physical surgery with the exception of no bleeding or unbearable pain.

"And you can't be a doubter, I found that out the hard way. There was one occasion when Dr. Murphy operated on me and I thought to myself, 'Well, I hope he helped it.' That was the wrong attitude! As soon as I hit that bed he 'helped' it. The pain was almost too much to bear, yet I had to lie there. From now on I *know* they can help me."

Dr. Murphy? Dr. Chandler? Who were these invisible medical men?

"There are twenty-eight specialists who use this body," Reverend Brown said matter-of-factly; "some are heart specialists, others deal with bones, eyes, nerves, muscles, etc. Dr. Murphy is a diagnostician but he's also started to do some surgery. He's become fascinated with ophthalmology in the last few years; perviously, he had turned all those cases over to another doctor, and he still defers to others when he comes up against a real tough case. But mostly he gives injections with invisible syringes and calms the patient down. He's got a great sense of humor."

"You make him sound as if he were still alive," I said. "He is dead, isn't he?"

"No! He is not dead!" Reverend Brown said sharply. "He does not have a physical body per se, but uses my physical body as though it were his own. He is, nevertheless, very much alive! How could a physically embodied person take over my body?" He glared at me and then continued. "There is Dr. Spaulding, who is my protector. He doesn't operate but stands by this body to see that no malevolent entity takes it over while I am away from it. There is Dr. Livingstone, too. You know, the one that Stanley went looking for in Africa. Dr. Thorndyke works on abdominal problems. He's a very serious gentleman, almost the exact opposite of Dr. Murphy, who jokes around a lot. Dr. Chandler is an orthopedic. Dr. Fredericks is a heart specialist. Dr. Cushing is the most recent one to join the group. He was an American."

"Have you ever checked into their stories?" I asked. "Have you ever dug up information about them to prove that they were who they say they were?"

"What good would that do?" he asked quickly. "I don't think it matters one little bit who these people were or what they did while they were in human bodies. What matters is what kind of results they bring about now. Their biographies may be interesting reading matter but most of them won't be found in history books. Let's not forget that most people who are cited in history books—I call them hysterical books myself—are there simply because they did nothing to be proud of. Most of them are there for the horrible things they did to one another. I've had people who wanted me to backtrack on my doctors, but I've put that down because I think it's impertinent and I can't see what would be gained by it. Many of them were on this planet at a time when all hope of resurrecting any physical evidence would be impossible. I refuse to worry about that side of it. They do what they say they do. That should be enough proof."

I nodded. "When Dr. Murphy takes over, do you change in any way? Have people noticed that you've changed physically? Do you have your eyes shut?"

"You keep using the second person there and I have to correct you. When you say do *you* do this or do *you* do that, no *I* don't. It is not *I* who is doing any of these things."

"All right then," I retreated slightly, "when Dr. Murphy takes over your physical body does he change your physical body in any way that would be noticeable to a third party?"

"I can't honestly answer that. I don't know. There is only one thing I can tell you to help you out: We are two different personalities, and when he takes over, you know it's not Bill Brown talking. He has his idiosyncrasies and I have mine."

"Have you ever been filmed while . . ."

"Not *me*, no."

"Has *he* ever been filmed?" I rephrased the question. "Now you're getting me confused." He laughed and I was glad. The ice had been broken for the rest of the interview. "Would you please leave the room and let me talk to Dr. Murphy?" I said, and he laughed again. "Has Dr. Murphy ever been filmed?"

"No, I don't believe so. Not on movie film. Once at a demonstration in St. Louis some people were shooting flash pictures and he made them stop. Their cameras refused to work after that."

I swallowed at that one, for I had heard of such things happening. A friend of mine once tried to take pictures of a Haitian voodoo ceremony and his camera jammed. Once I tried to interview a Brazilian spirit priest and he jammed my tape recorder. The tape came up and out of that machine like spaghetti.

"Has it ever happened that more than one of these doctors have had control of your body at the same time?"

"No. How could they? Two persons or objects do not occupy the same space at the same time. One has the control, and when he leaves, another comes in."

"Is there a determined length of time between one leaving and the other taking over?"

"About as long as it would take for me to get up from this chair and go sit in that one over there."

"But you're not there when this transference takes place?" I asked.

"How could I be?" he said, giving me one of his stern looks. "How can two things occupy the same space at the same time?"

"Well," I tried to reason it aloud, "one has left for a few seconds and you realize it's gone . . ."

"No," he interrupted, "I'm not there. There is no realization on my part at all."

I sighed, seeing how difficult it was to interview this man. Not that he wasn't co-operating, far from it, but I was asking him questions about events that took place while he was literally out of the room. I decided to try a different tack. "How do people hear about you if you don't get publicity?"

"I don't know. I really don't know. I guess most of it is by word of mouth. I have given a few lectures and my address has been given out afterward and, of course, that magazine article that I didn't want, but I think that when people are ready to hear about these doctors they just hear about them. That's all. There is a planned order to everything, you know. When knowledge should be given to you, it is. People will write to me and I'll reply, but I'll tell them I can't guarantee anything. I make no promises. I have no control over what the doctors will do or not do. All I can do is to promise to lend them my physical body as a channel for the doctors while the patient is here.

"I'll set up an appointment for the operation and I

expect them to check in here at my home the night before. We want them to stay here. We have four bedrooms set aside for them. It's not that we want a house full of people all the time but the doctors want it that way. They want the patient to be rested and mentally ready for the operation. If they travel a great distance to get here, they check into a motel, spend the night there, get dressed in the morning, find a cab or drive over to our home, get undressed for the operation, it's just too much racing around. It takes them too long to unwind. My wife Nancy is a perpetual hostess. Dr. Murphy calls her the Mother Superior. I call her Florence Nightingale."

He doesn't eat any breakfast before the operation, nor does Nancy, who acts as recording nurse. The patient is also not allowed to eat anything beforehand. He can have a little water or some fruit juice but the doctors want the body as light as it can be, without a lot of heavy undigested food in the stomach. Cigarettes and coffee are also forbidden.

There is a ritual before the operation. There is recorded sacred music and Reverend Brown asks the patient to repeat the "Lord's Prayer" with him, "slowly, so as to understand the meaning of each word." Then there is what he calls the "Affirmation of Faith." It too is said aloud and in unison.

The patient, dressed in a hospital gown, then gets onto a blue massage table that has been draped with a white sheet and made more comfortable with a pillow. Reverend Brown sits in a chair near the table and listens to the soft music playing in the room. Then he slumps over, his head hanging between his knees, and when he rights himself it is no longer Bill Brown but a departed entity who is inhabiting his body.

The first visitor is always Dr. John Geoffrey Spaulding. His job is to see that Bill Brown's body is protected from any outside, unwanted influences. He is introduced to those present in the room by Nancy.

Then he leaves and a new entity takes over. The second visitor is always Dr. John Murphy, the Irish diagnostician. Dr. Murphy tells the patient what is wrong—where and what shall be done about it. He gives invisible injections to prepare the patient for the surgery that is to come. When he leaves, another doctor comes into the body and performs the actual operation.

Reverend Brown's hands never touch a patient. They are always working quickly in the air a few inches over the body. The surgery takes place on the etheric and not the physical level.

The etheric body is an exact copy of the flesh and blood body with every muscle, bone, organ, and nerve reproduced but in a finer density. The principle is that this body, being more basic than the physical, can be adjusted more rapidly and bloodlessly. Each condition corrected in the etheric body is reflected back into the physical body, thus adjusting the physical back into health.

While the doctors work, you can see Bill Brown's hands (powered by the entities) moving quickly. You watch as his hand picks up an invisible knife from an invisible side table and can almost see it sink into the flesh as it makes a rapid incision. You almost see the assistants standing on the other side of the table who take the used instruments and hand him the necessary new ones. You watch as the fingers remove something and toss it on the table, and you sit fascinated as the fingers stitch up the invisible wound with a needle and thread. All this time Bill Brown, the man, has his eyes shut tight, yet his voice makes comments about conditions, and he points with great accuracy to various sections of the anatomy.

Patients are encouraged to answer the surgeon's questions but are warned not to try and carry on an unnecessary conversation. His time in Bill Brown's body is limited and he has come for work, not for chitchat.

After the operation has been completed, a Dr. Davis shows up to give a closing prayer. The body is sitting down at this point and soon its head falls forward between its knees. This time when the head comes up it is Bill Brown once more. He sits calmly for a few minutes, then shakes his hands rapidly and opens his eyes. He says, "The hands feel larger than when I normally occupy the body."

After this the patient is allowed to get off the table and, putting on a bathrobe, is taken to a bedroom for several hours of rest and sleep. It is very important that this rest period be one of absolute repose, because once the etheric body starts reflecting the newly made changes into the physical, some discomfort, shock, or even pain will be felt. This reaction seems to depend on how far the patient has progressed spiritually in this lifetime. Nonbelievers, it appears, suffer much more than those who have accepted these things as a natural part of God's laws.

The four recuperating bedrooms are each decorated in a different color. One is all in blue; walls, rug, curtains, bedspread, lamp shades, towels, and even the pictures on the walls. The others are in lavender, yellow, and green. If a person has had a certain type of heart operation, or something with his respiratory organs, such as emphysema, he is placed in the lavender room. The blue room is used for cardiac cases. Yellow is an active color used for renewing energies and to influence circulatory and digestive organs. The green room is primarily for tranquilization. Those who are especially nervous calm down when put in there. It is pastel green, not the heavier green, for Reverend Brown has found that the lighter the shade the more relaxed the atmosphere. "Obviously, if they are in a highly agitated state, it makes it just that more difficult to heal whatever the problem may be. It's not straight surgery per se that renders the complete result. It's a combination of things. The person's environment has much to do with it." Some people can't stand the lavender room, they find the vibratory rate too high for them. They become restless and want to escape, rather than stay put and relax.

His bedside manner is almost nonexistent and brings comments that he is unsympathetic toward his patients once the operation is completed. He offers his reasons. "I don't go near them after it's over for two reasons. First of all, I don't want to pick up whatever it is that's bothering them. This body is highly sensitive and becomes even more so once the work has been done. If I went into that person's room and they had an 'uhhh' someplace then I'd 'uhhh' right along with them. I'd draw their attention to their problems rather than away from them. The second reason is that an integral part of this whole process is repose. They must be quiet and be by themselves for a change. Some of them, for the very first time in their lives, learn to shake hands with themselves. When they are in this self-imposed envelope of color they learn that they are their own worst enemy and their own best friend. If and when they succeed in doing that they'll find it much easier to shake hands with everyone else."

I had a question ready. "Doesn't it take a strong person to realize that many of his illnesses, if not all his illnesses, have been brought on by himself over the years?"

"I think that everyone has a lot of strength that is untapped, strength they don't know about," he replied.

"Yes, but to come out and say that I have a cancer because I am the way I am! We love ourselves too much to ever admit that we would do such a thing to ourselves."

"That's probably true with most individuals," he said, "but the strong ones come here and understand where their illnesses came from. And that makes them stronger. People have a lot more strength than they at first realize."

I was ready to argue. "But don't you think that you get the majority of the strong ones? People come to you to be cured who have been told by their own doctors they were incurable, yet they refuse to believe it and continue searching. They have not given up, these medical rejects, and they come to you as the last resort."

"You said that, I didn't," he replied, and then laughed. "I can tell you this much. That any person, no matter who he is, or where he is, or what it is he does, if he wants help from any direction, he must ask for it.

"Everyone is familiar with the old truths, 'Seek and ye shall find,' 'Knock and it shall be opened unto you,' 'You must ask before you receive,' and ad infinitum. But few healers realize that Jesus Himself gave a clue in matters of this kind when he said, 'Whatever you do unto the least of these you have also done unto Me.' What that means is this: that when you learn to externalize yourself away from your own wants, cares, desires, problems, and so forth, long enough to come to someone else's aid and help him with his problems, you are so involved in the activity of helping that other person that your own problems do not exist all during that time. Because of your own absence from your problems, they are taken care of while you are helping someone else solve his. This is why anyone who is aware of this will never want."

"Will never want on what level? The spiritual?"

"On any level. You told me earlier that many of the healers you've talked to were crying poor. Perhaps this was the reason and they don't understand it."

"But they seemed to be out doing things for others," I added quickly. "Their lives are occupied with healings in churches and going into hospitals and having patients come into their homes."

"But underneath all this, as you are telling me now," he argued, "they have gone and offered. They haven't waited for the person to ask. That's a different matter. You see, it's not a point of being officious nor a question of being filled with self-importance. It's a question of complying with God's laws as they are. These we cannot change even if we want to. Certainly they are not going to move over just because of a personal whim. A healer must conform to it and wait for people to ask. They must want it themselves. Why? They have reached an arbitrary point at which they are willing to get out of their own way for a change. To let go and let God. In this manner they can become passive enough to allow the forces to take over."

"You mention God and Jesus quite a lot," I said.

"Why shouldn't I?" he answered sharply.

"Okay," I conceded, "but suppose someone comes and wants a healing but doesn't necessarily believe in God or believe that Jesus was the Son of God?"

"I've had those, too," he said.

"Then what happens to them physically? Anything?"

"The best way to answer that is to give you an example. I remember a lady who said she was an atheist. Now frankly, I don't believe there is any such thing simply because they are people who don't wish to be labeled as being a Baptist or a Presbyterian or a Catholic or something like that. They refuse to be identified with a particular religious-ism. These people take pride in themselves as being intellectual wizards. They have figured out, all by themselves, what the world has been pondering for centuries. Anyway, I didn't know anything about her religious problems and I didn't want to. When she started to talk, I couldn't help but think about Abe Lincoln when he made the remark that it's better to keep your mouth shut and be thought a fool than to open it and remove all doubts.

"When she got on the table Dr. Murphy told her what was what and she didn't deny one bit of it. He gave her a complete diagnosis and told her everything her physical doctor had told her. Word for word. One of her problems was diabetes and that's not a surgical matter. It's chemical and my doctors wouldn't touch it. She had an abdominal tumor that she could feel with her own fingers. It was making elimination very difficult. She had been taking enemas every day for eighteen years."

"God," I interrupted, "the situations people get themselves into."

"Don't they though? Well, Dr. Thorndyke came in and he went about the business of straightening her up. During the operation something was said about her husband getting a job with a large university. Closed-circuit TV was mentioned, too. Anyway, that night she knew something had happened because she had pains that she never had before. In the morning she started poking around and she couldn't find that lump. From then on she had no more problems with her elimination.

"Now about four months later her husband got a letter that he had been accepted for the position of sociology professor at a university down in Florida and that because of the student body being so large many of his classes would have to be held over closed-circuit television. The last time I heard from her she wrote, 'I've not thought to thank God for anything since I was a little girl at home. Now I've changed my ways.' Remember I did nothing to discourage or encourage her religious beliefs. I remained completely impersonal. She saw what God's power could do and she saw it much better than I could ever have told her. My advice to you, as well as anyone else, is don't try to persuade anybody to believe anything they are not capable of. It's a waste of time. Yours as well as theirs."

The next morning we went to a small town in North Carolina. On the way, he told me a funny story about a very wealthy and very famous lady who lives in New York. Her best friend was the sister of a well-known movie star. The sister was ailing and Reverend Brown was asked to come to Manhattan to see what he could do. He asked her if everything was ready for the operation. She said it was. Then he asked about the operating table. She didn't have any such thing in her apartment. Wouldn't a bed do? No, a bed would not do because the doctors required a steady surface for their patients and a bed gave way under a body. She promised to get him a table and said she would send her chauffeur for him. When the chauffeur arrived, he had an ironing board from Macy's. That was to be the operating table. Reverend Brown laughed as he remembered going down Park Avenue in a magnificent limousine and with an ironing board sticking out the side window. "If those doctors in all those expensive offices along the way would have known where I was going and what I was going to do with that ironing board they would have had a fit!"

"Have you ever drawn blood?" I asked.

"Drawn blood? How could I do that?" he asked.

"Well, maybe there was a slip through the etheric body down into the physical body and blood was drawn. Like they do in the Philippines."

He looked at me as if I were crazy. "No, that never has happened. I question the sanity of everyone including myself, but I don't question the sanity of the doctors. I have misgivings about everyone else, but the doctors know what they're doing."

When we arrived in Mooresville, North Carolina, we were met by Vaughn Boone, a gentleman with a deep voice who is a direct descendant of Daniel Boone. He drove us to a shop called Plastastics, where his wife Millie sells art and crafts supplies. In the back room, piled high with lead paints, beads, macramé yarn, and decals she told me how Bill Brown's doctors had saved her life.

"The first time I ever met Bill Brown was at a dinner party in Charlotte. We were talking about something or other when he suddenly remarked that somebody at the table was having a terrible backache. Well, it wasn't me and as I looked around the room I caught my husband's eye. He had had a kidney stone attack that very afternoon but wanted to come to this party so badly he didn't tell me anything about it. I'm a skeptical Taurus and have to see things to believe them but when Vaughn spoke up and said it was *his* back I thought, well, that man's pretty weird.

"Well, I had something like a whiplash in my neck and Vaughn was having trouble with his kidney stones so he suggested that we go over and see what this strange man could do for us. I'm curious enough to agree to anything, so we phoned for an appointment and went.

"I had a knot on the back of my neck. I mean I could feel it under the skin when I touched it. There was a lady there from California that day and she felt it too. I got on his massage table and his surgeons came in and worked on me. Well, when it was over the first thing I did was reach back there and feel that thing had *gone*. Well, you better believe it that there was no one more surprised than me, but somehow I couldn't understand what had *really* happened.

"Vaughn then had his operation and we both were put into one of those colored rooms. We hadn't felt anything during the operations but oh how we suffered that night! Both of us were in terrible pain and Vaughn is sure he left his body. He said he looked back and saw this form on the bed and it was himself. He told himself that he couldn't die because it would be a shock to me and secondly because he didn't want to spoil Bill Brown's reputation by having a patient die on him."

Everyone laughed and I turned to Reverend Brown. "Why is this pain necessary?"

"I've given it a lot of thought," he said slowly, "and it seems to me that there is no other way for the skeptic to be convinced that something has actually happened."

"But Millie reached around and felt that knot was gone," I argued. "That should have been enough proof."

"She told you that she didn't believe it even then," he said. "That's why she had to be shown that something happened."

Millie Boone is a handsome woman with light hair and infectious laughter. It's hard to believe that she has had so much physical pain, yet she was once at the place where she couldn't walk across a room or even sit in a chair. The intense pains started in her abdomen and worked down her leg along the sciatic nerve. She was going to a chiropractor every other day and he would work on her lower back. He wasn't able to do anything but take her money. Finally she decided to let Reverend Brown's surgeons try to erase this pain. Armed with the X rays the chiropractor had taken she went to see him. He agreed with her chiropractor that it was an impingement of a nerve in her back that transversed the nerve ending and was bringing great pain to the groin area. But when he allowed Dr. Murphy to come in an entirely new diagnosis was given. It was not a nerve problem, the Irishman stated flatly, but that the sigmoid valve on the lower portion of the colon had a growth on it. Both Nancy and Millie protested that Dr. Murphy was wrong and he told Nancy to press her fingers on a certain spot in Millie's abdomen. Millie screamed. The two women were convinced and Dr. Thorndyke came in and operated. There was almost no pain that night and Millie not only was able to sit and walk, she was able to run without the slightest bit of discomfort.

"The third time I was operated on," she said, "was after my doctor found a lump in my breast. He wanted me to go into the hospital right away but I held him off. He made me fill in all the forms and re-

serve the operating room in two weeks and I was sure
he was wasting time, both mine and his. I knew what
I was going to do but of course I couldn't tell him. I
called Bill Brown and said I needed some help again.
He told me to come in on Thursday for a Friday-
morning operation.

"I went back to my physical doctor on Monday. He
asked me what I was doing there because I didn't
have an appointment. I told him I wanted to cancel
the surgery because the lump in my breast was gone.
After he examined me he had to admit I was right.
He asked me what had happened. I knew he
wouldn't believe me if I told him the truth so I just
said that I had a lot of people praying for me and
that I was a firm believer in the power of positive
thinking."

Her husband spoke up. "I think it's interesting to
note when Millie had that growth on her sigmoid
valve that Bill agreed with the chiropractor, yet when
he was under the influence of Dr. Murphy the diagnosis changed entirely. It shows that Bill's personality
is completely suppressed when one of the doctors
comes in. I'd like to tell you a story, if I may."

"Please do," I said.

"Well, there is a lady here in town who was born
with a defect in one of her hip sockets. One of these
sockets turned outward. The doctors tied her legs together so that they would grow into the normal position but all it did was make it worse. As she grew up
she had seven different operations on that hip joint.
The last one, they ran a fourteen-inch steel rod down
her leg and fit it into a steel plate they put in her hip
socket. Well, she was in terrible pain and her doctors
finally said that the only thing left was to amputate
the leg once and for all. Even though it would have
taken away her pain she is a fighter and she heard
about Reverend Brown and asked me if I'd take her
there.

"When she got on the table Dr. Murphy asked me

how much difference I thought there was between
one leg and another. I said it looked like as much as
an inch and a half. Well, after her etheric surgery she
got off that table and her legs were even. She was
able to walk across the floor as normal as you and I.

"Later she went back to her doctors and they
couldn't believe what had happened. They took X
rays which showed that her hips were exactly even,
which in itself is rare in anybody. She's off crutches
now and all the pain is gone. And her doctor told her
I had been wrong. Her legs weren't an inch and a
half off, there was a *two-and-a-quarter-inch* difference
in them before Reverend Brown's surgeons worked on
her."

"I don't know why you're so all-fired up about what
X rays say or don't say," Bill Brown spoke up. "This
business of 'proof' gives me a pain. The 'proof' is
there when the patient knows he's been helped. Some
things never show up differently on X rays or in laboratory reports, yet the person is healed. He *knows*
he has been healed. And who knows better than the
person who's been suffering all his life?"

Mr. Anthony Brooke of London, England, is a
world traveler, lecturer, and investigator into the occult. He spent eight days with Reverend Brown and
his wife in 1966 and came away amazed at what he
saw. That same year he gave a lecture on Bill
Brown's abilities at the convention of Spiritual Frontiers Fellowship in Chicago. He told a story about an
American chiropractor whom he calls simply "Dr. A."

"Dr. A. is fifty-four years old. He is a chiropractor.
In August of 1965 he began to experience pain in his
lower back and prostate and in September he went to
a Chicago clinic for a complete medical checkup. X
rays and other tests revealed a condition of cancer in
the pelvic girdle. The prostate was tender and swollen and he was told that his condition 'could be
cancerous.' He went to another clinic for a recheck,
and his condition was in every respect confirmed. His

suffering in the back and prostate gradually increased and he began to develop other disagreeable symptoms. In October and November the condition slowly spread to the lower rib cage and his pain was intensified until in December it became excruciating. He then developed a bony tumor in the head, which was perceptible both to sight and touch. The inflammation spread to his chest and in January 1966, his feet began swelling. He went for another checkup in a third clinic and by this time he was suffering from high fever and profuse perspiration. At the end of seventeen days spent in this clinic he went home because nothing more could be done for him. By this time he was convinced he had cancer and he continued with laetrile treatment at home. His wife had heard of Reverend Brown and began a correspondence with him. The weather at that time, however, was extremely bad, and for other reasons, too, Dr. A. felt disinclined to undertake the long journey from Colorado. Finally, however, as he told me himself, he was 'psychologically ready' to visit Mr. Brown, and the date for his examination by the etheric specialists was set for the twenty-sixth of April.

"When Dr. Murphy took over the Reverend Brown's body to make the initial diagnosis, he asked, without touching the patient's body, that the following adjustments should be made by a chiropractor six weeks hence: third, fourth, and fifth cervicals out to the right 1¼ centimeters; fourth, fifth, and sixth dorsals out to the right 3 centimeters; second lumbar out to the left 1½ centimeters; and the coccyx inverted and hooked to the right.

"Himself a chiropractor, Dr. A. realized that such a diagnosis could not normally be made with such detailed precision without the assistance of X rays and a centimeter ruler.

"As regards Dr. A.'s more serious condition, Dr. Murphy made the following diagnosis and a series of operations were performed accordingly: tumor in the left frontal lobe of the brain; palpitation and regurgitation in the right ventricle of the heart, involving calcium deposits in the mitral and tricuspid valves, carcinoma involving transverse, descending, and ascending colons and prostate gland; massive sarcoma in eleventh and twelfth ribs and throughout the pelvis. The pelvic sockets were replaced with bone graft from the right tibia and two cysts behind the pancreas and six lithstones were removed from the gall bladder.

"Before operating on the brain tumor, Mrs. Brown, Mrs. A., and myself were invited to feel it, which we all did in turn. After the etheric operation the tumor seemed, when reexamined, immediately to have been dissolved, as the patient himself confirmed. The three of us, and the patient himself, were also invited to check by means of a stethoscope the palpitation and regurgitation of the heart. We each noted the unmistakable periodic swishing sound. After the etheric operation on the heart, which took about seventeen minutes, but when carried out physically might have taken about three hours, the heart was found to have been immediately freed from its palpitation and from all irregularity. Mr. Brown later admitted that it was unusual for the effect of an etheric adjustment of such a serious nature to take effect so quickly in the physical body.

"It is, I think, significant to note that Mrs. A. had worked in the Medical Branch of the WAC during World War Two, as a surgical technician. She had witnessed innumerable operations and testified to us all that the quick and deft movements of the hands when operating were exquisite to watch. She does not possess etheric sight but could recognize without any difficulty and with heartfelt admiration the precision and quality of the surgical work that was being done."

I had heard about another chiropractor who came to Reverend Brown with gastric ulcers. The very night after his operation he was eating hot dogs with pickle relish and loving every bite of them. This same man saw another operation with results that he could not believe possible. "I am medically trained and this elderly gentleman had an S curve in his spine. A C curve is fairly normal but to have it go in both directions is abnormal. I saw something happen there that is medically impossible. In order for the arm to move," he explained, "one muscle has to shorten and the other has to elongate. I saw *both* muscles elongating and both muscles contracting as if a giant hand had hold of this body and was bending it out into a straight line. There was no possible way that the muscles themselves could have made this adjustment based solely on mental attitude. When they got through there was a slight C curve but the S curve had disappeared completely."

How many such stories like this could be told, I don't know, but Reverend Brown says he's worked on more than 6,500 people. He has a filing cabinet bulging with patients' names and addresses, letters of appreciation, and reports of followups from their own doctors as well as hundreds of certified laboratory reports and X rays. He wouldn't let me study them or copy them. "The information here was given in the strictest confidence for my eyes alone," he said. "People don't want their names bandied about. They came here for a healing and most of them got what they came for. It would be breaking my oath to them to let you or anyone else read and publish this material."

And I had to agree with him.

The next day was Sunday, and while Reverend Brown doesn't usually perform operations that day, he did it because I was there and Chuck had to return to work. I showed up at the Brown home at seven-thirty in the morning. I remarked to myself that there was a rooster crowing someplace. I hadn't heard any roosters since starting the interviews for this book.

Reverend Brown was wearing white. White trousers, white shoes and socks, and a white hospital coat. His wife Nancy was wearing a white nurse's uniform. Chuck was wandering around in a pale green hospital gown under a bathrobe.

I was asked to go into the surgery room and take a seat. I was told that I would not be permitted to tape anything that was said. When I asked if I could take pictures, Reverend Brown said it was all right with him but he wasn't sure if it would be all right with the others. I wondered what that meant as I sat silently looking around the room.

It was papered in gold and green with a pattern of blue flowers. The tone of the room seemed to be blue and white or blue and gold. The rug was blue, the chairs were covered in blue plastic, and the portable massage table was in turquoise blue. While Nancy put a sheet and pillow on the table and then added a light white blanket, I took in what was on the walls. There was a large brass censer hanging with a blue light in it. It had been the gift of a Catholic bishop who had been healed. There was a painting of Christ. There was Dali's painting of the sacrament of the Last Supper. There was a portrait of a spirit guide with the Star of David on his headgear. There was a portrait of a magnificent Egyptian and still another picture of Christ. There was a chart with the twelve signs of the Zodiac and several small statues of the Virgin Mary. There was a white dove in ceramic and a painted and beribboned shillalah sent from Ireland to Dr. Murphy by a satisfied female patient. There were three different sizes of praying hands in various materials. On the small table between the chairs that Reverend Brown and Nancy sat in rested an open Bible. The Bible is kept open to the Book of Isaiah. Reverend Brown claims that the only place in the entire

Bible where spirit teachers are mentioned is to be found in Isaiah, Chapter 30, verses 20 and 21.

Chuck came in and sat beside me, and as soft music played Mrs. Brown took her place in a chair at the foot of the table and Reverend Brown sat in a chair against the wall, on the opposite side from me. The chair was about two feet from the operating table.

He asked us to repeat the "Lord's Prayer" in unison but to pay attention to the words and what they were saying. Then he began the Affirmation of Faith, which we repeated after him. I glanced at Chuck. He was fidgeting in his chair. I got my camera ready.

The music stopped playing and there was silence. I kept my eyes glued to Reverend Brown's face. His eyes were closed and he was breathing deeply. His hands were palms down on his knees. His feet were flat on the floor and slightly apart. I glanced at Nancy; she was sitting in the same attitude but with a pencil and notebook on her lap.

Then, suddenly, Reverend Brown fell over. It was a quick and unexpected movement. He just doubled from the waist, his head down between his knees. It was almost like the actions of a puppet whose string had suddenly gone slack.

Then slowly, but very slowly, his head came up again. Finally he was back in an upright position but his face seemed somehow changed. His eyes were closed. His mouth opened and a deep voice came out. Nancy greeted it as "Dr. Spaulding," her husband's protector. He was introduced to me and then greeted Chuck and Nancy.

His face grimaced for a second and then relaxed.

"Top of the morning to you," the thick brogue came out of the Southerner's body. Nancy and Chuck both greeted Dr. Murphy. "Who is that sittin' over there?" he wanted to know, pointing a finger at me.

"It's a researcher, Dr. Murphy," Nancy said. "He's come to watch us work. He's writing a book."

"A researcher is it now? Why are you wastin' your

time this lovely Sunday morning sittin' in here when you could be outside with the pretty colleens?"

I explained that I was writing a book and that I had come for information, not colleens.

"That's the pity of it," he said. "When you are young enough for colleens you prefer your books. Someday when you're old you'll prefer the colleens to your books but it won't be any use at all." He laughed. "Anyway, I'm glad to meet you and happy that you are here. Be welcome."

"Thank you," I said. I was surprised to see Reverend Brown act like this and to speak with this light Irish voice. While he has a sense of humor and likes to tell jokes, he is not the type to put on an accent and call attention to himself.

Dr. Murphy asked who was going to be operated on that day and Nancy said it was Chuck, but she had been having trouble with her big toe and would he look at it? He told her to get up on the table. Bending down low to look at the toe—but with his eyes shut tight—Dr. Murphy told her that it was infected. She said she didn't think it was because it didn't feel like that.

"Now, Nancy," he said, "don't be tellin' me my business. That thing is infected and I am going to have to give it a shot."

I got my camera into focus and quickly took three pictures. The shutter made a booming noise (to me anyway) but Dr. Murphy didn't seem to notice. At least he didn't object.

He looked down past the end of the table and seemed to be searching for something. "There it is," he said, "under that other stuff." He reached down and lifted an object from the table. An invisible object from an invisible table, I must add. He held it like a hypodermic syringe and, lifting it up, he squinted against the light as his finger pushed a drop up and out of the needle. Then he told her to lie still. With his eyes closed he came within a few inches of her aching toe and forced the invisible liquid into the toe of her etheric body. He pulled out the needle and placed it back on the invisible table.

"That'll hold ya for a while," he said, and motioned for Nancy to get off the table. "Now who's next?" he asked.

"It's Chuck, Dr. Murphy," said Nancy; "he's had trouble with an old operation that some physical doctors performed on him. He hopes you can help him."

"I hope so too," he said. "All right, my lad, get up here now. Let's have a look at ya."

Chuck took off his bathrobe and swung himself onto the table. Nancy covered him with the white blanket. Dr. Murphy told her: "I'm going to have a look at his private parts, Nancy. If you don't mind." She left the room and he pulled Chuck's gown up to his chest, then he pulled the blanket down to just below the groin. "You've a lot of scar tissue in there," he said. "No wonder it's been causin' ya troubles." He looked at Chuck. "But why are ya so nervous, my boy? You've been here before and we didn't hurt ya, did we?"

"Not on the table," Chuck answered, "but it sure ached later."

"But it's the fire that tempers the steel, haven't you ever heard of that?"

"I've heard of it, Dr. Murphy, but I'm not made of steel and I don't like being tempered."

Dr. Murphy put back his head and laughed. "Well, we'll calm you down a bit with some of this." He reached over and picked up another invisible hypodermic syringe. Deftly he injected its unseen contents into the young man's neck. Then he put it down and picked up another. This one was injected into the other side of the neck. "Now count from ten to one slowly," he ordered. Then to me. "You! Mr. Researcher! Come over here and feel this young man's pulse."

I rose and came over to the table. Reaching down,

I took his wrist in my hand and placed my fingers on his pulse. It was beating strongly. I told Dr. Murphy so.

"Well, just wait a few moments and see how fast it's beatin'," he said. "I put enough material into him to calm him all the way down."

Sure enough, as I stood there, my thumb pressing firmly on Chuck's pulse, I could feel it getting weaker and weaker and weaker. Finally it was almost impossible to find.

Dr. Murphy motioned me back to my chair. I went willingly (I've never liked watching operations anyway) and got my camera ready for some more pictures. Reverend Brown's body was returned to the chair and sat down. His hands fell to his sides. Then his features relaxed and his hands began to move again. "Good morning," said a soft voice with a definite British accent. "I'm Dr. Thorndyke. Shall we begin?"

He worked quickly and silently. Like a skilled surgeon with an invisible assistant who knew his every move in advance, he picked up a knife, made an incision, and clamped it open.

I put my camera up to my eye and pressed the shutter. It didn't move. Scowling at it, I checked to see that I had advanced the film all the way after the previous picture. I had. Again I pressed the shutter. Again it failed to click. Dr. Thorndyke worked rapidly and I, just as rapidly, examined my camera to see what the trouble was. This was a fine time for the damned thing to go wrong, I thought, and I kept pushing on the shutter release and getting angrier the more it refused to budge.

Then I knew what was going on.

Dr. Murphy didn't mind having his picture taken while he was there but Dr. Thorndyke had other ideas. He wanted no snapshots, so he had jammed the camera. I didn't know *how* he did it and I didn't care.

All I knew was that he had managed to stop me from photographing him.

Chastened, I sat quietly and watched the rest of the operation. Dr. Thorndyke pulled something out of the wound. I could see Reverend Brown's hands going through the motions. Then he was handed something so thin that it must have been a needle. He ran the fingers of his left hand down the invisible thread attached to the needle and began to stitch up the incision. Then he patted Chuck's abdomen and pulled his gown down as he pulled the blanket up to cover him. He began to tell him what he wanted him to do. Things like no running or high reaching, etc.

The camera sat in my lap. Idly I pushed the shutter release. There was a click. The camera was working again! Now that the doctor had finished the operation, he permitted my camera to function once more! The temptation was to try to catch another shot of him but he went away quickly and in came Dr. Davis. He advised us that it was time for Reverend Brown to return to his body. He gave the benediction and departed. The face grew red and then bent suddenly from the waist down. The head hung there between the knees for a few seconds and then started back up again. When it opened its eyes it was Bill Brown in charge once more. He shook his head and hands as if to clear away the cobwebs and looked over at me. "Did you get anything worthwhile from this session?" he asked.

"I certainly did," I replied, "everything except photographs of Dr. Thorndyke operating on Chuck."

"Why didn't you take them? I said I didn't care."

"It wasn't you," I protested, "Dr. Thorndyke didn't want them. He jammed my camera so it wouldn't work."

The Reverend William Brown let out a loud laugh. "Well, I'll be . . ." he said. "Did Dr. Murphy pose for you?"

"I don't know," I replied truthfully. "The camera worked when he was here but I don't know what I got. Maybe Dr. Thorndyke loused up the entire roll."

"I'll be interested to see what comes out," he laughed again. He left the room to change his clothes.

Chuck was still sitting on the table, looking whiter and weaker than he had before. He said that he had felt as if a rubber band had been stretched across his stomach. Aside from that, the operation was painless. He shuffled off to the green room and in a few minutes was fast asleep.

The body that is used by these various surgeons on the other side was born in Pittsburgh, Pennsylvania, on February 24, 1914. Its father was an electrician who moved to Florida to take part in the housing boom. In spite of his northern birth, Bill Brown considers "everything north of the Mason-Dixon line as foreign territory."

Yet it was while he still lived in Pennsylvania that the training for his life's work began. "I remember it as if it were yesterday," he told me. "I was only three years old and I was wandering in the woods near our home. I saw this man. He was just an ordinary-looking man. No fancy raiments or costumes or anything. He started talking to me and, of course, my vocabulary was pretty limited but I understood everything he said. This was my first meeting with Dr. Spaulding, my friend, teacher, and protector. He was a Presbyterian minister and he passed over in the year 1800. About six months later I met Thundercloud. He was a medicine man with the Sioux Indian tribe and he was all decked out in a fancy feather headdress and buckskin clothes. He was tall, too, over six feet. Just the opposite from Dr. Spaulding. I learned a great deal from him. He was stern but very gentle. He taught me about nature and how it plays an important part in our human development. He told me how Indian medicine men could read auras and that when a boy baby was born, if the aura was right, the medicine man would take the child and raise it as his own, teaching it all he knew so he would eventually take his place in the tribe."

"Then Thundercloud was looking to make you into a medicine man," I suggested.

"No, not in those terms. It was simply an education in appreciating life and forms around me. He showed me the electromagnetic fields of different types of plants. He told me that plants were not only living things but capable of emotion as well. Plants can weep as humans weep, or react as humans react. It's only recently that scientists are beginning to discover this for themselves. I remember one episode in which he pointed out poisonous plant life versus nonpoisonous or what we call today toxic and nontoxic. He showed me a poison ivy plant and it had a greenish-brown hue for a magnetic field around it. I could see this and he knew I could see it. He explained that the Great Spirit had designed plant life in a wonderful way so that there was always an antidote for toxic plants no more than three feet away. He showed me another plant near the poison ivy. It had a magnetic field of turquoise with white streaks. He said that was how the medicine men fought the poison of all natural plants."

"Did you tell your family about this?" I asked.

"I tried to, but like everyone else at that tender age I learned to keep my mouth shut. I have two brothers and they didn't believe anything I told them about the Indian. They still look with a jaundiced eye upon what I'm involved in. Thundercloud never hinted that someday I would heal or anything similar and he stayed with me for years, he still does, no matter where I go. You see, there were many ways I had to be tried before my life could be settled in any one direction."

Many ways indeed. He never studied medicine but wanted a more adventurous life. He served in the

Merchant Marine and learned to fly a plane. He was ordained a minister, in 1954, of the Spiritualist Episcopal Church and traveled the evangelistic circuit. Now, because of policy changes in that organization, he belongs to the Church of Revelation.

When he met Nancy he felt an incredible urge to be with her. They both had been studying metaphysical subjects and reading books on the psychic and occult world and knew they were fated to be together. He married her in spite of the fact that she was horribly broken and marred by an automobile accident that her doctors said would give her precious little time to live. Nancy was his first patient.

"We had been studying for quite a while," Nancy told me, "and one night I was informed that I was going to have an operation. I was surprised that I had been chosen as the first patient but not surprised when I saw Bill go into trance and heard another voice come from his body. I had many things wrong with me and one of them was a huge tumorous bulk that was caused by one of my operations. I stood for an hour and a half with two people holding me up while Bill's doctors operated on me. When it was over, the ugly lump was gone. The doctors told me that they were going to rebuild my body as much as possible so that I could stay on earth and help Bill in his work. They performed fifty-two operations on me over the years until they were all through. I'm here today only because they wanted me to stay."

The doctors experimented with Bill Brown's body in fourteen different ways until they finally decided that they worked best by having him leave it. Apparently he was chosen not because of his being a minister or his metaphysical studies but because the chemical make-up of his body was compatible to their purposes. He insists that he didn't ask for this and made no effort to obtain it. He was more surprised than Nancy when he came out of it and she told him what had happened.

Then his teachers showed him the Akashic Records, the fabled books where each soul's life pattern is carefully recorded. "The healing work had to be resumed in this life," said Nancy, "because Bill had failed five times before."

"I didn't fail," he put in, "I just quit."

"The same thing!" she said quickly. "You failed in your Karmic missions because of the lack of understanding of the people around you in those various lifetimes. I was with him in each of them, that I know. They showed us that in the Records. They told us that the lives had been lived in Atlantis, Egypt, and England. Once we had to flee the authorities in ancient Egypt and hide in a cave because of jealousy from the temple priests."

"When you are helping him and his body has been taken over," I asked, "do you see the various doctors as they come and go?"

"No, I don't. If I saw a drawing of what Dr. Murphy looked like while he was on this earth, I wouldn't recognize him. I do see their hands and sometimes see the instruments and I can tell from their movements exactly what they are doing and what they are removing."

"When they cut out a tumor, for instance, and throw it aside, what happens to it?"

"That question has been asked many times. It simply disintegrates. There is a constant cleansing and cleaning up going on all the time in there. The parts and pieces are not left lying around on my level."

"What is the longest that they have used your body?" I asked Bill.

"About five hours," he replied matter-of-factly. "It took me about two and a half hours to come back to normal after they had left."

"What about fees?" I asked. "How much do you charge?"

"Not a cent," he answered. "I don't charge one red cent for the work the doctors do and if anyone tells you differently you can tell them that you heard it directly from me. People give me donations, what they can afford and what they think the operation is worth to them. I do tell people when I write, however, that we expect a donation for the use of the bedrooms to maintain their upkeep and wash the linens and such, but I never ask for a fixed amount."

"You have been accused of being impersonal with your patients. How do you reply to that?"

"Well, I have to be. Getting emotionally involved in their problems doesn't help them and it hinders me. I believe in doing something about a problem, not worrying about it. When you reach that impersonal state you become misunderstood. There is a difference between compassion and sympathy. When you're compassionate you've reached the mental spectrum of being objective. Being sympathetic means you are caught up in the maelstrom of that personality, and you're not doing them a bit of good. It's not easy."

"If it's not easy," I suggested, "why don't you stop?"

"And come back and have to do this all *over* again? I did stop five times before and I know the consequences. Like so many others I went off the path that had been laid out for me. This time around I'm going to stick it out to the end."

"And you won't come back another time?"

"I don't have any plans to do so."

"But do you think," I asked, "that once you are in limbo, so to speak, that you will be doing with other humans what your doctors are doing with you? Will you be taking over the body of a Bill Brown somewhere in the future?"

He paused for a few seconds. "I rather doubt it," he said. "My own personal interests, for whatever it may be worth, are in cosmic law and philosophy. These are the areas in which my own *personal* interests lie. Not in the area of medicine or surgery. I hope that being as I have no personal involvement in those areas that I'll be permitted to do something else after I've left this body for good."

*   *   *   *

Reverend Brown's wife Nancy died shortly after the hardcover edition of this book was published. For awhile he traveled around the nation healing others and "trying to find where I was to go." In 1975, on a trip to Los Angeles, he met a woman who saw his doctors and assisted perfectly at his operations. Maria Nicolosi wed the Reverend Brown in the spring of 1976. They now live in the small southern town, "alone yet with all my doctors."

# A Physician's Statement

Dr. Walter C. Alvarez is the venerable (over eighty years old) medical doctor who writes a syndicated column for many respected U.S. newspapers including the Los Angeles *Times*. Often he says what other doctors half his age are afraid to admit. His column dated December 5, 1971, was such an example:

## Spectacular Cures by Faith Healers

Every thoughtful physician must admit that sometimes a sick person has been cured spectacularly by a faith healer, a layer-on-of-hands. Sometimes thoughtful physicians will wonder, when a patient gets well, whether he got well because of the medicine that was given or because of the psycho-therapy that went with it.

I have known how powerfully the mind can affect the body ever since my childhood in Hawaii. I used to hear my doctor-father telling about some young Hawaiian who, after having been told that a Kahuna (witch doctor) was "praying him to death," sat down, stopped eating and drinking and in 10 days died.

Then when I was 14, my father taught me to give anesthetics while he operated. I had a fright when a man came in who said that he "knew" he would die on the table. With the first whiff of ether he stopped breathing, and Dad and I had to perform artificial respiration for some time before we could get him out of danger. Since then, I have seen a number of people die quickly after an operation when, for some reason, they felt they "had" to die. Curiously, at autopsy we could not find any physiological reason for their death. They had apparently "willed" their own death.

## MENTAL UPSET

During my many years as a gastroenterologist (stomach specialist), I found that in perhaps a third of the patients who came to me with physical symptoms, the trouble was arising in their brain. They sometimes had very severe symptoms due to a mental upset, great unhappiness or great anxiety. What such a person needed was not medicine or an operation, but help with his mental distress.

There are many forms of hysteria that can cause strange symptoms in persons, such as a loss of the voice, loss of the ability to smell, painful and lame joints, deafness and blindness, paralysis, loss of memory and a "lump" in the throat. These persons can have intense pains in various parts of their bodies. No medicine or surgery will cure such a person; what he needs is psychotherapy, and it is conceivable that a faith healer can bring relief of the symptoms.

I know that I have cured hundreds of patients who came to me with what I thought was a functional disease (functional means that the symptoms are due to a disturbance of the mind). In these cases other doctors, who did not believe much in the existence of functional disease, had tried to cure them with medicines or with operations, but without success. . . .

Although I am not advising people to entrust their health to persons who are not medically trained, I do feel that there is much more to medicine than laboratory tests and X-ray examinations. I think that it is sad that today many doctors are so busy that they depend on the results of lab tests for their diagnosis. And then, according to the polls, many of them give a patient on an average, only four or eight minutes in time for a consultation, which certainly isn't enough.

In the past, I have known people who went to a well-known quack, and I asked them, out of curiosity, why they did that. So often the person said, "I know that the man is listed as quack, but he was nice to me, and he gave me half an hour, during which time he listened to what I had to say. I will always be grateful to him for that."

# X
## Alberto Aguas:
## Healer from Brazil

I was in the office of the Society for Psychic Research in Beverly Hills, California, when the post cards started coming in. "Cured. Cured. Better. Better. Cured." And the comments written on them, squeezed on the bottom in ink or pencil: "very relaxed, felt high heat," "heat in the affected areas," "relaxation was above average and I still have a warm glow feeling," "I am now at peace with myself and with the outer world. I am sure that I am healed, that all is well."

These were a few of the positive reactions to the extraordinary powers of a young healer from Brazil named Alberto Aguas. A young man whom I have watched through the years, on two continents, grow from a beginning channel to a powerhouse of transmitting energy.

"We are moving into a strange period," he once told me. "A period of much unrest and confusion. People need to know the material world is not the only world. They need to have hope in the darkness. If I can act as one small light to make their darkness less fearful, I will do it. The time has come when all of us in the spiritual world must come forward and be ready to help."

As the newly elected president of the Society for Psychic Research, I became immediately aware of the need for this help Alberto spoke of, but I also knew that the public, skeptical even in its need, demanded factual documentation concerning those who were there to guide them. Too many charlatans infest the psychic world ready to prey on the suffering and the unsuspecting. As an investigator, and now as president of the most prestigious psychic society on the West Coast, I knew I had to have the "facts." That's why, when Alberto told me he had been booked for a week's healing service in Sacramento, I asked for documentation and written proof. Even professional writers can be blinded by the glare of publicity-seeking self-promoters.

Alberto's first meeting in the California capital was a lecture at the fashionable Mansion Inn, sponsored by the Alpha Club of Sacramento. Alice Crowdis, editor of the club bulletin, expected about 30 people at the lecture. Instead, almost 100 showed up. Alberto, admitting he was nervous and worried about his English, began to speak on his life as a healer. "Soon," he recalls, "there was so much love coming toward me that I forgot about my nouns and tenses and the words just poured out. I hadn't intended to give a healing demonstration that night, but it seemed to come naturally. Soon everyone was holding hands and building the energy in the room. I think I helped many people."

I *know* he did, for I received the individual handwritten reports. Mary Bidwell wrote: "This man is beautiful and kind and sincere. He helped me tremendously." Bernice Salladin: "My vibrations were strong on my right from my hand to the left side of my lower back and that is where I have my troubles." Juanita Eisler: "While we made a chain as a group, I felt healed in my lungs and throat." Regina Collins: "He is probably one of the few psychics that have reached me and helped me to understand the psychic world." Ellen Fries: "That night Alberto made my skin cancer disappear."

Other reports came to me from his healing service

at the Sacramento Unity Oaks Church that same week. Mary Nowell: "That was a great vibration and my hands, legs and abdomen really tingled. I know I have been helped and will be able to walk better." Amelia Smith: "While he was working on some individuals I saw bits of tiny dark clouds or spots just float out and turn into a beautiful golden God color." One woman wrote to report on her friend, Mrs. Velma Ackley: "She is able to control her eyes better and arthritic conditions have improved. She looks years younger and has a glow of health." And from an unsigned note in masculine script: "The energy is quite unmistakably there, even for one as skeptical and insensitive as myself."

Dr. Harvey L. Rose also lives in Sacramento and he has been using the Edgar Cayce methods to research body healings. Working with energy testing machines developed by Dr. William Tiller at Stanford University, Dr. Rose claims that pre-school children have "uni-polar energies". He says that the energy movements over a child's right shoulder are the same as the energy movements over his left shoulder. It is a stronger and more active energy than the adult "bi-polar" field. In an adult, Dr. Rose says, the energy moves in one direction over the right shoulder and in another over the left. Seldom does an adult have the pure "uni-polar" forces. Dr. Rose tested Alberto's energy and was amazed to find that "his is the rare 'uni-polar' adult force field. His energies are most unusual."

I first met this "unusual" young man when I was living in Brazil. He was introduced to me through one of the country's best known actresses. He came into my life at a time when I needed him—or someone—to help me over a psychic wall that had been built up around me and that I not only couldn't see but refused to believe existed. I've told the full story in the last chapter of *Drum and Candle*, and it was quite simply that someone had put the "evil eye" on me and I was slowly dying. It took Alberto and his contacts to show me the way out of that frightening situation. First they had to educate me, then they were able to help me. Or I should say, then I was able to help myself.

Alberto opened doors for me and got me interviews with many of the top Brazilian mediums and "voodoo" priests. If it hadn't been for his know-how and his reputation in the psychic field down there I would never have had the personal experiences and seen the fantastic ceremonies that I did.

I felt I owed him a debt of gratitude and so when I decided to leave Brazil and return—after almost 13 years—to my own country he asked if he could come with me. The political and economic situation of Brazil, at that time, was at an unprecedented low and Alberto felt his future lay elsewhere. It was a brave thing for him to do. He left his family and all his friends to come to a country where he couldn't even speak the language and knew only one person: me.

I settled in San Francisco and started researching *The Psychic World of California*. Alberto practiced his English. One day the Metaphysical Bookshop on Sutter Street asked him to lecture on Brazilian spiritism. It was such a success that they booked him for private readings. He wasn't too keen on the idea but I insisted he go along with it. He doesn't like being mistaken for a medium, even though his mediumistic powers are quite strong. I wanted my fellow Americans to see how a South American psychic worked and Alberto didn't fail me.

Translating at his lectures was easy. It was when I had to translate at his private readings that things became touchy. Sometimes he would tell people things that I didn't think he should and I, as a true Libra, tried to soften as I translated. I remember the very first private client he had in San Francisco. It was a young woman who was very nervous, almost in tears. She told us she was worried about the type of education she was giving her small daughter and wondered if she was doing the right thing. I translated this into Portuguese.

"Ask her if she's married," Alberto said.

"I can't do that!" I protested. "I don't want to insult her. Anyway, she's wearing a wedding ring."

"Ask her if she's married," came the command in Portuguese.

I swallowed and verbally groped my way. "Uh ... he wants to know ... uh ... he wants to know if your husband is helping you choose your child's education," I stammered, red in the face.

"I have no husband," the young woman replied. "I'm an unwed mother."

After that I knew my place. I gave strictly literal translations from then on.

As his fame in the Bay Area grew, so did the number of those who sought his advice. He was booked solid for a month in advance and the telephone at the apartment where he was staying rang at all hours of the day and night. He went to other cities (San Jose, Sacramento, Berkeley, Los Gatos, Richmond) and other states (Ohio, New York, New Jersey) and wherever he went, it seemed everybody needed help. One night, at a "Psychic Fair" in San Francisco, a nervous and badly dressed man pushed his way into Alberto's reading room. Alberto was alone. The intruder didn't even bother to sit down, but blurted out: "When am I going to die?"

Alberto was so startled by this man's unexpected appearance that all he could do was tell him there was nothing to worry about. "But I know I'm going to die," the man insisted, "and I think you can tell me when and how."

"I can't tell you anything like that," he replied. "I don't tell fortunes. But you have many years left. Now go in peace." The man left as hurriedly as he had entered.

The next morning the San Francisco police came

calling on Alberto. Could he give any further details about that man? His age? Describe his face? Alberto said the only thing he remembered was that the man was nervous and poorly dressed, more than that he couldn't recall. The police thanked him and told him to be careful. That man, they said, was probably the dreaded "Zodiac Killer."

That did it for Alberto. He decided that it wasn't worth using his talents if he would be prey to criminals and police investigations. He felt drained by the American public. It was different from Brazil where people wanted spiritual guidance. Here everyone wanted to know about their jobs, their new car, if they would move and who their boyfriends were sleeping with. "I wasn't trained in my country to be a teller of fortunes," he told me. "These countrymen of yours are not like my people. I will not be drained anymore."

And so he stopped giving readings.

But he was unable to stop his psychic abilities.

Once when I was in California and he was in Brazil, I awoke from a dream where I had seen him running in front of an enormous tidal wave. I knew something was wrong and tried to phone his Rio apartment. There was no answer. Worriedly, I sent a telegram to a mutual friend, Miss Isel de Carvalho, asking her to see what was wrong with Alberto. Two days later he called me. It was the first time he had been able to leave his apartment. There had been a flash flood in Rio and live electrical lines had blown down around his building. The water had been past the second floor. The flood had come just about the time I had dreamed it. "I was thinking of you," he told me, "and wondered who would tell you the news if I drowned."

During the 1972 presidential election he was back in California, and while Nixon was soaring at the height of his popularity, Alberto became quite upset. "That man is going to ruin the country!" he groaned.

"He will be elected by more people than has ever voted for one man before, but soon the American people will wish they had never heard of him! Oh, the poor American people! How they are going to suffer!"

"Nonsense," I argued. "He is a great man. Look what he did to end the Viet Nam war. And see how he opened Red China and has improved relations with the Russians. He's the best thing that ever happened to the United States."

Alberto would only shake his head and mutter: "Poor American people."

There's no use elaborating on *that* prophecy.

With more confidence in his command of the English language (he speaks it quite well now, with an intriguing accent), he began to give readings again, but only to close friends or friends of friends. The turning point in his life came one night in Venice, California. "I was with a group of people and one woman began to complain of a headache. I had always fought against healing in the U.S. because I didn't think I was worthy of it, but that woman was in such pain that I went over to her and placed my hands close to her head. Immediately I could feel the tremendous heat. So could she. Her headache vanished."

After that members of the group brought friends who were ill and Alberto worked on them. Often he would leave late at night, driving for miles along the freeways, to give healings. When I asked him why he put himself out like that he would answer simply: "People need me." The night visits became more and more frequent, finally he was accepting people into his apartment. The phone calls didn't stop. "I feel good again," he told me. "Like a horse back in a familiar harness. I was afraid to begin healing because I was afraid I would fail. But there haven't been any failures so far. 'They' are giving me energy."

The mysterious "they" he refers to are the powers that have been with him ever since he can remember.

Like many Brazilians he grew up *knowing* that there was a spirit world out there ready and willing to help humans resolve their problems, be they financial, medical or spiritual. His mother was a believer and an active practitioner in a "white table" (high Kardek Spiritist) church. "I was born very late in her life," he said, "and my father was always traveling because of business. When my mother went anywhere she took me with her. My brother, who is much older than I, wasn't interested in spiritism. He is like my father, practical and with both feet firmly planted on the ground. My mother and I always had our heads in the clouds. So when she took me to these spirit sessions I watched and learned. Sometimes she would even let me touch the patient's body when she did. My mother gave healing to many people. She would visit their houses or they would come to ours. She didn't go into trance or anything like that and when they asked her where her powers came from she would simply say 'the other side.'"

Alberto is an excellent dresser, a gourmet cook and a meticulous host. He collects antiques and paintings. He also has a photographic memory and can recall names, dates and events that happened years ago. No wonder then that he tried to emulate the passes and cures he saw his mother giving. He vividly recalls his first healing experience. "Well, I was six years old and there was a neighbor who complained to me about her migraine headaches. As I had seen my mother do the laying on of hands so many times, I did the same thing with this woman. Her headaches went away and her migraines never came back. She was astonished. So was I."

I asked him if he told his school friends about these abilities. "I suppose so," he answered, "but I never went out of my way to tell them either. You see, in Brazil, we don't make such a fuss about healing and metaphysical things as you do here in this country. Because there you know that your father was cured through a healer or that your grandmother goes to a spirit session. I mean in Brazil this all develops in a *normal* way. They don't have that *fanaticism* that you have up here. There are none of those intense metaphysical-intellectual types down there that there are up here. There is so much carrying on up here that instead of helping the common citizen your psychic intellectuals just confuse them. Eighty percent of my countrymen have gone to a spiritist session. Maybe they don't go all the time but they sure do go when they need help! The last time I was home I was amazed to see how many *German* people were into Macumba and the predominantly Black religions. You know David," and he pointed a finger at me, "*you* know what a powerful country it is! I'll tell you I haven't found anywhere in the world where the mediums and healers are as good as they are in my country. This is not just my patriotism speaking. There are many here in the United States and they are good. But in Brazil they are *fantastic!* Even my Aunt Mariquinhas used to go to them."

Alberto's piercing dark brown eyes glow when he speaks of this aunt. She was a real character, a page out of *Auntie Mame* and *Travels with My Aunt.* There was nothing she didn't dare do, and no convention she didn't dare flaunt. She drove the first open air car in Brazil. She had lovers who left her fortunes in their wills. She came to Hollywood and starred in several silent films. She spent her money as if it was water. When she died she was a recluse, living alone with her memories and a suicidal mongrel dog that she had saved from drowning by jumping, fully clothed, into a river to rescue. She died the way she had lived: under her own terms.

Her father, Alberto's grandfather, was a minister to Carlos I, King of Portugal. He had been sent to govern one of the African colonies when the King was overthrown. Revolutionaries and natives pursued the family. Alberto's grandmother died and his grandfather, in order to save his children, put them on a boat and sent them to Brazil. He never saw any of them again. Mariquinhas, at 18, became the sole support and mother to her two younger brothers and a sister. They arrived in the rubber rich Amazonian state of Para and stayed, for awhile, with a wealthy uncle. But soon Mariquinhas had her own mansion and her own bank account. She was a beauty who spoke several languages fluently and knew how to make men squirm in her presence. Soon she had moved to the capital city of Rio de Janeiro where she quickly became the toast (and the talk) of the town. She parlayed her talents and her business sense into houses, ocean front property, manufacturing and imports. Alberto recalls being in her mansion when crates of Chinese urns, French gilded furniture and African ivories arrived. She entertained lavishly and her kitchen was stocked with such items as English teas, French champagnes, Greek olives and Persian caviar. When she went to Europe, (as she did 16 times in 22 years!) she took the most luxurious suite aboard the ship. Her maids and hairdresser took the second most luxurious suite. Nothing was too good for her and she wanted the best for her brothers and sister. That's why she was incensed when one of them married "beneath" him. It was when Alberto's father married his mother.

"My mother was from a fine, wealthy old family in the north of the country," Alberto told me. "My grandfather was a surgeon and the director of one of the largest hospitals in the area. My great-aunt was the *first* woman lawyer in South America. We had lots of money and the family mansion was so important that trains made regular stops in our front yard. The back yard sloped down to the river bank where fresh produce from our farms used to arrive daily. We were important people then. We were related to the Brazilian Emperor and many of my aunts and uncles are buried in the royal cemetery. But I had an uncle, my mother's brother, who insisted on getting involved in politics. He stirred the people up against the central government. He talked of equal distribution of wealth and revolution. One day the soldiers captured him and took him out to sea on a government boat. When the boat returned my uncle wasn't on it."

After that the government put tremendous pressures on the family. His grandfather lost his position at the hospital. Taxes were raised to an absurd sum. Old friends avoided them for fear of their own lives. Finally they sold what little remained and moved to a little town near São Paulo where his grandfather became the company doctor for a group of Englishmen building a railroad. In order to bring in extra money Alberto's mother took a job teaching elementary school in São Paulo. It was a two hour train ride. One day she stuck her head from the carriage window and saw a man with his head out another window staring at her. She got off at the next stop. So did he. He introduced himself and took a small religious medal from a chain around his neck and gave it to her. (Alberto wears that medal now.) With amazing speed for South American courtships, they were married ten days later.

Aunt Mariquinhas was furious because she had another bride in mind for her youngest brother. While she was impressed with his wife's family background, she wasn't at all happy that they were under political pressure and penniless. She calmed down, eventually, and financed several factories and businesses for Alberto's father. He, an astute financier, increased their value several times over. Alberto was able to grow up in the lap of luxury: huge homes, maids, gardeners, fancy cars and the very best schools. But things came to a full circle in the late 1960s when mismanagement and unscrupulous partners forced his father to the edge of bankruptcy. Gone are the houses and cars. The servants have been reduced to one trusted maid. Alberto's mother sits home alone now, never talking of her days as a healer or her connections with the spirit world. She's taken a new religion that has given her the consolation to face defeat and death.

Alberto gets emotional whenever he talks of his parents. "She used to look like Susan Hayward and my father looked like Clark Gable. Now they are both old and tired. She has become very bitter in her last years because she and my father don't have a peaceful relationship. They are still married but he goes away for long periods of time. She stays alone in the old mansion and is very lonely since I came to this country. I love her very much but it was meant to be and now has to be this way."

Alberto made a name for himself very quickly in this country. He has appeared as banquet speaker at the annual Phoenix Psychic Fair, has been interviewed on radio and television all across the country and now has the same agent as does psychic Jeane Dixon. He has lectured and given healings in such diverse spots as Eugene, Oregon and St. Louis, Missouri. Wherever he goes, crowds wait for him for private appointments or just to touch him. "What I admire in him," says Los Angeles agent Lee Atkinson, "is his sincerity. He doesn't have any of that giant ego that so many in this field have. He wants to help others and he *does* help them. He said something very beautiful at a lecture the other night. 'You cannot heal if you do not love.' What a metaphysical truth that is!"

I have been privileged to watch a few of Alberto's healings. He doesn't like to have anyone there, just observing, because he feels it is a most intimate moment when the energies come through him for a specific client. It was at his Hollywood apartment and a patient had come from Indiana in great pain. The man, in his late fifties, had rheumatoid arthritis and couldn't raise his arm more than a few inches without suffering. Alberto told him, quite candidly, what he tells all his patients:

"Let me explain the way I give my healings. I will ask you to lie down on the healing table. Don't cross your legs or your arms and when I start please close your eyes. I will place my right hand half an inch in the air over your solar plexus and my left hand half an inch away from your forehead. Usually I don't change the location but sometimes I have the urge to change and if I have that urge I will change the position of my hands and place them at other locations on your body. I want to tell you that I don't promise you anything. Anything! I want to make sure you understand what I mean. Many people come to see me with a very great variety of illnesses. I give them the healing, they have lots of faith, they don't have any reaction and they are not cured. And I have people who come to me, very negative, very skeptical, have no reaction at all toward the healing and they are cured. I want you to know that the period of treatment is between 20 and 25 minutes. When the top of my hands feel very warm and my veins start to pump up I feel I have channeled enough energy for this period and you don't need more. I will leave the room, wash my hands and come back and place your name and address and the kind of illness you have and your reactions—if you have reactions—in my appointment book. Once a day for the next thirty days I will send absent healing to you and to the other people in my book. If you have any questions, or if you could not follow everything I said to you, let's talk and be very clear before I start. If you don't like the way I give my healing I can recommend you to other healers in town. I want you to know that I believe if somebody takes so long to get an illness they should not expect to be cured in one treatment. I believe six treatments is the ideal but this is up to you. You have my telephone number and you are the one who has to decide. I have many people who come to me one

time and they are cured. And others come six times
and they are cured. I have people who come six times
and they are not cured. I send them to other healers
and the other healers send people to me when they
cannot do anything for them. Most of the time I am
able to help."

The gentleman from Indiana listened and accepted
this. He stretched out on the table and closed his eyes.
I saw Alberto's lips move in what I knew was a silent
prayer. Then he placed his right hand over the man's
stomach and the left hand over his forehead. His
hands did not touch the patient's body. After a few
minutes I saw the man relax, saw his muscles lose
their tenseness and the tight expression at the corners
of his mouth disappear.

Alberto concentrated on sending the energy and as
he did I watched in amazement. (Will I ever get used
to seeing these things?) as his body turned a deep
red color. Alberto was wearing a white short sleeve
shirt and the redness, against his dark hair and the
white cloth, was profound. He looked as if he was filling up with some inner fire and would be consumed
in a flash once it ignited with the oxygen of the room.

The man twitched under the heat of Alberto's
hands. He sighed deeply and wrinkled his brow in
puzzlement. I was sure he was experiencing the energies that so many had told me about. It must be a
unique sensation to feel these rays coming from the
open palms of an "ordinary" human being.

Alberto moved his hands to the area of the man's
shoulder. He concentrated and the redness of his skin
intensified. I thought some of the color had been
transferred to the mans' face. He seemed to be flushed
and glowing. Then I noticed the veins atop Alberto's
hands begin to swell. That was the sign. The sign
that all the healing energies needed had been put
into the patient's body and now the body was refus-
ing any more energy. It was returning to Alberto.

The young Brazilian looked down and saw what

was happening. He smiled at the man, turned and walked past me toward the bathroom where he always went to wash his hands. As he passed I couldn't help but comment to him on the redness of his skin. He glanced down at his hands, made a well-what-do-you-know gesture and walked down the hall. But as he passed I picked up the overpowering scent of camphor and menthol! There was the unmistakable smell of medicine in the air! I waited patiently for him to return and spoke up—in Portuguese—immediately.

"Look Alberto, you aren't allowed to use medicine in this country. That's a no-no. I smell the salve you rubbed into his muscles."

Alberto exploded. He being Latin I expected it. "What medicine?" he demanded. "I haven't used any medicine! What salve are you talking about? And how can I rub someone with salve if they don't even take off their shirt? You see stains of salve on that man's shirt?" He glared at me and I shrank back.

He was right. There were no stains on the man's shirt. The odor had come from another source, a source far removed from a pharmacist's mixing table. (I have a psychic nose. I pick up odors like roses and perfumes while other people see things. It's a nice thing to have but it can be annoying at times. This was one of those times.)

The man said he didn't smell anything and, frankly, he was so delighted with the healing that he didn't care if he had missed out on the scent. "Look!" he shouted and raised his arm. "I couldn't do that before I came here! And there is no more pain! Look!" and he waved his arm and grinned broadly. The next day his daughter telephoned to report that her father had had the first pain-free night in months and without taking painkiller pills. She gave Alberto's "psychic Ben Gay" the full credit.

Another case that interested me—and Alberto—from the very beginning dealt with a young mother who was dying of cancer. A friend of hers called him to

see if he could do anything to help, even though the
woman was in the last advanced stages of the disease.
Alberto went to her home once and that very night
the woman got out of bed, dressed and sat with her
family for dinner. It was the first time in months they
had all been together at the table. A week or so later
she called Alberto again and he went to see her, gave
her his energies but also gave her a stern lecture on
using those energies. "I told her the energies were for
her and not to be wasted on foolish things. I told her
to take those energies and keep them inside her body.
But she didn't pay any attention. The very next day
she got dressed and went to see her daughter who
was in an amateur play. She came home and collapsed."

A few days later the woman's friend called Alberto.
She had some sad news. The woman was dead. Alberto was crushed. He wondered whether he was in
the right profession. He wondered whether he really
was doing any good or whether it was all a sham. But
the friend refused to listen to him. "Look," she said,
"Elizabeth asked me to give you this message before
she died. She said she knew she would never recover
but you had helped her to see her daughter in that
play and she wanted that more than anything else in
the world. Elizabeth was also grateful because you
changed her husband from a skeptic into a believer.
He saw what your energies were able to do for a person. She asked me to tell you that you helped her die.
She was at peace with herself and prepared for
death. All her pain was gone. She didn't need any
tranquilizers. She was lucid right up to the last. For
that she and her family blesses you."

Alberto's voice chokes when he tells of Elizabeth F.
"She was the first patient that I ever had who died. I
learned a great lesson from her. I learned that healing
die. Perhaps a healer cannot help them remain alive
once their time has come but we can certainly help

them die in peace. Once I understood that I felt much better."

I asked him if he knew where this power came from.

"No, I don't have any idea. I know ... the elementary conception that I have is that I think this power comes from an energy that I have around me. An *intelligence* that I have around me. It's not because I *want* it to be there. It just *happens* to be there."

"Is it around you all the time or only at certain times of the day?"

"It seems to be stronger in the afternoon or evening, yet it's been there when I've had clients in the morning as well."

"Have you ever needed it and it *wasn't* there?"

"No."

"You say it's an energy, an intelligence, yet your mother thought her healing energies were from the spirit world. So isn't it just silly superstition on the part of the Brazilians to give credit to the spirits?"

"Not at all!" he replied, his voice rising. "Some people call on Jesus, others call on Buddha and others ask Khrishna for help. Everything comes from God. I believe this power of mine comes from God. And no matter what you call it, it's there. That's the important thing. It's there! The French author Saint Éxupery said in *The Little Prince:* 'You need rituals. Rituals make things important.' If those spirit rituals make the Brazilian healers important then why should they stop?"

"Yes but scientists ..." I started to say.

He was out of the chair with a bound, paced across the floor and turned to face me. "Scientists!" he almost shouted. "Please don't tell me about scientists! There are many people in this country in the scientific field, the parapsychology field, who try to test psychics and healers but their tests are inadequate. Their methods and their machines are inadequate. Even Mrs. Thelma Moss at UCLA agrees with this.

The Kirlian photography she is doing there is not like the Russian photography. You know that. And they all play the Devil's lawyer ..."

"Advocate," I said.

"Advocate?" he repeated the new word, letting it roll around on his tongue for a few seconds. "Yes. They all play the Devil's advocate. What they should do is toss away their negativity and say, 'Hey, I'm not sure of what you are doing just like you aren't sure of what I am doing so let's work together and find something.' But all the time they are putting people down. If a scientist would come to me and admit that he doesn't have the proper machinery but was open minded enough to see what would happen, I'd work with him. He would give a little and I'd give a little and possibly something could be born of that investigation. But these 'scientists' (and he made a face as he said the word—it didn't taste as good as 'advocate' had) these scientists doing investigations just like to scream at the top of their lungs that everybody's a fraud. You know," he added, sitting down and calmer now, "you know there are no popes in this field. Everybody makes mistakes. These researchers should understand that they need us to make their living. We—the healers and the psychics—don't need them to make *our* living. They would be out of a job without us!"

"Speaking of jobs," I put in quickly, "do you make a lot of money as a healer?"

"Oh David! Come on! You know me better than that! If I had to depend up till now on the money I make as a healer to survive, I'd have been dead and buried long ago."

"This seems to be the general pattern in healing," I told him. "Healers aren't wealthy. People expect a miracle from them and when they get that miracle they sometimes don't even bother to say thank you."

"You're telling me? Listen. I don't charge a set fee. I work by donation only. I accept whatever a person wishes to give me and do you know what?" He didn't wait for my reply. "The rich people are the worst ones in this. The rich come with the big problems that their expensive medical doctors couldn't cure and they are the greediest when it comes to giving me anything for my time. I had a millionaire from Beverly Hills who came with three members of his family. They told me about their mansion, their swimming pool and their tennis courts. I worked all afternoon on them and they didn't even say thanks when they left."

"Maybe you didn't do them any good," I suggested.

"No *good?* Then why did they call me a few days later and want another appointment?"

"Did you give them one?"

"Yes. They came and told me how much better they were feeling. I gave them a second healing and they went away. The same thing. Not even a thank you. The poor people give me something for my services but the rich? Forget about it!"

That Latin temper of his calms down just as rapidly as it builds. "You know, I love people. I really do, but I am very much afraid for them. They get on such confusing psychological trips and screw up so many things with their fantasies. Their minds play such tricks on them because they *let* it happen. Sometimes it's a wall they hide behind. Whenever I have a new client I try to discover what happened in their past to bring on the problem in their present and there is *always* something. Their mother died or their husband left them, or something. The mental is what's bothering them and it shows up on the physical. A lady came to see me one day and she was so negative. Very, very negative. She had these terrible pains in her spine. For fourteen years she had these pains and no doctor had been able to find the reason or deaden the pain. The doctors wanted to sever some nerves in there. Imagine! Anyway, she came with her husband and as I gave her the treatment I talked to her. Her husband was sitting right there, looking on. So I said to her, 'You've had these pains for fourteen years. What happened in your life that was so negative fourteen years ago?' She thought and said, 'Nothing. Nothing happened fourteen years ago.' I went on with the treatment when suddenly she said in a loud voice: 'My God! Fourteen years ago? That's when I married *him!*'"

I asked Alberto if there were certain illnesses he was unable to cure.

"Oh yes, many things, but I will try to work on *everything*. What I cannot help I will refer to other healers. Not every healer can cure every disease just like every medical doctor cannot cure every patient that comes to him. I will even work on animals. Some healers think they are too important to work with animals but if I have a free space in my schedule and someone wants to bring a dog or a cat I'll take them. Why not? They are God's creatures just like man is. They have feelings and need love just like man does. A lady brought me a cat once that was limping on a back leg. The cat had cancer in that leg and the veterinarian wanted to amputate. After a few minutes here with me and my energies that cat was running all around the apartment. And you know what?" and here his voice broke again, "he was so grateful that he went into my bedroom and curled up on my pillow and went to sleep! Wasn't that something?"

I had to agree that it was.

"So everything and everybody is worth a try. I once went to hear a lecture of healers and there was a young man in the audience who had diabetes. He was only about twenty-two and already on daily insulin injections. He asked one of the healers if he could cure his diabetes. And you know what that healer said? He said, 'Well, diabetes is so complicated that it would take too much time to work on it. I don't bother with it.' Can you imagine? What a terrible negative way to answer! He could at least have *promised* that young man some hope. Instead he planted the negative seed that his diabetes would *never* be cured. That's not fair to do to anyone. You must build up hopes if you expect to cure bodies.

"And another thing. I read an interview the other day of a healer who claimed he could cure everything. He said there wasn't anything he couldn't heal. Well, I thought that was a sad statement to make in a national magazine because I happen to know that in that healer's family there is someone who has been afflicted by a horrible disease and the last time I saw that person he was crippled by this illness. I don't see that this healer was able to do anything for this person, this person he loves so much. If he can heal *anyone* why doesn't he start at home?

"And another thing. The other day I was astonished to hear someone in the metaphysical business tell me, 'You know, I don't care too much for healers.' That person is a medium and has never been healed by a healer yet this same medium will go out and work as a *healer* if someone calls for such a service. I find that very strange indeed. Let me tell you something. I think mediums and healers are very important but if I had to make a choice I would say that healers are *more* important. They help people very much. Mediums give readings but most of the time it's for people who don't want to take the responsibility for their actions and want the mediums to make their decisions. What is better: to pass your problems off onto another person or to be made physically whole so you can face anything that lies in your path?"

One of Alberto's most memorable healings took place on November 14, 1974, in Phoenix, Arizona, and was witnessed by a church full of people. The day before he had been seeing private clients at The Universal Series Center, which is owned by Norma Graham and is the hub of metaphysical activity in that desert city. A young man named Steve Kelly came to him. He had fluid in his lungs and the lungs were collapsing. His breath was short and seemed to gurgle. Alberto knew the man was dying and when he showed no reaction from the treatment Alberto was positive that death was imminent.

The next day, around 3:30 in the afternoon, Steve's girlfriend called and insisted on speaking with Alberto. She was in tears. Could he please come immediately to see Steve? The priest had just left. He had given Steve the last rites. Steve lived in Tollison, about ten miles away. Alberto told her it would be impossible for him to make it out there. He had a full afternoon of clients and was to hold a service at the Spiritual Frontiers Fellowship church that evening. The girl was desolate but there was no way Alberto could have made the twenty-mile trip.

"I went back to my hotel about six o'clock," he remembers, "and as I was getting dressed for the church service the phone rang. It was Steve. He could hardly talk. He was gasping for breath. It was like hahhhhh ... hahhhhh. Horrible! He said he was dying and kept pleading with me to help him. I said, 'Steve I can do just so much for you. I can send you absent healing.' I told him to hold the phone close to his ear and to be silent."

Then Alberto concentrated like he had never concentrated before. He pictured Steve getting well. He pictured Steve's lungs whole and functioning normally. "I kept sending him energy and praying that he would be healed. When I finally hung up I was so exhausted that I was dizzy. I almost fell on the floor from lack of energy."

He went to the church and spoke with Rev. Paul Wilkinson before the service started. He told him about Steve and asked him to find someone in the congregation who would drive him to Tollison as soon as the service was over.

Alberto was sitting in the back of the church, near the door, waiting to be announced from the pulpit. He heard the Rev. Wilkinson ask for a ride to Steve's place and heard the minister explain why. A lady volunteered. Alberto said thanks to God. Then the minister started to introduce Alberto.

He vividly recalls what happened next. "I heard the door to the street open and I turned around to see who it was that was coming so late. My heart jumped into my throat and all my breathing stopped. For there stood Steve Kelly! I said to myself, 'My God. Steve is dead and his ghost is here to tell me so!' But the ghost walked toward me and was smiling. I jumped up and ran over to it. I grabbed one of its arms and it was Steve! He wasn't dead! He was breathing normally and was smiling! The absent healing had worked a miracle! I almost ran down the aisle of the church shouting to everyone that Steve had been healed. Here was a man that everyone knew was dying. He had been given the last rites. That very afternoon. Yet he was alive and well and had driven that distance to tell the congregation of his miracle. Don't ask me to explain this because I can't explain."

Alberto looked at me, tears were in his eyes. "Can *you* explain?" he asked softly.

# Undiscovered Energies

In 1966 Mark L. Gallert wrote a book titled *New Light on Therapeutic Energies*, which was published by James Clark and Co., Ltd., and was largely ignored. Too bad, for the man had a great deal to say. For instance:

"The concepts of scientific research as developed by the Western world in recent centuries, with the emphasis on established principles and the efforts to fit newly observed facts into those principles insofar as possible, has had the effect of encouraging the study and use of certain types of energy—namely, those with widespread uses in material or non-organic science, such as heat, steam, short-wave, etc., and has had the effect of discouraging the study and use of other types of energy.

"It is becoming apparent, from research in various fields, that the characteristics of the living organism embrace more types of energy than has previously been realized, and include some energy types that have not entered into the field of non-organic science."

# XI
# Dr. William McGarey and the Cayce Techniques

It's the only one like it in the world. It looks like an ordinary doctor's office or "professional building." It sits on a rather quiet street in a residential section of Phoenix, Arizona. A small sign outside identifies it as the A.R.E. Clinic. The patients going in and out the front door look like patients going in and out of clinics anyplace else. Even the waiting room, with its comfortable chairs, pictures on the walls, and outdated magazines on the table looks like every other waiting room across the country.

It doesn't seem to be any different from a thousand other clinics until you hear the white-clad doctors and nurses talking about castor oil packs, reincarnation, acupuncture, three-dimensional man, and Edgar Cayce.

What makes it different is that this is the location of the Medical Research Division of the Edgar Cayce Foundation.

It is difficult to read much about America's psychic heritage without, sooner or later, coming across the remarkable figure of Edgar Cayce. Or rather, the marvelous unconscious mind of Edgar Cayce. He has been dead since 1945 yet his ideas and his readings are more alive today than ever before.

Too many books have been written about this man to go into great detail here. Every bookshop and library in the country has at least one book about him or else one book dealing with the impressive messages that were channeled through him. Unlike many psychics the contact on the other side never gave himself a name. And no one around Cayce thought to ask if it had one. So the messages are attributed to "an intelligent source." But a source that could immediately locate any living person anywhere in the world, look into their physical bodies and tell, in minute detail, what was wrong and how that wrong could be righted. Cayce's was not a healing power as others in this book. It never brought about an instantaneous cure. It worked as a diagnostician and as a general practitioner and would only *suggest* what to do. If the patient didn't follow instructions that was no fault of the message giver.

Edgar Cayce was born on a Kentucky farm near the small town of Hopkinsville on March 18, 1877. He was no ordinary little boy but one who told of seeing visions and of communicating with relatives and neighbors who had passed away. Rather than study, he would put his schoolbooks under his pillow and absorb the information while he slept. But even with talent like this he was forced to leave school after the seventh grade and get a job.

He worked at many things, few of them successfully. It seemed that he was searching for something. What it was he didn't know, but his wife and children had to be supported. When he was twenty-one he was working as a salesman. Then as things were going smoothly, illness struck. His throat muscles went into slow paralysis and he was afraid he would lose his voice. Local doctors were unable to do anything to help and finally he asked a friend who was also a hypnotist to put him into the same kind of sleep that he entered when he was a schoolboy and memorized his lessons.

Cayce went into trance and a voice came out giving a detailed explanation of his throat condition and recommending certain medications and therapy. This was done and the illness went away.

In a small town news travels quickly and soon doctors were asking him to go into trance to diagnose *their* patients. He was able to do this successfully time and time again. Then it was discovered that the patient did not have to be present at these sessions and all that Cayce needed to know was his name and address. He was able to tune in, using this unconscious mind source, to anyone who requested a diagnosis anywhere in the world. A young medical doctor, Wesley Ketchum, wrote about this ability and submitted it to a clinical research society in Boston. The *New York Times* got wind of it, sent a reporter and a photographer to see for themselves, and the result was two pages of pictures and headlines in the issue of October 9, 1910. Suddenly this humble man was famous. People came for miles around waiting to be healed through his readings. Letters poured in from all over the country. The more he did, the more work he had to do.

He gave almost fifteen thousand readings, which helped at least that many people, yet his own life was filled with financial problems, illness, and accusations from nonbelievers. He was talked into setting up a research center and, along with his wife, tried to run his talents on a businesslike basis. Not to make any money—for he never did—but just to organize and co-ordinate his abilities.

His technique was simplicity itself. He would go into a room, take off his shoes, and stretch out on a small bed. He would close his eyes, cross his hands over his chest, and go into a trancelike state. His wife Gertrude and a stenographer would be at his side. His wife would ask the questions and the stenographer would take down the answers in shorthand.

It always began the same way when he was asked to diagnose. Gertrude would give him the name and address of the person and add: "You will go over this body carefully, examine it thoroughly, and tell me the conditions you find at the present time; giving the cause of the existing conditions, also suggestions for help and relief of this body. You will answer the questions that may be submitted, as I ask them."

There would be a brief pause and then he would say, "Yes, we have the body."

Then would follow a detailed examination of the person, telling what bones were broken, what muscles or nerves out of place or what disease was destroying it. Then he would suggest ways to put the body back in balance. More often than not these ways were highly unorthodox methods calling for such things as raw apples, castor or olive oil.

There would be an immediate follow-up by his staff and the illness would be confirmed in writing by the person who had had the reading. He was seldom wrong in his diagnosis. (The patient would be told in advance that he was to be read for at a definite time and if he was not sitting quietly awaiting the visit of this unconscious mind Cayce would get upset. Several times he commented on the fact that nobody was there. Once he chuckled about a loud pair of pajamas and once, to prove to a doubter that he had been there, he gave the contents of a letter that the man had on his desk while the reading had been going on.)

Cayce died in 1945 in Virginia Beach, Virginia, and left 14,328 documented readings. Of these 8,976 are physical health readings; the others have to do with religion, reincarnation, mental attitudes, philosophy, etc. (There are also an estimated 500 readings that were never recorded and therefore have been lost.) These readings are one of the largest and most impressive records of psychic work ever left by one individual. Under the guidance of his son Hugh Lynn Cayce they have been compiled, cross-indexed, printed, and placed at the disposal of anyone wishing to study them. The A.R.E. headquarters (Association for

Research and Enlightenment, Inc., P.O. Box 595, Virginia Beach, Virginia, 23451) sees a steady stream of doctors, psychologists, theologians, writers, and just plain folks coming to study these messages from an unknown but higher source. Hugh Lynn travels around giving lectures and making television appearances, talking of his father's contact with the other world while the rapidly expanding staff keeps a voluminous correspondence going with A.R.E. members and home study groups all over the world.

Since 1965, when the Medical Research Division of the Edgar Cayce Foundation was established, Dr. McGarey has been its director. Dr. Bill received his medical degree in 1947, just two years after Cayce's death, yet he never heard him mentioned. They could have met personally many times because Dr. Bill (as everyone calls him) was born in Ohio (Cayce came from Kentucky) and went to college in both Arkansas and Ohio. (Cayce was a short distance away in Virginia). It's a shame the two men didn't get to meet each other, for Dr. Bill's entire life—both personally and professionally—revolves around concepts evolving out of Cayce's readings.

Dr. Bill was born in Wellsville, a small town on the Ohio River, in 1919. He was more interested in athletics and writing than in medicine in those days and got a job as sports editor and reporter on the Wellsville *Union*. He went to the College of the Ozarks in Clarksville, Arkansas, and got his Bachelor of Science degree in 1944. He got another piece of paper worth framing a year earlier: a marriage license. He met and wed Gladys Taylor, who was also studying medicine. Gladys, an attractive woman with a soft voice, was the daughter of a medical missionary to India, where she was born. She got her medical degree from Women's Medical College in Philadelphia in 1946. A year later he got his from the University of Cincinnati. Dr. Bill went to the Korean conflict as an air force flight surgeon and after two years of that, he and Gladys moved to Phoenix, Arizona, where they set up a general medicine practice.

Dr. Bill had always been a religious man. In fact, when he first entered college it was to be a Presbyterian minister. "But I switched from religion to medicine not because I was disillusioned with the ministry but because I was disillusioned with myself. I just didn't feel I was good enough to be a preacher."

He would have made a great preacher. He is tall, slim, and blue-eyed. The warm Arizona sun has given him a permanent tan, which sets off white sideburns and the slight wave of white hair over each ear. Uncomfortable in a dress shirt and tie, he likes to wear sports shirts, and when he has to look more businesslike he'll slip a double-stringed slide, with a silver and turquoise clasp, under the shirt collar. He has been in the west long enough that all the Ohio farm boy in him has been baked out. His voice is deep and soothing. It gives him a great bedside (or pulpit-side) manner.

He was as surprised as anyone when he switched from religion to medicine. "I have been a religious man for many incarnations but there was no memory of ever being a doctor," he told me. "I had never thought about the medical profession and no one in my family had ever been involved in it. Now our oldest son is studying to be a doctor at the University of Miami. I'm very proud of him and the fact that he has seen our work and likes it enough to carry on in the same field."

The work that he refers to is the careful follow-up and research of the many Cayce readings, but Dr. Bill was an established medical doctor long before he ever heard of "the Miracle Man of Virginia Beach."

It was in 1955, ten years after Cayce died, that someone loaned Bill McGarey a copy of Gina Cerminara's book *Many Mansions*. It told of Edgar Cayce the psychic and of Edgar Cayce the medical diagnos-

tician. Bill was intrigued. "I was utterly fascinated
with the idea that this man could have seen into the
bodies of others and told what ailed them. As a doctor I had often wished that I had been able to do this
very thing. People who came to me and couldn't tell
me what was wrong were as bad as small children
who couldn't talk at all. But I didn't do anything with
the Cayce readings because I figured that the man
had been dead ten years and that his ideas had died
with him. I didn't know that an organization called
A.R.E. even existed. Then one day I saw a poster
saying that Hugh Lynn Cayce was to be in Phoenix
on a lecture tour. There was a phone number to order
tickets. Well, I called the number and told one of the
lecture sponsors who I was and my interests in the
Cayce material. I was so interested that I couldn't
wait to hear the lecture. So Hugh Lynn came over to
my office, perched himself on a stool, and we talked
for hours. I felt I was on to something but I couldn't
see at that time how I could use it in my own practice."

The friendship with Cayce's son kept on via the
mails and telephone calls but it wasn't until three
years later that Dr. Bill managed to get some time off
to attend a seminar at Virginia Beach. There, for the
first time, he was able to see the vast files of readings.
"I found the spiritual ideas in them more interesting
at first," he admits, then adds, "perhaps I still do."
But Hugh Lynn wanted Dr. Bill to do more than just
read them. He wanted him to study them and try to
put some of them into practice. As a bonafide member of the American Medical Association, Dr.
McGarey was in a position to try the practical aspects
of the readings as well as savor the intellectual aspects. Dr. Bill insisted that he couldn't look into a
person's body and apply the Cayce prescriptions. He
told Hugh Lynn, "the readings are different with each
patient. Your dad gave individual readings and individual medical advice. Sometimes he changed his ad-

vice completely when he gave a person a second reading. I can't look inside the body and I won't be given a second chance. I am not a psychic."

Dr. Bill admits that while he couldn't fathom how the readings could be used in their entirety, he did start experimenting with some of the more standard prescriptions. In the beginning, most of his time was devoted to the effects of castor oil.

Cayce had often advised castor oil packs for his unseen clients. While they were unheard of here in the States, they had been known in the folk medicine of some European countries. Naturally, university-trained doctors had ignored them, and if they ever prescribed castor oil at all, it was as a purgative. Dr. Bill dug into the history of this oil, from the seed of the *Ricinus communis*, and found out that the ancient Egyptians used it in their cosmetics as well as a form of eye drop. Yugoslavian folk medicine had it rubbed into tired feet and used it as packs on the abdomen for a variety of complaints. Early settlers in New England found it good for eliminating warts, removing moles, fading brown age spots, and increasing the flow of mother's milk.

While Cayce, (or rather his unconscious mind) had recommended the oil taken internally a few times, the majority of his prescriptions called for it to be placed on the *outside* of the body in heated packs. For some reason the heat forces the oil into the skin and sets up a kind of chain reaction with the muscles, nerve endings, and blood cells. It may even work like acupuncture needles, stimulating a certain point to cause a beneficial reaction in another part of the body.

Dr. Bill worked on eighty-one different cases using caster oil packs and wrote a report on his study. The illnesses ranged from abscesses to appendicitis to threatened abortions to hemorrhoids to hepatitis to bursitis to ovarian cysts. In almost all instances he had dramatic results.

A nine-year-old boy was taken to his clinic with a

severe abdominal pain. He was throwing up and couldn't eat. As the pain increased, there was no doubt that it was appendicitis. Then a castor oil pack was placed on his abdomen and his parents were instructed to keep it on constantly during the night. He slept well, no pain. In the morning all pain was gone, he was hungry and had no complaints. The packs were used for three nights in a row—with no other medicine—and on the third day he went back to school.

A twenty-five-year-old housewife, three months' pregnant, came to see Dr. Bill after she had been bleeding from the vagina for an entire day. There was a profound ache in her pelvic region. He sent her home, telling her to put castor oil packs on her lower abdomen three times a week for one-hour intervals. The pain went away, there was no recurrence of the bleeding, and she had a normal delivery six months later.

A seventy-five-year-old lady, the resident of a rest home, complained of severe pain from a furuncle in her left armpit. She had been to other doctors but they had been unable to drain it. A year earlier she had been hospitalized with the same thing under her other arm. That furuncle had been cut out by the surgeon's knife. She did not want to go back to the hospital but the pain was so severe that she could barely raise her arm. Dr. Bill put her on the castor oil packs twice a day for an hour and a half for seventeen days. The pain and the swelling subsided after the third day and the furuncle gradually cleared up until it disappeared altogether. There was no scar and there was no external draining at any time.

In his 135-page medical monograph "Edgar Cayce and the Palma Christi" (literally "the palm of Christ"; another Latin name for the castor plant), Dr. McGarey tells of these successes—and the failures— with the castor oil packs. He points out that they can treat other things than just the physical:

The peacefulness which several of the group noticed when they applied the packs to the abdomen, particularly the first time, may point up a relationship between emotion and body that needs comment here.

Case number 16 is relevant. This 51-year-old woman was nearly overwhelmed by the stress of her marital break-up and it was mirrored in her body by the depression, nervousness, numbness, anorexia, abdominal cramps, distention, mucus and diarrhea which she was experiencing. The treatment with the packs over a four week period brought the physical body a long way back toward normal. The pressures at a mental-emotional level, however, were not solved, so a recurrence came about some time later on. These observations are saying, in effect, two things: first, that turmoil in the emotions will produce a turmoil in the body, as physical disease; and second, that the packs in cases like this, bring into being a peace throughout the nervous system that reverses the emotional impact on the body for a period of time, but unless they are continued, the effect will not last.

Dr. Bill believes that people set in their ways will not likely respond to the packs (or probably not to other treatments either) even though the packs bring peace to the body "and this is a measure of grace. Those who are set in their ways cannot let go of their own wills long enough to sense that it is the will of God that they be healed through grace."

He feels that those who are receptive in their nature will benefit most from the packs. "Being receptive is being as the little child. He has faith without even knowing why, and so accepts all things as if he knew this is the will and the graciousness of God acting in his life. And the peace comes to him, throughout the whole of the earth—his earth."

I asked him if he had been doing any of the Cayce methods before he had heard of Cayce. In other words, doing them unaware that Cayce had proposed them.

"Diet," he said. "Cayce has diet as the underlying basis for most everything. He wanted us to take care of ourselves with a proper diet and he always urged people to pray and meditate. I had not started to meditate before I read Cayce but I had been praying all my life. But concerning the most basic concept that I'd found in his readings, I hadn't even started on that. You see, it's a mechanism of the mind he was really talking about. It's what you're aiming for that's most important in his readings and it's so delicate. For instance, let's say you are flying in a plane going at one thousand miles an hour. You flick the steering mechanism just a little bit and keep on going. If you don't correct your course, you're not going to land anywhere near where you originally wanted to be. Well, the difference in direction between aiming your efforts at the rehabilitation of the physical physiological body is one concept and aiming your efforts at destroying bacteria and viruses is another idea. They may be close when you begin but when you get to the full implementation of the ideas, they are worlds apart. One builds up a normal self-sufficient body and the other only destroys an illness. And the body may not be better for it. I think the true practitioner puts these both together in their proper perspective. I learned from Cayce's readings how to approach a disease and rehabilitate a body, not just how to eliminate that disease and leave the body to struggle on its own."

"You didn't learn that in medical school?" I asked rather surprisedly.

He shook his head. "There was no talk of the spiritual side of healing when I went to school. Nor was there given the concept that the body has the amazing potential for regaining its normal balance and integrity. There was also no talk of miracle healings or the power of faith to heal. The professors never even hinted that this could be possible. I still don't think it's mentioned in medical curriculum anywhere. It's an unusual professor that would want to stimulate his students thinking along those lines. Anything that is not understood is called 'spontaneous remission.' It's a kind of wastebasket term, in a sense, because we doctors feel that in medicine everything must be understood; and, if you don't understand it, get rid of it. When you think about it there is much in modern medicine that we don't understand, so we classify it, giving it names to clarify it in our minds, and then we *think* we understand it. There is much about the human body and the human brain and the human soul that we don't know and those who profess to know are kidding themselves."

This coming from a member of the AMA was intriguing, so I asked the next, and most obvious, question. "Do you think the majority of American doctors today really know what they're doing in the majority of the cases?"

"I think that considering what the medical doctors have to do, they do to the best of their abilities. Cayce puts it this way, that all healing comes from one source whether it be by knives or medicine or prayer or the laying on of hands or electrotherapy. It all comes from one source. In other words, from God. So healing the body by penicillin is not, in my estimation, any different than healing the body by prayer. It's just the difference by which the healing power comes into the body. This power brings an awareness to the *cells* of the body." He stopped talking and looked at me, anxious that I understand what he was talking about before he continued. I shook my head that I was with him. "This upgraded consciousness of the cells of the body, this awareness, is what we call healing. Each cell has a brain and each atom has an awareness.

"Cayce said that man is a product of creation and that all things in a created world are brought into creation by what you might call bipolar activity. In other words, positive and negative. Every atom has a positive and negative side. The electron is negative, the proton is positive, yet this atom is more nothing than it is something. It is energy but it is also an active solar system like the sun and the earth and the planets, but there is more force to it than there is substance." He paused again. "Do you understand?"

"I think so," I said, not at all sure that I did.

"We are something *material*," he gestured with his hands, "and yet we are nothing. We are manifested energy stopped in time and space in a three-dimensional world, becoming a 'real' part of that third dimension so we can live in it. Each atom is an aspect of our total consciousness in the three dimensions. Our total consciousness is not perfect; therefore, our minds and bodies are not perfect. There are cells in our bodies that have not yet become aware of this. Most of them have not. But because we are constantly striving to become more aware or striving to become something to ourselves, we must upgrade our self-awareness or we're sunk."

This I understood and shook my head in agreement.

"This ties in with our religion," he continued, "because as we enter a state of a greater self-awareness we transcend and move away from what religions call 'sin.' A self-aware person is still only partly aware and partly unaware, and yet," he laughed, "we're not even aware which parts *are* aware."

"But," I interjected, "a laying on of hands or a penicillin shot does, therefore, awaken these cells and make them aware of their function."

"That's right. When a human being has been given help he sees a whole new world opening up in front of him. He has felt miserable and the help that you have given him has made him feel better. Then he begins to wonder about the *source* of this new-found betterment. Often when a person is literally brought back from death he will have a higher awareness of life. When the body is healed, then, no matter how it is healed, the person is filled with gratitude and gratitude means the person gets out of himself and thanks someone else, thus taking his consciousness out of himself. As long as a person keeps his entire awareness centered on himself he is not growing."

"How many patients do you have," I asked, "that when they are healed by the Cayce method give thanks to God for it? Or how many of them say, 'I'm glad I went to that doctor because *he* healed me.' How much gratitude actually goes back to the Supreme source?"

"I don't know and I don't think anybody does," he replied. "But don't forget, God is acting *through* a doctor. The patient may not recognize it as such because his awareness may not be great enough to see that this doctor is merely acting as an instrument. Even the doctor may not be aware of it. Only God may be aware of it. The thanks is there no matter how it's directed."

"But doesn't this put the doctor in a bind," I asked, "because he has to realize that it is not he himself that should take the credit?"

"It does indeed," he said. "It's an ego smasher to realize the truth behind this. But many doctors know this and use it in their daily practice. I have no doubt at all that thousands of doctors get the wonderful results they do because they consciously act as a channel for God's power. Their main desire is to make their patient well again and they let God use them no matter if they are cutting with a knife or prescribing pills. Their method works because they *want* it to work.

"We haven't measured any of this in medicine yet, so *formally* you don't hear this idea being talked about. Many doctors think they have to be 'scientific' and science is not sufficient where God is involved.

"We must put into modern medicine the understanding that healing is not the destruction of the disease process but rather healing is to bring life to the human body. When it brings more life and more awareness to the human body then the health of the human body does not deteriorate into sickness. It's when the emotions are wrong, the attitude is wrong, and the actions are wrong that illness comes about."

"But if the emotions are what's wrong," I put in, "are you saying that all illness is psychosomatic?"

"No, because to me psychosomatic is not an effective term. It's easy to say an illness is psycho—of the mind—and somatic—of the body—but it doesn't talk about the spirit there. I subscribe to the view that the body, the mind, and the spirit are one. So what affects the psyche affects the soma, certainly. What affects the soma affects the spirit too. I think that illness is built because we move away from our ultimate destinies without knowing it."

"You mean our Karmic life pattern?"

"Exactly. Sometimes we move because of fear and when we do that we are hurting ourselves. When we are moving because of self-desire then we are also hurting ourselves."

"But how do we *know*," I asked, "when we are on the path or not on the path? If it is so important that it can seriously affect us physically, there must be a way of telling us when we've strayed."

"I've heard it said that the easy way becomes the hard way and the hard way becomes the easy way. The way I understand that is that if you know you are not supposed to do something, you put a check on it. For instance, when someone insults you and you want to assault him or call him a dirty name or to lower him because of what he's done, you must remember that it's not right to do this to another human being. It's hard to do, but you must forgive him. Forgiveness, you see, is the law. I can't explain this in just a few words but after you've done this for a while you will find that you are able to be kinder to everybody. And you'll say, well, gee whiz, this is getting easier. The hard way becomes easy. But what happens if you do it the easy way is that when you feel like slugging the guy, you slug him. Now that becomes hard because he may slug you back, twice as hard."

Of all the personalities in this book, Dr. Bill was the most reticent when it came to talking about his professional life and his works. He is a medical doctor and, because of this, has a standard of ethics regarding interviews that other healers do not have to abide by. He feels that undue emphasis on himself and his clinic could be considered as an advertisement. He wishes to do nothing that would jeopardize the fine relationship he shares with the other medical men of his area.

He was reluctant to tell me that his clinic is the only one of its kind in the world. I had to get that information from sources on the East Coast. Sources other than the unassuming Dr. Bill told me that the clinic has eight examining rooms and one emergency room. More than fifteen thousand charts of patients, both active and retired, are filed in the front office. As of mid-1974 there was a staff of six medical doctors, seven registered nurses, four therapists, five receptionists, two secretaries, two in the outpatient residence, plus a librarian, an accountant, and a clinic manager.

Patients must know about Edgar Cayce and his methods before they will be admitted. The R in A.R.E. stands for "research" and the clinic is mainly devoted to researching the various Cayce suggestions.

Dr. Bill became quite interested in the ancient art of acupuncture when he began wondering what Cayce meant by such statements as "the system needs to be balanced" or "the liver is not in balance." He was struck with the acupuncture idea of "balancing" the body's nervous energies by applying needles to certain vital points. So interested has he become and so thoroughly has he researched the subject that he recently published a book on it. *Acupuncture and*

*Body Energies* was issued by Gabriel Press in Phoenix. It's a fascinating treatise and one that should make the subject more understandable (by clearing away some of the present mumbo-jumbo) than most of the books on the market today.

Dr. McGarey feels that the trancelike readings of Edgar Cayce have added a new dimension to medical therapy. "Much of today's therapy is very helpful," he said, "but it's only being applied at the end of the trail when people are starting to fall apart. There has never been any really satisfactory preventive medicine elaborated. The only preventive measures have been inoculations or in sanitation. There has been no concentrated activity to show the individual how he can prevent disease and maintain his health. It *is* possible to maintain good health. A patient should be shown how to take care of himself to avoid future illnesses. He needs to be taught that health in the human body can actually be built."

At the A.R.E. clinic if a patient needs an antibiotic or other orthodox medicines, it would be administered along with the Cayce method, but they have found, with the castor oil packs for example, that some medicine administered along with the packs cuts down the packs' effectiveness.

The method of making a castor oil pack is no jealously guarded secret and Dr. McGarey notes that it can be used in a variety of common ailments. You take a soft flannel cloth and fold it until it's about eight inches wide and twelve inches long. It shouldn't be thicker than three layers. (This is the size for the abdominal area, smaller areas like the neck or arm get smaller size packs.) Pour some castor oil onto the cloth until it is wet but not dripping. Apply the cloth to the area needing treatment. Cover this with a piece of plastic cloth and apply a heating pad. Start out with "medium" heat and go to "high" if the body can stand it. The pack should remain in place for about an hour and a half. It helps if you wrap a towel around the things to hold them in place. Wash the skin afterward with two teaspoons of baking soda in one quart of warm water. You can keep the flannel and use it over and over again. (The time left on as well as the number of times the pack is used depends on the illness. It is used most commonly for an hour to an hour and a half. Cayce suggested this in his readings and Dr. Bill also described it in his research.)

Cayce's remedies didn't always call for castor oil. Here is his prescription for removing scars:

> Two ounces camphorated oil, 1 ounce peanut oil, 1 teaspoon dissolved lanoline. Warm ingredients in a pan and put into blender. Rub into the scar two or three times a day until the thing goes away.

Medical doctors have trouble getting rid of the common cold without penicillins and injections. Cayce suggested one take two ounces melted lamb fat, two ounces spirits of turpentine, two ounces spirit of camphor, mix well and rub some of this mixture on throat, chest, and soles of feet. Put a flannel on the chest and throat and wear an old sweater or sweat shirt. Put heavy socks on the feet. It works better if one takes a hot bath first, quickly towel dries, hops into bed and applies the potion. Drink citrus juices and take lots of vitamins for a day or two.

"Where did Edgar Cayce stand on the subject of surgery?" I asked Dr. McGarey. "Do you operate?"

"I'm not a surgeon," he said, "but Cayce was not against surgery, that's something most people don't understand. He didn't say surgeons were a lot of nogoodnicks. In fact, he recommended surgery on himself in one reading when his attending doctors reported he didn't have appendicitis. He went into trance and out came the message that his body had to have surgery immediately or it would die. They opened him up and took out his appendix, which was ready to burst. In those days, had it ruptured, his chances for survival would have been very slim."

"Dr. Bill," I asked, "have you ever found Cayce to be wrong?"

"I'm sure he was wrong a few times. It's the nature of man to be wrong. Even Jesus said, 'Why call thou Me good? Only the Father in heaven is good.' I think it's the nature of the third dimension to bring about error—so everyone has been wrong. Cayce was not a perfect channel, but he was about as good as you can find anywhere. I think he was in contact with universal forces and I think at times God was speaking through him much like He spoke through the prophets of old. Yet the things that Cayce brought through him were subject to some error. The reason? Because of himself and the people who were surrounding him and were with him that he gave readings for. I think all these people added something to the environment that slightly altered the reception of some of his readings."

"Do you think," I asked, "that because he passed away in 1945 that his information is limited? I mean that it hasn't kept up with man's progress in modern medicine?"

"That's a hard question to answer, but I think that what he implied in his readings was that there are certain techniques to be followed to bring about a balance of the human body and a co-ordination once again between the functions of the human body and thus a restoration to normal health. He showed that this can be done in any one of a variety of ways. He also said that it is important that this regeneration be brought about with a variety of things at once and that's what makes it difficult to approach in a research manner. Scientists usually eliminate everything and just test one part of a theory at a time. Well, his readings said that there are several things working together that bring back the balance. He cited diet and low voltage electricity, or maybe massage or Atomidine, maybe hot castor oil packs, maybe epsom salt baths singly or in varied combinations.

"While his suggestions are not current chronologically up to today, his *concepts* are, because they have been viable since the beginning of the world. They are, in a sense, timeless."

"Do you see the Cayce methods being used more and more by American medical doctors?" I asked him.

"They seem to be getting a greater acceptance as time goes on," he replied. "Since 1968 we have sponsored symposia here in Phoenix for physicians. The material offered in these four- or five-day events deals with concepts from the Cayce readings which seem to add significantly to the understanding of the human body and which are important in a holistic approach to the treatment of the body. The readings, you see, have much valid material to offer concerning the physical body, its functions, its derangements, and offer a variety of therapeutic measures designed to restore the body to a state of health once again.

"American doctors want to grow and learn. I'm quite sure of that. We know our limitations. Today we look back and say, 'Twenty-five years ago we really didn't know very much,' and I'm sure twenty-five years from now we'll look back and say the same thing about medical knowledge today. A good doctor has to be honest with himself and admit that he doesn't have all the answers. If he does that while keeping his eyes open to learn about new things, he will become a better physician."

Dr. Bill is a busy man and had taken valuable time from his patients to talk to me. I appreciated it and I told him so. I also told him that I admired what he was doing and was pleased to find an accredited medical man using information from a psychic source as a method to be tested and validated.

"Do you want to know what my definition of 'healing' is?" he asked. I told him I did. "Healing may really be peace—a peace that comes to rest in the body, that is a reflection of the 'peace that passeth understanding.' We see it come to the body much as peace is allowed to come to the earth: a nation here and a nation there. When we find real peace on the earth, we may see a state of health having come to all bodies."

# From a Book on Yoga

I bought a bunch of old books on yoga one time and while I never read them, I kept them for reference.

As I pondered one evening on some of the things that the various healers had told me, my attention was pulled to a small worn volume on yogic healing. I thumbed through it and when I came to the very last page I found the following written in faded pencil marks, by a hand that shook with age:

"The Eternal Force is neutral. It does not, it cannot, take sides nor be partial nor selective. It Exists. *It is*. The use of one's Powers depends entirely upon oneself—whether we ignore it, or use it for ill or good purpose."

# XII
# Summing Up

There are many more healers in the United States than I have, or could have, interviewed. To give them all a separate chapter would have made this work larger than the Manhattan telephone book. Those given the full chapter treatment are people I have chosen based on their reputations, their documented healings, and the deluge of letters I received from their former patients. But others deserve to be mentioned.

The late Kathryn Kuhlman, for instance, was probably the nation's top healer if size of audience, size of organization, and amount of signed testimonials are any indication. I did not give her a complete chapter because there are at least four books already published about this great lady that tell much more than I have space for, also, her organizational managers made it difficult for me to interview her by dragging their feet and keeping me at bay. I wasn't surprised, for this lady was bombarded by thousands of requests every week for interviews, prayers, and healings.

The first time I saw her was in Los Angeles at the mammoth art-deco Shrine Auditorium. I had been promised four seats by the Kathryn Kuhlman Foundation in the specially reserved section. I was to be accompanied by my friend from Brazil, healer Al-

berto Aguas, and movie actress Ann Miller and
her mother. (Annie later cancelled out when her
mother became too ill to leave their Beverly Hills
home.)

There must have been almost ten thousand people
jamming the area around the auditorium that Sunday.
They came in cars, in chartered buses, and on foot.
Many were in wheel chairs, some were on crutches.
Some were even flat on their backs on portable hospital beds. They were all ages, from tiny babies in their
mothers' arms to elderly grandmothers supported on
the arms of their children. It was a racially mixed
crowd as well, with blacks, Latins, and Orientals
sprinkled amid the mostly middle-class whites.

The doors opened and they surged in, flowing like
lava from some noisy volcano. In less than twenty
minutes the seven thousand seats were filled. The
ushers pushed the unlucky ones back outside and
closed the doors. "Jesus has often healed through the
loud-speakers out here," the disappointed crowd of at
least three thousand was told. Some mumbled and
left. Others sat on the ground, making room for the
ones on crutches and in wheel chairs.

Inside, from my reserved seat in the first-row balcony, the service was about to begin. For at least an
hour the two-hundred-voice choir had been singing
hymns. Their voices filled the vast auditorium before
the people did, setting up vibrations and creating an
atmosphere.

When it was time for the service to begin, amid
very little fanfare, Miss Kathryn Kuhlman walked out
onto the stage. No, it was more than just walking out;
it was a quick, energy-laden movement almost like
the arrival of a volt of electricity. She was wearing a
white blouse with light, puffy, wrist-length sleeves.
She wore a simple knee-length, pleated, white skirt.
High-heeled white shoes were on her feet and her au-
burn hair was hanging freely to her shoulders.

The choir behind her began to sing and she sang

right along with them in that deep throaty voice that had become familiar to so many television viewers. She wasn't asking for anything, or even that you believe in what she was about to do. She was singing because she was happy to be there and to be beginning her service.

After that she told a few stories about her childhood and showed a gift that she had received from one of her small nieces. She loved those girls and wistfully told all of us that it was a shame that she had never had any children of her own. (She was married once, years ago, but it ended in divorce.) From there a male vocalist sang two songs and she rested a bit. She must have been tired for she hadn't stopped moving, talking, praising, since she had first appeared.

Then she began to preach. It was from the book of John and told of Christ's tribulations. As she was speaking, she suddenly stopped and pointed out into the audience. "Someone out there has been cured of a fused disc in the spine. He is wearing a body truss and it is beginning to burn. Take it off! Jesus has touched you! You have been blessed by the touch of the Lord!"

There was a murmur as heads turned to look at a man who was struggling excitedly to his feet. He began to unbutton his shirt as she went back to her sermon. "Up there," she pointed to the other side of the balcony, "there is a woman who can see again! Oh, praise Jesus that this dear soul has been given her sight. Praise him!" and back she went to her message.

This happened several times during the sermon. She announced—she didn't go down there and touch, but announced from the stage—that a hip socket was well, that an ulcer had vanished, that a severe itching had ceased, that a swollen throat had returned to normal, that a broken ankle was well, that a migraine headache had stopped, etc., etc., etc. People cried out, others shouted praise to Jesus, others sobbed or sat there praying that this miraculous power would touch them, too. They had come for a miracle. They were praying to get what they came for.

Her oft-interrupted sermon over, she had them pass the collection plate as the choir sang. Some people put in checks, others threw in large-size bills. Most people dropped in a few coins and those who didn't have anything to give at all let the plate go by.

Then she asked that those who had been healed, who had "been touched by Blessed Jesus," come forth onto the stage. All over the auditorium people rose and moved toward the aisles. They came down to the steps leading up to the platform. Many carried canes and crutches in their hands. One woman was pushing her own wheel chair. Ushers at the steps asked a few brief questions before they permitted the healed to come up next to Miss Kuhlman.

With a portable microphone around her neck, she began talking to those who said they had been healed. A woman began sobbing as she told her story of feeling a stomach tumor burn up and go away. "All the pain is gone," she kept saying. "It's the first time in months there hasn't been any pain."

Then Kathryn Kuhlman did something extraordinary. She reached out and prayed for the woman, but as her fingers touched the woman's forehead the woman fell backward. She seemed to be jolted by an unexpected lightning bolt that knocked her off her feet and into the waiting arms of one of Miss Kuhlman's helpers. She lay there, on the stage, for a few seconds before regaining consciousness. When they helped her to her feet, she, still in tears, thanked Miss Kuhlman again. "It is not me, my dear, that you must thank," said the evangelist. "I have no power. It is the power of Jesus that cured you. Please don't give me your praise. Give it to the Lord." And she reached out again and again the woman fell over backward onto the floor.

And that's the way it went for another two hours. A

steady parade of people who claimed to have been instantly cured *before* she ever touched them, cured while she was preaching her sermon. And as she prayed for each of them, over onto the floor they went.

A young girl came up a specially constructed ramp, pushing her own wheel chair. She was with her teen-age sister. Both were in tears. Miss Kuhlman managed to get their story through the sobbing. The girl had been crippled since she was six years old and confined to that wheel chair for life. Then two years ago, when she was sixteen, the doctors had discovered cancer. Desperate for anything that would help, their brother had heard of Kathryn Kuhlman and had paid their airplane expenses from Arizona to California. Miss Kuhlman asked the brother to come on stage and a young sailor, wearing his summer whites, joined his two sisters. He was also crying. Miss Kuhlman began to pray for all three and as she did, she reached out and touched them. One at a time they fell over backward, sisters and brother alike. They lay on the stage as she continued to pray for them.

Then there was a young Mexican boy whose mother confessed she had taken him from the state hospital for incurables that morning on a pretext of a family picnic. The boy was in his late teens and he had been unable to walk. He felt something surge down through his legs as Miss Kuhlman was speaking and told his mother he had been cured. Miss Kuhlman asked that he run down the ramp and up the aisle to the rear of the auditorium and back to the stage. As his mother sobbed and cried out, *"Gracias a Dios,"* the young man—incurable just minutes before—raced up and down the aisle.

I had noticed a woman with a withered leg as I came into the auditorium. One leg was normal, the other was like a dry stick, and about three inches shorter. She walked with a heavy limp, leaning on a thick wooden cane. Now she came onto the stage. She walked evenly. There was no more limp. The difference in the leg, somehow, was gone. One leg was still withered, but it gave her support. She held out her cane and Miss Kuhlman took it, touched her on the forehead, and she fell over backward. There wasn't a dry eye in the house.

As time drew to a close, there were so many people jammed on stage that she couldn't listen to each individual story. She started praying and as she did she walked into their midst and began touching them on the forehead, with both her right and left hands. They began falling. The stage, when she was finished, looked as though a farmer had toppled bundles of wheat. She stood there, standing alone, triumphant and praising Jesus.

Afterward, I was taken backstage to see her. I wanted to ask her if she would be willing to be interviewed for this book. Guards at the door had my name and, when one group left, I was ushered in with my friend from Brazil. I told her what I wanted and she readily agreed, telling me to contact her secretaries whenever I wished to see her. As I was leaving, Alberto asked for a favor. (His eyes had been as wide as saucers all during the service. He'd never seen anything like it in his life . . . but then, who had?) "Please, lady," he said, "will you pray for me?"

She smiled and came over to Alberto. She began to ask Jesus to watch over him and she put her hands up above his ears. Alberto fell over backward. There was a man there waiting to catch him and push him back onto his feet. She continued her prayer and over he went again; he was righted and then over he went again. She removed her hands and thanked Jesus. I turned to leave for the second time and she came over to me.

"Jesus, bless this young writer and the work he is doing. Illuminate his mind as he researches this most misunderstood subject. . . ." Her hands came up to my temples, I went over backward. She was still praying when I was righted and she said something about "understanding of the public" and over I went again. It wasn't an electric shock like others had described but more an overwhelming feeling to relax as if it was pure foolishness to stand up when I could be lying down.

What did this woman have? What was the source of this incredible power? She had been curing people (and many medical doctors have attested to these cures) for years. She said it was the power of Jesus. She said it's something Jesus gave her to help others. She didn't know how to start it or how to turn it off. (I fell over in her dressing room *after* the service had been concluded.) Her greatest desire was to one day heal everyone who came to her services, but her batting average never got that high. She was afraid that someday this power would be taken away from her. She wanted to heal as many as possible before that.

Skeptics said it was all a show. A great big flashy carnival show to bring in the money to keep her offices and homes and airplanes and assistants and nationwide television program paid for. It *was* a show. But I live in Hollywood. I have been around actors all my life. No director could get the week-after-week Academy Award performances that she got by paying people to come on stage and pretend that they were healed. It *was* a show, but a natural show like the show of thunder and lightning or the show of a spring meadow all in bloom.

Those into metaphysics claim that her power came from her very audience. That the two-hundred-voice choir sang vibrations into the air that she converted into energy. That the prayers and desires of those who came for healing created a source of energy that she tuned in on. They say she used this energy the way a radio set uses transmissions from the main tower and she was able to direct this force like a laser beam, as she pointed toward those who needed help. The aura of the ill person got recharged, the physical body was healed. An interesting and, in the light of other incidents in this book, a plausible explanation of her powers. But Miss Kuhlman wasn't looking for an explanation. She was sure she had one. "My power is from Jesus Christ," she said. "A Christian would never doubt it."

Another big name in Christian healing is Oral Roberts of Tulsa, Oklahoma. This man began as a humble evangelist and parlayed his talent into his own university, with a large campus, closed-circuit television, and a nationwide television show. It is said that he does very little healing personally now, but his professors teach that healing is possible.

Leroy Jenkins, of Delaware, Ohio, is another of the big-time healers. He is building one of the largest cathedrals in the Midwest. Reports of his ability are mixed but he brings in the crowds.

Olga Worrall is the second half of a husband and wife team that worked for years healing people in the state of Maryland. The subjects of several books and innumerable magazine articles, the Worralls have hundreds of cures to their credit. Ambrose Worrall died recently, and Olga has devoted most of her time to lecturing and public explanations of the work they did so well together. At a prestigious seminar at the University of Southern California in Los Angeles, Olga Worrall was the only nonscientific healer invited to speak on a platform studded with doctors, scientists, and researchers. And she held the audience in the palm of her hand.

Lawrence Le Shan works with the American Society for Psychical Research in New York City. He had long been interested in metaphysical things so he *taught himself* to heal others. He claims that he can teach others, too, and holds classes regularly.

Oskar Estabany has also been written up in numerous magazines and Sunday supplements for his work with Franciscan nun Sister Justa Smith. The sister is chairman of the National Sciences Concentration at Rosary Hill College in Buffalo, New York. She heard of Hungarian-born Estabany when he began to do seemingly miraculous things with his hands at McGill University in Montreal, Canada. Just by holding mice in his hands, he was able to prevent growths from forming in them after they had been treated with a chemical that distends the thyroid gland to ten times the normal size. He was also able to make barley seeds germinate by the powers from his fingers after they had been soaked in a salt solution that ordinarily would have stunted their growth. With Sister Justa he showed that he could activate enzymes in a test tube. So impressed is she with this aged man's work that she has gone across the country lecturing on his unusual powers. It's a little startling to see a black-robed Catholic nun on a platform talking about healing and not claiming it comes directly from a belief in God's only son.

The Reverend Ted Pierce lives in Yarnell, Arizona, and does absent healing as well as the direct laying on of hands. His wife classes him as a "Karmic eraser," in that he "drains off misqualified energy within a person that is causing illness in the body, mind, or spirit. Healing often follows. A large percentage, if not most, of the misqualified energy is from past-life experiences," she says.

William Finch, lives in Sedona, Arizona, and is a long-time student of metaphysics and an organizer of psychical seminars. He is the compiler of a who's who in the psychic United States. He and his charming wife Elizabeth are into what they call Photochromotherapy. They believe that colors play an important part in the healing process and that a person can be restored to health if the proper colors are around him. Many ancient peoples believed this as well. The Zuni Indians of New Mexico used to hold a colored shell between the sun and the ailing person so that the rays would shine through and fall on the patient. Mr. Finch claims that the great stained glass windows of European cathedrals were used for this very purpose. While the AMA has repudiated all color healing (in spite of strong evidence that it does work), scientific experiments in Japan proved that young guinea pigs grow more rapidly in red light than blue light. In Canada, Dr. P. D. McClure, chief blood specialist at the Hospital for Sick Children in Toronto, uses blue light on babies born with bilirubin in their blood. The blue light is able to disintegrate this substance, which is fatal to the baby, causing brain damage and cerebral palsy. The only treatment prior to the blue light was a complete blood transfusion.

Also in Canada, the Re-Education Centre in Surrey, B.C., has been working with very little public fanfare. The director is Mrs. E. Hager and she says that "for nearly ten years the elimination of many different kind of diseases, including cancers, glaucoma, arthritis, back trouble, bladder infection, ovarian cysts, undiagnosed stomach conditions, and others has taken place through various kinds of therapy. I suppose that some of this has been accomplished by 'faith healing,' although from our point of view the faith of the client is not essential. According to the need of the condition, we use the method most appropriate. For example, if a malignant disease is in later stages we use everything we can to help the organism renew itself. This may include the laying on of hands, prayer, and the *all-essential counseling*, which finds the cause in the subjunctive emotional attitude of the person. When the cause is brought up into the consciousness of the individual, nature's own healing power does the work."

And I met a young minister and his wife from a western state who told me of their work with tiny abandoned and orphaned children. Tots so small that they could not possibly comprehend what the minister was saying would get well as he spoke words of love, affection, and security to them. "We think," he told me, "that babies don't understand when we talk to them, but they do. They are acutely aware of everything that is going on around them. It is we adults that don't understand *them*."

Healing, the kind that I have reported on all through this book, is not new. It's been going on for generations, ever since man became ill and turned to a friend for help. It may seem new to us today because we have been kept out of contact with it. Churchmen and scientists have told us for too long that it doesn't work.

Healers are not infallible. They don't cure one hundred per cent of their patients and they are the first to admit it. But doctors, with their four-year courses and their period of internship and their daily contact with illness and accidents also cannot claim one hundred per cent success when it comes to curing their patients.

Quacks—fraudulent healers—who are out to make a fast buck and know that ill people are easy targets do abound all across America. I've heard all the scare stories. The man in Texas who charges (and gets!) five hundred dollars for two drops of his magic cancer-curing liquid in a glass of water. The woman in New York who has a magic stone that she rubs on arthritic joints at twenty-five dollars a session. The farmer in Missouri who has a "blessed stream" running through his property and who will let anyone wash away their disease at thirty-five dollars a bath. Then there are the "candle healers," who will burn candles for you at a price of ten dollars a candle, and you usually need six or more all going at once to do the job. There is a man in San Francisco who has an electric healing box. It's big enough to crawl into and he'll turn on the healing rays if you have an appointment and fifty dollars. And I mustn't forget the healer who passes his hands over an ill person's body and he gets worse. Instead of giving new energies, he *takes* them. A large university who investigated him calls him "a psychic vampire."

I will be the first to agree with the AMA that we need licensed physicians. Most healers cannot stop the flow of blood, cannot take care of a ruptured appendix, do not handle emergency cases like drownings, shootings and automobile accidents. We must have doctors in hospitals ready to take care of accidents and illnesses.

But nothing will change the AMA's stand against healers until the general public decides it has a right to the type of cure it wants. Until then healers will be considered criminals. It is against the law for a healer to diagnose. Even if he sees a tumor on the side of a man's face, he is legally prohibited from telling the patient that he has a tumor. It is illegal for a healer even to suggest the taking of an aspirin, for that is considered "prescribing medicine without a license" and is subject to a jail term, a heavy fine, or both. No wonder then that most healers obtain a "minister's license" and set themselves up under the protective umbrella of a "church." The law still permits church activity without interference.

We are living in a scientific age and have been conditioned that if science can't find it at the end of a test tube, it doesn't exist. If our scientists say it is not so, then it is not so. After all, they are our hierarchy and our leaders.

Some dogmatic scientists are beginning to have second thoughts where healing is concerned. While few have come out and openly said it was possible, several have admitted that "there might be something there." A courageous parapsychologist named Dr. Thelma Moss at U.C.L.A. has dared to experiment with healers and healing in the university laboratory. She has succeeded in photographing healing energies coming from a man's finger tips. Then she went one step farther and showed these pictures at a symposium where the general public was invited. The first time she did this six thousand people showed up in two days! Dr. Moss makes no claims. All she does is present this information to the doubting scientific world.

Dr. William A. Tiller, chairman of the Department of Materials Science at Stanford University, studies brain waves and body energies. At a seminar in Los Angeles in 1972 he startled many of his colleagues by showing a rather complicated slide-graph and casually remarking that "possibly this idea will someday prove the theory of reincarnation."

Lockheed Aircraft Corporation, Palo Alto, California, has set aside funds and scientific talent to investigate psychic phenomena with a heavy emphasis on healing. They call their group "The Academy of Parapsychology and Medicine" and their seminars, with some of the top names in the metaphysical field, have attracted literally tens of thousands. Its president is Dr. Robert A. Bradley of Denver, Colorado, who aside from advocating healing, spirits, and hypnosis is also a licensed physician and member of the AMA.

Astronaut Edgar Mitchell has his own foundation that is delving into the "whys" of healing.

We are stepping into a new era. An era where dogmatism—whether from the pulpit or the laboratory—will no longer be accepted at face value. We have become disillusioned with our priests and our scientists and many of us have started to examine our old-fashioned beliefs and found them wanting.

Abraham Lincoln said: "To believe in what you can see and touch is no belief at all; but to believe in the unseen is a triumph and a blessing."

# Addresses of Healers

Here are the addresses of the healers mentioned in this book, with the exception of the Reverend William C. Brown, who did not wish his address listed. It is *always* better to write them rather than telephone. While a limited few send healing over the phone, they can pay more attention to a letter.

Let me make an important point. *None* of these people charge a fixed fee for their work, but *all* of them have to pay the rent and put food on their tables. They live by donations and "love offerings." There is no reason to expect them to work free of charge for you or your loved one. The butcher, the baker, and the candlestick maker all receive money for what they do. *You* earn your money from your profession. If a healer helps you, give whatever you think that help is worth. A healer does not have an obligation to heal you but *you have an obligation* to thank them for his time and talents. (Note: No one in this book asked me to add this. It's just that I've seen too many cases of financial abuse with healers. Once a patient has been cured, he forgets how urgently he needed help.)

## In Alphabetical Order

Alberto Aguas
P. O. Box 39392
Los Angeles, California 90039

Dorie D'Angelo
P. O. Box 4713
Carmel, California 93921

Charles Cassidy
Box 39722 Griffith Station
Los Angeles, California 90039

Ethel de Loach
P. O. Box 2071
Morristown, New Jersey

Willard Fuller
P. O. Box 7556
Jacksonville, Florida

Dr. William McGarey
A.R.E. Clinic
4018 North 40th Street
Phoenix, Arizona

Bob Hoffman
The Quadrinity Center
1005 Sansome St.
San Francisco, Cal.

Rosita Rodriguez
714 South Scoville
Oak Park, Illinois

Dorothy Vurnovas
264 West 5th Avenue
Sun Valley, Nevada 89431

The following healers have either been briefly mentioned in the last chapter or else have been recommended to me by interested parties. In some cases the addresses are not complete but by doing a little digging you ought to be able to find them.

Oral Roberts
Tulsa, Oklahoma

Reverend David Epley
P. O. Box 323
St. Louis, Missouri

Leroy Jenkins
Box F
Delaware, Ohio

Reverend T. L. Osborn
Osborn Foundation
Tulsa, Oklahoma

Olga Worrall
Baltimore, Maryland

Reverend Ennio Cujini
Clayville Church
North Scituate, Rhode Island

Lawrence Le Shan
The American Society for
   Psychical Research
5 West 73rd Street
New York City

Reverend G. M. Farley
P. O. Box 167
Williamsport, Maryland

Oskar Estabany
Rosary Hill College
Buffalo, New York

Mr. Harold A. Hilton
385 Waterloo Street
London, Ontario, Canada

W. J. "Bill" Finch
P. O. Box 1529
Sedona, Arizona

Mr. A. Nelson Patterson
Lancaster, Ohio

Mrs. E. Hager
Re-Education Centre
17981-96 Avenue
Surrey, B.C., Canada

Ted Owens (the P.K. Man)
Box 48
Cape Charles, Virginia

Mrs. Charlotte Friedman
501 West 189th Street
New York City

Reverend Don Stewart
The A. A. Allen Ministry
Miracle Valley, Arizona

Mr. Vaughn Boone
Route 2, Box 452
Mooresville, North Carolina

Mrs. Helena Bower
Saybrook, Ohio

Mr. Harold Kupel
San Jose, California

Mrs. Shirley Harrison
West Buxton Road
Buxton, Maine

Mr. James Benoit
Mountain View, California

Mr. Ray Jaegers
2723 Sutton Boulevard
Maplewood, Missouri

Reverend Lynn Radcliff
Omaha, Nebraska

Dr. Merritt W. Terrell
Cambridge Springs,
    Pennsylvania

Reverend Elizabeth Chaves
Tuscon, Arizona

Mrs. Betty Carpenter
Cove, Arkansas

Reverend Richard Lee Reed
Sanctuary of Healing Light
P.O. Box 1114
San Marcos, California

Mr. Martin Cloor
San Francisco, California

Reverend Douglas Johnson
951 Michel Torena
Los Angeles, California 90026

Reverend Pearl Shannon
Western Spiritual Science
    Church
44 Page Street
San Francisco, California

Magnolia Ellis
Truth or Consequences,
    New Mexico

Dr. Dolores Krieger
New York University
Division of Nurse Education
New York City

Norbu Chen
Houston, Texas

J. Joseph
104-40 Rossen Circle
Dallas, Texas

Ted Whitesell
1618 Huntington Drive
Alhambra, California

Sherry Goldberg
P. O. Box 39621
Los Angeles, California 90039

Janann Clanton
405 Kimberley Drive
Greensboro, N. Carolina

Bryce Bond
410 E. 65th St.
New York, New York

Fred Stoessel
Box 5012 Woolsey Station
Long Island City, New York

Bill Boshers
c/o Dr. Eileen O'Ferrell
Cincinnati, Ohio

Reverend Alex Holmes
215 N. Aymer St.
Caro, Michigan

Universal Series Center
4340 N. 7th Avenue
Phoenix, Arizona

Phoenix Book Center
524 Westheimer
Houston, Texas

Sol Weiss
1128 So. Doheny Drive
Los Angeles, California 90035

(And, I would appreciate it if you would send me any other names and addresses for future editions of this book. You may write to me in care of Doubleday & Co., Inc.)

# ABOUT THE AUTHOR

DAVID ST. CLAIR was a *Time/Life* reporter for six years. His previous books include: *Child of the Dark, Safari, The Mighty, Mighty Amazon, Drum & Candle, The Psychic World of California* and *How Your Psychic Powers Can Make You Rich*. He is president of the Society for Psychic Research and is currently working on a documentary film about the psychic world.

# PSYCHIC WORLD

*Here are some of the leading books that delve into the world of the occult—that shed light on the powers of prophecy, of reincarnation and of foretelling the future.*

| | | | |
|---|---|---|---|
| ☐ | 12466 | THE GOLD OF THE GODS<br>by Erich Von Daniken | $2.25 |
| ☐ | 12604 | EDGAR CAYCE: THE SLEEPING<br>PROPHET<br>by Jess Stearn | $2.50 |
| ☐ | 11866 | PSYCHIC DISCOVERIES BEHIND<br>THE IRON CURTAIN<br>by Ostrander & Schroeder | $2.25 |
| ☐ | 11991 | YOGA, YOUTH & REINCARNATION<br>by Jess Stearn | $1.95 |
| ☐ | 12931 | SETH SPEAKS<br>by Jane Roberts | $2.95 |
| ☐ | 11856 | THE SETH MATERIAL<br>by Jane Roberts | $2.25 |
| ☐ | 12369 | YESTERDAY, TODAY, AND FOREVER<br>by Jeane Dixon | $2.50 |
| ☐ | 12868 | LINDA GOODMAN'S SUN SIGNS<br>by Linda Goodman | $2.75 |
| ☐ | 10696 | THE NATURE OF PERSONAL<br>REALITY by Jane Roberts | $2.75 |
| ☐ | 13005 | A COMPLETE GUIDE TO THE TAROT<br>Eden Gray | $2.25 |

# WE DELIVER!
## And So Do These Bestsellers.

| | | | |
|---|---|---|---|
| ☐ | 11256 | **HAYWIRE** by Brooke Hayward | $2.50 |
| ☐ | 12261 | **DR. SHEEHAN ON RUNNING** | $2.25 |
| | | by George A. Sheehan, M.D. | |
| ☐ | 12528 | **GODS FROM OUTER SPACE** | $2.25 |
| | | by Erich Von Daniken | |
| ☐ | 12868 | **LINDA GOODMAN'S SUN SIGNS** | $2.75 |
| ☐ | 11660 | **THE AMITYVILLE HORROR** by Jay Anson | $2.50 |
| ☐ | 12427 | **THE MOTHER EARTH NEWS ALMANAC** | $2.50 |
| | | by John Shuttleworth | |
| ☐ | 12220 | **LIFE AFTER LIFE** by Ramond Moody, M.D. | $2.25 |
| ☐ | 11150 | **THE BOOK OF LISTS** by D. Wallechinsky, | $2.50 |
| | | I. & A. Wallace | |
| ☐ | 12285 | **NIGHT STALKS THE MANSION** | $2.25 |
| | | Westbie & Cameron | |
| ☐ | 12136 | **PAUL HARVEY'S THE REST OF THE STORY** | $1.95 |
| | | by Paul Aurandt | |
| ☐ | 12521 | **THE ONLY INVESTMENT GUIDE YOU'LL** | $2.50 |
| | | **EVER NEED** by Andrew Tobias | |
| ☐ | 12991 | **PASSAGES** by Gail Sheehy | $2.95 |
| ☐ | 11656 | **KICKING THE FEAR HABIT** | $2.25 |
| | | by Manuel J. Smith | |
| ☐ | 12218 | **THE GREATEST MIRACLE IN THE WORLD** | $1.95 |
| | | by Og Mandino | |
| ☐ | 12250 | **ALL CREATURES GREAT AND SMALL** | $2.50 |
| | | by James Herriot | |
| ☐ | 11001 | **DR. ATKINS' DIET REVOLUTION** | $2.25 |
| | | by Dr. Robert Atkins | |
| ☐ | 12942 | **JOAN CRAWFORD: A BIOGRAPHY** | $2.95 |
| | | by Bob Thomas | |
| ☐ | 11291 | **THE LATE GREAT PLANET EARTH** | $1.95 |
| | | by Hal Lindsey | |
| ☐ | 01137 | **THE PEOPLE'S ALMANAC #2** | $9.95 |
| | | by D. Wallechinsky & I. Wallace | |

**Buy them at your local bookstore or use this handy coupon for ordering:**

Bantam Books, Inc., Dept. NFB, 414 East Golf Road, Des Plaines, Ill. 60016

Please send me the books I have checked above. I am enclosing $_____
(please allow 75¢ to cover postage and handling). Send check or money order
—no cash or C.O.D.'s please.

Mr/Mrs/Miss _____

Address _____

City _____ State/Zip _____

Please allow four weeks for delivery. This offer expires 2/80.

NFB—8/79

# How's Your Health?

Bantam publishes a line of informative books, written by top experts to help you toward a healthier and happier life.

# BE A WINNER
# IN THE RACE FOR
# FITNESS

These physical fitness titles give every member of the family the guidance they need for getting in shape and keeping fit. Choose the program most suited to you whether it be yoga, jogging, or an exercise routine. You'll feel better for it.

| | | | |
|---|---|---|---|
| ☐ | 12261 | **DR. SHEEHAN ON RUNNING**<br>George A. Sheehan | $2.25 |
| ☐ | 12382 | **GETTING STRONG** Kathryn Lance | $2.50 |
| ☐ | 12289 | **RUNNING FOR HEALTH AND BEAUTY**<br>Kathryn Lance | $2.25 |
| ☐ | 11166 | **JAZZERCISE** Missett & Meilach | $1.95 |
| ☐ | 13061 | **LILIAS, YOGA AND YOU** Lilias Folan | $2.25 |
| ☐ | 12546 | **NICOLE RONSARD'S NO-EXCUSE**<br>**EXERCISE GUIDE** Nicole Ronsard | $1.95 |
| ☐ | 12540 | **AEROBICS** Kenneth H. Cooper | $2.25 |
| ☐ | 12468 | **AEROBICS FOR WOMEN** Cooper & Cooper | $2.25 |
| ☐ | 11902 | **THE AEROBICS WAY** Kenneth H. Cooper | $2.50 |
| ☐ | 12360 | **THE NEW AEROBICS** Kenneth H. Cooper | $2.25 |
| ☐ | 12322 | **CELLULITE** Nicole Ronsard | $1.95 |
| ☐ | 11282 | **THE ALEXANDER TECHNIQUE**<br>Sara Barker | $1.95 |
| ☐ | 11246 | **INTRODUCTION TO YOGA**<br>Richard Hittleman | $1.95 |
| ☐ | 11976 | **YOGA 28 DAY EXERCISE PLAN**<br>Richard Hittleman | $2.25 |

**Buy them at your local bookstore or use this handy coupon for ordering:**

# RELAX!
## SIT DOWN
## and Catch Up On Your Reading!

| | | | |
|---|---|---|---|
| ☐ | 11877 | **HOLOCAUST** by Gerald Green | $2.25 |
| ☐ | 12206 | **THE HOLCROFT COVENANT** by Robert Ludlum | $2.75 |
| ☐ | 12859 | **TRINITY** by Leon Uris | $2.95 |
| ☐ | 12262 | **ACT OF GOD** by Charles Templeton | $2.50 |
| ☐ | 12550 | **THE MEDITERRANEAN CAPER** by Clive Cussler | $2.25 |
| ☐ | 12683 | **EVEN COWGIRLS GET THE BLUES** by Tom Robbins | $2.75 |
| ☐ | 12152 | **DAYS OF WINTER** by Cynthia Freeman | $2.50 |
| ☐ | 13176 | **WHEELS** by Arthur Hailey | $2.75 |
| ☐ | 11966 | **THE ODESSA FILE** by Frederick Forsyth | $2.25 |
| ☐ | 12490 | **TINKER, TAILOR, SOLDIER, SPY** by John Le Carre | $2.50 |
| ☐ | 12573 | **THE DOGS OF WAR** by Frederick Forsyth | $2.50 |
| ☐ | 12489 | **THE HARRARD EXPERIMENT** by Robert Rimmer | $2.25 |
| ☐ | 12513 | **RAISE THE TITANIC** by Clive Cussler | $2.50 |
| ☐ | 12855 | **YARGO** by Jacqueline Susann | $2.50 |
| ☐ | 13186 | **THE LOVE MACHINE** by Jacqueline Susann | $2.50 |
| ☐ | 11886 | **PROFESSOR OF DESIRE** by Philip Roth | $2.50 |
| ☐ | 12433 | **THE DAY OF THE JACKAL** by Frederick Forsyth | $2.50 |
| ☐ | 12941 | **DRAGONARD** by Rupert Gilchrist | $2.25 |
| ☐ | 12399 | **THE CULT** by Max Ehrlich | $2.50 |
| ☐ | 13017 | **THE CHINA SYNDROME** by Burton Wohl | $1.95 |

**Buy them at your local bookstore or use this handy coupon for ordering:**

---

Bantam Books, Inc., Dept. FBB, 414 East Golf Road, Des Plaines, Ill. 60016

Please send me the books I have checked above. I am enclosing $_____
(please add 75¢ to cover postage and handling). Send check or money order
—no cash or C.O.D.'s please.

Mr/Mrs/Miss _____

Address _____

City _____ State/Zip _____

FBB—8/79

Please allow four weeks for delivery. This offer expires 2/80.

---

# Bantam Book Catalog

Here's your up-to-the-minute listing of over 1,400 titles by your favorite authors.

This illustrated, large format catalog gives a description of each title. For your convenience, it is divided into categories in fiction and non-fiction—gothics, science fiction, westerns, mysteries, cookbooks, mysticism and occult, biographies, history, family living, health, psychology, art.

So don't delay—take advantage of this special opportunity to increase your reading pleasure.

Just send us your name and address and 50¢ (to help defray postage and handling costs).

# CARIBBEAN BLUES

Lady Hannah from Havana is the fabulously wealthy owner of the exclusive Cuban resort The Perfumed Garden. She is cruising aboard the Cunard *Countess*, and rumor has it that her meeting with attorney Hy Court and accountant Richard Ledger involves an international expansion of her famous "spa."

A recent companion to Fulgencio Batista, Lady Hannah is also the owner of the priceless Caribbean Blues. Discovered by adventurer Jules Finder in Siam in 1926, these three perfectly matched sapphires are said to carry an ancient deadly curse.

Accompanying Lady Hannah will be her personal secretary, Willa Wright, noted psychic Madame Deja Bleu, the popular blues singer and bandleader Scats Allegro, and her personal maid, Susie Tong.

Shortly after departure from San Juan, Puerto Rico, Lady Hannah is found dead and the Caribbean Blues are missing!

Coincidentally, a group of private investigators is on board trying to form an international association with a referral network. They must solve the murder, if only to save face, and must work together in order to bring the guilty party to justice.

## The most novel novel
## in the history of the mystery

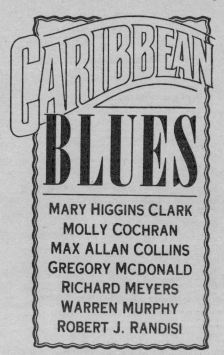

# CARIBBEAN
# BLUES

**MARY HIGGINS CLARK**
**MOLLY COCHRAN**
**MAX ALLAN COLLINS**
**GREGORY MCDONALD**
**RICHARD MEYERS**
**WARREN MURPHY**
**ROBERT J. RANDISI**

## Prologue & Epilogue
## by Mary Higgins Clark
## Based on a scenario
## by Karen and Bill Palmer

*PaperJacks* LTD.

TORONTO    NEW YORK

# AN ORIGINAL

## *PaperJacks*

## CARIBBEAN BLUES

*PaperJacks* LTD.

330 STEELCASE RD. E., MARKHAM, ONT. L3R 2M1
210 FIFTH AVE., NEW YORK, N.Y. 10010

First edition published March 1988

# THE PERPETRATORS

| Writer | Character | Chapters |
|--------|-----------|----------|
| Mary Higgins Clark | | Prologue, Epilogue |
| Molly Cochran | Chico Mangini | 5, 10 |
| Max Allan Collins | Nate Heller | 4, 12 |
| Max Collins with Bill and Karen Palmer | The Solution | 18 |
| Gregory Mcdonald | Ph. d. Phlem | 8, 14 |
| Ric Meyers | Andy Baltimore | 7, 13 |
| Warren B. Murphy | Devlin Tracy Leslie Dither | 1, 2, 3, 6, 11, 15, 16, Postscript |
| Robert J. Randisi | Jack Miles | 9, 17 |

# WHODUNIT?
## BY BILL AND KAREN PALMER

The two of us had just returned from a Bogie's Murderous Mystery Tours weekend at the Parker House, in Boston. In addition to Warren Murphy, Molly Cochran, and Marian Babson, Robert B. Parker was also a guest of honor. Bob had just received an award for his work in helping adults learn to read.

We had become very aware of the shocking statistics of illiteracy, and decided that we would like to do something to make the rest of the country more aware of this terrible condition. Twenty-seven percent of all Americans are functionally illiterate!

There we were, a few weeks later, sitting over a couple of drinks at our restaurant, Bogie's, with Warren Murphy, who was busily scribbling notes on cocktail napkins. Following through on one of his better ideas, Warren suggested that we write a murder mystery scenario to be perpetrated on board a cruise ship. The authors portraying the characters would each write a couple of chapters for a book to be published; the book would be written as if the murders were actually taking place during the cruise. PaperJacks publisher Tony Seidl, who was also sitting with us, immediately agreed that he "could do that."

A few months later, the Cunard Line hired us to perpetrate a murder mystery during a Caribbean cruise. From May 16–23, 1987, we would be littering "murdered" bodies on the Cunard *Countess* (British Registry), and around the Caribbean islands! The perfect opportunity to realize our plans!

Each author we invited on the cruise was told about our plan to write this book and to donate the advance to help fight illiteracy. Mary Higgins Clark requested that the donation be made to the New York City branch of the Literacy Volunteers of America. Each of the authors immediately volunteered to write at least two chapters of the book! Max Allan Collins suggested that each author choose a fictional private eye to investigate the crime, and he or she would interrogate the suspect whom the author was portraying.

As the book progressed it became a true genre crossover. Our basic scenario, as enacted on the ship, was written in the classic "whodunit" style, while in the book, the case is eventually solved by a group of private eyes!

Now, we realize that multiple collaborations have appeared before (about fifty years ago in the mystery genre), but they were written in a round robin. That is, the first author wrote the first chapter and then passed it to the second author who then wrote the second chapter, etc. What is truly unique about this novel, however, is that for the first time a book has been written *simultaneously* by several authors! Never before has a book been written in this manner — by so many authors, on a ship, and all in one week!!!

Upon disembarkation in San Juan, the book was complete.

And how do the authors feel?

Greg Mcdonald probably best expressed it when he said, "It reminds me of the politician's wife, who, a week after the publication of her book, when asked how she liked it, replied, 'I don't know, I haven't read it yet.'"

# PROLOGUE

It is May 16, 1938. In Europe, war clouds are gathering. But as in every era, the rich are getting richer and a favorite delight of the privileged is a cruise through the Caribbean. Today, that jewel of a luxury liner, the first Cunard *Countess*, is sailing at eight P.M. Only a few of the passengers who boarded the ship that sunny May afternoon knew that this trip would be different.

On board, there came the usual sprinkling of café society folk, the celebrities, who years later would become known as the "jet set." Up the gangplank in stately procession marched the fabulously wealthy, surrounded by their personal entourages, secretaries, maids, companions. The stunning Lady Hannah is clearly the most exotic of these passengers to embark. Besides the usual fawning lackies, her personal psychic also accompanies her. And oblivious of the covetous eyes that follow her, she triumphantly glides aboard wearing the exquisite matched sapphires known throughout the world as the Caribbean Blues.

The socially impeccable, absorbed in themselves, the honeymooners absorbed in each other, the middle-income travelers, thrilling to the realized dream of the cruise they'd saved for all these years; the distinguished captain; the charming and efficient officers; the superbly trained staff. It ought to have added up to a week of pampered luxury and relaxation.

But within hours of sailing, chaos broke out. Murder most foul destroyed the serene atmosphere of the floating liner. Inexplicably, the lights went out. A shriek was heard. The dance floor in the salon, so accustomed to gliding feet, experienced the stumbling, shuddering steps of a man as he collapsed into the fearful darkness that is death. The climate of murder has been set, and before it is over it will claim more victims.

Was it simply fortuitous that seven of the most famous and infamous private investigators were aboard this cruise? Was it sheer coincidence that they had decided to hold the first convention to exchange views of methods of detection and then found themselves bonded in an effort both reluctantly cooperative and fiercely competitive to solve the case of the Caribbean Blues?

Lady Hannah, the flamboyant beauty who had clawed her way from a tenement walk-up through various lovers until she managed to catch the eye and capture the heart of Demitrio Finestra, the hotel builder who was reported to be Conrad Hilton's keenest competitor, caused great interest. But anyone who knew Demitrio broke into raucous laughter at that fable. Demitrio was a bumbler, dependent on the brains and acumen of his three partners, and when the stock market crashed, he, like so many of his peers, threw open the window of his office and tumbled into eternity.

Two of Demitrio's partners are on the cruise at the invitation of Lady Hannah. The third was recently deceased.

What of Hilda Johnson, the inquisitive, ladylike journalist? The eccentric clergyman whose verbal attack on Lady Hannah shocks the elegant gathering that first evening in the salon? The mysterious import-export tycoon?

Who are these other people in Lady Hannah's entourage? The personal psychic who did not contact her spirit guides and Tarot cards in time to give warning. The moody secretary who had bailed out Lady Hannah after the insurance company refused to pay Demitrio's multimillion-dollar policy? You see, it didn't cover suicide. The Oriental personal maid who believes so avidly in the curse of the sapphires? The bandleader from Cuba who knows so much about Lady Hannah's affairs? The titled big-game hunter without a farthing in his pocket?

Each and every one of them intimately involved with Lady Hannah at some point in their lives. All of them resenting her. Some of them hating her. One of them in that most awful of human predicaments, loving and hating her with equal and agonizing fervor.

The ship glides through the seas to the fabled islands that are the playgrounds of the rich. The private investigators band together to solve the deaths, to keep the killer from striking again. The exquisite cerulean blue of the sea and sky darken at night to a velvety blackness ablaze with stars, stars that almost equal the fire of Lady Hannah's sapphires.

A warning blast of the horn trumpets throughout the ship. Last call for visitors to go ashore. We invite the rest of you to become our fellow passengers, to join us on our cruise. Come. Let us sail away.

# CHAPTER 1

The giant cruise ship had arrived during the night at the pier on the edge of San Juan's Old City in Puerto Rico.

Throughout the hours of darkness, the ship's crew had cleaned and polished and restocked, and when the brilliant Caribbean sun exploded over the waterfront in the morning, the Cunard *Countess* sparkled white and trim as she rocked gently in the light Puerto Rican trade breezes, waiting for her passengers to arrive.

It was 1938 and the captain and crew of the *Countess* expected that this would be their last leisurely vacation run through the Caribbean. Any day now, they expected the teletype to spit out orders that would send them home to England, where the *Countess* would be refitted as a warship of His Majesty's Navy.

And all because of some silly-looking moustachioed rotter who was jackbooting it around Germany and had them all fired up there with his talk of world domination. Well, Great Britain would simply have to teach him a lesson, as it had taught lessons to so many would-be world conquerors before. This one might even be easy. It shouldn't take more than a couple of weeks to give that lunatic little paperhanger what-for.

But that was the future. For the present, the Cunard *Countess* was the world's most elegant warm-water cruising ship. And if this was to be its last peaceful voyage, the officers and crew were determined to make it the best cruise yet.

*So let it all be fun and games*, the ship's captain thought. *Time for death later.*

By late afternoon, all the passengers had come aboard and the giant ship had slipped its moorings and gently rode a rising tide out into the turquoise waters of the Caribbean. As the *Countess* cruised calmly past the scarred battlements of El Morro Fort on the tip of Old San Juan, cocktail parties started up all over the ship, as the 750 passengers prepared to put aside, for at least a week, all the worries of the outside world. For the next seven days this 17,500-ton behemoth would be their universe, and let the rest of the world, with its troubles and problems, keep its distance.

In one of the lounge rooms on a top deck of the ship, two separate small parties were under way.

At one end of the room, near a service bar staffed by a red-faced round man who seemed to have no discernible bones in his body, six men were sprawled out in heavily cushioned chairs. A young woman, with Oriental features and long blue-black hair, stood at an observation window, looking out over the sea as El Morro Fort slowly disappeared behind them. She was the only one of the seven who did not have a drink in her hand.

"Trace, come here," she said. Her voice was soft and musical.

"Yes, sir," grumbled a tall, light-haired man who sat about ten feet from her. He got slowly to his feet, holding tightly onto a glass of straight gin on the rocks, and walked to the window alongside her. He leaned there, looking back around the room, as the young woman said, "Isn't it beautiful?"

Devlin Tracy said, "Sure is."

But he was not looking at the ocean outside. His eyes were fixed on the other end of the lounge, where a dozen people were milling about in a private cocktail party of their own. The people seemed to be moving about at random, but a trained eye could see that the locus of their movements was a petite dark-haired woman. She was wearing a red dress with matching hat and shoes. The hat was gargantuan and seemed designed to display half the annual agricultural output of Puerto Rico. It was fixed to her hair with a hatpin that seemed to be a foot long, and anyone looking at the woman would not have been able to take his eyes off the monstrous hat had it not been for two things: first, the woman was magnificently beautiful; and second, around her neck she wore a very elaborate necklace, created around a centerpiece of three giant blue stones.

The woman's eyes met Devlin Tracy's briefly.

Then she turned away with an expression of total disinterest on her face. It was a wonderful face, Tracy thought, and who knew? On a seven-day cruise, he might just be able to change that disinterested look.

"So this is the way it's going to be?" asked the young Oriental woman standing next to him.

"What? Did you say something, Chico, my dear?" Tracy asked.

"Yes, I did."

"Would you mind repeating it? My mind was elsewhere," Tracy said.

"Of course it was, and I know where. Listen. We have barely pulled out of port and already you're giving the eye to other women? That's what I said. Is this the way it's going to be for seven full days?"

"Chico, listen," Tracy said as he nodded toward one of the loudspeakers mounted high up on the wall of the room, over the main entrance doors. "They're playing our song. 'I Only Have Eyes for You.' "

"Well, thank you, idiot," she said. "But they're playing 'Take the A Train.' "

Tracy shrugged. "I knew it was something like that. And anyway, don't get upset with me already. We just started our vacation and I couldn't help looking at that woman. You know, it's like scenery. You like to look at old castles and water that's got fish swimming around underneath it. I like to look at women. It's all scenery."

"Just don't try crawling around in the

scenery," the young woman said. "And especially her. Look at her. A blue stone necklace with a red dress. She looks like something out of the chorus line at Minsky's."

"Minsky's should be so lucky," Devlin Tracy said.

Another voice pitched in.

"She could buy and sell Minsky's," the speaker said.

"Yeah. Tell her, Heller," said Tracy. "Tell her I'm not ogling some refugee from a burlesque show."

Heller, the new speaker, was a tall, sandy-haired man with a vaguely professional look, but there were scars around his eyes and on the backs of his hands that made it clear he had spent at least some of his life hitting something other than books.

"That's Lady Hannah from Havana," Heller said. Chico looked impressed, but Tracy said, "Who exactly is Lady Hannah from Havana?"

Chico said, "Oh, Trace, you don't know anything about anything. Lady Hannah runs a world-famous resort and nightclub in Cuba and is fabulously wealthy."

"I don't hang out in nightclubs," Trace said.

"No," Chico said. "I've noticed. Cheap gin mills and blue-plate-special restaurants are more your speed. What could you be expected to know about money and class?"

"To refresh your memory, my dear Miss Michiko Mangini," Trace said, "I am not the person who was complaining about her wearing blue stones with a red dress."

"That was before I knew she was real rich,"
Chico said.

"That necklace," Heller said. "Those stones
are the Caribbean Blues."

"I thought the Caribbean Blues was a
baseball team," Trace said.

"Three perfectly matched sapphires," Heller
said. "Some people say they have a curse on
them."

"Yeah," Chico said. "Wear them and you go
color blind. You start wearing any color dress.
And look at that hat. Will you please look at
that hat she's wearing? Quick, call Hollywood.
Tell them not to renew Carmen Miranda's contract."

"Suppose we drop this subject," Trace said.
"I just don't know what your fascination is
with that woman anyway, Chico. Listen, Heller,
rescue me. Tell me about this organization."

Heller nodded but he continued to watch
Lady Hannah at the far end of the room. She
was accepting a glass of champagne from a
tray held by a ship's officer who wore a sparkling white uniform with three strings of gold
braid around the cuffs.

"The reason I've invited you all along,"
Heller said, "is that I think it's time that we
private detectives had an organization of our
own."

"If you're starting a union, count me out,"
Trace said. "I don't trust unions. They're all
Communists."

"He thinks everybody's a Communist,"
Chico explained. "What's the point of the

organization, Heller? Hey, what's your first name? I just can't keep calling you Heller."

"Nate," Heller said. "Anyway, no, not like a labor union. More like a professional association. We could trade techniques; share information. We could help each other in different cities. And maybe we could think about raising our fees."

"I'm for that," Trace said. "This living on twenty-five dollars a day plus expenses isn't for me, especially since Chico seems to want me to start taking her to expensive nightclubs."

"So that's why I got you all here," Heller said. "You two with your agency in New York City and Jack Miles over there. He's in New York, too." Heller pointed to a stocky man with a mashed nose who was sprawled on a sofa, drinking beer from a bottle.

"We don't travel in the same circles," Trace said, looking at Miles. "I go more for tony clients."

"Not quite," Chico said. "We go for anybody who can pay the bill."

"Like the rest of us, I guess," Heller said as he nodded and continued. "And I'm from Chicago, and Andy Baltimore is from Los Angeles. Phil Phlem works out of Boston. And Leslie Dither pretty much specializes in overseas work. I think we've got a pretty good group here to form an organization."

Trace looked around at the other detectives, rating them quickly. Phil Phlem looked dry, humorless, about what Trace would expect from a Boston private eye. The only real crimes committed in Boston were committed by politicians, and nobody ever needed to hire a detective to find out about them. Public corruption in Boston was just that — public, and everybody above the age of five knew all about it. Boston P.I.'s must specialize in divorce cases if they didn't want to starve, Trace thought.

Jack Miles, the other New York private investigator, had the face of the prizefighter he had once been. His clients, Trace knew, were generally people who were down on their luck, the losers of the world, the old pugs and the bimbos and cashiered cops and jockeys who took bribes, the kind who paid one off in thanks and good wishes and by saying a novena at the local church. If they sobered up enough to get there.

The unfortunate truth was that Miles's client list sounded a lot like the one for Trace and Chico's agency. Except Miles seemed to want them as clients. Trace wanted only multi-millionaires; it was just the luck of the draw that he and Chico also seemed to attract bums into their office.

Leslie Dither looked like no one in the field that Trace had ever met. He was a short man with eyeglasses, not physical-looking. His face was fixed in a constant smile, and his hands kept reaching for a bowl of peanuts next to his lounge seat. But there was something vaguely foreign, almost elegant, about his mannerisms, and Trace could understand how he might do most of his work in Europe.

Andy Baltimore was from Los Angeles,

Heller had said. He was another stranger to
Trace, but his mannerisms were pure California,
in Trace's book. Californians always seemed to
be doing one thing while they were actually doing something else. Right now, for instance,
Baltimore was busy talking to Phil Phlem, but
his eyes were looking past the Boston investigator, fixed on the far end of the room
where Lady Hannah was holding court. And he
had a beard. Trace thought only degenerates
and Vikings wore beards.

About Heller himself, Trace knew little. The
man had a pretty good reputation as an
operative in Chicago, America's toughest city.
And his reputation had gone sky-high in
Trace's mind when Heller had called and offered him and Chico a free Caribbean cruise to
discuss the new private detectives' association
he wanted to form. Trace thought it was a
stupid idea, but for a free cruise he would listen
to any kind of stupid idea. Hell, for a free cruise
he'd listen to someone who wanted him to in-
vest in radio . . . with pictures.

But Trace had a suspicion. He had a suspicion that Heller had something more in mind
than just talking to them about the United
States Private Eye Association. There weren't
any free lunches — despite that madman
Roosevelt in the White House — and Trace felt
pretty certain that Heller was going to ask
them to do something for him.

# CHAPTER 2

"You're Tracy, aren't you?"

Jack Miles spoke with an accent that would have been at home only in Hell's Kitchen on New York City's west side.

He had seen Tracy and the beautiful Oriental woman talking to Heller, and now that Heller had sort of drifted down to the other end of the lounge where that party of rich folks was boozing it up, Miles thought that this Devlin Tracy might have some answers for him.

Like what were they doing here, for openers? Nobody had ever yet given Miles a free cruise to anywhere, except to the hospital, and he didn't expect that this trip was going to be any exception. He'd wind up paying for it; he'd like to know how and when.

"Right. Devlin Tracy," the tall blond man said. He glanced over his shoulder to look for the pretty Oriental, but she was talking to that guy from Boston. The guy from Boston had moved right in. Miles thought he was pretty smooth, even if he did look like a car thief. "Jack Miles?"

"The one and only," Miles said. "So now you've been talking to Heller. Tell me, what did you find out?"

"About what?"

"About what we're doing here," Miles said.

"He says we're forming a new association of private eyes," Trace said.

"And you believe him?" Miles asked.

"No, I didn't say that," Trace said.

"No, I didn't think you were that dumb," Miles said. He took a long draft from a fresh bottle of Rheingold beer, which the ship had stocked especially for him. It was a local New York beer and it was cheap and good and predictable, and Miles didn't like surprises. Which was why he was talking to this Tracy, a guy who was obviously born with a silver spoon in his mouth, never had to worry about where his next meal was coming from, and probably played private detective to fill up the time between the checks from Daddy's trust account.

"I'd expect you to be an expert," Trace said.

"What? Expert?"

"In dumb," Trace said.

Miles took another long sip of beer before answering. "Tracy," he said finally, "you know, this can be a long trip or a short one. Or, for you, it can be a short one that seems awfully long. I think we'll all have a better time if you keep your snotty remarks to yourself."

"What weight did you fight at?" Trace asked.

"One-forty-seven and a half," Miles said.

"What do you weigh now?"

"One-forty-seven and a half," Miles answered.

"Were you any good?" Trace asked.

"Except for a lousy manager, I coulda been a contender."

"Okay, if you were good and you're still at your fighting weight, let's be friends," Trace said. "What do you think we're here for?"

"Something sleazy," Miles said.

Trace shrugged. "Naturally. Why else would they call *us*?"

"And somehow, I think it has something to do with that party down at the other end."

"How's that?" Trace said.

"Because Heller knows more about all those people than their relatives do. He's here for something to do with them and he's dragged us along to help out."

"You know the way I look at it?" Trace asked.

"How's that?"

"Nobody's been knocking down my door to hire me. So if somebody's going to give me a free cruise and free booze and a free room, what the hell. Count me in."

"I just don't like being used," Miles said, "unless I know who's using me and for what."

"Well, maybe we'll find out if we go down there and circulate," Trace said.

Miles rose from the gray chair and started to walk with the taller man toward the other end of the room. But first he tugged at Trace's arm. "The little Chinese girl. Aren't you going to bring her?"

"Do yourself a favor, Miles. Japanese, not Chinese. And I wouldn't get ten steps before she finds out I'm missing and she's after me."

"Are you two — what does Walter Winchell say? — 'an item?' "

"Partners and items," Tracy said. "Why do you ask?"

"Well, if she's taken, I won't go running around after her."

"Good thinking," Trace said. "She's taken."

# CHAPTER 3

Leslie Dither thought that it was odd. He and the other private detectives had followed Trace and Jack Miles down toward the other end of the room and were mingling with the guests in the other party.

Dither had said, "Why not, old chaps? It looks like they're having more fun than we are."

But what was odd was the ship's officer. Dither had sailed across the Atlantic many times on ships, and by the three stripes on the man's sleeve, he could tell he was a high-ranking officer. But instead of being "officerly," he was standing around, holding a tray of drinks, obviously unwilling to take his eyes off Lady Hannah. He stood at her side all the while, and when Dither took a drink of champagne from his tray, the officer kind of glared at him.

Very strange behavior, Dither thought. But his brief puzzlement didn't stop him from tasting the bubbly. It was dry and light. A very good wine, he thought. Lady Hannah, whoever she might be, had good taste in wine, if not in ship's officers. The man looked nothing like a ship's officer. He looked hard and weather-bitten, and while ship's officers might look weather-bitten, they also always seemed to have a veneer of sophistication, poise. This man did nothing but stand and stare.

Maybe that wasn't so unusual. Lady Hannah, Dither thought, was certainly worth staring at. He guessed her age at the mid-thirties, but she could have been anything from twenty-five to forty-five. Her skin was flawless, and although it seemed healthily tan, it was absolutely unwrinkled by either age or sun. Her eyes were dark, a velvety brown, and her lips were full and sensual. Her body was trim and shapely, rather than full and lush, but the way she moved under her red dress gave the impression of a woman of animal smoothness and strength. She seemed to smile a lot, but when her gaze turned on some members of her party, there was no good humor in her glance.

Something was going on here, Dither thought. But he didn't know what.

There was a shout from the doorway and everyone turned. A short man, red-faced to the point of apoplexy, ran into the room. He wore a dark suit and a clerical collar.

Only Dither was sure what the man had shouted. To the others in the room, it sounded like a guttural shout, but to Dither it was clear. The man had shouted, *"Ich brauche, ich brauche"* — "I need, I need."

Before anyone could stop him, he had raced across the floor and had come toward Lady Hannah. The ship's officer, who was still hanging around, handed his tray of champagne glasses to someone else and stepped in front of the small woman.

The sudden appearance of the big man in the white uniform in his line of attack seemed to slow down the mysterious minister. He stopped, seemed to think for a moment, then pointed an accusing finger at Lady Hannah.

"You must give them back," he proclaimed in thick German-accented English. He pronounced give as "giff."

Later people would remark on how cool Lady Hannah seemed to be. She merely smiled; she did not flinch from the man's physical assault, and said, "My dear man, give what back?"

"You know. You know. Those jewels. You must repent and return them, before the curse strikes you."

Hannah laughed, a sparkling laugh that seemed at home at a champagne party.

"Curse?" she queried. "The only curse I know is when the bar runs dry."

"Hussy," the clergyman said. "Shameless, sinful woman. I was there, you know. And I read the inscription: 'Death to all who violate this resting place.' You must return those jewels or your life is forfeit."

"Please remove this man," Hannah said coldly to no one in particular.

Nate Heller stepped forward and said, "I think that's just about enough of that." He looked to the ship's officer. They nodded to each other and then each grabbed an elbow and dragged the clergyman toward the door.

He shouted as they pulled him away, "Death to all who violate this resting place! Death, you hear me! Death!" Then he was gone through the door.

"Well," Trace said aloud, "the party's complete now. We have our comic-opera German."

Lady Hannah glanced at him and smiled. Chico moved up closer to Trace's side.

Looking at Trace, the woman with the blue jewels said, "I want to apologize to everyone for this interruption. I hope we'll all just go on with the party." Chico saw her incline her head ever so slightly toward Trace. "I hope I'll be able to make up for it to all of you later. Somehow."

Chico pulled Trace away. "Somehow. I'm sure she could figure out just how without too much trouble."

"I'll bet he was a Nazi," Trace said.

"Nazis? For five years you've been seeing a Communist under every bed. Is it now going to be Nazis everywhere?"

"There's a lot of it going around," Trace said.

"Forget that," Chico said. "Did you see what happened?"

"Of course I saw what happened. I was right here."

"Did you see Heller?"

"What about Heller?"

"He took charge," Chico said. "He said it was time to get that madman out of here, and it

was only after he said it that the ship's officer
made a move. It was like he was taking orders
from Heller."

"I think something's afoot around here,"
Trace said. "And I don't like it. I think it's going to mean more work for us."

The ship's officer in the white uniform and
Heller came back into the room. Everyone
turned toward them, and the officer cleared his
throat nervously, as if he were unaccustomed to
speaking to large groups of people.

"Ladies and gentlemen, the man who was
just here is Father Peter Blue. Mr. Heller and I
have calmed him down and he has apologized
for his outburst. He blames it on his long trip
from Europe to Puerto Rico to board this ship.
He has gone to his room to rest and said he
would return in a few minutes and apologize in
person. He has promised us that there would be
no more such outbursts."

"A Nazi," Trace mumbled. "Nazis are always
making promises. I don't trust him."

But, true to his word, the Reverend Peter Blue
came back twenty minutes later. He looked
abashed by his behavior and went quietly to
one of the windows looking out over the
darkening Caribbean Sea. As Andy Baltimore,
the Los Angeles detective, watched, Father
Blue seemed to be making a herculean effort
not to look at Lady Hannah or the jewels
around her neck. For her part, if Lady Hannah
even knew the man was in the room, she certainly gave no indication of it.

Baltimore saw that the Reverend Blue was concentrating most of his attention on another of the guests in the room. The man he was looking at was tall, with graying sandy hair and an aquiline nose. He wore khaki shorts and a bush jacket. His face was ruddy — the kind of face gotten by a man who was exposed to the sun a lot but didn't have the kind of skin that tanned well.

"Who is that guy over there?" Baltimore asked an attractive blond woman who was standing next to him. He introduced himself and learned that her name was Willa Wright.

"You mean Lord Hunter."

"A lord?" Baltimore asked.

"Yes. That's Sir I. B. Hunter, the world-famous explorer and big-game hunter. Why do you ask?"

"Because right now he looks like the hunted. Our little German friend with the holy collar can't seem to take his eyes off him."

"Maybe they're old friends," Willa said casually, then turned and walked away.

Leslie Dither noticed that the ship's officer was back at his usual post, hovering around Lady Hannah's elbow. Every so often the man would glance over his shoulder, as if to reassure himself that Reverend Blue was staying in the corner as he had promised. The minister showed no signs of going anywhere. His face was still red, still apoplectic, but he seemed to be keeping himself under control.

It was dark out now. The party seemed to be

winding down. People were taking their last sip
of their last glass, when, suddenly, the lights in
the lounge went out.

A couple of voices were raised in protest.
"Hey! Who turned the lights out? Turn them
back on."

"Hey! What's going on?"

Trace was near the door. He fumbled for the
light switch, found it, and flicked it back on.

The lights flooded the room again.

There was a scream.

It came from near Lady Hannah, and Trace
ran forward. There was a body on the floor at
Lady Hannah's feet. The ship's officer in the
white uniform lay there on his stomach, his
arms sprawled out at his sides. Nate Heller was
kneeling alongside him, searching for a pulse at
the man's throat. Trace knelt next to the officer. The man gasped and sputtered a sound.
"She . . ." he seemed to say, then was still.

Heller looked up and his face and voice were
anguished. "He's dead," he said.

"Dead?" Chico said. "What? A heart attack?
What?"

Lady Hannah shrank back from the dead
man at her feet.

Heller said, "There was nothing wrong with
his heart. I think he was murdered." He stood
up and looked around. "I'd appreciate it if no
one left the room."

Chico looked at Phlem, the private detective
from Boston. They nodded to each other

because each had recognized the significance of something: How had Heller known that the ship's officer did not have a bad heart?

The Cunard *Countess* docked at Road Town,
   Tortolia at 11:30 A.M., Sunday, May 17,
      1938.
The sky was overcast, the weather hot and
   humid.

# CHAPTER 4

*Excerpt from operative's report, case file 714, date May 17, 1938. To the attention of George Donahue, vice-president, Cunard Line. Reporting operative: Nathan Heller, president, A-1 Detective Agency, Chicago, Illinois. Written en route during Caribbean cruise aboard Cunard* **Countess.**

*Okay, George, the first thing we have to get straight is that I'm not going to write you a formal report. We've been friends too long, and I'm going thoroughly bughouse on this goddamned cruise of yours, thank you very much, and I'm just going to give it to you straight, like it or not. When this affair is behind us, I will, if you insist, write up an overall, formal report that you can share with your superiors. Something clean and tidy and polite.*

*Which is more than can be said for the first night on your goddamned cruise.*

*I blame myself, to a degree. I wasn't watching Jonesy, I was watching your precious Lady Hannah and her lousy goddamned "Caribbean*

Blues," and that's exactly what I have right now. But I figured Jonesy could take care of himself, and why shouldn't I? I've known — make that I had known — the tough little bastard since our days together on the pickpocket detail of the Chicago P.D. Sure, he took a bribe now and then. But then I'm repeating myself, aren't I? I already said he was a Chicago cop.

Anyway, after the ship's doctor and some stewards gurneyed out what used to be Jonesy, the captain ordered that fancy chrome-and-leather nightclub cleared of all passengers. This was against my advice, as I thought every man jack of 'em (and every woman jack, too, for that matter) ought to be held and questioned. They were witnesses to a probable murder, after all. But grilling the guests, as opposed to the guests' filet mignons, would be a bad show, don't you know. Bloody British.

I asked the various detectives I'd invited aboard for the Private Eye Convention (as the ship's daily programme referred to us) to hang around the club.

It was time to give them the lowdown.

I stood on the shiny dance floor, like an entertainer, and made my speech, while the half dozen in my audience lounged at tables and in booths nearby.

"Maybe you were wondering why a bunch of down-at-the-heels private dicks got a free ride on a boat like this," I said with what I hoped was a tone of wry but good humor.

"That's 'ship,' Heller," Miles said, screwing

up his bulldog's puss. *Everything I said, the ex-pug took wrong. All I had to do was say hello and he got that sniffing-the-base-of-a-tree expression going.*

"Is it a coincidence that a killing took place with us on board?" Baltimore asked, his bearded mug a mask of ingenuousness. "Or am I crazy?"

"Does one necessarily rule out the other?" Trace asked from his booth, one hand wrapped around a drink, the other draped over the bare shoulder of *the beautiful Oriental dame that I took for his secretary.*

"That ship's officer that was killed," *I told them,* "was no ship's officer. He was one of us."

"What do you mean, one of 'us'?" Miles demanded, balling his fists, *which is one of the better things to do with a fist.*

*I sighed.* "He's an operative, too," *I said.* "Or he was. He was working with me. We were partners in the A-1." *They exchanged glances that were at once surprised and annoyed — but there was a general tightening around the eyes, too, including the haunting ones of that Oriental dish.*

*One of our own was down.*

"I got all of us free passage on this 'pleasure cruise,' " *I told them,* "by agreeing to do a little work on the side. It was nothing Jones and me couldn't handle on our own — that's what I thought, anyway."

"How shrewd," *noted Leslie Dither. Dither was the British representative of our little group. Bloody British.*

"*It wasn't supposed to involve any of you,*" I went on lamely. "*A jewel thief's been hitting the Cunard Countess — the last three cruises. It's an embarrassment to the line — they can't do an aboveboard investigation of a thing like that without putting all of their passengers under suspicion. You saw tonight how unwilling they were to do that in a murder case, let alone a theft. So, anyway, I swung this deal with an old friend of mine, name of Donahue, who used to work in Chicago for the transit system but landed a sweet job in New York with this steamship line. When this thief started working the Cunard Countess, George called me with the job. I happened to be working on putting this association of private investigators together, and, hell, it seemed like an ideal way to get us all under one roof, even if it was a floating one. So I worked a deal with George — kind of under the table, so not a word to anybody else, okay?*"

"*You did say George was from Chicago,*" said Dither, "*so under-the-counter activities are certainly in character. One might say your mentioning it is a bit redundant.*"

He left off the "*old chap.*" Thank God. Bloody British.

"*So I told George we'd catch his thief and in return he'd give our 'convention' a free ride.*"

"*Looks like your pal Jones did have to pay for his passage,*" Phlem pointed out acidly.

The British settled Boston, you know.

"*Jones was my partner,*" I said. "*He's not your responsibility — any of you. Finding his killer is up to me. If any of you want to give a hand, I wouldn't turn it down. But when the one who did it is brought to bay, I want him."*

"Revenge, Mr. Heller?" the pretty Oriental asked. What the hell kind of name was Chico for an Oriental, anyway? What the hell kind of name was it for any woman? On the other hand, if she had a sister named Harpo, I was interested.

"Let me put it this way," I said. "When a man's partner is killed, he's supposed to do something about it."

"Oh yeah?" Miles asked with his usual dull-edged sarcasm. "What if you hated his guts?"

"I didn't hate his guts," I said. "But it doesn't make any difference what I thought of him."

"He's your partner," Phlem said, nodding, "and you're supposed to do something about it."

"Then it happens we're in the detective business," Chico said.

"I thought you were a secretary," I said.

"She's my partner, okay?" Trace said testily.

"Are we letting women into the association?" Baltimore wondered aloud.

"I don't think that's the issue," I said. "Putting the bylaws of our association together goes way on the back burner. I've had somebody in my organization murdered, gentlemen . . . and lady."

And Chico said, "Well, when one of your organization gets killed, it's bad business to let the killer get away with it."

"*It does happen that we're in the detective business,*" Miles admitted grudgingly.

"*Letting the killer get away with it,*" I said, "*is bad all around. Bad for my organization, bad for every detective everywhere. . . .*"

"*And,*" Chico said, the smartest of us all, obviously, "*this association which we may or may not be organizing — which I may or may not be allowed the honor of joining — is going to be made to look like a prize boatload of saps should word about this get out.*"

"*Damn!*" Miles said. "*She's right! A private eye gets bumped off under the noses of a roomful of his fellow eyes. We are going to look stupid!*"

"*For some of us that comes easier than for others,*" Trace pointed out, and sipped his drink.

"*I got to agree,*" Baltimore said ambiguously. "*We have to pitch in on this thing. Heller, I'm willing to help you out — and I won't get in your way when the killer shows himself.*"

"*Or herself,*" Chico added.

"*Mr. Heller,*" Dither asked, "*did you and Mr. Jones know that Lady Hannah would be on board?*"

"*Yes,*" I said, "*we did. That's one of the reasons Jonesy and me thought this thing would fall in place so easy. With those rocks around her neck, Lady Hannah was the cheese, and all we had to do was hang around and wait for the rat to make his move.*"

"*Maybe the rat in question,*" *Phlem said,* "*is that eccentric reverend who made that scene earlier — if he is a reverend.*"

"*I'll have a go at the father, if you like,*" *said Dither.*

"*Thanks,*" *I said. God bless the British.*

"*Now you're trying to recruit us into this farce,*" *Trace said, standing, none too sturdily, but standing.* "*I want none of it. A man's gotta do what a man's gotta do, right? Well, you're the man, Heller . . . do what you gotta do. Me, I gotta find a men's room.*"

"*That's 'head' on a ship,*" *Phlem said.*

"*It's not for my head,*" *Trace said.*

*Chico reached out for his hand and said,* "*Trace, we really ought to give Heller a hand.*"

"*I couldn't agree more,*" *Trace said, and put down his drink and began to applaud.* "*Let's hear it for him! Nate Heller, the con man who got us all on board to do his security work for him.*"

"*That's not true, Detective,*" *I told them.* "*The security job was mine and Jonesy's. The investigators' association is something apart from all this. It's an idea we need to get back to, when I've put this mess behind me.*"

"*I agree with Heller,*" *Phlem said.* "*We need this association so we can link up with each other, and compete with the big boys. Here we all are, a sorry lot of one- and two-man operations, each in a different city — well, if we can refer clients to each other, call on each other for out-of-town stuff, then we have a network. We can give the likes of Pinkerton and Hargraves a run for their money.*"

"*That's what I have in mind,*" I said. "*It's just that I don't think we're going to get down to business until the guy who killed my partner is brought to justice . . . justice as I see it, anyway.*"

"*Where does our jewel thief fit into this?*" Baltimore asked.

"*He's the killer,*" I said flatly.

"*You think he was tipped to what you and Jones were up to?*" Miles asked.

"*I don't know,*" I admitted.

"*Even if he did,*" Trace said, reluctantly drawn into it, "*why murder? No, it has to be more than that.*"

"*I think it's in the best interests of all of us to help Heller out,*" Chico said.

"*No way in hell,*" Trace said. He turned to her, exasperated. "*Look, I let you talk me into taking this crummy cruise just because you say I never take you anywhere for fun. Well, fine, we're here, but I'm here for fun, not work. I got bigger things on my mind!*"

She smirked at him. "*Like what, for instance?*"

"*Well, this guy Hitler. I think he's a problem.*"

She rolled her lovely eyes, shook her head.

"*I don't need any help,*" I said. "*Let me do some sniffing around myself. . . . If I find there's more to this than just my jewel thief, I'll see if any of you still want to lend a hand.*"

"*Look,*" Chico said. She had great eyes, inci-

*dentally.* "*I'll talk to Lady Hannah tomorrow. . . .
The woman's touch might be helpful there.
This all started with her — with her jewels.*"

"*The Caribbean Blues,*" Phlem said, nodding, *as if the rest of us might have forgotten.*

"*Bloody curse,*" Dither said.

"*A curse didn't kill Jonesy,*" I said. "*A
murderer did.*" Then I smiled at Chico. "*I
would appreciate your help with Lady Hannah.*" Did I mention her eyes?

She smiled back at me. "*Glad to.*"

Trace rolled his eyes, which weren't lovely
unless bloodshot was one's idea of a good time.
"*I'm finding the john, or head, or whatever the
hell,*" he said, and shambled out.

"*Do talk to Lady Hannah first thing in the
morning,*" I said to Chico. "*I'm going to spend
the next few hours talking to the ship's crew,
the staff. . . some of whom were aware of Lady
Hannah, her ice, the jewel thief, all of it. It's a
place to start poking, anyway.*"

"*Good luck,*" Chico said.

They began to wander out of the showroom,
and one by one, each of them to a man (and
woman) — despite what they may have thought
about me or the circumstances under which I
had got them here — said a word about my
partner. Even Miles. And Trace, too — he stopped back in to say it was a damned shame.

And it was and is.

For the rest of this entry, George, I can say
only that the evening — what remained of it —
was spent by me grilling the various crew members, an effort that produced not a damned

*thing. Afterward, I drank some rum, which I'm putting on the expense account, and went to my cabin and went to bed, leaving this report till this morning. I dreamed about my dead partner, and then I dreamed about Trace's live one. Both of them made my heart ache.*

# CHAPTER 5

Chico woke up, as she did every morning since she'd made the colossal mistake of agreeing to sleep with Devlin Tracy, by propping her back against the wall, drawing her knees in close to her body, then slamming her legs out in front of her with sufficient force to roll Trace's dead weight onto his own side of the bed.

Trace responded with a snore, the decibel level of which set up a vibration in the brass fitting of the bed, creating a high-pitched, tinny hum. Only there was no empty bottle on the nightstand.

Something was very wrong.

She shook Trace awake. "Are you awake?" Chico asked.

"No."

"Are you sober?"

"Hell, no," Trace said. "Leave me alone."

"We're on a ship," Chico said with sudden clarity.

"Give the lady a see-gar."

"And there's been a murder."

Trace sat up, red-eyed and hulking. "There's

going to be another one if you don't stop piping. Pipe, pipe, pipe, in that little short person's
voice of yours. It drives me crazy."

"Trace, this is important. The ship's officer,
remember? The guy named Jones. He wasn't a
ship's officer at all. He was a private eye, like
us."

"Like me," Trace said. "You're a private pain
in the privates."

"I've got a license," Chico said sullenly.

"Gotten through deceit and cajolery. You
Orientals are masters of cajolery. You start cajoling and piping, and people end up giving you
whatever you want just to keep you quiet.
Pipe, pipe, pipe. Cajole, cajole, cajole."

"Dickhead, dickhead, dickhead," Chico said.

Trace wrapped his pillow around his face.
"Why do I put up with this?"

Chico kissed him. "Because you love me."

Trace grunted.

"And because I love you."

She kissed him again. Trace grunted again.

"And because no one else could stand to live
with either of us."

In the distance a church bell chimed eight
times, then pealed out "A Mighty Fortress Is
Our God."

"It's Sunday morning," Chico said, bounding down the length of the bed to look out the
porthole. "We're in Tortola. Come look."

"I can't. I'm using all my energy to keep
from throwing up while you do gymnastics on
my thighs. Look, why don't you go to the dining room and eat a few dozen breakfasts? I'm

sure you can cajole the chef into roasting a pig for you."

"Very funny. As a matter of fact, I am leaving. This cabin isn't big enough for me and your breath."

"Remind me to keep breathing."

"And I've got an investigation to conduct — although breakfast doesn't sound like a bad idea." She leaped, naked, out of bed and slipped into a white sundress.

Chico always wore dresses. She had been a dancer once, and was still vain about her legs. It was one of the things Trace liked about her, along with her waist-length black hair and the fact that it never took Chico more than four minutes to put herself together for any occasion.

What Chico liked about Trace was that he was tall and blond and, on the rare occasions when he wasn't plastered, sensible. Trace was the only sensible American man Chico had ever met. He didn't exercise, believing firmly that a man was born with an allotment of just so many heartbeats and exercise just squandered them. He didn't waste his money on expensive solitary hobbies like fancy cars or small planes, preferring the more sedate joys of speakeasies and gambling dens. And he didn't believe in women's rights, which made it possible for Chico always to get her own way. He was a sensible man, and Chico adored him.

"Tell you what," she said brightly. "I'll go chat up Lady Sadie from Haiti —"

"Lady Hannah from Havana," Trace corrected.

"Whatever. The one with the gorgeous sapphires." She stuck her thumbs into her belt. "Anyway, shweetheart, I'm going to crack this case and find out what's the poop on this Jones stiff, got it?"

"Pipe, pipe, pipe." Trace sighed. "Humphrey Bogart doesn't pipe. But listen, you go do it. Hannah's the killer."

"How do you know that?" Chico asked.

"I heard the dead guy say 'she.' Who else?"

"There are a lot of women on this ship," Chico said.

"All peasants," Trace said. "Trust me. Hannah's the killer. Go get her."

"Okay," she said. "And then I'll meet you in the dining room in one hour. One hour, got it? I'll give you the lowdown then." She swaggered out the door. Before she reached the end of the corridor, she could hear Trace's snoring and the high-pitched hum of the bed fittings. The man was a menace on the open seas.

The aroma from the dining room was almost enough to distract Chico. Food had that effect on her. Food and tall blond men, in that order. She wouldn't have minded three or four Danish pastries, some eggs and ham and sausage, and a few croissants to tide her over until midmorning brunch. A carafe of orange juice. Maybe some French toast. But she had an investigation to conduct.

Actually, it was Chico's first investigation.

She didn't like to admit it, but Trace had been right about cajoling her way into becoming a private detective. She had cajoled Trace into pulling enough strings to get her a license. He hadn't had to do it. He could easily have refused her, told her that detectives were well-trained professionals, that a background as a dancer at the Moulin Rouge in Paris and as a blackjack dealer in Monte Carlo were not exactly the proper credentials for an investigator in crime. He could simply have refused, and grown accustomed to the small discomforts that came from living with a dissatisfied woman, such as a bed covered with broken peanut shells or a liquor cabinet stocked exclusively with near beer.

But no. Trace was a good man. A sensible man. He had come to his senses after only three weeks of near beer and peanut shells. One week after Chico had taken to waking him at six A.M. with a bugle call. Three days after his ex-wife called him demanding more alimony, having received his unlisted phone number anonymously in the mail. Five minutes after Chico had refused to lend him two hundred dollars for a sure winner at Aqueduct.

What a guy.

She would have to do right by him now and show Trace that his unswerving faith in her detective abilities was not undeserved. Conducting her first investigation, then, was a top priority for Chico, even more important than food.

Prepared to face starvation in order that

justice be served, she snatched only one sticky bun from the buffet near the door of the dining room and ate half of it before she reached Lady Hannah's stateroom.

The other half flew out of her hand and rolled down the corridor when she heard the scream.

It was Susie Tong, Lady Hannah's maid, and she was standing in Hannah's open doorway, wailing like a banshee. Chico rushed over, licking caramel syrup off her fingers. "What's the matter?" she asked.

Susie pointed a trembling finger toward the floor. There, near the bed, lay the mysterious woman known as Lady Hannah from Havana. Quite dead.

"Cheez-o-man!" Chico said, taking in the scene. Lady Hannah was wearing the same red dress she had worn to the cocktail party the night before. Her hat lay beside her in a pool of blood.

Aside from the presence of the corpse, though, nothing in the room seemed to be out of kilter. There were no signs of a struggle. The room was immaculate and tidy, except for an envelope and a deck of cards on the bureau. The envelope bore a Boston postmark and was addressed to "Mrs. Hannah Finestra" in Havana.

There was one other thing. The sapphires Lady Hannah had been wearing were not around her neck.

She turned to Susie Tong, and the two pairs

of Asian eyes locked. "Where are her jewels?"
Chico asked.

Susie stopped shrieking in mid-wail and
gasped. "The Caribbean Blues!" she whispered. "The curse is true."

"What curse?" Chico asked.

Susie Tong screamed again. "There . . .
there!" she said, pointing at the deck of cards.

Chico examined them more closely. They
were not ordinary cards. It was a Tarot deck,
used to tell fortunes.

"The card on top . . . it is Death," Susie said.

The picture on the card showed a skeleton.
Another card, depicting a man and woman
holding hands, had been pulled forward from
the deck. "What's this one mean?" Chico asked.

"The Lovers," Susie Tong said, and began to
wail again.

Chico grabbed her by both shoulders and
shook her. "Get a grip on yourself, Susie," she
said. "How about a little Oriental passivity
here?"

The woman nodded, choking back her tears.

"Now, what was that about a curse?"

"It's the stones," Susie said quietly.
"Everyone who has ever owned them has died
violently. The last owner was a Cuban
millionaire. When his wife was beaten to death
on a street in Havana, he gave the jewels to the
government. In Cuba, of course, 'the government' means Fulgencio Batista."

"So?" Chico said. "Batista got hold of the

Caribbean Blues. How'd Lady Hannah end up with them?"

Susie's gaze lifted upward toward a picture on the nightstand beside the bed. Chico went over to examine it.

It was a photograph of Hannah, taken in some lush tropical nightclub. The well-dressed man beside her, his arm around her shoulders, was General Batista, already the most powerful force in the history of Cuba.

"Were they lovers?" Chico asked.

"I think that's enough," another woman said from the doorway. She was blond and attractive despite her prim mode of dress. Chico recognized her from the night before as part of Lady Hannah's entourage. "What's the matter with you, talking about those things with strange —"

She looked past Susie to see the body of her employer on the floor. "Oh, my God!" she whispered, and rushed forward to crouch over the body. "Well, don't just stand there!" she called to Susie. "Get a doctor."

"I think it's too late for that," Chico said as the maid retreated down the hallway.

"Who are you?" the woman asked acidly.

"I'm Michiko Mangini, one of the private detectives on board. Are you a relation of Lady Hannah's?"

"If you are referring to Mrs. Finestra," she corrected primly, "no, I am not a relative. I am — was — her personal secretary. My name is Willa Wright."

Chico took a notebook out of her pocketbook

and began to write. "You said Lady Hannah's last name was Finestra? Is her husband on board?"

Miss Wright sighed. "Mrs. Finestra has been a widow for nine years. Her husband was Demitrio Finestra, the Boston hotelier."

"Boston? I thought Lady Hannah was from Cuba."

"She was an American," Miss Wright said wearily, "of Cuban descent, like her husband. We — that is, Mrs. Finestra, Susie Tong, and myself — moved to Cuba after Mr. Finestra's death." She bent over the body. Chico could see the woman's shoulders heaving as she sobbed quietly.

"I'm sorry," Chico said, "but the sooner we get the facts, the more likely we'll be to pick up Lady Hannah's murderer."

"Oh, do stop calling her that," Miss Wright said viciously. " 'Lady' Hannah!" Her words tumbled from her in a seething rage. "Her title was as much an affectation as her outlandish hats. Lady Hannah, indeed. . . ."

Suddenly she looked up at Chico, as if seeing her for the first time. "Oh dear," she said, wiping her nose with a lace handkerchief, "I'm afraid I don't know what I'm saying anymore. It's the shock of it all, I'm sure."

"I'm sure," Chico said sympathetically. "How did Mr. Finestra die?"

Miss Wright stiffened. "He fell from his office window," Willa said finally.

"Fell?"

"The official report was that Mr. Finestra

was depressed about the stock market crash and committed suicide. That was what his partners said, at any rate.''

"Who were his partners?"

"Two of them are on this ship. Hy Court and Rich Ledger," Willa said. "The third, Ernest Friendly, died earlier this year. Heart attack.''

Chico scribbled furiously. "Didn't you believe them about Mr. Finestra's suicide?"

Miss Wright shrugged. "The insurance company did. The Finestra Hotel had gone bankrupt earlier that year. He was virtually penniless. They refused to pay a dime on his policy.'' She shook her head, remembering. "There were so many suicides of that type in 1929.''

Chico looked around the first-class cabin. "I had the impression Lady Hannah was rich," she said.

"Oh, she was, eventually. We made a go of things, despite everything.'' There was a gleam of pride in her eyes. "She owned The Perfumed Garden, you know.''

"You're kidding!" Chico exclaimed. "I've been there!''

"Oh?" Willa visibly warmed toward her.

"It's the best resort in Havana. Great casino, fabulous food, fantastic music. . . .''

"Yes, indeed," Willa said. "When were you a guest there?"

"Well, I wasn't a guest, exactly," Chico said. "I was a dancer in a cabaret revue once.''

Miss Wright's expression frosted over again. "Oh.''

There was a timid knock at the door. Susie Tong had returned. "I'm sorry to have taken so long, Miss Wright," she said diffidently. "I had to track down the doctor. He's on his way now."

"It's about time," Willa Wright said.

The doctor swept in a few moments later. While he was examining the body, Chico took Susie aside.

"I didn't kill her, really, I didn't," Susie wailed.

"Settle down," Chico said. "I just want to ask you if you and Miss Wright were the only people traveling with Lady . . . er . . . Mrs. Finestra."

The maid smiled with relief. "Oh, no. Lady Hannah always liked a lot of company. Madame Deja Bleu is with us. So is Scats Allegro, the bandleader from The Perfumed Garden."

"You called her Lady Hannah," Chico said. "Doesn't that name bother you?"

"Bother? Why should it? Everyone called her Lady Hannah." She looked over her shoulder at Willa Wright. "Except for that priss," she added in a whisper.

The doctor stood up. "Gunshot wound," he said disgustedly.

A murmur rose up from the corridor. By this time, a number of passengers had gathered around the doorway to gawk and speculate. "Coming through," came an authoritative voice. Two young men in ship's uniform made their way through the crowd. One of them went directly to Lady Hannah's body and began to tape its outline. The other spoke to the passengers, ordering them to disperse.

"You, too, miss," he said to Chico.

"Okay. Just one second. Doc?"

The doctor looked up in annoyance. "There's nothing to be said about this death at the moment," he said. "Go join the rest of the passengers."

"Not this death. The other one, the P.I. named Jones. What did he die of?"

The doctor scratched his head. "Well, I guess that's going to come out sooner or later, anyway. Mr. Jones died of poisoning."

"Poisoning? Like food poisoning?"

"There is absolutely no danger of food poisoning on board this ship," the young officer said. "Now, if you will be so kind as to join the others at breakfast. . . ."

"Not food poisoning," the doctor said. "Curare. It's a rare poison, very fast-acting. Curare showed up in his blood work."

"Curare," Chico mused. "That's a South American poison, isn't it?"

"That's enough, miss," the ship's officer said, taking her arm.

"One more question, Doc!" she shouted as the young man dragged her away. "Have you ever examined anyone who died from a curse?"

"A curse?" the doctor asked irritably. "What are you talking about? Nobody dies from curses."

But the last face Chico saw as the officer forcibly extricated her from the room was Susie Tong's, and in those Asian eyes there was no doubt.

# CHAPTER 6

*"Dominus vobiscum. Et cum spirituo tuo."*

The words were Latin, but the voice uttering them had a different accent, more guttural even than the old Church Latin.

He had heard the voice somewhere before, so Leslie Dither stopped in the passageway outside the ship's theater, which doubled as its chapel, and listened for a moment longer.

He recognized the voice when it spoke again. It was the Germanic voice of that Reverend Peter Blue who had accosted Lady Hannah the night before in some sort of silly brouhaha about the gems she was wearing.

Nasty turn of events, all that. First that private operative had gotten himself killed, and then Lady Hannah herself had been gifted with a new navel. Thirty-eight caliber. Not a cracking good start to what he had hoped would be a pleasure cruise, Dither thought.

And now all these American detectives were racing around, comparing notes and theories, and blustering about having to solve the crime to avenge their fallen compatriot. What perfect twiddle. If he knew Americans, they would just keep on about this until the entire cruise had been ruined. And at the end, they would have very little to show for it. Americans were just not so very efficient, after all.

Perhaps the only way he was going to get any peace at all would be to solve the two murders himself, so Leslie Dither, latest in the proud line of Dither family detectives who traced their history back to before Sherlock Holmes, walked into the chapel.

Father Peter Blue was standing at the portable altar, before the movie screen in the theater. A surprisingly large crowd of three dozen who had attended mass had risen to their feet and, having received the benediction, were on their way toward the doors and toward whatever waited for them out there. Dither walked to the front of the temporary chapel and waited there, soundlessly, until Father Blue looked up.

*"Guten tag,"* Dither said.

Dither was a small round man, but Father Blue was even shorter and rounder. He looked at Dither with a pleasant expression and responded, *"Sprecken sie Deutsch?"*

*"Ja,"* Dither said with a nod. Then he switched languages and added, "But my English is better."

"Good. Then we will speak in English." He pronounced his *w*'s as *v*'s, Dither noticed. "I need the practice," Blue said.

He said *"der* practice," and Dither thought how much his accent sounded like that of Jack

Miles, that pugilistic private detective from New York City. Miles also said "*da*" for "the." Dither pondered it for a split-second, just long enough for the thought to reinforce his long-held opinion that Americans did not speak English at all, but actually some kind of foreign, and therefore lesser, tongue.

"You are a detective?" Father Blue asked.

Dither nodded. "Have you heard this morning's news?" he asked.

Father Blue shook his head. "I have been here all day, at the prayers. Many come late, you know, and I would provide mass for all of them."

"Lady Hannah is dead," Dither said.

"*Ach. Gott in Himmel,*" Blue said. He crossed himself.

"English, remember. We are being civilized. You did not know until now?" Dither asked.

Blue shook his head. "I pray that God will forgive the poor woman," he said.

"Poor woman?" Dither repeated. "Seemed like a pretty rich woman to me . . . sporting all that jewelry."

"Not hers," Blue said vehemently. "Not hers at all. Maybe now it goes back to the rightful owner?"

"Somehow I doubt that," Dither said. "It's been stolen."

"Oh, my God." Father Blue sat down heavily in one of the front-row theater seats and stared glumly at the blank movie screen.

"Perhaps you would tell me why the jewels are so important to you?" Dither asked.

Blue hesitated a long time before answering. "Why do you think they are important to me?" he asked finally.

"For one thing, friend cleric, because you made a scene about them last night in the cocktail lounge. For another, because when I just told you they were stolen, you almost fainted."

"Ah, there is no fooling you. You are a detective."

"The only one on this ship, too," Dither said. "Now, why don't you tell me about it?"

"Am I . . . what do you English say, a suspect?"

"Not yet," Dither said, lying casually as generations of Dither detectives had done.

He sat down next to the corpulent priest. It occurred to him that anybody passing by and looking in at the two small round men might think they looked like Tweedledum and Tweedledee.

He waited and finally Father Blue released a long sigh. The story followed. It came with a rush, as if Father Blue had been waiting, wanting to tell it to someone.

When he was done, he sighed again and looked over at Dither. "So that is it," he said. "Am I now the prime suspect in these murders?"

Dither shook his head. "Not in my mind," he said.

"But in the eyes of your friends? To them I am maybe the killer?"

"They're not my friends," Dither said. "I'm an Englishman. And heaven only knows what they will think. But I promise that I will try to keep these American cowboys away from you."

"I would appreciate that very much," Blue said. He stood. "Now you will excuse me," he said. "I must say prayers for the dead."

"Even for Hannah?" Dither asked.

"Especially for Hannah," Blue said.

"Why 'especially'?"

"Because she needs them the most," Blue said as he walked heavily away.

The other detectives insisted upon knowing what Dither had learned from Father Blue, and even though the Briton was sure nothing he had learned would help this rabble solve any crime, and even though he was convinced that Father Blue had nothing to do with any murder, he found himself forced to give them a report on his earlier conversation with the priest.

He told the story quickly, paraphrasing, shortening it, as if trying to get rid of an unpleasant task as rapidly as possible.

Father Blue, he reported, was born fifty-two years ago in Siam, the only child of German missionaries who had been living in Siam for ten years before his birth. He was raised in Siam and grew to love the country as his own, and it was with great reluctance that he returned to Germany at age eighteen to study for the clergy.

"There," Dither reported with a straight face, "he fell in with bad company and became a Roman Catholic."

"Oh, the shame of it all," said the one known as Devlin Tracy, and Dither looked at him for a long second before deciding that the poor, misguided man must be a Catholic too. How odd that people would be Catholics when there were so many acceptable religions to belong to.

He shrugged off the thought and returned to his story. Father Blue, after being ordained to the priesthood, returned to Siam to assist his missionary parents in their work. They were not thrilled with his change of religion but swallowed their pride and worked with him, until they died soon after, Mrs. Blue of cholera, and her husband from having been trampled to death by a rogue elephant.

In 1926, everything changed for Blue. The unopened tomb of an ancient King of Siam, King Chauvalit Pardist, had been discovered by a team of archeologists led by adventurer Jules Finder.

There were reports of great treasures being found, and Father Blue went to the tomb to talk to Finder. He was allowed to enter the tomb and saw, etched in stone over the entrance, the words: "Death to All Who Violate This Resting Place."

In the tomb were the intricately carved statues of the three gods who were to convey the long-dead king into the afterlife, and in the center of the forehead of each statue, radiating a soft blue light, was a huge perfect sapphire.

Father Blue begged Finder to donate the treasures to Siam's national museum, but Finder laughed at him and said that his discovery must be shown to the world.

Jules Finder never left Siam alive. Three days after entering the tomb, he was dead.

"The cause of death," Dither said quickly, "was never determined. But foul play was not ruled out."

The sapphires, though, had gone. Finder had called them the Caribbean Blues because they so closely matched the color of the Caribbean Sea.

"According to Father Blue, they have had a most bloody history," Dither said.

"It looks like they still do," said the one called Andy Baltimore. God, Dither thought, but he hated Americans, and of all Americans, he hated Californians the most. Adventurers, the lot of them. And this Baltimore chap looked like a pervert to boot.

"Yes, yes," Dither said. "At any rate, Father Blue has been tracking down the gems for years after deciding that it was up to him to get them back. He followed them to London, where their most recent owner, Lady Harriet Cartwright, had just fallen off London Bridge while wearing the necklace made of the three gems. Then he heard that the stones had turned up in Amsterdam. He followed them there and everywhere, but was always a step behind, a minute too late."

"Colorfully put," Chico said. At least some-one in this group had some taste, Dither thought.

Dither reported that Blue had found out just a few months ago that the stones were in the possession of Lady Hannah Finestra in Cuba, but when he got there, he found she had left for San Juan to take the cruise aboard the Cunard *Countess*. He arrived in San Juan just in time to catch the ship.

"And there we are, chaps," Dither said. He nodded toward Chico. "And lady."

"That's it?" Heller asked.

Dither shrugged. "More or less," he said.

"Pretty much less," Heller said.

"I look forward to your enlightening me, Yank," Dither said sternly, trying to keep the hard edge out of his voice.

"First of all," Trace interrupted, "did Blue know any of these people traveling with Hannah?"

A lucky guess, Dither thought. "Well, actu-ally, yes. He had seen Sir I. B. Hunter, the ex-plorer. He was at the opening of the tomb when the jewels were found."

"And you didn't think that was important enough to tell us?" Trace asked.

"I didn't want to bog you down with details," Dither said.

Trace shook his head in a manner Dither thought most boorish.

"If the jewels were in statues of three pagan gods, why the hell did Father Blue care about the curse or getting them back or anything like that?" Jack Miles asked.

God, his pronunciation was atrocious, Dither thought. He said, "It's for his adopted country, Siam. Not because of the curse. He doesn't believe in such curses, he told me, although he did admit that this curse seems to have more teeth in it than most such curses do."

"It ought to put its teeth in your leg," Miles grumbled.

"Where, Mr. Dither, was Father Blue when Lady Hannah was murdered?" the young Oriental woman asked him softly.

"He had returned to the ballroom in time for the murder of Private Investigator Jones," Dither said. "Then he drank a little too much, and at midnight he seems to recall he was playing the slot machines up in the casino."

"Great," Trace said. "A whisky-swilling, casino-haunting priest. Nothing suspicious there. You don't think he had anything to do with either of the murders?"

"No. I'm sure of it," Dither said.

"Your being sure of it makes him number-one suspect in my mind," Phil Phlem said. Another savage, Dither thought.

Everybody else around the table nodded. Even the cheeky little Oriental woman.

Dither excused himself. To blazes with all of them. Father Blue had killed no one. Dither was sure of that. But how to tell them why he was sure . . . that he was certain of Father Blue's innocence because Father Blue was German and the Hun was notoriously neat, while both these murders were rather sloppy?

He would not tell them that. He would not tell them anything. Let them look anywhere they wanted. Dither could see he would just have to solve this murder on his own or else watch his free cruise be ruined.

Americans were savages.

When Dither left the small meeting room, the other private detectives remained. Heller said, "Well, at least we know one thing: The jewel thief that Jones and I were looking for is on the ship."

"Maybe," Miles said. "And maybe not. The one you're looking for never killed anybody before, so maybe this is somebody else."

"This is too complicated," Trace said. "I'm going to bed."

"You just got up," Chico said.

"That's right. And all of you have already made me nuts enough for one day. I'm leaving."

He did. Chico stayed.

DATE: Sunday, May 17, 1938
TIME OF DEPARTURE: 9:30 P.M.
DESTINATION: St. Maarten
TIME OF ARRIVAL: 8:30 A.M.
DISTANCE: 94 nautical miles
WEATHER CONDITIONS: Rain, lightning,
    and thunder.

# CHAPTER 7

Andy Baltimore was not a particularly happy person at the moment. He wasn't happy about the way the ship was lurching through the sea like a Peugeot hitting potholes on La Cienega, he wasn't happy about the nasty little turn this supposed vacation was taking, and he was especially unhappy about this big, ruddy-faced Irishman who had the bad taste to purloin his partner's name. This bonehead spelled it wrong, though.

"No, you can't wait until we get back to San Juan," Devlin Tracy was bellowing, waving his arms. "Do it now. You've got to do it now."

*Who died and made you Aimee McPherson?* Andy wondered irritably. *Do it now, do it now.* He sounded like a Melrose housewife on her fourth day with the milkman.

This was just not Andy's cup of yogurt. What did he know about stolen jewelry and murder? He was a missing-persons expert — co-director of the nation's (make that the world's) best (make that the only) twenty-four-hour rescue service. Abduction Anonymous —

more officially known as Lost and Found Incor-
porated (L.A.F.). That was, Andy and his partner worked *only* in the first twenty-four hours
before the police were able to enter a missing-
persons case. Because they knew that if something . . . untoward . . . was going to happen to a
kidnapped individual, it would happen in the
first twenty-four hours.

Andy longed to see his partner right then
and there. Tracey Tailer had a way of knowing
when to make an entrance. And how! She was,
after all, slightly psychic.

"Oh, yeah, Miss Deus Ex Machina of 1938,"
Devlin had said. The first of many such endear-
ing occurrences between the obsessive victim-
hunter from Los Angeles and the overbearing
mick from New York.

"I know what's going to happen," Devlin
was continuing. "We'll get back to the States;
then you'll all get sidetracked with your real
work and this'll never get done."

Yeah, right. This Tracy knew *himself* real
well. But as the little yellow bird with the big
feet said, "He don't know *me* very well, do he?"

"Just be glad I don't give you that weird
reverend, Baltimore," Devlin ranted on in that
ingratiating way of his. "No, I'm a nice guy.
Out of the kindness of my heart, and at great
personal expense, I let you pump Lady Hannah's good-looking blond secretary. Ho, ho,
ho."

Pump. Andy bet he thought that was clever.
What Andy thought was that the only reason
he was going to interrogate Willa Wright was

that if Devlin's companion, Chico, found the Irishman within a parsec of the platinum looker, Trace would be chum for the cuttlefish.

"Ah," said Andy. *"Mangez la porte."* It was French for "eat the door." Andy knew how to say "eat the door" in seven languages. Even when the persons he was talking to knew the language, it always took them a second to realize he was speaking nonsense. Devlin Tracy did not know the language.

"You're welcome," Trace said with a big, satisfied smile.

Baltimore wandered the ship in search of Lady Hannah's personal secretary. That he could do. Andy was real good at finding missing women. What he was not good at was finding bodies. In fact, he was fairly staggered by how the rest of his unfraternal companions dealt with the corpse as if it was "just another" dead body. They seemed to look upon it like a chef looked upon a filet mignon. What was this case going to be: rare or well done? That sort of thing chilled Andy to the bone. He was used to warm, misplaced, breathing bodies and sad, mad perverts. To tell the truth, the idea of a person who calmly and deliberately poisoned one person and shot another in the chest, *just* for personal gain, scared him excrementally.

No, it was safe to say this trip was not going well. His partner, Tracey, the real brains of the L.A.F. outfit (at least that was one thing Andy had in common with Devlin), insisted he R.S.V.P. the invite after a solid fortnight of tracking down a half dozen missing prostitutes

who were the intended victims of some nut case
with a hacksaw. That, of course, meant that
Andy had gone two weeks with almost no sleep
and was ready to ceremoniously disembowel
anybody who even told a dirty joke.

"G'wan," his staggeringly attractive half-
Irish, half-Spanish partner had said. "Take the
cruise. It'll be fun."

Some fun. Complete strangers were being
dropped dead, and the cruise had become a
cross between church camp and prison. If only
Tracey were here, he moaned to himself for the
sixteenth time that day. She could tell him how
to proceed and he could concentrate on his
specialty — how to best launch the alleged per-
petrator's nose into his brain.

Andy climbed stairs. The ocean liner was
knotting into the wind, through unusually
adverse weather for this time of year. He passed
old people feeding their faces in the football-
field-sized dining room, he passed middle-aged
people feeding quarters into equally ancient
slot machines, and he passed young people
feeding nickels in the penny arcade.

It wasn't until he got to the seventh level of
the ship that he saw a feast for the eyes.
Various firm members of the staff were leading
various flaccid members of the passengers in
morning exercises on the deck.

These female crew members, mostly English
girls, had none of the steak-and-kidney-pudding
look their countrywomen were famous for. As
Andy watched the hard bodies bouncing rhyth-
mically up and down in their skimpy outfits,

his mind effortlessly glided into overdrive. It would be easy to silently ambush these sweet, fresh-faced, peach-skinned girls one night and secret them in one of the lifeboats or in the ship's bowels until they could be carried ashore inside duffel bags or laundry hampers and prepared for sale in the Caribbean white-slavery market, where the price for Occidentals was still at a premium. . . .

Andy smacked himself on the side of the head. He had been a ransom-buster too long. All work and no play made Jack a perverse boy. He had saved so many people from fates worse than death that he saw kidnapping conspiracies everywhere. Maybe a little lesson in interrogation skills would do him some good, after all. So where was Willa Wright?

He found her in the steam room. His heart sank when he looked into the foggy window of the booth that was stuck down next to the whirlpool baths (which were, in turn, next to the puddle-sized, five-foot-deep swimming pool on the upper deck). She sat there, luxuriating, legs out, head back, with only a small bone-colored towel covering her torso, from her upper thighs to her chest.

Andy knew the routine. Ceremaic skin the color of alabaster (and, no doubt, the feel of butter). A shape that went to the center of the male hormonal system. A face that made one feel paternal and passionate at the same time — big blue eyes that had that "golly-gee-who-me?" intensity, a nose so perfect that a caricature artist wouldn't even bother drawing

it, and naturally rosy lips that got a man thinking about serious, repeated contact. And the
hair: naturally blond hair on the head, over the
eyes, on the arms, and God knew where else.
She was the kind of girl one would snake-walk
through ground glass to see straighten a hem.

So much for new experiences. Andy Baltimore was back in his element. Without even
considering taking off his L.A.F. jacket (the
one with the company's motto, "Saving a
Reluctant World," stitched over the front
pocket), he pushed open the door and stepped
inside.

Bingo. Her eyes moved to his without surprise, shock, or even irritation at the intrusion.
She had been expecting someone, and just
waiting to see which someone. Andy swallowed
a smile. Suddenly he was eager to see how well
she lied . . . to him and/or herself.

"Pardon me," he said. "I'm Andy Baltimore,
one of the detectives on board. Do you want me
to come back after you're dressed?"

"No," she replied. "That's all right. I mean,
it's a public steam room, right? I mean, I knew
one of you would probably like to talk to me,
and . . . well, uh . . ." She swallowed quickly and
smiled, her features relaxing. "Well, I was hoping it would be you," she finished warmly.

Andy was gripped by the sudden desire to
break into the first few bars of "Dancing Cheek
to Cheek," complete with soft shoe. "Heaven,
I'm in heaven. And my heart beats so that I
can hardly speak . . ." Yeah, right. She was
Carole Lombard and he was Clark Gable. She

was Jean Harlow and he was James Cagney. More like she was Ginger Rogers (what a dancer!) and he was Peter Lorre.

"Well, isn't that nice," he gushed, coming forward and leaning on the slick tile wall opposite her. He nearly slid down to the floor, but his sneakers gripped at the last minute. She didn't even have the sense to titter sweetly behind an upraised hand. She was too busy playing the earnest witness who had fallen in like at first sight. "What was it?" he wondered aloud. "My thick, round glasses? My mottled salt-and-pepper hair? My big, round head? The little tiny hairs on my nose?"

She stared at him in stunned silence for a second, the wheels of her brain breaking down her mind's viscosity, until she decided he was hitting on her funny bone. She giggled. "I knew you were different from the others," she said with pseudo relief. "I knew you would understand."

She was making this easy. "Understand what?" he asked vacantly.

"Why, the stress and pressure I've been under," she replied. "This has been a terrible ordeal for all of us. And as much as I hate to admit it, your friends running around acting as if this is some kind of surprise party designed just for them hasn't helped."

Andy pictured the others in his mind. "They're not my friends," he said, "although I kind of like the ex-boxer. He's so transparent. Anyway, I can't tell you how sorry I am. I really can't understand why anyone would purposely

kill anyone for any reason . . . outside of self-
defense. I mean, what could be so important?"
It was true. Andy knew only of death by
perverted passion. Cold, premeditated murder
most foul was an aberration of nature.

Willa Wright was momentarily taken aback
by his earnestness. This guy was not pulling
her leg. For a moment, her carefully thought-
out presentation was disrupted. "It was
revenge," she blurted out.

"Revenge?" Andy echoed. "For what?"

Willa was immediately circumspect. She
leaned back, clutching the towel to her as if she
had suddenly realized she was sans sartorial
splendor. "I'm . . . I'm sorry," she stuttered. "I
shouldn't have said that. I shouldn't say anything."

"What do you mean?" Andy retorted, leaning intensely. "What are you talking about?
What revenge?"

Willa looked as if she was trying to lean
through the wall. "Please, Mr. Baltimore," she
pleaded. "Mrs. — I mean . . . Lady Hannah . . .
trusted me."

"Lady Hannah is dead!" Baltimore shot
back, outraged. "You tell me what revenge,
or . . ." — Andy's eyes became unfocused as his
mind whirled — ". . . or I'll pull your heart out
through your mouth."

The woman suddenly realized that he was
not in there alone with her, but she was in there
alone with *him*. Baltimore was not a shy push-
over. He was a repressed actor auditioning for
psychosis.

"Please, Mr. Baltimore . . . Andy . . . calm

down," Willa begged. "I'll tell you the truth."

"I'd appreciate that," he said as if he didn't think she'd actually announce when she was lying. The sweat that was pouring down all over only added to his ambience.

"I became Hannah Finestra's personal secretary nine years ago, after her husband died," she revealed.

"Who was her husband?"

"Demitrio Finestra."

"Who was he?"

"You don't know?"

"Was he a known sex offender?"

"No!"

Andy shrugged. "Then I don't know."

"He was the owner of the famous Finestra Hotel in Boston," she sniffed proudly.

"Boston, huh?"

"You know it now?"

"No. We were called in on a copycat Jack the Ripper case on Beacon Hill."

Willa recoiled even farther from her interviewer, edging on the slatted wood seat. Her entire right leg appeared from under the towel, dappled in golden beads of perspiration, like gems set in every ivory pore. Andy was beginning to enjoy himself — it was fun to enhance his reputation as an extremely dangerous sort. It often prevented him from actually having to do anything.

The woman hurried on, smitten with an overwhelming desire for the sea air. "Mrs. Finestra and I moved to Cuba, where we opened a hotel called The Perfumed Garden."

"*We?*" Andy interrupted.

"I beg your pardon?"

"You said 'we.' Not her, not she, but *we*."

"Uh . . . yes. Mrs. Finestra was virtually penniless, so she borrowed a few thousand from me. I got a percentage of the resort. Ten percent. I quickly made back my investment. The club at The Perfumed Garden was one of the most exclusive Havana night spots."

"I'm sure," Andy said dryly. "Gambling, right?"

Willa's demeanor became equally chilly in this oven. "Mrs. Finestra catered to the needs of her influential clientele."

Andy's face was a sour mask, his glasses completely fogged, his close-cropped beard raining. "Terrific. Go on."

"Mrs. Finestra became friends with people from all over the world. Among them was Irving Baxter Hunter, the famous African explorer."

"Ah, yes," Andy said. "The *schnorer*."

"Excuse me?"

"Hurray for Captain Spaulding, the African explorer," he suggested quickly.

She stared at him as if he were a water bug. "Ah. Yes. Amusing." It was obvious she had never heard the Marx Brothers song.

"You don't get out much, do you?"

"I'm *very* busy." The atmosphere in the sweltering box had changed. She had wrested back control of the conversation. Andy had all but handed it to her. "At any rate, that was Mrs. Finestra's first serious relationship since the death of her husband."

"Is he the guy who was getting revenge?"

"I'm sure I don't know," Willa said coyly. "All I know is that Mrs. Finestra spurned him."

Andy just stood there, dripping. "Let me get this straight. This guy waits a couple of years, then comes on this cruise, poisons a Chicago private eye who happens to be around, then blows her heart out?"

Willa's attitude had sunk from cold to dry ice. "I don't know what you're talking about."

"You ever been shot?" He didn't wait for a reply. "It's a hunk of lead traveling faster than sound that tears through your skin and rips through your body. Can you imagine what that feels like? Can you imagine your heart, your own heart, being torn apart? Like two hands grabbing your heart, and tearing it in half?" He grabbed an imaginary organ in front of him and rent it, sweat splashing off his hair as if ejected from a shower head.

Willa choked.

Baltimore's glasses slipped off his face and fell to the hard tile with a clatter.

He just stood motionless, his small, haunted brown eyes appearing in and out of the mist. He couldn't see her face. It was just a soft, ethereal blur. But he could imagine her expression. He wasn't far wrong.

"You didn't like Hunter, did you?" he asked. It was an easy question. What was there to like?

"I didn't like or dislike him." Her tone was hard and flat.

"Your trusted employer is dead," Andy

seethed. "Eternity in the darkness. Forever. Nothing. Her body is decomposing —"

"Stop it!"

"You talk to me!" he yelled.

"No! I didn't like him! He was an effete snob. He didn't even treat me like a human being."

"Why don't you try acting like one?" Andy snapped. Then he continued immediately: "Cheap shot, cheap shot, I know. I'm sorry."

He leaned down and retrieved his glasses. When he put them back on, he saw that she was crying, her beautiful body shaking beneath the towel. "I don't care what the others are doing," he told her. "I'm not doing this for fun. I didn't know these people . . . and now I never will. And I'll never know whether I would have liked them."

"My God!" Willa sobbed, trying to stop crying. "You care, don't you? You actually care."

Andy couldn't understand what she was asking. How could a human being not care? What if it was she the murderer had wanted? What if it had been him? How could others *not* care?

Willa took a few deep breaths, providing Andy with an entertaining balcony scene. She regathered her defenses and prepared to survive the next onslaught. "Mrs. Finestra started an affair with General Batista of Cuba. Hunter couldn't compete. He went back to Africa."

"Okay," Andy said reasonably. "So?"

Willa looked trapped and helpless, an expression with which Andy was all too familiar. "Jeez, I don't know," she almost whined, squirming. "These were just two of the affairs I knew about. How many other men did Miss Hannah spurn? Maybe the private eye who was murdered was watching her. Or maybe he was hired to protect her. Or someone who wanted to steal the Caribbean Blues had to kill both of them to get them. Do I have to do all your work?"

He looked down at her, smiling, although his eyes were dead. "Am I going to have to tell you what happens to your guts when you're poisoned?" he said pleasantly.

"What do you want from me?" she cried.

Andy's gaze took on pity. "How was Demitrio Finestra killed?" he asked quietly.

She gasped. "How did you know he was killed? How did you know he didn't just die?"

"I won't be coy," Andy promised, "unlike somebody I could name." His explanation was tinged with bitterness. "Finestra was in business. Businesses are insured. If there wasn't something screwy with his death, Lady Hannah wouldn't have needed your lousy few thousand. Now tell me what the heck is going on, or I'll tell you what the bladder does just before death."

"Please," Willa replied, holding up her lily-white hand in acknowledged defeat. "Demitrio Finestra died in a fall from his office window."

"Jumped or pushed?"

"I don't really know," Willa said wearily.

"What happened to his hotel?"

"Bankruptcy. So, you see, she needed my 'lousy few thousand.' "

Andy opened his mouth to say something more, but then his teeth snapped together with an audible click. When he spoke again, his tone was the original, solicitous one with which he had entered the steam room. "There. All finished. Now, that wasn't so bad, was it?"

"Do I get a lollipop?" Willa answered with a tired smile.

"Bad for your teeth," Andy said, smiling back. "Sugar clouds your mind. And I want you to think about something. If you haven't been completely 'up front' with me, or won't keep me 'abreast' of things, I may have to come back and get a few things off your chest."

Andy was richly rewarded for his crudity. Her expression mingled fear, defiance, and a certain competitiveness. She sat up, letting the towel drop to her stomach.

When she spoke, her voice was husky, her eyes smoky.

"I've got nothing to hide," she said.

Andy Baltimore looked at the sad little girl ... who was both literally and figuratively at sea. Vamping him was like trying to sell binoculars to a blind man. He walked to the door. But, at the last moment, he stopped, turned, and stared purposefully at her undeniably beautiful breasts.

"Thanks, four eyes," he told her. "My mom had two of those."

When Heller first saw the little man by the rail, he thought he was going to jump. Then the Chicago P.I. realized that Andy Baltimore was simply stiff with tension. The lost finder was scanning the rippling sea as if communing with Neptune.

Initially Heller was going to ignore the strange guy. He couldn't shake a slightly distasteful feeling every time he saw him. Baltimore was the kind of man who not only wore his heart on his sleeve, but his liver, spleen, and intestines as well. Heller had the unmistakable sensation that someday, someone would have to put Baltimore down like a mad dog. He was simply too similar to the people he chased.

"You're wasting your time," he growled, coming up alongside Andy. "You won't find any answers there."

Andy's voice was distant. "I talked to Willa Wright."

"What did she tell you?"

"It's what she didn't tell me. It's what she worked very hard not to say that worries me." He turned to look directly at Heller. "She flashed me."

"Lucky you," Heller said, scowling.

"No. Unlucky me. I look in the mirror, Heller. Nobody sticks their chest out for me. Not unless they're trying to distract me." He told the detective what he had found out.

"Sounds like a lot of air," Heller decided sourly.

"Yeah," Andy agreed. "She chose her words very carefully. She didn't say whether she knew Finestra was murdered or committed suicide. She said she didn't 'really' know."

Heller was incredulous. Baltimore was getting worked up over one word? But before he could walk away from Andy in disgust, the angst-oozing little man continued, staring out to sea.

" 'Bankruptcy.' One second her back was so straight about that luxury Boston hotel you could iron shirts on it. Then, just like that, it's bankrupt."

"What are you getting at?" Heller asked him pointedly, exasperated.

Baltimore looked at the avenging investigator, his expression empty.

"Damned if I know," he said. "Yet."

# CHAPTER 8

"Pull!"

Bang-bang.

Phlem watched the leathery-faced, paunchy man in the safari jacket and bush hat on the fantail of the Cunard *Countess* reload both barrels of the shotgun before the crockery he had shattered mid-sky hit the water.

"Pull!"

Two more of what Phlem understood to be skeets soared above the horizon aft of the ship.

Bang-bang.

Before they had a chance to enjoy freedom so sweetly tasted, both saucers were blown to shards.

"Pull!"

Philip d'Artagnan Phlem (for such was the spelling of his name his mother had given him; which spelling he had accepted utterly until the age of eighteen, when, about to be sent overseas, he received a note from his mother, the first he'd ever had, which read: "Phil, dear, When you are in Phlanders Phield, please do me the phavor of phinding some nice phlowers

for the grave of your phather's new phloosie";
since then he had been less certain) had left
school in the fourth grade for a package of
cigarettes and had never returned, as he was
caught smoking them while driving a Ford he
had stolen.

Phlem felt akin to shards. He knew how it
was to have that initial feeling of soaring
toward freedom, shucking the gravity of
school, looking down at the horizon for a short
moment only to be shot down, shattered, forced
to fall back into the sea of humanity.

Drafted out of the reformatory, Phlem served
a hard two years in the infantry in France
before being dishonorably discharged for per-
mitting a gun caisson to roll over the shiny new
boot containing the never-before-broken foot of
a shiny new second lieutenant.

Ph. d. Phlem (as he preferred to sign his
name on those infrequent occasions when he
had any reason to do so; he hoped doing so
would indicate, implicitly, of course, an education beyond his own degree), in shards at twenty, decided to enter the profession of private
detective.

Good thing his motive was not money. He
made little.

Good, too, he felt little urge to serve Justice.
If that had been his intention, Justice was as
unserved as Oliver Twist asking for seconds.

Philip d'Artagnan Phlem's sole purpose in
becoming a private detective at age twenty
was to detect and reveal unto the world nasties

and naughties about all the people in the world
who stood straighter than he, walked with a
brisker step, spoke more clearly, were cleaner
in limb and dress, more clever of mind, noble of
ambition — and that *was* all the people in the
world.

Despite poverty, hard work, long hours, the
loneliness of an irregular, bachelor's life, Philip
d'Artagnan Phlem had had for twenty-two
years what he considered a satisfactory career.

He had caused the ruination of a good many
nice folks.

"Pull!"

Bang-bang.

Now Sir I. B. Hunter (for such was he
smashing crockery off the fantail with a
double-barreled shotgun), to Phlem, clearly fit
into the category of acceptable nice folks. So
nice, in fact, Phlem had heard His Majesty, the
King of England (Phlem's education having
gone up in smoke in the fourth grade caused
him to think George III was always and
therefore still King of England), had invited
Hunter to his digs for a boilermaker and bop-
ped him on the shoulders with a sword and
declared that henceforth everyone was to call
him "Sir," whether one felt like it or not.

Indeed, to Phlem, Hunter was a piece of
crockery soaring high above the horizon.
Hunter looked decent enough to ruin.

By Phlem's count, Hunter's score was ten
shots, ten skeets, which bested Phlem's own
professional tally of twenty-seven shots, one

burglar, sixteen taxis, five pedestrians, one department-store-window mannequin, one traffic policeman, and three unknowns.

"Sir I. B.? Sir Hunter? Sir?"

Hunter's bloodshot eyes noted Phlem as might a lion noting a dik-dik when his lioness has been rather slow about returning with a gazelle.

"Pull!"

Bang-bang.

Broken crockery hit the water in so tight a pattern Neptune could dine off it without reaching for the glue.

"One of the snoops, are you?" Hunter asked. "Thought one of you convening dicks might crawl along choked up with suspicion. Hardly expected to see you in daylight, though. Don't you chaps generally take to the dark corners?"

"You like to shoot things," Phlem asserted while watching Hunter reload.

"Rather good at it," Hunter said. "Might say I shot my way off the family farm in Scotland and out of Edinburgh University. Found the pursuit of sheep and their skins rather tame sport. Much jollier traipsing about in the bush giving the gift of death to more admirable beasts: the lion, the elephant. Well, one must use what talents one has."

"You like to kill things."

"Only some things, old boy. Some things look better dead than alive." Again, Hunter surveyed Phlem. "Others are beneath concern. Pull!"

Bang-bang.

Hunter said, "No good questioning me, old

sod. Couldn't possibly be the sack you're after. I'm as innocent as the desert's dry."

"I've never seen a desert."

"Not given to introspection, eh?"

"Listen, Sir I. B. —"

"If you don't know how to use a title, old chap, then don't address the card. In fact, you'd save us both a lot of trouble if you'd wait to be properly introduced."

"Someone said you're a big hunter —"

"Wrote the book on it, I did: *Hunter on Hunting*. Knighted for it. For that, plus certain jobs I did for zoological groups hither and yon. You'd think such a book would bring me a decent pension, wouldn't you? Gambling palaces have such a nice ambience. They make you feel so rich, until you get outside and check your pockets. Sometimes there's hardly enough left over for the full case of gin."

"You're not rich?"

"Good Lord, man. Knighthoods don't carry stipends. If anything, they raise the tailor's bill. If ever offered a knighthood, I wouldn't accept, if I were you. The raise in your tailoring bill would be astronomical."

"Are you broke?"

"As light in the pocket as the day I was born. Lighter, in fact. Sold off the paternal seat in Scotland last year. The Prince of Monaco had put a black check next to my name till I rectified a run of bad luck at the casino that pays him rent. Some chaps in Cuba were prowling rather glinty-eyed, too. No way you could lend me a tenner, I suppose?"

"Me? Lend you money? Ha!"

" 'Ha,' is it? Never mistake you for a gentleman, I wouldn't. Rather put you down for a
doormat."

"Hunter —"

"That's my name; that's my game."

"Where were you Saturday night when Jones
earned his wings?"

"Standing right next to him, old chap.
Thought he'd gone down to do my boots."

"You were?"

"I was. They could have done with a bit of a
brush-up."

"You know who he was?"

"Figured it out. I had just greeted Lady
Hannah. Hadn't seen the old thing in years.
Arranged to meet later, in quieter circumstances. Noticed she was wearing the blue sapphires. The Caribbean Blues. Sounds like a
dance tune, don't it? A slow two-step, I should
say. Recognized those stones immediately, of
course. Then that Johnny Collar came up to her
and began reading her out —"

"What's a Johnny Collar?"

"The cleric chap. The missionary, vicar —
whatever he is. The one who looks like
unkneaded bread in a black wrapper."

"The priest. Father Peter Blue."

"Um. Blue in black. He recited the litany of
the grief the Blues had brought everybody over
the years. Don't doubt what he said. Cursed
things."

"How did you know what the gems were?"

"In on their discovery, old boy — 1926, it

was. Twelve years ago. This wallah, Jules Finder, came along to me at the Explorers' Club in London. Wanted me to lead an archeological expedition to Siam. Hot to discover the tomb of Chauvalit Pardist, he was. Taboos against disturbing tombs, of course. Never believe in going against local taboos, I don't. I've never drunk gin on the south side of Mount Kenya. At the time, the West End bookie school was after me for giving them false information on which horses would win which races before the fact. . . ."

"You needed the money."

"I didn't, old chap. But the bookies said they did, you see. All insisted they had wives and children to support. That's their bad luck."

"You ran out on your debts."

"You are a nasty piece of package, aren't you? Always keen to think the worst of one. Doubt you've ever seen a gentleman before. You give no sign of it. I needed to assure the bookies I had gainful employment and they could afford to feed their anticipation."

"To get the sharks off your back you took a job doin' something you didn't believe was right."

"Accusatory little toad, aren't you?"

"Your being a fancy knight, big famous hunter, cuts no mustard with me, mister."

"I rather feel I've just cut the razor. You know what that means, old chap?"

"You going to tell me?"

"As if I've just stepped in spoor."

"What's spoor?"

"I am, alas — 's poor me. Pull!"

Bang-bang.

"Anyway, this Finder wallah turned up the tomb, 1926 — that was, broke into it, despite the motto over the entrance: 'Death to All Who Violate This Resting Place.' Rather a chilly welcoming mat, wouldn't you say? I mean, hardly a hello, won't you come in and wet your whistle, is it? Finder proceeded to plunder away like a Zulu in a Masai's shamba."

"Were you with this Finder guy in the tomb when he found the jewels?"

"No, no. Would have put my foot down at the plundering, old chap. Great believer in leaving the natural habitat pretty much as I find it. Douse the campfire, feed the cigar butts to the hyenas — all that. Not one to contract a nasty curse, if I can help it. When the Siamese people discovered what was going on, of course, they were fit to be Thai'd. I understand that Father Blue happened on the scene about then."

"So when did you first see the sapphires?"

"Finder brought them back to the hotel bar to me, old chap, where I had just gone to sample the local. Had them in his hand. Showing them off like the schoolboy who had just won all the aggies. Three sapphires. Each had been in the forehead of carved statues of three gods assigned to escort old King Chauvalit Pardist to his final campground. Shocked, I was. Made me switch to doubles. I left the area next day. I had been having poor luck predicting the outcome of the local snake races, anyway."

"And what happened to this Finder guy?"

"Never laid eyes on him again. Believe he never made it out of the country. Heard something about his skin being slipped off while he still breathed and set to crisp. Too bad, too. Treated right, his skin would have made a half-decent pair of boots, size thirteen wide, I should say. Never heard what happened to the rest of him. Pull!"

Bang-bang.

"And you never saw the sapphires again, until Saturday night?"

"Right you are. Think of that. There's me old pal wearing the baubles I'd helped discover twelve years ago in Siam."

"Where did she get them?"

"Around her neck, old boy."

"I mean, where did she have them from?"

"Don't know. Running with a Cuban politician in recent years, lizard named Batista, and you know those politician types have sticky fingers. They're apt to pull anything out of their knickers. Threw me over for him, in fact. Had to have something in his knickers besides his manly parts."

"You were that intimate with Lady Hannah?"

"Now, now, old sod. Gentlemen don't tickle and squeal. Used to stay at her resort in Cuba, The Perfumed Garden, don't you know. No matter how warm the days, the nights were just as long, if you catch my drift."

"And you were the knight?"

"Not then, old chap. Just working on it."

"You hated Lady Hannah for throwing you over for this Batteryista guy."

"No such thing. One is always wise to mind

the local politics. And politicians. A lesson old Jules Finder spent his skin in tuition to learn."

"You wanted to get together with her again."

"Thought crossed my mind. Heard she was taking this cruise. Old boy, I said to myself, this may be a good time to renew acquaintance with the Lady Hannah. Time I came in out of the sun, don't you think? Pushing forty-eight in the years department. Time I took to the shade, bottle of rum by the elbow. Eighty proof."

"You're tryin' to tell me you came on this cruise to get together with Lady Hannah again?"

"Something like that. 'Getting together' is a bit of imagery I leave to you Yanks. Sounds a bit like salad-making to me."

"You came on the cruise to steal the sapphires."

"Did I?"

"You know where the Caribbean Blues are now?"

"No idea, old chap. You're on the wrong spoor altogether. I wouldn't purloin the Blues."

"You're broke! You said so yourself!"

"The Caribbean Blues are as cursed as a bookie's kids."

Phlem ticked off on his fingers. "You led the expedition that found the Caribbean Blues in Siam. Maybe that makes you think you have some rights to their ownership. How many times over the last years, Hunter, have you had the sharks breathing down your neck and you wished you had your share of the Blues?"

"Elephants breathe down the neck, old man. The odd lion will warm your back collar. I think sharks approach one in an altogether different manner. Catch me, if I'm wrong."

Ticking a second finger, Phlem said, "This Hannah dame —"

"Dame Hannah would be closer. I warned you before — don't play in fields if you don't know where the rocks are."

"This phony broad — the departed — chucked you out for some Cuban politico, which you couldn't have liked all that much —"

"Didn't like him at all. Rather reminded me of a pool player I once knew, in Nairobi. He knew the velvet was thin."

"I mean, you didn't like being chucked out."

"Old boy, if you were a gentleman, you'd know you have no rights to a lady's affections unless you're willing to guide her down the aisle and agree with what is there said."

Phlem gave up ticking off his fingers. "Where were you Sunday night?"

"In my bunk, after the casino closed. Trying to raise my fare, if you understand me."

"You weren't in Lady Hannah's cabin anytime Sunday night, Monday morning?"

"Pull!"

Bang-bang.

Phlem ticked off one of his fingers again. "You knocked off one of the detectives hired to protect the Caribbean Blues."

"Could have, easily enough." Hunter's speed

in reloading the shotgun was amazing to
Phlem. It usually took him three double bour-
bons to load his Detective Special. "Standing
right next to him. Worm probably deserved doing in. Put him out of his bloody misery. All
you window peepers convening on this cruise
look damaged by life to me. Ought to have a
major hunt aboard. Wouldn't half mind putting out a few lights on this cruise."

"You saying you killed Jones?"

"His head would not grace my walls. The
startling lack of intelligence in his eyes would
lower the impression of intelligence in the
whole exhibit. Surely you can understand that.
Oops, forgive me. Forgot you've already confessed to a lack of introspection."

"He was poisoned by curare. You know
about curare?"

"Of course. Some of my best friends in the
jungles of South America use it every time
they dispatch a spear. Works wonders. You
nick a jaguar with curare and, believe me, it
stays parked."

"And you have access to the substance."

"Naturally. Customs wouldn't notice the odd
bit of curare next to my tooth powder."

"There was curare near Lady Hannah's corpse,
too."

"Must have been a penny sale on. Amazing,
the bargains in some of these free ports. But
you're all wrong about me, you know. Shooting
for sport requires some respect for what you
kill. I shoot lions, not window peepers. Haven't

enough respect for your sort to do in P. I. Jones. Not worth putting oneself out for. I wish you'd understand that."

"And Lady Hannah?"

"Why, we were old pals. I was looking for blissful retirement on her veranda. Why would I do her in?"

"For the jewels. You need the money. Probably some shark after you."

"I thought I'd made it quite clear I've always paid my debts, no matter what it has taken."

"Give me one clear piece of evidence sayin' you didn't kill Lady Hannah."

"You've got it."

"What?"

"Notice the weapon used."

"A handgun."

"Right you are. Now tell me, who uses a handgun?"

"I use a handgun."

"Right again. You go to the head of your class. Toads, weasels, worms, window peepers — all use handguns. Not a sporting weapon, old chap. Not a proper weapon for a gentleman at all. You'd not catch me with a handgun, dead or alive."

"Says you."

"You can take the word of a gentleman. If I were you, I'd have a close look at that judge wallah. What's his name? Hy Court?"

"You got any evidence against him?"

"Absolutely. Sneaky eyes. Low brow. If I

came across him in the brush, I'd shoot him in a second. Pull!''

Bang-bang.

"You missed! Both of 'em!''

"Um,'' said Hunter. "My mind was elsewhere.''

Late Monday afternoon, Ph. d. Phlem reported to the convention of other toads, worms, weasels, peepers, and dik-diks that Sir I. B. Hunter definitely was the murderer of P. I. Jones and Lady Hannah of Havana. He recommended that an immediate search for the Caribbean Blues be undertaken in Sir I. B. Hunter's stateroom, because Hunter was also, obviously, the jewel thief.

Jack Miles sneaked into Hunter's cabin later. The jewels were not there, he reported.

# CHAPTER 9

Jack Miles thought the whole thing was ridiculous.

First a bunch of half-baked P.I.'s — and he included himself in that general description — gets together on a cruise ship to form some sort of United States P.I.'s Association: "The Loyal Order of Dicks, Shamuses, and Gumshoes"? All they needed was a handshake.

And then not one but two murders take place right under their noses. To top the whole thing off, as badly as Jack wanted to be somewhere else, it irked him that the killer — or killers — had the gall to think that they were all "blind" eyes as well as "private" eyes.

Jack Miles himself was no prize, he was the first to admit. He was a busted-up ex-pug turned gumshoe for lack of training to do anything else, but some of these others were real pips!

First there was that fast-talking drunk, Trace, and his Japanese geisha girl friend, who thought she was a female Sherlock Holmes; then that Andy Baltimore clown who just wanted to bust someone in the chops; Philip d. Phlem, who thought wealth was measured by the number of ex-wives one *didn't* pay alimony to; that Limey twerp, Dither, who thought he was better than everyone else; and, finally, Nate Heller, who called his Chicago Agency Z-1 or A-2 or something as silly.

These were the people — the "colleagues" — that Jack had agreed to spend a week with because someone sent him a free ticket for a Caribbean cruise. That would teach him *not* to look a gift horse in the mouth. Next time he'd know better.

This time, though, he had some murders to solve because none of those others could figure their way out of a pair of pants.

Yeah, it looked like old Jack Miles was going to figure this one out if they were going to get any peace at all.

And speaking of "piece," Jack was on his way to interview a neat one, that little china-doll maid of the deceased Lady Hannah, Susie Tong.

He'd had his eye on Susie from the moment he first saw her at that first-night cocktail party where the first murder had taken place. Now it had fallen to him to question her about not only that murder, but the murder of her employer, Lady Hannah.

He tried her cabin first, but there was no answer to his knock. It was still early, so maybe she was up on Eight Deck, or whatever they called it, taking in the ship's exercise class. Wouldn't that be something? Out of a job and being calm enough about it — and the murders — to take an exercise class? If she was, of course, which he was going to check right now.

He took one of the ship's two elevators as far as it would go, to the Boat Deck, which everyone simply called "Seven," and then walked up to Eight Deck, where the casino and fitness center were.

He didn't find a class going on, so naturally he couldn't very well question Susie's taking the damned thing, but when he looked up to the very top level of the ship, where the shuffleboards and chaise longues were, he wondered if the little darling might not be sunning herself. Wouldn't that be a sight?

He climbed the steps to that top deck and saw a lone figure lying on a chaise longue. Wouldn't you know? It was Susie Tong herself.

"Well, hello," he said, approaching her. "Remember me?"

She turned her head to look at him, and he took the opportunity to look at her. Cute little body she had, with bigger breasts than one usually saw on a Chinese girl. He wasn't complaining, though, no, sir, not when she had a face to go with it. Be a hell of a thing if she turned out to be the killer.

"I'm sorry —" she said, which he took to mean that she didn't remember him.

"I'm Jack Miles, the P.I. from New York. I saw you Saturday night at the cocktail party, just before Jones bought it."

"Bought it?"

"Got bumped off, killed, died."

"Oh, that was horrible," she said, shivering deliciously in her gaily colored bathing suit.

"No more horrible than your own employer buying ... I mean, getting killed."

"Please ..." she said, closing her eyes. "I am very upset about that."

"I can see that," Jack said. "It's really putting a crimp in your tan."

"My tan? Oh, you think because I'm tanning I didn't care about her? You are wrong. I am simply trying to relax. I have been very tense since that first night."

"Well, I could always help you relax," Jack offered.

"No, thank you."

She said that in the same tone of voice Trace's Japanese bimbo had used when Jack had offered to give her some lessons in investigative technique. Cold, both of them. He wondered if all Oriental women were frigid.

"Well, then, I'll just have to sit here and ask you some questions," he said, sitting in a chair next to her. The sun was already brutal and he was sweating gallons in his white pinstriped suit — the only suit he owned.

"Questions about what?"

"About the murders."

"What would I know about them?"

"Ah," Jack said, "but that's where the questions come in."

"I'm sorry," Susie said, grabbing her towel, "I have to go —"

He put his hand on the towel, pinning it to the chair, and said, "I'm afraid I'm going to have to insist."

"You're not a policeman. I don't have to talk to you."

"Honey," Jack said nastily, "as far as you're concerned right now, I'm God. There's just you and me up here, with no witnesses. Get my meaning?"

"You . . . you're threatening me."

"Hey, you catch on fast. You're not as dumb as some people say."

"Who said —" she began, then caught herself and looked chagrined.

"Did you know Jones, Susie — may I call you Susie?"

She ignored the second part of the question.

"I did not know him."

"But you knew Lady Hannah."

"Of course —"

"And had reason to kill her."

"What reason?"

"That's what I'm asking."

"I had no reason, and I did not kill her."

"But you found her."

"I did."

"And we only have your word that she was dead at that time."

"It's the truth!"

"What about your boyfriend?"

"What boyfriend?" she asked, her attitude very guarded. So she did have someone on board she was seeing. Jack vaguely recalled some exchanged glances between her and Dan Risi that first night. He hadn't thought anything of it at that time, but now . . .

"Dan Risi."

"Dan and I —" she said very quickly. Then she finished lamely, ". . . are friends."

"Oh, come on, Susie, don't give me that. You're a lot more than friends." They had to be, or else why would she have turned *him* down just moments ago?

"Very well," she said, lifting her fine little chin defiantly. "We are lovers. There. I said it. How do you like it?"

*Please*, he thought. Risi was as slimy an eel as Jack had ever seen. What did this fine piece of china see in him?

"Maybe you found out that Risi and Lady Hannah were seeing each other, as well?"

"That is a lie!"

"And that would be motive enough to kill her."

"I did not!"

"What about Risi?"

"What about him?"

"Maybe he killed her."

"Why would he do that?"

"You tell me why he wouldn't."

"He has no motive."

"Risi's background looks pretty shaky to me, Susie." It was just a guess, but it seemed to hit the target. Susie's tan cheeks flushed.

"Meaning what?" she asked.

"Meaning that he hasn't always been a stickler for doing things the legal way."

"You don't know Dan the way I do."

"And thank God for that."

"You are disgusting!" she said with feeling.

"I've been called worse by better, lady. Let's stick to the matter at hand. What makes you think that Dan Risi wasn't interested in something else besides you?"

"Because I know how he feels about me. I know how we feel about each other."

"How?"

"A woman knows when a man loves her," she said wisely — and naïvely, as far as Jack was concerned. She seemed incredibly naïve for a woman who had to be in her mid-thirties. Possibly she'd never had to deal with a man like Dan Risi before.

Jack looked down at the towel they were both holding on to. It would have been very easy for her to let it go and leave, but she seemed intent on holding on to her end of it with a white-knuckled grip. Maybe she wanted to talk, after all.

Jack released the towel and waited to see if she would leave. She didn't. She seemed confused about what to do.

He decided to stop pushing and try a different tack.

"Tell me about you and Lady Hannah, Susie."

Susie explained how her parents had immigrated to the United States from Hong Kong before she was born, and later died in 1919, when she was sixteen years of age. At that point, Susie quit school and began looking for a job.

"A maid's job was all I was suited for," she explained. "I worked in several households, usually as an upstairs maid."

Jack didn't know what that meant. Was that a lesser position than a downstairs maid? Dealing with maids and butlers and the households that employed them was far from his daily business.

Susie continued her story.

In 1928 her employers moved overseas. She went to an employment agency and was sent to the home of Mr. and Mrs. Demitrio Finestra. She started at a good salary, and eventually graduated to "personal" maid.

"A year later Mr. Finestra died in a fall from his office window."

"A fall?"

"The police called it accidental, but Lady Hannah didn't believe it."

"Did she suspect anyone?"

"Mr. Finestra had many business enemies."

Jack decided that this incident probably was not related to the murders on board. After Demitrio Finestra's death, Lady Hannah moved to the Finestra villa in Cuba with Susie and her husband's secretary — now her own personal secretary — Willa Wright.

"Mr. Finestra's hotel went bankrupt and the insurance company refused to pay because he was supposedly a suicide. That didn't stop Lady Hannah, though. She borrowed money and turned the villa into The Perfumed Garden, a resort."

"This is getting too involved," Jack said finally. "When did you meet Dan Risi?"

"You're not going to start on Dan again, are you?"

"I just want to get the facts straight."

"We met a year ago, and fell in love. It's as simple as that."

"Who told him that Lady Hannah was going to be on this cruise?"

"I did," she replied, a bit too forcefully. "What's wrong with that?"

"Nothing — unless he was here just to steal the Caribbean Blues."

"He's not!"

"He's here because of you."

"Is that so hard to believe?"

"For a man like Dan Risi, yes — and that has nothing to do with you. I think you're fine-looking, and any man would be proud to have you for a lover."

She seemed taken aback by his kind words. Jack himself thought that saying this might help him get to first base with her — or home plate.

"Dan said that this cruise would be the perfect chance for us to spend some time together."

"Susie, during the course of your relationship, has he asked you a lot of questions about Lady Hannah?"

She paused just long enough for him to know that she was going to lie through her teeth — and *in his face!*

"No."

"No?"

"That's what I said — no!"

"He's never asked you any questions about her?"

"Well . . . of course he *has* . . ."

"But you just said he hadn't."

"I meant that he hadn't asked me the kind of questions you're thinking about."

"What kind are those?"

"The kind that would help him steal from her."

"So you've considered that, too?"

"Of course not!"

"But you just said —"

"You're trying to confuse me!" she shouted.

"Maybe you're confused enough without my having anything to do with it."

She stood up then, pulling her towel away before he could grab it.

"I'm not confused at all, Mr. Miles. Not at all. I'm very happy with the relationship Dan and I have. Maybe you're just jealous because you have no such relationship with anyone."

As Susie stalked away, heading for the stairs, Jack called out, "Tell me about Lady Hannah's hats."

Susie turned and stared at him with a puzzled frown.

"Her hats?" she repeated.

"Yes, her hats."

"Why do you want to know about her hats?"

Jack stood up and approached her. He felt wet enough to have fallen in the ocean.

"The autopsy report says that her hatpin was tipped in curare. Was that a common practice of hers?"

"I don't know — of course it wasn't."

"Then who did it?"

"I don't know."

"P. I. Jones was killed by curare. Could Lady Hannah have killed him?"

"Why would she?"

"You lived with the woman, Susie, not me. You should know her better than anyone."

"I do — I mean, I did."

At that point three people came up to the deck, two men and a woman, all clad in bathing suits. Jack pulled Susie aside to the railing that overlooked the outdoor bar below.

"Would Lady Hannah have been capable of killing someone?"

"Yes," Susie said without hesitation.

Jack's surprise was evident on his face. He didn't think she would admit it freely.

"You're surprised."

"Yes."

"You shouldn't be. I told you that she didn't believe her husband committed suicide. If she ever found the man who killed him, she would happily kill *him*."

"The 'man' who killed her husband?"

"Man, woman, person — whoever."

"So you're saying she was capable of killing Jones?"

"If he was the man who killed her husband."

"Did she think that?"

"You're confusing me again."

"Well, that makes two of us."

She frowned in annoyance.

"I simply used Jones as an example. She would only have killed him if she found out that he killed her husband, or had something to do with the death of her husband."

"But you're not saying that he did."

"How could I say such a thing? I have no idea if Lady Hannah had even met Jones before."

"I see."

"I really have to go now, Mr. Miles. Are you finished with me?"

"To meet Dan Risi?"

She didn't answer, but compressed her lips tightly together so that they formed a pale, thin line.

"All right, all right, go ahead. I'm through."

She turned and walked to the stairway, then stepped aside to let two more people ascend. When the way was clear, however, she didn't move. Jack watched her and waited. She finally turned to look at him.

"Do you know who did the killings, Mr. Miles?"

"No, I don't know."

"Do you think you know?"

"Are you asking for you yourself, or for your boyfriend?"

Again she compressed her lips, this time in anger, and hurried down the steps, almost

knocking over a fiftyish man with a huge
potbelly hanging over his bathing suit.

"Bloody rude!" the man said angrily.

"If you're gonna say things like that about
people, Pop, spend some time in the gym,"
Jack said, slapping the man's belly as he passed
him. The man winced from the stinging force of
the blow.

When he reached the deck below, Susie was
just going through a far door, back into the
bowels of the ship. He could have followed her,
but he was sure she was going to see Dan Risi,
and he had to question the man later on,
anyway. At least this way Miles would know
where to find Risi, since the only place the pair
could get together was in one of their rooms.

He'd give them a chance to get comfortable.

Jack went back to the Showtime Lounge,
where he would report to the other P.I.'s on his
conversation with Susie, and his insights — if
his insights didn't go entirely over their collec-
tive heads!

DATE: Monday, May 18, 1938
TIME OF DEPARTURE: 5:30 P.M.
DESTINATION: Guadaloupe
TIME OF ARRIVAL: 8:30 A.M.
DISTANCE: 178 nautical miles
WEATHER CONDITIONS: Partly sunny with
   some periods of rain.

# CHAPTER 10

While Phil Phlem was ordering a drink from the waiter, Chico reached over with her fork and stole the pork chop off his plate.

"Now, that's really disgusting," Trace said. "You ordered two for yourself, you ate mine, and now you snatched Phlem's meal just because you know he's too dense to notice."

"Trace, please," Chico mumbled between mouthfuls. "You're embarrassing me." She was already casting around the table for new victims. Jack Miles saw her and snaked his arm around his plate protectively.

"Don't try it with Miles," Trace said. "He bites. That's how he won his last ten fights."

"Pooh on him," Chico said. "This morning, all I asked him for was his toast. His *toast*. Do you believe he wouldn't even give up a measly piece of toast?"

"That was after you wolfed down all my bacon," Miles said sourly, peering up over his elbow.

"It was the least he could do for me, after I

gave him all that valuable information from my investigation. For free."

"Hey, Charlene Chan, I gave you information, too, remember? And mine was a lot more valuable than that ancient history crapola you brought in."

"Ancient history?" She turned to Trace. "Are you going to let him get away with that?"

"Well . . ." Trace waffled. He didn't want to lose friends. Either of them.

"Really, Trace," Miles said, "your girl's a looker, but all she got out of those people was a lot of bunk about the stiff's past."

"It's not bunk!" Chico shouted. "Lady Hannah's history has got to be important to this case. Someone who knew her killed her."

"So? Anybody could've found out what you did by going to the library and reading through some old newspapers. You were at the scene of the crime when the body was found. A golden opportunity. And you blew it. Zero."

"Why? Because I didn't find a murder weapon?"

The ex-fighter shrugged.

"And *you* would have, I suppose," Chico challenged.

Miles resumed eating. "That's what private investigators are trained to do. *Real* investigators."

"Come on, Jack," Trace began.

Chico talked over him. "That's not fair. I did find clues."

Miles snorted.

"Many clues."

"Right. An empty envelope and a deck of fortune-telling cards."

"And blood," Chico added.

"Oooo, big clue." Miles's face hardened into a scowl. What do you think comes out of bullet holes? Cheerios?"

Chico tossed down her napkin.

"Sorry, kid," Miles said. "But you screwed up."

Trace could see tears glistening in Chico's eyes. "Excuse me," she said quietly. "I'm not hungry anymore."

She left. Trace rose to follow her. "I think this is serious," he said.

"Must be." Miles sopped up his gravy with a piece of bread. "Got her to stop eating."

Trace found Chico on the deck. Her white dress was billowing out behind her like an angel's wings, and her head was bowed into the wind. Trace knew she was crying.

It always took him by surprise to see her defeated. Chico so rarely let down her defenses that he had grown to think of her as invulnerable. Now, though, she looked like a lost child. Trace longed to put his arms around her and comfort her, but he knew she would never permit that. Her pride was such that she would take a punch in the jaw before she would accept a shred of pity from anyone, including the man who loved her.

He sidled up next to her at the rail. "Want to fool around?"

She shook her head. Her long black hair

swirled past his face. It smelled of her perfume.

"Not even from the waist up?"

She smiled despite herself, then wiped her eyes with the back of her hand. "Trace," she said shakily, "you're the best friend I ever had."

"Wait a minute. Only nine or ten hours of heavy drinking produces statements like that. Pork chops don't cut it."

"I wanted so much for you to be proud of me," she went on. "I wanted to conduct a great investigation."

"And you did, Chico. Don't let Miles get under your skin. He's just sore because I wouldn't let him hit on you."

"What?" The sorrow in her eyes was instantly replaced by burning fury. "That bum? I wouldn't go out with Jack Miles if he had the last hamburger on earth."

"Take it easy. I'm just telling you how men think." Trace lit a cigarette. "Besides, you would so go out with him for the last hamburger on earth."

"Well, maybe."

"Anyway, you did a fine job."

"You don't really think so."

"Dammit, Chico! You don't know what I think."

"I do so. I can tell by the sheepish look on your face. You looked sheepish while Miles was dumping on me. Like you were watching one of your kids running with the ball toward the wrong goalpost during the big game."

"What do my kids have to do with anything?

My kids can't even play football. They haven't mastered drooling yet. When the oldest one graduates from high school next year, I'm going to give him a pair of training pants."

"Don't change the subject. In your heart, you agreed with Miles about my not being a *real* detective."

"Jesus! Chico, you don't make anything easy, do you?"

"All I want is the truth."

He tossed his cigarette overboard. "Okay. The truth — the naked, unvarnished truth — is that I don't care. I wish you would get that through your thick Eurasian skull. I don't give a flying finger through a rolling doughnut whether you're a private dick or public enemy number one. I love you, Chico. That's all that matters to me."

She looked up shyly at him. "You do?"

"I do," he said, and he kissed her. "Even though you are squat and funny-looking."

"You don't think I'm a bimbo?"

"Of course not," Trace said gently. "You're far too flat-chested to be a bimbo."

"Okay, then, tell me what was right about my investigation."

"What was right?"

"Yes. Miles could find plenty of things that were wrong. If you really meant it when you said I was okay, you ought to be able to tell me the things I did right."

Trace thought about it. "Okay. Three things. Point one: The room where Hannah died was probably clean. It's unlikely that a murderer would drop a lot of clues in a place the size of a ship's cabin.''

"There were clues, though," Chico reminded him.

"Yes, I know. Many clues. An envelope. I think that's stretching things.''

"It was from Boston. And the deck of Tarot cards. Death was on top. No doubt an important clue," Chico said.

"Maybe, maybe not," Trace said. "Hannah may have been reading her own fortune, for all you know. At any rate, I think you found out as much as you could.''

"Don't forget the picture of her with Batista. He probably gave her the sapphires.''

"Somehow, I doubt that the Cuban military dictator smuggled himself aboard the Cunard *Countess* to do in Lady Hannah.''

"Maybe he wanted the jewels back," Chico offered.

"Why don't we just drop Batista, okay? Point two: You were right about Hannah's past being important. There are an unusual number of people aboard this ship who knew her. I wouldn't be surprised if she was killed for something that has to do with one of them. Some old slight, maybe. . . .''

"Ancient history," Chico said. "That's what Miles called it. Ancient history. A lot he knows.''

Trace ignored her. "The only thing that bothers me is Jones.''

"Jones?''

"Jones," Trace repeated, waving his hand in

front of Chico's blank face. "The P.I. who was killed on Saturday night."

"Oh, him," Chico said. "I forgot all about him. Lady Hannah's much more interesting."

Trace closed his eyes and breathed deeply. "Nevertheless," he said, "Jones is dead, too."

Chico took a lipstick out of her pocketbook and applied it perfectly without the aid of a mirror. "Hey! I've got an idea. What if Jones's murder was tied in somehow with Lady Hannah's?"

"Be still, my heart," Trace said, fanning himself. "Do you really think so?"

Chico gave him a disgusted look. "Are you saying you came up with the same idea?"

"It may have crossed my mind. In primitive terms, of course. However, I give all the credit for the idea to you."

"Good," she said. "Trace, it looks like I'm going to crack this case after all."

"How's that?"

"You said it yourself. Point one: My clues were good. Point two: Jack Miles is a bum."

Trace allowed a moment for this to sink in. "I never said Miles was a bum."

"Well, that's what it comes down to. He said I could have found out everything I learned from the scene of the crime in a bunch of old newspapers. He's a bum."

"He's not a bum," Trace said. "And he happens to be right."

She narrowed her eyes. "You *men* —"

"Don't use that suffragette stuff with me. Miles *was* right. There must be all kinds of information on Hannah Finestra in the morgue of a newspaper office."

"Trace, I don't want to spend a week in a newspaper morgue. I want to crack the case now."

"Well, if you could stop interrupting me for three seconds so I can finish point two, I'll tell you how."

"How?"

Trace nodded toward a group of people standing at the far end of the rail. "The woman in the white sweater. I overheard her at the cocktail party on Saturday night telling some people she was a reporter for the *Boston Bugle*. I think her name's Hilda Johnson."

"Did she kill Lady Hannah?"

"Dammit, Chico! *I* don't know. But she's got access to the *Bugle* morgue. All she has to do is send a telegram to her office asking for background information on Lady Hannah, and they can send it right to the ship. If you can cajole her into doing that, you might come up with some interesting tie-ins."

"Like Jones."

"Who?"

Chico punched him. "That's perfect," she said. "You know, Lady Hannah once lived in Boston. And remember the envelope from Boston."

"Even better."

"I'll get on it right away. And I'll be a real detective this time, Trace. No girlish namby-pamby. You'll see. Anyway, you know, we all make mistakes."

"Not me," Trace said.

"No? Remember? You thought Hannah killed Jones because Jones said 'she' when he died."

"I don't remember that at all," Trace said.

"I do. And I'll remind you often." She pecked him on the cheek and started away, then turned back. "Wait a minute," she said. "What about point three?"

"Point three?"

She crossed her arms impatiently. "You said there were three things that made me great on this case. Point one, good clues. Point two —"

"All right, all right, I remember."

"So what was point three?"

"Point three is that we're not getting paid for this case, so it doesn't matter if you screw up or not."

Chico's lips tightened into a thin red line. "You know, Trace, I hate to be the one to tell you this, but your attitude is really unprofessional. You'd better watch it." She tossed her hair and flounced away.

Mrs. Hilda Johnson was the sort of woman other women invariably described as "lovely." Soft-spoken and charming, she possessed an air of unaffected good breeding from her intelligent eyes to her sensible shoes.

She was even polite to Chico, despite being accosted like a thief during an arrest.

This was part of Chico's new approach to private investigation. There was no room in this business for a scatterbrain. She would be tough. She would be hard. She was a professional. She would show Jack Miles. She would show them all.

Chico Mangini had come of age.

By the time she dragged Hilda into the lounge for a grilling, Trace was already there. He was standing at the bar with two women whose chest measurements qualified them as bimbos. Chico gave him an evil look.

After several minutes, Hilda cleared her throat. "Er . . . do you know that man?" she asked, observing the ferocity of Chico's gaze.

"He's just some degenerate," Chico said. "We'll ignore him." She continued to stare.

Hilda Johnson looked at her watch. "Well, Miss Mangini, I'm certainly willing to cooperate with the commissioner of the New York City Police Department, but . . . by the way, when were you appointed? I don't believe I've heard your name before."

"We're keeping it under wraps," Chico said, "for when I work undercover."

"I see," Hilda said. "Are you working undercover now?"

Chico nodded in what she hoped was a brisk and authoritative manner. "I'm pretending to be a lowly private investigator, hobnobbing with the bums and reprobates of that profession." Her eyes were still trained on Trace.

"Yes. Uh . . . I understand there are a number of them on board — detectives, I mean."

"They're my helpers," Chico said. "We're here to solve Lady Hannah's murder."

Hilda looked puzzled. "But wasn't Lady Hannah killed after we sailed? That is to say, after you and your . . . er . . . helpers were already on board?"

Chico had to think hard. "We were afraid something like this might happen," she said, shaking her head solemnly. "All I can say is, it's a good thing I was here. There were good clues to be found, you know."

"Clues?"

"Many clues." Chico raised one eyebrow.

"Yes. Well . . . as I was saying . . ."

"And Lady Hannah's past is very important to unlocking the key to her murder."

"I'm sure it is," Hilda said. "However . . ."

"That's where you come in." Chico winked at her. "You're going to help me crack this case wide open, shweetheart."

She slammed her glass of ginger ale down onto the tabletop. Liquid splashed out of it into Hilda's eye. The woman covered her face, as if hoping that when she took her hands away, the obnoxious Oriental woman who insisted that she was the New York Police Commissioner would have vanished.

It didn't work. When Hilda managed to open both eyes, Chico Mangini was still there, doing a bad impersonation of Humphrey Bogart.

"Here's the lowdown, babe," she was saying. "You're a newspaper gal, reet?"

"Reet?"

"Right?"

"Right? Oh, right."

"I need you to get the square poop on Hannah Finestra."

"The square what? Oh, yes. I mean no."

Hilda shook her head in a frenzy. "No, I can't do that."

"Why not?" Chico asked out of the corner of her mouth. "Got something to hide, sugar cake?"

Two red blotches appeared on Hilda's cheeks. "No, I do not have anything to hide," she said, barely managing to contain her anger.

"Then I suggest you get on the horn, pronto."

"Miss Mangini, I said before that I was willing to cooperate, but I simply don't know anything about Lady Hannah, and I don't know how to find out. As a matter of fact, I came on this cruise hoping to interview her for a free-lance magazine article."

"But your newspaper morgue," Chico said, forgetting her phony accent.

"Believe me, I've checked that. There's been next to nothing in print about her. That's part of what made her such a fascinating woman. All I know about her is that she went to Cuba without a dime in her pocket, and she became one of the richest women on the island. She owned a big resort, had numerous lovers, and wore a set of three perfectly matched sapphires worth millions."

Chico's face fell. "Cheez-O-Man, I knew that much," she said.

Hilda held up her hands helplessly. "I wish I could tell you more. I'm sorry. I really do have to go now." She took out her wallet. "I'll pay for our drinks," she offered graciously.

Chico's eagle eye noticed the monogram on the wallet: H.F.J. "That your wallet, doll?"

Hilda's two blotches reappeared. "Of course

it's my wallet. Those are my initials." She plunked down two bills. "Good day, Miss Mangini," she said in a huff.

"Call me chief," Chico said.

When Hilda was gone, Chico went over to the bar and dispersed Trace's two companions with threats of physical violence to their persons.

"What'd you do that for?" Trace protested. "I was just explaining to them about my new invention. Listen to this. It's going to turn detective work on its ear."

"Like the bottle opener that doubles as a razor, I suppose," Chico said flatly.

"Even better than that. A microphone. A microphone that you can attach to your clothes, so that you don't have to take notes all the time. Isn't that the damnedest idea you ever heard? You could disguise it so that people you're talking to won't know it's a microphone."

"Disguise it as what?"

"Anything. A boutonniere. A tiepin."

"A foot-long tiepin. Cute, Trace. Very cute."

"You could put decorations on it. Paint it to look like a fish. A frog, maybe. Nobody'll know."

"What about the electrical cord?" Chico asked.

Trace examined the corners of the ceiling for a long time. "Well, I haven't really worked out the fine points yet," he said. "Just the broad outlines."

"Come with me," Chico said, prying his

fingers from his glass. "I want to see your broad outlines."

"Find out anything?" Trace asked as they walked down the corridor toward their cabin.

"Yeah. Hilda's middle initial is F."

"Nothing gets past you, Sherlock."

"I'm a bust as a detective, Trace."

"Hey, you're not going on another insecurity jag, are you?"

She took his hand. "I've been thinking."

"Oh, God."

"About point three," she said.

"Point three?"

"We're not getting paid for this."

"Not a red cent, shweetheart," Trace said.

"So why am I knocking myself out? I mean, maybe I should let some of the other P.I.'s have a try at this case."

"Now, that's a really noble thought."

"I'm glad you think so. I could use a little relaxation. Only . . . "

"Only what?" Trace asked.

"Only, how will we fill up our time? There's nothing to do on this ship except drink and eat and dance and gamble and swim and get suntanned and shop and visit beautiful islands." She giggled.

Trace opened the door to their cabin and kissed her. "Step inside," he said. "Maybe I'll think of something."

# CHAPTER 11

The ship had left port after sunset, and minutes later the elegant small casino had opened. When Trace arrived at eleven P.M., there were only about a dozen people there, most of them clustered around the long, ornate roulette table.

Somebody was missing a bet, Trace thought as he looked around the room. Gambling — legal, high-class gambling — could someday be a high-ticket item, with a lot of profit for the people farsighted enough to get in on the ground floor.

Right now, in the United States, gambling had been legalized only in Nevada, but the single place that specialized in it was Reno, and Reno was a grubby little roadside town, with no charm, lousy hotels, and nothing to pull tourists from the rest of the country.

But Trace had heard that some mobster — Buggy or Bugsy or something — had his eyes on starting a string of casinos in Las Vegas. Maybe that town would amount to something someday. And if anybody could pull it off, The

Syndicate probably could. Sometimes Trace
thought that The Syndicate was the only group
in America that really knew what the hell it
was doing. Certainly, that lunatic Roosevelt in
the White House and all those cuckoo clocks he
had surrounded himself with didn't know
anything. Maybe that was the way to end the
depression: hire organized crime and tell them
to figure out a solution. It might work. Anything was better than all those Communist
stunts that Roosevelt was trying.

Trace saw the man he was looking for sitting
alone at a blackjack table. Blackjack was an
old French gambling game, vingt-et-un, which
was just starting to become popular around the
world. The idea of the game was to get cards
totaling closer to twenty-one than one's op-
ponent's, and Trace had grown up playing it
with his grandmother using bingo markers as
chips. One of the great sad days in his life had
occurred when he found out his grandmother
cheated. But by the time Trace was smart
enough to figure out his grandmother was a
cheat, he was also smart enough to have
figured out that a player didn't have to cheat.
Blackjack was a beatable game if the player
knew what he was doing.

As he walked across the room, he thought
again about that Syndicate thug, Buggy . . .
Buggy . . . Bugsy Siegel. That was it. He hoped
Bugsy got Las Vegas gambling going in a
hurry, because as soon as he did, Trace was

moving to Las Vegas and playing blackjack for a living. Screw being a private investigator.

He slid into the seat next to Hy Court and handed a twenty-dollar bill to the dealer, who gave him back a stack of twenty one-dollar chips.

As Trace took the chips, Hy Court looked around at him.

"Hey, you're one of those private detectives, aren't you?"

Trace nodded. "Devlin Tracy," he said. "Call me Trace. You having any luck?"

The lawyer shook his head. "Nah. I was going to ask you the same thing. You find out who the mad killer is aboard this ship?"

"Not yet. But we will," Trace said. He stacked two one-dollar chips on the rectangle in front of him on the table. There was an ashtray in front of Hy Court and it was overflowing with cigarette butts. An almost empty pack of Pall Malls was on the table. The green felt was littered with ashes. A large water tumbler half filled with whisky, neat, no ice, was at his left hand.

The dealer, an elaborate tanned redhead in a black evening gown, had finished reshuffling the single deck of cards she was using and offered them forward for Trace to cut. Trace divided the cards into two piles, nodded to the dealer, and said to Court, "They say you were an old friend of Lady Hannah's."

Even though it wasn't a question, Trace

waited for an answer. Most people, he knew, got nervous unless conversation filled the air, and after only a few seconds Court replied, "Good friends with her husband, Demitrio. Haven't seen her much since his death."

"Oh, yeah. He's the guy who tried flying out the window, isn't he?"

Court nodded and drank from his tumbler of whisky. "He was wiped out in the crash, like a lot of people. I guess he just couldn't take being broke."

"You were his partner. Did you go broke, too?"

"You can be sure of it," Court said. "All of us."

"Who were the others?"

"There was Rich Ledger. He's on the ship now, too. And me. And Ernest Friendly. He was the hotel general manager. We each owned fifteen percent. Demitrio had the big share, fifty-five percent. We were all old college buddies. Boston University, you know."

The dealer had placed two cards in front of each player, one face up, the other face down. The face-up card in front of the dealer was a six.

Trace glanced at his cards. He had a ten and a jack, which totaled twenty by blackjack's rules. He told the dealer, "I'll stay with these."

Court's up-card was a seven. He peeked at the face-down card as if someone were watching, then sighed and leaned back in the chair. He had twenty dollars in the betting space in front of him. He thought for a few moments, then showed Trace the hidden card. It was an ace, which counted as one or eleven in blackjack.

"What would you do?" Court asked Trace.

"Double down and take one card," Trace said.

"What?" Court's face registered his astonishment at what he clearly thought was incredibly stupid advice.

Trace shrugged. "Do what you want, but I've got this game figured out, and the right play is to double down."

"Just once, Trace, because you look like a nice guy." He took twenty dollars in five-dollar chips and put them alongside his regular bet.

"Go ahead," he told the dealer. "Double down. You heard him." The young dealer smiled. Obviously, she thought, the man called Trace knew absolutely nothing about blackjack. She dealt Hy Court another card face down, and then turned over her own downcard. It was an ace, which gave the dealer a total of seventeen. She was not permitted to take any more cards.

Court turned over his new card. It was a ten. The ten, ace, and seven gave him a total of eighteen. He was the winner.

"Yahoo!" he cried as he pushed his cards forward and the dealer started matching his chips to pay off the bet.

"Maybe you're on to something, Trace."

"I'm a student of the game, Mr. Court," Trace said. "If I concentrate, I can't lose."

"How come you're not rich, then?"

"I have trouble concentrating," Trace said. "Something to do with alcohol. Anyway, you were telling me about the partnership."

"Yeah. The hotel was doing real well and we were all making money, and then, at the end of the twenties, just about the time of the crash, things got tight. I guess Demitrio just couldn't take the thought of being real poor, so he jumped out the window. All of us were there, too. It was awful. He just said, 'I'm not going to take this anymore,' ran to the window, and dove through it. And that was the end of him."

"You all seemed to survive all right," Trace said.

"Not that easy, young man," Court said. "Ernest Friendly had a heart attack soon after and he was laid up for years. He just died a few months ago up in Boston. And Rich Ledger and I . . . well, we had to scratch around for a long time making a living. There weren't any easy times. I even thought for a while about letting my wife, Sue, go back to work. Hey, how would you play this?"

Trace glanced down at the table. He had forgotten to remove his money after the last hand, so his bet was four dollars. Again, he had two face cards and he nodded to the dealer that he would stand on those. The dealer's up-card was a nine. Trace looked at Hy Court's two cards. They were both eights.

"Split them," Trace said.

"Split?"

"Split," Trace insisted.

"You heard him," Hy Court told the dealer.

He reached into his pocket and pulled out a stack of five-dollar chips. He counted off forty dollars' worth and matched his original bet.

The dealer dealt one card atop each eight. Hy Court got two tens. Each hand totaled eighteen.

"I stand," he said hurriedly.

The dealer turned over her hole card. It was a three. She drew again to her total of twelve and pulled a five. The dealer again had seventeen, and Hy Court had won both hands. This time, as she paid off, the dealer wasn't smiling. Trace took one of Court's five-dollar chips and tipped the dealer. She resumed smiling.

"I tell you, Trace, maybe we should take this show on the road. I'll bet, you play, and we'll clean up," Court said.

"I'll think about it," Trace said. "Is your wife with you on the cruise?"

"Sue?"

"I guess so," Trace said. "Right name for a lawyer's wife."

"Yeah. She's around somewhere. I think she went for a walk on the deck with Rich Ledger. Two walking fools, those two. Me, I like to sit down with my smokes and my drink and my cards and enjoy life."

"Different ways to enjoy life," Trace said. "So you met with Lady Hannah the night she was killed."

Hy Court looked at Trace through narrowed eyes. "Are you implying something?"

"Not me. I'm just wondering."

"Yeah . . . well, we met with Hannah. Sure we did. Rich and I went in there. I never liked that woman, and now she had this weird idea that somehow Rich and I were responsible for her husband's death."

"How'd she get that idea?" Trace asked.

"Ernest Friendly. I guess he must have gotten senile just before he died, because he wrote her some kind of letter and said that we were cheating Demitrio and he caught us and we threw him out the window. A lot of crap like that."

"And what did Lady Hannah do?" Trace asked.

"She said she was going to make us sweat. That someday she'd go to the police, but we'd never know when. That she'd just let us dangle, slowly, slowly, swinging in the wind."

"That must have upset you," Trace said.

"You can believe that. I was furious." He stopped for a moment, then chuckled. "Very clever, Trace. But no cigar. We didn't kill her. We told her where to get off, and Rich and I left. Rich went for a walk and I went to the bar. The bartender will tell you I was there until the place closed. And when was she killed? Around midnight, they said? I was into about my third Scotch by then." He lit a cigarette angrily.

"Anyway," he said, "those rumors about Demitrio's death were kicking around for a long time. The hell with them. Nobody ever believed them before, and I don't know why anyone would believe them now. I'll tell you, it made it damned hard for me to make a living, those rumors. The police finally called it a suicide, but my reputation was hurt. None of the big firms would hire me. I had to go into private practice, ambulance chasing, to make a living, and one way or another, I'm still at it."

He blew a large, lazy cloud of smoke and coughed, the dry, raspy cough of the heavy smoker and drinker.

"Christ! Listen to me," he said. "You'd never know I was a college swimming champ at Harvard, would you? My lungs must be filled with macadam by now." Trace pounded him on the back until the coughing jag had stopped.

"So how'd you get to come to this ship?" Trace asked.

"Rich and I got invitations from Hannah. She said she wanted to talk to us about plans for a new resort, so we jumped at the chance to come along. We didn't know she was plotting some kind of silly revenge."

"One thing I wonder," Trace said.

"What's that?" Court asked.

"Right after Hannah's body was found, you told one of the ship's officers that you and Ledger talked in her cabin about her new resort. That was a lie, wasn't it?"

"Okay, so it was a little white lie. But you know, if I said that she was going to blackmail us or something, it would have made us look like suspects. So we lied. But we didn't kill her. She was alive — real nasty alive — when we left, and to hell with her. The only thing I'm sorry about her death is that I didn't get a chance to kill her myself. Rich Ledger, too. We're close friends, spend a lot of time together, and I know he feels the way I do. But

we didn't kill her. Now, are you going to grill
me all night, or are you going to make me rich
by telling me how to play blackjack?"

"Probably both," Trace said as he nodded to
the dealer to deal their cards.

It was well after midnight when Trace found
the other private detectives sitting together at
a table in a corner of the cocktail lounge. A
handful of waiters was busy cleaning up the
rest of the room. Only a scattered handful of
drunks was still in the place.

As he slid into a seat and picked up somebody else's drink, Trace said, "It's all done.
You guys can stop working now. I've got it all
solved."

"Oh?" Heller remarked. "You got the
killer?"

"Yeah," Trace said. "Hy Court. That
lawyer."

"Did he confess?" Dither asked.

"No. He didn't have to. I know a guilty man
when I see one," Trace said.

"You should," Chico said. "Before you tell us
how you allegedly solved two murders, why
don't you fill us in on this lawyer?"

"Sure," Trace said. He pulled a cocktail
napkin out of his pocket. "You know," he said,
"someday, somebody's going to invent some
kind of little recording device that you can
keep notes on and stuff, so you don't always
have to write on cocktail napkins."

"Why don't you go invent one?" Chico said.

"It sounds like a better idea than most of your get-rich-quick schemes."

"Hey, calm down, lady. You're talking to a guy who won fifty dollars at the blackjack tables tonight. As well as solving two murders. Anyway. Hy Court. Fifty years old. Born in Boston. Father a judge, mother from England. Harvard. Friends and partners in a hotel with Hannah's husband; Rich Ledger and Ernest Friendly. They were all together when the lady's husband, Demitrio Finestra, decided to fly through a window. Since then, private practice, a little hard times, but still kind of lives above his means. Wife. Used to be Sue Banister. Been married thirteen years. She's from New York. Her folks owned a furniture store, but they got killed in a car accident in Italy about eight years ago."

Trace looked up. "In case I never told any of you this before, don't ever drive in Italy. Those Italians are crazy."

"Get on with it, Trace," Chico said.

"Right, right. So, anyway, Court is scratching out a living. His wife used to be a writer and editor, and he thought for a while about sending her back to work, but changed his mind. So then they get an invitation from Hannah to come on this cruise. She tells them that she wants to talk to Court and Ledger about being partners in a new place she's opening. They come and they meet with her Saturday night, at about eleven o'clock. But it turns out that she doesn't want them to be partners at all. What happens is that she's got a letter from Ernest Friendly. He was the other partner. Just before he died, he wrote a letter that told her that all three partners in the hotel had been cheating her husband, and when he found out about it, Rich Ledger and Hy Court threw him out the window. Finestra didn't commit suicide; he was murdered. Anyway, Hannah told them that she knew and that she was going to make them sweat before she called the cops."

Trace looked up from the cocktail napkin, then crushed it and put it into his pocket. "Hah? Hah?" he said triumphantly. "Is that a motive, or is that a motive?"

Heller said thoughtfully, "It sure as hell sounds like a motive for killing Lady Hannah. But what about my partner, Jones? What would that have to do with killing him?"

"You people always do this," Trace grumbled. "You always bother around with details. I tell you this guy's the killer."

"If he was, why would he bother telling you all about this?" Andy Baltimore asked.

"Well, he said the bartender could give him an alibi for the time Hannah was killed. He said he was at the bar here and didn't leave until closing." Trace waved a hand derisively. "But you know . . . that's all hogwash. He did it."

Chico left the table.

Phil Phlem said, "I thought that Court and Ledger said that they *had* discussed a new partnership with Lady Hannah."

"That's what Court said at first," Trace said.

"But he finally admitted he was lying. They were afraid somebody would think they had killed her. Well, they were right. I do."

Trace finally got the waiter's attention and ordered a drink.

Heller said, "They still had no cause to kill my partner . . . unless they're jewel thieves or something and he got on to them, but I don't think so. I don't know." He looked through the lounge windows out at the Caribbean.

Chico came back and sat at the table again.

"Back to the drawing board, Trace," she said. "This is the same bartender. He remembered Court. He said he never left the bar Saturday night until it closed."

"Oh, that's hog bilge," Trace said. "How can he remember a thing like that? People get up and go to the bathroom. Bartenders don't remember things like that."

"This one did," Chico said. "He said that he and Court were talking about it, and Court said he never went to the bathroom while he was drinking because he had the greatest kidneys on earth. It was like a joke. Sorry, Trace. And besides, didn't you say the murderer was Lady Hannah because the dead man, Jones, mumbled 'she'?"

"An uncommon momentary slip on my part," Trace said. "I've rethought it. Jones didn't say 'she'; he said 'shy' — for shyster. That means Hy Court, don't you see? And that's not all. There's lots of evidence."

"Like what?" Chico asked.

"All right. A. Hy Court's a lawyer. They're

all criminals, especially all those ones in Washington working for that lunatic Roosevelt. B. Court needs money and he gambles. C. He smokes far too much for any trustworthy person. D. He drinks like a fish. Case closed and proved. He did it. Hy Court is your killer." He leaned back, sipped someone else's drink, lit a stolen cigarette, and demanded, "How could anybody not suspect a man with such terrible habits?"

"You've got me, Trace," Chico said. "You truly have."

"Lucky guy," Heller said.

DATE: Tuesday, May 19, 1938
TIME OF DEPARTURE: 6:30 P.M.
DESTINATION: St. Lucia
TIME OF ARRIVAL: 8:30 A.M.
DISTANCE: 133 nautical miles
WEATHER CONDITIONS: A storm is brewing
    and the seas are choppy.

# CHAPTER 12

*Excerpt from operative's report, case file 714, date May 20, 1938. To the attention of George Donahue, vice-president, Cunard Line. Reporting operative: Nathan Heller, president, A-1 Detective Agency, Chicago, Illinois. Written en route during Caribbean cruise aboard Cunard Countess.*

*Today, George, I thought maybe I had the son-of-a-bitch.*

*This bird Trace may seem half-witted and half soused half the time, but he also seemed half smart and half sober.*

*So when he said he knew who killed Jonesy, I had to take him at least half seriously, right?*

*Wrong. The sum and total of his theory was this (Are you ready, George? Sitting down?): Attorney Hy Court was the killer because Trace has run into lawyers before who were killers. To this he adds that this particular lawyer drinks and smokes too much, making him especially prone to character flaws. This view I can accept, since Trace himself drinks like a fish and smokes like a smokestack, to put it tritely but accurately.*

*Nonetheless, I did, as I said, take him half seriously. In Chicago I've had occasion to run into a disreputable lawyer now and again. That was understated sarcasm, George — put your eyebrows down, and while you're at it, sit down if you haven't already. This goddamned report on this goddamned case on this goddamned cruise is about to take a turn. A goddamned turn.*

*Tuesday night, after Trace imparted his brilliant theory, based upon nothing substantial at all, I couldn't sleep. My cabin was a cell. The ship was careening through whitecaps taller than the Trib Tower and, since I was too much the he-man to take any of those sissy seasick pills, my stomach was careening, too, and so was my mind. This guy Court — he could be the killer. Trace could be right. So why waste time with niceties? My partner was dead, and Court was a lawyer. Rousting a lawyer wouldn't do my conscience any damage. Some threats of violence and maybe a little violence itself might get me the answers I was looking for. Why waste time trying politely to interrogate a mouthpiece who knew all the tricks of the trade?*

*Shaking him by the front of the shirt till all the shyster tricks were shook out of him made sense to me.*

*I asked around the ship — checking in the*

*dining room, the library, the casino (not yet open for gambling, but in free use as a lounge), and finally, in the latter, that dishy little blonde, Willa, sitting reading an Agatha Christie, said she thought Court had gone up for a swim in the pool on Eight Deck, the top deck.*

*"The pool doesn't open till ten," I said. "It's barely eight."*

*She just shrugged and made a pretty face.*

*I growled her my thanks and went on up. The wind was chilly, but the climate was otherwise hot and humid. So when a gust of wind pushed at you, you felt a chill; the rest of the time you baked. This is the last cruise I ever go on, incidentally, George — I like it better in Chicago, where the weather usually stinks, but at least you know where you stand: Cold is cold, and hot is hot, and the hell with this tropical noise.*

*I climbed the steps to the upper deck, heading to the pool, when that massive truck of a guy, that would-be white blues singer, Scats Allegro, stepped out of the steam room. He was a block of flesh in a terry-cloth robe, body beaded, white hair damp. He grinned at me like Satchmo and rubbed his Buddha belly.*

*"The Scatman ain't havin' much luck losing this life preserver, Heller, my man."*

*"Scats," I said, "I don't like you. I didn't like you in Chicago, and I don't like you here."*

*"Hey, man, what's the problem? What did the Scatman ever do to you?"*

"*You lifted every lick in your pathetic bag of tricks from* real *blues singers on the South Side.*"

"*Heller, those cats are primitives — it's the Scatman who truly knows how to wail.*"

"*You're a phony and a bigot, Scats. If you'll excuse me . . .*"

"*Bigot? Moi? I done the black man a favor, man — I took his crude jungle boogie and gave it a* real *audience. . . .*"

"*A white audience, you mean.*"

"*Yeah,*" Scats said, his round, pale face a ball of confusion. "*Ain't that what I said?*"

"*I notice you're not sitting in with the band on the ship. . . .*"

"*I don't play with those cats.*"

"*Those* colored *cats?*"

"*Hey, I don't pay no attention to their color, man. Are you kidding? It's just I'm way past 'em.*"

"*They don't have a handle on jazz and blues like the Scatman, right?*"

"*All root,*" Scat said, flashing his big white grin.

I just shook my head and went on past the gym to the pool. The area was empty — the lounge chairs, deck chairs, sunning themselves, metal gleaming; the bar across the way unattended. The blue-and-white mosaic of the pool glistening, wetly; water splashed about, though no swimmers were present. Odd. I moved closer and saw that I had been wrong.

*There was a swimmer.*

*Only he wasn't swimming.*

*"Scats!" I called out. "Haul your fat butt up here!"*

*His voice called out, somewhat distant. "Say what?"*

*I said what, again, and knelt by the pool, where a body floated, face down.*

*"Damn!" I said, and jumped in. (My seersucker suit was ruined by this act of bravado, George, leaving me with one suit for the rest of your damned cruise. Replacement cost will be on my expense account. No discussion on this point or I'll sue your butt. Of course, I'll have to use a lawyer other than Hy Court.)*

*Hy Court, whose body this was — and it did seem to be a body, as lifeless as a dead fish floating in a stagnant pond — would not be answering any of my questions.*

*"Heller, what the hell, man, what the hell..."*

*Scats was at the edge of the pool, leaning over, hairy hands on bare knees, eyes wide and marble-round, mouth open as if he were about to start spouting one of his phony-baloney bebop riffs.*

*"Give me some help, you dumb lardass!"*

*He scowled at me, but stripped out of his robe and jumped in, the water geysering as his bruiser's body dropped in. He paddled over and helped me haul Court onto the tile near the pool. I climbed on the lawyer's back and began trying to give him some artificial respiration, his arms butterflied out while I kept up a rhythm on his back. Scats watched with an expression of surprise and concern, then began shaking his head. "It ain't gonna do you any good, man. Cat's dead."*

*I turned the body over and began to shake it. "Talk, you lousy goddamned shyster! Talk!"*

*I don't know how long I did that, George, I haven't hidden that this is a personal matter. That I might not be at my most collected. My most detached.*

*But after a while I felt a hand on my shoulder and a sweet voice said, "Stop. He's dead, Mr. Heller."*

*I glanced back and Chico was standing there, in a black swimming suit, towel over her arm, a study in grace and beauty. Me, I was just a schmuck in a wet seersucker trying to slap some truth out of a corpse.*

*Standing behind her in his suit, towel over one arm, cigarette in a casual hand, was a befuddled-looking Trace.*

*"Maybe Court isn't the killer," he said.*

*I stood. "That theory," I said, "will hold water."*

*And I went to get the captain.*

# CHAPTER 13

If Andy Baltimore had been expecting the morgue to be a sterile, pristine area just off the hospital, he would have been disappointed. It was a dark, gloomy, cramped room in the very bowels of the ship, at the end of a long, meaningless corridor. Andy trudged down it, feeling as if he were marching through the craft's tainted soul.

To get there, Andy had to go down every step in the place and pass a half dozen doors marked "Do Not Enter," "Private," and "For Crew Only." He also had to pass the Negroes in the galley, the Cockneys in the crew quarters, and the Chinese in the laundry. Each of them had looked up from the huge, hot, steamy machines they were manning to stare, expressionless, at the obsessive little man who strode past.

Each one of them knew Andy didn't belong down there.

Nobody stopped him.

Andy grabbed the warm metal latch of the big, thick, unmarked metal door, pushed down, and pulled. His already low-slung heart sank as he stepped inside the crypt. To his immediate right was the morgue — a single steel refrigerated tomb the size of a small submarine. There was refuse around its base. To the left were link-fence cages crammed with electrical and plumbing equipment.

*Death among the toilets*, was Andy's first thought. A soul-stirring, second-to-last resting place.

Andy looked sourly at the freezer door. He thought about what had led him to this ignominious trespass. The investigation had stopped days ago as far as he was concerned. Nobody cared about the victims anymore . . . if they had cared at all. It had now degenerated into an infuriating exercise in     maintenance. Trace was all but bragging about his deflated lawyer theory. Chico had her hands full just keeping him upright. Dither and Phlem were busy oozing smug all over their nice clean floors. Miles may have had his heart in the right place, and certainly his fists, but who knew where his head was?

And Andy was even unsure about Heller. How much of his crusade was in memory of his partner, and how much sinful pride? Besides, he was being forced to play scout master more than Sam Spade.

As for the others . . . Who *wasn't* lying? The idea of talking to those people any more made Andy sick. They were covering their behinds and uncovering their breasts. Better he should talk to dead people. *Yeah, let's see what the corpses had to say*.

Andy was welcomed to the underworld by a blast of sickeningly stale air as he yanked open the morgue tomb. He averted his head and almost fell back as the stench of death hit him in the face. Through tearing eyes, he saw the furnace-sized interior crammed with macabre shapes.

For a split-second, Andy thought he had finally gone off the edge. But as he stepped aside, he realized that the freezer wasn't even on. Andy stumbled forward, grabbing for the tomb's top. His fingers fell on a pile of cloth as his other hand went for the small, screwed-on box beside the mausoleum's door.

All he had to do was touch it. The orange plug stuck in the top, then shifted, and the electricity surged on. Cold air, growing frigid, immediately started pumping out of the interior's sides.

Andy leaned back against the link-fence wall, gasping and blinking. He let his hands drop to his sides, still holding the cloth. He looked down to see a light jacket in his grip. It was Hy Court's jacket.

Okay, fine. This gave him something to do while he waited for the bodies to ice. He did a thorough body search of the inanimate object. Andy knew immediately that no one had thought of doing even this most rudimentary example of detection. No, they were too busy talking to liars.

There it was. Folded in the inside pocket. A one-page letter. Succinct. Simple. Suicidal.

Jan. 5, 1938

Dear Mrs. Finestra,

Although it has been many years, I'm sure that you will remember me from happier days at the Finestra Hotel. As one of your husband's partners in the hotel, I feel that I must take some of the responsibility for Demitrio's death.

Having recently learned that my next heart attack will be my last, I will instruct my sister to send you this letter after my death.

I hereby confess to the embezzlement of hotel funds, along with Hy Court and Rich Ledger. When D. Finestra confronted the three of us with his allegations, Hy Court and Rich Ledger killed him! They threw him out the office window, and proceeded to destroy all evidence of the embezzlement. Court and Ledger then told the police that Finestra was depressed over the stock market crash and committed suicide by jumping.

Although I was not directly involved in the murder, I was threatened into silence by the other partners. I know that by keeping their secret, I became an accessory to the crime. This has weighed heavily on my conscience, especially since insurance companies won't pay on suicides.

Now that I know I am dying, and while I can still make things right, I am putting this all down on paper. Take it to the police, or do whatever you want with it. I shall be able to die knowing that I have made restitution for my sins.

With Deepest Regrets,

Ernest Friendly

Naked in death, vulnerable to the slings and arrows of outrageous eternity, the corpses lay atop one another as if resting on an invisible bunk bed. This was a morgue built for one that was now triple-teamed. They made a perverse Havana Hannah sandwich: the poisoned P.I. on the bottom, dried spittle over his lower lip; Lady Finestra in the middle; and the freshly killed attorney on top.

Yes, dammit, killed. The odds that Demitrio Finestra walked out of that office window under his own power, then the Chicago P.I. coughed up his guts, Lady Hannah was nailed to the deck, *and* Hy Court took the long dive of his own accord were astronomical. Especially in light of the letter.

Andy reached into the tomb the way he would in a stopped-up toilet. He found himself holding his breath as he fondled Hy's head. One lump or two? None. Dead end. Yeah, but what was that? A pimple? On the back of his neck? What could the ship's doctor be thinking of? That Court was attacked by a vampire with a missing denture?

It was at times like this that he fervently wished he had a Larry and Curly. What joy to go through life with someone to slap, slug, and poke the eyes of. Moe and he understood each other. *Spread out, Willa Wright, here comes Andy.*

He tried to calm down by walking as fast as he could and breathing deeply. Andy Baltimore did not hit women. That was what Tracey Tailer was for. But Tracey wasn't here, curse the luck, and at least some truth would have to be extracted. This thing would haunt him for the rest of his life if justice wasn't served in some fashion.,

As Andy searched and searched and searched, his anger lessened and his anguish rose. This was a plot against him. Everyone was hiding just beyond his vision, giggling into their hands. A vision of his haunting a ghost ship flashed through his brain.

All the old, familiar places were deserted of suspects, and he didn't want to start pounding on a passenger out of sheer frustration. So his quest continued on the very outskirts of the vessel, practically praying he'd find an innocent captive, bound and gagged in a lifeboat, whom he could rescue.

Andy stepped out onto the portside deck expecting to find it as empty as all the others. But there, all the way down by the "No Passengers Beyond This Point" sign, was Scats Allegro.

What sort of a stupid name was Scats? Looking at the hulking bonehead, Andy imagined his parents had taken one look at him in the crib and cried "Scat! Get that kid outta here!" Andy felt stupid enough without yelling that artificial moniker.

"Hey!" Andy shouted at him. "Willie boy!"

Scats, who had been staring vacantly out to sea, acted as if he was just plugged in. He started, looked around wildly, spotted Andy, and ran as fast as he could in the other direction.

"Hey!" Andy howled with delight, tearing after him. "Great! Thank you, thank you, oh, God, thank you . . . !"

Scats raced along the narrow deck, beneath the gigantic, hanging lifeboats. He ignored the "No Passengers" sign, leaping over the low gate. Andy kept after him, maintaining an even pace so he wouldn't end his fun too soon. Scats was surprisingly quick for such a big man, but years of running after captive-filled trucks along Sunset Boulevard won out.

Andy caught up with him just as Scats was about to round the corner of the ship's bow. "Oh, Willie boy," Andy cried, as if he were Jack Benny calling Rochester, his hand just touching the burly singer's shoulder.

Scats grabbed a life buoy off the wall and swung it at Andy's head. Andy ducked under it and it slammed back into the wall. Andy stood, his head inside the doughnut hole. He smiled and jerked back his neck and torso. The heavy, padded life buoy was yanked out of Scats's hand as if it had been pulled by a rope.

*Ooo*, Andy thought of himself. *You show-off, you*. He let the buoy fly back off his head, behind him, as Scats pulled back his arm for a straight-arm punch. Andy's head snapped back upright, seeing the punch coming like a Hitchcock shot.

Andy cocked his head to one side. The ham-like fist went past his ear, just grazing the lobe.

Decisions, decisions. So much target, so little time. *What would Miles do?* Andy wondered. Shot below the belt? Shot to the solar plexus? Kick to the shin or knee? Night drop (between the legs)? Rabbit punch? The fabulous nose bone-into-the-brain maneuver with flat of hand or forehead? All of the above?

Andy dropped to his knees. Scats's gut filled his vision like a cellulite sky. Andy gave a short, explosive punch to Scats's bull's-eye.

Scats made the sound that made New Orleans famous and started the birth of the blues. Andy straightened, took his arm, and led the out-of-breath, doubled-over man to the starboard side.

"Here," he offered pleasantly. "Let me introduce you to the wonderful world of internal bleeding."

Scats folded over the railing and shot his lunch into the blue Caribbean.

"That was wonderful," Andy prattled on. "I'm refreshed. I'm renewed. I'm revitalized...."

"I'm retching," Scats growled wetly, raising his slightly greenish head. He looked like an unripe tomato. "What did you slug me for, man?"

"Oh, I'm sorry," Andy apologized profusely. "Obviously you were trying to save my life.

Just think, someday I might fall overboard and I'd never have to worry with that lifesaver lodged in my throat. Why, aren't you sweet? What did you run for?"

"Hey, man, I don't have to tell you anything. I'm sick and tired of you clowns giving me a hard . . . *urk!*"

Andy had stepped on the back of Scats's calf, forcing him to go down on one knee and smack his jaw on the railing.

A second later it was like it never happened. Andy was just standing there, smiling innocently, and Scats was back upright, little stars dancing before his eyes and little canaries singing in his ears. *Ah, yes,* Andy thought. *Life as a Warner Brothers cartoon. Nothing like it.*

"You're losing your accent, Willie boy," Andy warned.

Scats's eyes cleared and, sure enough, when he spoke his voice held little of the artificial gravel. "How do you know my name?" he asked tightly.

Andy was thunderstruck. "You mean that's it? Your name *isn't* Scats?" Maybe a bit of Tracey's delicate psychic ability was rubbing off.

"Middle name," the quickly recovering man said. "William Scats Allegro."

"You look like a William," Andy decided. "What sort of stupid name is Scats?"

"With a last name like Allegro, just be glad they didn't name me A Cappella."

"Well, William, Bill, Willie, Willie lad, Will honey, Billy boy. What are you running from?"

"Hey! Me, man? Nothing. You just spooked me is all." As his strength was returning, so was his totally artificial demeanor and voice. "It's just, you know, man, for the last couple of days, with all you crazies running around and all the bodies droppin', I just couldn't swing from all the stress and pressure."

Andy was dumbfounded. "I beg your pardon?"

"What, man?"

"What did you say?"

"About what, man?"

"You couldn't swing."

"No, man."

"Why not?"

"All the stress and pressure, man."

"Stress and pressure?"

Scats was looking at him as if he were retarded. "Yeah, man, stress and pressure. What's the matter with you?"

"Oh, nothing," Andy said sweetly. "Just the stress and pressure." Andy suddenly wanted to call China on the porcelain telephone. This . . . this pompous, posturing bullfrog and that beautiful blond secretary . . . ?

"Stress and pressure" were the words Willa Wright had used. Nobody else on board had used such an awkward phrase. That was what came of rehearsing too much.

"Yeah . . . well, if you'll excuse me, man," Scats was saying, edging away, "I gotta go teach those darkies in the orchestra how to really feel the blues."

"You'll sing now," Andy told him. "How

long have you been seeing Lady Hannah's secretary?"

Scats froze, looked at Andy, then burst out laughing. His mirth was cut off by his still-pained gut. "Argh. So you know, huh, man? How much did she tell you?"

There were a couple of ways to go with that one. Andy could lie and say she'd confessed all, but then why would Scats repeat it? Or he could lie and say that Willa had accused Scats of God knew what, but then he might not believe it, or clam up. Then there was part of the truth, where he could say that she hadn't said enough and try to browbeat Scats for more.

Then there was the real, practical, mercenary truth. Honesty was the best policy.

"She said just enough to get her in a scow-load of trouble," Andy revealed angrily. "She knows all about Demitrio Finestra's death and isn't talking. Fine with me. Let the San Juan police get it out of her. I hear their holding cells are lovely this time of year."

Scats laughed again. He reminded Andy of all those B-movie villains who gloated over everything that was said. "Hey, be cool, man." Andy thought of the corpses in the freezer, which only made him madder. "She was covering my rear, that's all, man," Scats concluded.

"I'm about to tear it off and play basketball with it, man," Andy seethed. "What absurd, pathetic reason do you have for withholding information and complicating things? No, no, let me guess. You're married, right? You and Willa are married, and Lady Hannah had some sort of stupid no fraternization rule.''

It was Scats's turn to be dumbfounded. "That's exactly right!" he announced incredulously. "How did you guess?"

"There's more," Andy announced. "Anything Wright knew about Lady Hannah, you knew. You knew how Mr. Finestra died, and you also knew Hy Court and Rich Ledger had a meeting with his widow the day before she was shot.''

"Yeah?" Scats said, his eyes veiled. "What of it?"

"You tell me," Andy demanded. "Right now.''

Scats started to laugh. Andy took a step toward him and the singer's mirth was cut off as he cowered. "No laughing," Andy said. "You give me any more of that ho-ho-ho and I'll push your tongue down your throat.''

"What do you want to know?"

"When were you born?"

"Eighteen ninety.''

"What's your sign?"

"Cancer.''

"What's Spanish for 'eat the door'?''

"What?''

Andy screamed incoherently.

"*Coma la puerta!*" Scats yelled in fear.

"Where did you learn Spanish?" Andy asked.

"Cuba, man, Cuba. Met Hannah there. In . . . 1933 . . . '34, maybe.''

"First time you met Mrs. Finestra?" Andy wanted to know.

"No, man. We met for the first time in Boston during 1928, just before her husband . . . died." Scats found himself almost kneeling before his persecutor. He puffed himself up, bragging. "Don't tell my wife or anything, man, but me and the Mrs. Finestra had a little tryst there."

Andy's countenance was horrible to see. It was a satire of a sickly leer. "You like women, don't you, Scats?"

"Uh . . . yeah, man. What's wrong with that?"

"Nothing," Andy said in a singsong. "Where were you on the day Mr. Finestra died?"

"Hey, you can't pin that on me," Scats insisted. "I was in Chicago, man. I was leading the band at Big Al's Speak E-Z."

"Al Capella's place?" Andy asked incredulously, his previous mood broken.

"Yeah, that's right," Scats said hopefully.

"You weren't there in early '34, were you?"

"No. I told you, man. I was in Cuba then."

"You sure you weren't in Illinois in '34, right?"

"I swear on my honor, man. I was wailing in Havana at The Perfumed Garden club."

"You weren't in Chicago moving moonshine and kidnapped teen-agers across the Illinois border into Sault St. Marie, is that correct?" Andy's eyes were shining.

"Oh, my God, no man."

"Girls who go out on dates for just a little illicit nip and the next thing they know they're chained to brass beds in Canadian brothels.

You weren't singing the blues to them, were
you, Scats?" Andy was all sweetness and light.
    Scats was horrified. "No, no, no. Cross my
heart."
    Andy looked him in the eyes.
    "Hope to die?"
    "Hope to die, man."
    Andy sighed, seemingly deflating before
Scats. The singer stopped holding his breath
and Andy stopped hyperventilating.
    "You okay, man?" Scats inquired, even risk-
ing putting a hand on Andy's shoulder.
    "Much better, thanks. Whew! That's a relief.
I would have had to push your Adam's apple
into your spinal column if you had been around
then and there."
    "Well, don't worry about that, man," Scats
chuckled. Andy put up a warning finger.
"Oops, sorry. No laughing. But don't worry,
man. I don't like my women chained down. I
like 'em walkin' and talkin' in their high heels
and tight dresses." He sighed. "Streets of
Paris, man. Streets of Paris."
    "Cuba in the year of 1933," Andy said.
    "Or '34," Scats added. "Ask Willa."
    "That's okay," Andy said wearily. Exhaus-
tion had come over him like a fog bank. It was
all too sad, too stupid, too useless. People killing one another for money. What a waste.
Andy couldn't wait until he got off this lurching purgatory and got back to Hollywood,
where people went nuts in the name of love. All
he wanted to do now was find Heller, give him

the letter, tell him about the needle mark on the back of Hy Court's neck, and report this conversation verbatim.

Later, Chico read the letter. "Well, this backs up what Hy Court admitted to Trace about his meeting with Lady Hannah. And it explains the envelope in Hannah's room postmarked Boston. This was the letter inside."

"Only one problem," Jack Miles growled.

"What's that?" Chico asked.

"It still doesn't tell us anything we didn't know. Like who the killer is; like who the jewel thief is."

Phil Phlem rose to his feet. "Well, maybe I'll figure it out," he said, "and save all you the trouble."

Trace hooted.

"Fat chance," Andy Baltimore said.

"We'll see," Phlem said.

# CHAPTER 14

"You appear a most understanding man, Dr. Phlem." While dabbing the corner of one eye with a pristine hanky, the grieving widow fixed the detective with the glare roosters shot to the East while announcing the dawn on slim immediate evidence. More than to assert fact, her statement was designed to make Phlem rise to the occasion.

"Yeah, yeah," Phlem said.

Having introduced himself to Sue, Mrs. Hy Court, as "Phlem, Ph. d.," he did not correct her calling him "Doctor."

Named for an expectoration, Phlem felt entirely justified in doing what he could to bring up expectation of himself in the surmise of other people.

"Dear Hy drowned only four hours and twenty-three minutes ago," said the grieving widow without looking at her wristwatch studded with rubies and emeralds.

Sharply, Phlem pounced on the point. "Drowned?"

Sue Court smoothed the dry handkerchief on

her knee. "Hy loved the water so. Been swimming since he was a boy."

"Must have been tired, ma'am."

"In college, at Boston University, they called him 'Hy Tide.' Captain of the swimming team, you know." She looked across the Showtime Lounge aboard the Cunard *Countess*. "I'm so grateful dear Hy died in the element he so loved."

"Ma'am?"

"I'm delighted the dear thing drowned."

Phlem shifted a little uncomfortably in his chair. "Then I'm afraid I have bad news for you."

"Oh?" Sue Court readied her hanky.

"Your husband didn't drown."

"But he was found in the swimming pool."

"Yes, ma'am."

"Face down."

"Yes, ma'am."

"Not swimming."

"Yes, ma'am."

"Not breathing."

"Yes, ma'am."

"Inert."

Phlem felt it was time to help out. "Deader than a mackerel."

"Dr. Phlem." Sue Court fixed her dry, clear eyes on her interrogator. "All that indicates, to me, drowning."

"Curare, ma'am."

"You mean Father Blue? He's a curare, isn't he? What does he have to do with it?"

"Curare is a poison, ma'am — as I get it,

featured by the Indians of South America. They dab their arrows with it when they shoot an animal, or an in-law — whatever. If their unwilling target moves and the shot proves to be just a grazing, they still have a kill." Phlem sat forward in his eagerness to bring charade to his exposition. "Soon as it hits the bloodstream..." With both hands Phlem grabbed his chest, then his throat, then his head. "Contortions..." He twisted his body in mock agony in his chair. "Convulsions..." Phlem proceeded to jerk his limbs and head to make convulsions real to the grieving widow. "Agony . . ." He rolled his eyes. "Gagging . . ." Phlem tried to cough himself up. "Death..." Phlem went limp in the chair.

"Well done, Phlem!" Sue Court clapped her hands.

"Thank you, ma'am." Phlem resumed his version of the vertical.

"How talented you are!"

"Had it from the ship's doctor, ma'am. A pathologist as a boy, he ran away and joined a traveling mime company before joining the ship."

"How very interesting."

"Yes, ma'am. The doc says your husband died of curare poisoning. His contortions and convulsions in the swimming pool caused him to take aboard water and appear to have drowned."

"Hy didn't drown?"

"Oh, no, ma'am. He suffered."

"Typical of Hy. Think he was doing one

thing when all the time he was actually doing something else."

"Never heard of curare, ma'am?"

Although Sue Court fit easily into the category of "nice folks" in Philip d'Artagnan Phlem's view, and therefore generally would have been marked for ruination, Phlem's viciousness toward his fellowman in this instance was tempered by a separate ambition.

It was Wednesday.

Phlem had been aboard the Cunard *Countess* since Saturday.

He had drunk his rye.

He had eaten his food.

He had detected the defects of as many nice folks as time had allowed, and reported them to whoever would listen.

But in all that time no opportunity had presented itself for Phlem to express physically his contempt for women by abusing one in bed.

He missed that.

When the convention of private investigators traveling aboard the Cunard *Countess* had raised the question as to who was going to impose upon the recent widow's grief to play the four *w*'s and one *h*, Phlem leaped at the chance.

Not only was Sue Court a widow, but Phlem, needless to report, had already detected (and reported, widely) what could be described as a moral defect in her way of life. As part of the subjugation Phlem considered seduction, he was eager to spring his knowledge on her.

Her moral defect boded well for Phlem's ambitions.

He had no intention of alienating the grieving widow totally until he had gotten her clothes off.

"Curare," she said blankly.

"Curare."

"Oh, yes." A tiny wrinkle appeared between her eyebrows. "Isn't that the stuff I use to remove nail polish?"

"Curare, ma'am?"

"I think that's the name of it." More assertively, she said, "Surely everyone travels with curare, Dr. Phlem."

"You must be mistaken, ma'am."

"Oh, no. I'm seldom mistaken about words. I used to be literary," she said, as one might admit once having had two heads. "I have my degree in English, from Boston University." Again Sue Court's smile sought understanding from Phlem. "In the Western Hemisphere, one does want one's degree in English from a Boston university, doesn't one?"

Phlem hadn't learned his language by degrees.

He'd got it with Original Sin.

"Before marrying Hy," Sue Court continued, "I was an editor at *The Ladies' Home Companion.* I was in charge of rejections." Sue smiled at the blank hanky on her lap. "Oh, no, don't be impressed. It was an easy job, really. It allowed me to do my nails all week. Then, between three-thirty and four-thirty, Fridays, I simply

stuck little notes to all the manuscripts that
had been sent in. The notes said, 'Regrettably,
your manuscript does not fit into our publishing needs at present. Thank you for thinking of
*The Ladies' Home Companion*.' The mail boy
did the real work. He had to carry them
downstairs and lick the envelopes.''

Philip d'Artagnan Phlem forced his mind
back above the waist.

"In fact, it was at a reunion of Boston
University alumnae that I met Hy, in 1923.
He'd gone on to Harvard Law School. We were
married in 1925. Dear Hy.'' The widow sighed.
"Such a man. He didn't want me to work, of
course. Thought it might reflect on his abilities
as a breadwinner. I've kept up my literary interests, of course. I write short stories. Send
them out to magazines. No, nothing published
yet. Somehow, my short stories don't seem to
fit anyone's present publishing needs. But I'm
certain I'll satisfy a need, someday.''

Quickly, Phlem crossed his legs.

"Hy, of course, was a very good provider. He
and some classmates invested in a hotel, and
did quite well with it. Of course, it went smash
in 1929. . . . Desperate, having tried to make
an honest living, Hy then had to turn to the
law. . . .''

"Who were your husband's partners in the
hotel, ma'am?''

"You see, that's the sort of thing I don't
know. Hy was so very protective of me. If ever

I asked a question about business, he'd say,
'Don't worry your pretty little head, sweetie.
Leave the worry to Hy.' "

"You didn't know any of them?"

"Well, Rich Ledger . . . ."

"I was about to bring his name up."

"Rich did my husband's accounting. He'd
come to the house, work with Hy. . . ."

"Yes?"

"I'd ask him things. . . ."

"So?"

"He'd answer. You see, unlike Hy, Rich discovered a genuine respect for my intelligence.
When Hy began traveling so much —"

"Traveling? Where?"

"I never knew, really. On business. Wherever
men travel, on business."

"What kind of business?"

"He never said. Anyway, Rich would continue his visits to the house even when Hy
wasn't there. To seek my advice."

"Is that what you call it?"

"Call what?"

"Hanky-panky."

"What which?"

"Hanky-panky, Mrs. Court. You're so good
at English. Didn't Boston University teach
you hanky-panky?"

"Of course."

"You and Rich Ledger were lovers."

"Whatever makes you say such a thing?"

"Your husband out of town a lot. His accountant visiting you all the time your husband was gone. Mrs. Court, your husband's accountant did a number on you."

"How do you figure that?"

Phlem initiated his subjugation. "I've seen you two by the pool. Neckin' like whoopin' cranes."

"You must be confusing me with —"

"This morning at four o'clock, I saw Ledger come out of your stateroom."

"He had come to discuss some business with my husband."

"Your husband has spent every night aboard this ship in the gambling casino. And other places. Dessert till dawn."

"Rich has been an especially good friend, this past year and a half. I've found him a great comfort."

"Look, lady, I didn't get no particular degree in readin' and writin' like you did, but I know what screwin' around means."

"A carpentry term, isn't it?"

"You and Ledger have been screwin' around, behind your husband's back."

"What an indecent expression. Really, Dr. Phlem, your imagery —"

"I don't mind."

"You don't mind what?"

"Any port in a storm."

Sue Court looked through a porthole. "What storm?"

"I mean, I don't mind if I do."

"Do what, Dr. Phlem?"

"I mean, as long as you're giving it out."

"Dr. Phlem!"

"Listen, lady, don't come all over virtuous with me. I can nail you one of two ways. Take your choice."

"You have nothing on me."

"Oh yeah?"

"Oh yeah!"

"You and your husband's accountant, Rich Ledger, have been playin' fiddle-faddle for years. You don't call that a motive for murder?"

"You mean, you think one of us . . . ?"

"The deceased married you, deprived you of your career, put you on a shelf like a laundered dress shirt."

"He was my husband. I was his wife."

"Wife? Ha! You spent your time between the covers with your husband's bookkeeper! The time came to bump your husband off with nail polish!"

"You think you're fingering me!"

"Not like I'm going to, lady."

"This smacks of blackmail. I don't care what happens to me. I'll not give in to your disgusting —"

"You care what happens to Rich Ledger?"

"Of course I care about what happens to Mr. Ledger."

"I've got you two lined up for conspiracy."

"That's rich!"

"Your husband had a five-hundred-thousand-dollar life insurance policy. Double indemnity. Isn't that true?"

"I've told you — my husband kept me in the dark about his business affairs."

"Yeah, but Ledger knew about them. Maybe

he even arranged the policy on your husband's life. You're in this together."

Sue Court made herself more comfortable in her chair. "What's your point, Dr. Phlem?"

"That's what I want to show you."

"Are you saying that if I don't abide by your obscene wishes, you intend to make trouble for Mr. Ledger and me?"

"You got it, babe."

"You can't be serious."

"Why not?"

"My husband chilling in the ship's freezer —"

"So? I'm not a home breaker."

"You're a private investigator."

"Just trying to get to the bottom of this affair, ma'am."

"If you had any real suspicion, or evidence that Rich Ledger and I had anything to do with my husband's death, you'd be duty-bound to report it."

"Duty shmooty. Ph. d. Phlem first; justice second: That's my motto."

"And how do you connect us to the death of P.I. Jones? He was poisoned, too, wasn't he?"

"Practice, ma'am, practice. You and Ledger were just practicing."

"And Lady Hannah? Why would we have shot Lady Hannah?"

"Oldest gag in the book. You kill several people, make the crimes look related, when your real purpose is to kill only one. In this case, the only one you and Ledger really wanted dead was your husband, Hy Court."

Sue Court's eyes narrowed. "You don't believe any of this."

Phlem smiled broadly. "No, ma'am, I don't."

"You just want to get me in bed with you."

"There you go."

"If I don't do as you say, you will make a lot of trouble for us . . . having seen Rich leaving my stateroom and all."

"A lot of trouble."

"Dr. Phlem, you are the most repulsive man I've ever encountered."

"Likely so, ma'am. What's a repulsive man to do?"

"You make murder occur as an excellent idea."

"You slay me."

"I just might."

"What will it be, ma'am?" Phlem leaned forward. He put his hand on her knee. He looked her square in the eye. "Exposure? Or, exposure?"

She brushed his hand off. "If it's the last thing I do, I'll see you in court."

"Uh-uh, ma'am." Phlem put his hand back on her knee. "You'll see me in Mrs. Court."

For a long moment, Sue Court studied Phlem's eyes. "If I do as you demand, won't I be admitting guilt?"

Phlem shrugged. "Who cares? Maybe you and Ledger actually did commit all these murders. If you bumped off Jones, fine with me. One less competitor in the field. Who cares who killed Lady Hannah from Havana? Who cares who killed Hy Court? As long as I get mine."

Studying Phlem's liquid orbs, Sue Court thought long and hard. "I have a dentist appointment next week."

"Oh?"

"Being delayed by the police in Puerto Rico would be a dreadful inconvenience."

"Yes, ma'am."

"Bad enough I'm going to have to lay out a Court."

"There's time for everything, ma'am."

Sue Court sat straight. "All right, Dr. Phlem. I accept your proposition."

"I thought you would."

"Meet me tonight. Eleven-thirty."

"Where?"

"Beside the swimming pool."

Philip d'Artagnan Phlem was pleased to report to his colleagues that he had interrogated Sue Court extensively, and had found no reason to consider her a suspect of murder or murders.

He so reported well before eleven-thirty that night.

# CHAPTER 15

The French were insufferable little pigs, but they did have a knack for the correct phrase, Leslie Dither thought. And the phrase he had in mind now was *Cherchez la femme*.

"Find the woman."

So when he had heard that bad American excuse for a bad American private detective — what was his name, Catarrh . . . no, Phlem, that was it — when he had heard him talk the previous evening about the possibility of Hy Court's wife, Sue, having an affair with Rich Ledger, Dither thought that the case was nearing its conclusion.

As he had expected, the Americans had done nothing but bustle about and learn nothing. But this business of Ledger and Mrs. Court being lovers — now, this could mean something to the trained intelligent operative.

Suppose they had killed the private detective because he had found out something about them, perhaps that they were the jewel thieves. Suppose they had killed Lady Hannah because she had surprised them trying to steal her jewels, the Caribbean Blues. And suppose they had killed Court to collect on his five-hundred-thousand-dollar insurance policy and to clear the way for them to take their romance public.

It all seemed highly logical to Leslie Dither and he was going to ask Rich Ledger about it.

He asked him about it at the bar on the back observation deck, where he found the balding husky accountant.

"That is quite simply the stupidest theory I ever heard," Ledger told Dither.

"I would have expected nothing less from you in the way of protestation," Dither said. "It is rare that a murderer will simply own up to his crime. Or crimes, as in this case."

"I really think you need psychiatric help," Ledger said. "Is there a psychiatrist aboard the ship?"

"I don't believe in that Viennese mumbo jumbo," Dither said. "Why don't you just confess to your crimes? It will make your head free and bring you great inner peace."

"I'll do it if you'll confess to your raving lunacy," Ledger said.

"Now, now, old chap. I really hadn't wanted this to degenerate into a name-calling contest."

"Then stop calling me and Sue murderers," Ledger snapped.

"How about *lovers*? Would you accept that label?"

Ledger turned and took a long swallow from the drink in front of him before answering.

"Sure," he said. "No secret about that anymore, not with old Hy dead now. Sure, Sue and I were lovers. And are lovers. But we would have taken our passion secretly to the grave rather than do anything to hurt Hy. He was my friend, you know."

"You have a curious way of dealing with friendship," Dither said.

"I don't think I want to talk to you anymore," Ledger said.

"I don't think you understand what's exactly at stake here," Dither said. Before Ledger could speak, Dither started to count off on his fingers. "First of all, there is a posse of American lunatic detectives running around, grilling everybody. Second, for some reason, the steamship line thinks that this is acceptable behavior. Third, you can be very sure that when this ship returns to port, the police are going to get a full report on Mr. Friendly's letter claiming that you murdered — with your good friend, Mr. Court — Lady Hannah's husband. Now, I and I alone can help you. Because of my international reputation as an investigator, I and I alone can prevent this snarling pack of jackals from bringing you down. Now I think it is in your best interests to speak to me."

Ledger considered that while finishing his drink and signaling to the bartender for another.

"All right," he growled finally. "I'll tell you anything."

"Okay, as you Yanks say. Did you kill Lady Hannah's husband?"

"No."

"Why did Ernest Friendly say you did?"

"The ravings of a dying man," Ledger said. "Hy and I killed nobody. Demitrio jumped because the hotel was losing money and he couldn't face the shame of being a failure."

"When did you start sleeping with Mrs. Court?"

"Eighteen months ago or so. Hy was out of town at a convention and I looked in on Sue to see how she was. She told me how her life had been wasted because Hy would not let her continue to be a writer. She was unhappy about it and couldn't tell Hy. So she told me. I comforted her and one thing led to another. Then we decided not to spend so much time together because neither of us wanted to hurt Hy's feelings."

"Did you kill Hy Court?"

"If I was worried about hurting his feelings, would I kill him? You ask stupid questions for a detective," Ledger said.

"You might think them stupid," Dither said. "But there is method to everything I do. Time will prove me right."

"If you're counting on time proving that Sue or I had anything to do with killing anybody, you're going to have to wait till the next millennium."

"We'll see. The night Lady Hannah died. It was midnight. Where were you?"

"Sue and I were out here, sitting near the swimming pool."

"Planning, no doubt, what to do with her inconvenient husband?" Dither asked.

"Wrong again. We were just talking about how sad things were sometimes and they never worked out. Why hadn't I met her before Hy? Maybe we would have been married and led a happy life instead of sneaking around. Stuff like that."

"Sounds very maudlin to me," Dither said.

"But it doesn't sound homicidal, does it?"

"I admit that it doesn't. When did you know that Hy Court had a half-million-dollar insurance policy on his life?"

"The day he applied for it. He borrowed money from me for the first premium. That was maybe ten years ago. If I wanted to kill him for the insurance, I would have done it before this."

"Why did Lady Hannah invite you on this ship to meet her?"

"I'm sure you know by now. We thought — Hy and me — that she wanted to talk about opening a new resort. Instead, she wanted to blame us for her husband's death. All because of that stupid letter from Ernest Friendly. We told her where to get off. We left. Hy went drinking. I went to find Sue and tell her what happened. That was that. I don't know anything more."

"You handled all the finances of the hotel?" Dither asked.

"Yes."

"Didn't you know the hotel was in trouble?"

Ledger hesitated. "Yes. I knew. But you couldn't tell Demitrio bad news. He only wanted to hear good news."

"Maybe some small dose of bad news, administered early enough, might have prevented him from jumping out a window."

"Maybe," Ledger said. "We'll never know, will we? Don't forget, he was my friend, too."

"Who do you think killed the people on this ship?" Dither asked.

"Talk to Hilda Johnson," Ledger said.

"Why?"

"Because all Hannah's talk about us killing her husband gave Ernest Friendly — Hilda's brother — a bad heart. I think she might have killed Hannah for revenge."

"Then why would she have had anything to do with Friendly's letter accusing you of murder?"

"I don't know. Maybe it was her way of clearing her brother's reputation. I don't know. Ask her." He finished the new drink in one long swallow, borrowed Dither's fountain pen to sign the check, and said, "I have to go now."

"I'd suggest that you don't leave the jurisdiction," Dither said ominously.

"How am I going to leave the ship on the high seas?" Ledger questioned. "You truly are an idiot."

Dither dutifully reported this conversation to all the other private detectives later that evening. None of them seemed interested. Too bad for them, Dither thought. When he solved the crimes, they would be sorry.

And he *would* solve the crimes. Of that he was sure.

All he needed was a good suspect, hopefully not an Englishman.

Chico had walked out onto the deck. Nate Heller noticed a slump to her shoulders and followed her outside.

"What's the matter?" he asked.

She raised her face to him. Her cheeks were tear-stained. "I'm a flop at this business," she said. "I talked to Hilda Johnson and never found out she was Ernest Friendly's sister. I saw the middle initial *F* on her monogram and never put it together. I'm worthless."

Heller put a consoling arm around her shoulder. "No, you're not. You're just young. And there's an easy cure for it."

"Yeah? What's that?" Chico asked.

"Just hang around. You'll get older. We all do."

They stood side by side, looking out into the night-darkened waters of the Caribbean.

"Yeah," Chico said not convincingly. "I'm just not much help in finding the murderer of your partner. I'm sorry, Nate."

"Don't worry about it," Heller said. "We'll get him. I know it. We'll get him."

DATE: Wednesday, May 20, 1938
TIME OF DEPARTURE: 4:00 P.M.
DESTINATION: Antigua
TIME OF ARRIVAL: 8:30 A.M.
DISTANCE: 201 nautical miles
WEATHER CONDITIONS: Rain and
    rough seas.

# CHAPTER 16

"No, I don't want lunch. I don't want anything," Trace snarled as he slid into his seat with the other private detectives and slammed his glass of gin-on-the-rocks down onto the dining table.

"You're in a fine mood," Chico said. "What's the matter with you?"

Trace used his napkin to wipe up the drops of liquor that had spilled from his glass.

"You know," he said, "someday somebody's going to invent a clear liquor that doesn't taste like juniper berries. I hate the taste of juniper berries. Who the hell ever heard of eating a juniper berry? Why should I have to drink one?"

"Why not drink Scotch, then?" Phlem asked.

"Because when I spill it on my clothes, it stains them and you can always tell I've been drinking. I need a clear liquor. I just want one that doesn't taste like juniper."

Dither said, "They have one. I've tasted it."

"Yeah? Where?" Trace asked suspiciously.

"In Russia," Dither said. "They make it out of potatoes. It's called vodka."

Trace snorted in derision. "Forget it," he said. "Nobody's ever going to drink some Communist rotgut made out of potatoes. If you're all smart, none of you will buy vodka stock."

"If you're finished with your lecture, are you going to tell us why you're so cranky?" Chico asked.

"Sure. I'll tell you. I was just with that phony fortune teller, Deja Bleu. And I thought I had the whole thing solved, but it didn't work out."

"Why not?"

"You know. Her folks were missionaries named Blue like the color, not that phony French spelling. And that Reverend Peter Blue — his folks were missionaries, too, and so I thought him and this woman were secretly related. But it didn't turn out that way. They're not related."

"Trace," Andy Baltimore said, "do you mind if I ask you a question?"

"Go ahead."

"Suppose they were related. What importance is that?"

"I don't know all the fine details," Trace said. "What I know is that if they were related and they didn't bother to tell anybody about it, then it *must* be important, and so they're liars, and if they lie, they probably killed everybody. It's obvious, isn't it?"

Chico looked at the rest of the table and held up her hands. "Don't argue with him, folks.

This is what he calls being logical. Trace, what happened with Deja Bleu?"

"Her name used to be Deena Blue and she grew up in Cuba. She's been reading palms and Tarot cards and stuff like that since she was about seventeen. She just up and walked away from her missionary folks. Then about five years ago, Hannah came to the hotel where this woman was working, had her read Tarot cards or something, and they became friends. So she offered Deja Bleu a job at The Perfumed Garden. She gave her the new name and bought her clothes to look the part. But not those silly hats. Deja said she wouldn't wear any silly hats with big hatpins."

Trace looked around the table for sympathetic eyes, but everyone was busy eating, looking down at their plates. He decided to wait until somebody was paying attention to him. He sipped his drink.

Finally, Heller looked up and said, "So? Get on with it. What happened with her?"

"Well, there's Deja at The Perfumed Garden, having a good time, being Hannah's friend and blah-blah-blah and like that. They were real good friends. Real good. Did you know that Hannah left Deja Bleu a hundred thousand in her will to set up some kind of psychic research center in Cuba?"

"Sounds like a motive to me," Jack Miles said.

"Well, maybe," Trace said. "But they were real friends, from all I can figure out. I don't think she is lying. She said Lady Hannah was a terrific person. Bad temper, don't get on her wrong side, and she carried a grudge, but if you were her friend, you were her friend."

"So? Any ideas? Does she have a suspect in mind?" Dither asked.

"Yeah. But I don't believe it," Trace said.

"Who's she suspect?" Chico asked.

"She thinks that Scats Allegro did it."

"But you don't buy it. Why?" Chico asked.

" 'Cause I know about things like this," Trace said. "It turns out that when Allegro came to the island in '35 to work for Hannah, Deja Bleu fell in love with him. But all he had eyes for was Willa Wright. So she's just saying that Scats did it because . . . well, you know . . . hell, fury, woman scorned — that stuff."

"They found those Tarot cards next to Hannah. Were they Deja's?"

"Yeah," Trace said. "She said she left there just before the cocktail party. Ignore them. She's just sore because the Lovers card didn't have anything to do with her and Scats. Three years and she is still carrying a torch for that guy."

"He's probably got rhythm," Chico said. "All musicians got rhythm."

"Maybe," Trace said. "But he's not beating on her drum. She's carrying a grudge. She told me that he was in some kind of trouble with the law in Chicago. She overheard him and Hannah talking about some gangster named Big Al Capella."

"I told you *that*," Baltimore said huffily.

"Yeah. I know. But I wasn't listening," Trace said.

"She doesn't seem to have a kind word to say for anybody?" Phlem asked Trace.

"Susie Tong. She thinks Susie is real sweet," Trace grumbled. "Everybody around here is real sweet. I'm going to waste this whole cruise looking for a damned murderer."

"Where was Deja Bleu when Hannah died?" Chico asked.

"After dinner she stopped in Hannah's cabin, but Hannah told her she had a meeting at eleven o'clock, so she kind of chased Deja. Then around eleven forty-five or so, she heard a noise in Hannah's cabin. Deja's got the cabin next door. So she went over and pounded on the door, but didn't get an answer, so she figured Hannah was taking a bath. I guess her psychic powers weren't working then. So she went back to her own cabin to go to bed and didn't know anything until she heard Susie screaming in the morning that Hannah was dead."

"Did Hannah tell her who the eleven o'clock appointment was with?" Chico asked Trace.

"No." Trace shrugged. "But we know it was with Hy Court and Rich Ledger."

"Who knows?" Chico said. "Maybe Hannah had two appointments."

"I'm annoyed," Trace snarled as he drank his gin. "I thought Deja Bleu might be the killer because of what Jones said when he died."

"What?" Heller asked. " 'She' for Hannah?

Or 'shy' for shyster? What's that got to do with Deja Bleu?''

"I thought he might have said 'shay,' like in 'shaman'... a witch doctor or fortune teller.''

Heller groaned. "Jones never said 'shaman,' '' he said.

"Don't confuse me," Trace said. "I'm confused enough already. I want to go home. I don't want to be here anymore. Do you realize that while we're cruising around the Caribbean, that lunatic Roosevelt is ravishing America? I want to go home.''

Heller looked up slowly from the other side of the table. His face bore a quizzical expression.

"I think pretty soon, Trace," he said. "I think we'll all be done pretty soon.''

"I'll believe it when I see it," Trace said.

"Stop complaining and drink your juniper," Chico said.

"Believe it," Heller said softly.

# CHAPTER 17

Thinking back to yesterday was a problem, especially considering the amount of time Jack Miles had spent in the casino bar. He knew that he had wanted to question Dan Risi yesterday, but he couldn't for the life of him remember why he had not.

That had to be done now, then.

Chances were good that Susie was sunning herself on the upper deck again. He'd give her time to finish and then go to meet Dan Risi, as she had done yesterday. He'd kill time waiting for her over a cup of coffee at the Starlight Café, on Five Deck.

Over his second cup Jack decided that he might know who killed P. I. Jones, but he was still stumped on Lady Hannah's murder. He was pretty sure they were killed by two different people, though, because of the two different M.O.'s. Whoever had shot Lady Hannah might have tipped her hatpin in curare to implicate her in Jones's murder, but he doubted it. He didn't think her killer had that much imagination. He'd turn out to be a slug-in-the-chest man, and not a crafty poisoner.

Checking his watch, he decided that Susie had had ample time to sun herself and would now be in the throes of passion in either her stateroom or Risi's.

He decided to try her room first, on Four-Deck, but as he entered the hallway he saw Dan Risi come out of her room. He ducked back out of sight, waiting for Risi to come to him.

As the man turned the corner into the "shopping arcade," Jack stepped into his path, startling him.

"Jesus Christ, man! Give a fella a warning."

"I'd like to talk to you, Risi."

The man's eyes narrowed as he studied Jack. Physically, both men were similar, average height, stockily built — both dark-haired and sporting facial hair, Jack a moustache, Risi a full beard and moustache. Not many people knew that Jack Miles's father's name was Milano, which Jack changed when he went into the ring.

Jack Miles knew a slimy dago when he saw one.

"You're Miles, the P.I. from New York."

"That's right."

"The one who's been bothering Susie."

"I don't know about bothering," Jack said. "I was asking her some questions."

"She told me."

"Good. Then you know what I'm going to ask you."

"You're not asking me anything, Miles, and you're not bothering her anymore, either."

"Come on, Risi, don't play hard with me, you haven't got the right equipment. You don't give a rat's tail for that girl."

"Believe me, Miles," Risi said, jabbing Jack's chest with his forefinger, "I can get harder than you've ever seen."

"Not likely."

Risi grinned and said, "Try me."

"Here?"

"Anywhere."

At that moment Jack thought he better understood Andy Baltimore. He would have liked nothing better than to bust Risi in the chops. In fact, he might be able to do that and still question him.

"The fitness center on Eight Deck," he said.

"Perfect. When?"

"Right now."

They walked to the elevators together, entered, and stood at opposite ends, eyeing each other like two fighting cocks about to be released. When they reached Seven Deck — marked "BR" on the elevator button for some reason — they got out and walked up the next level side by side, without exchanging so much as a word or a glance.

The fitness center was a small room equipped with some weights, a heavy bag and appropriate gloves, and a steam room. There were also some mats on the floor, placed there to guard against injuries.

Risi entered ahead of Jack.

Jack was saying "What do you want to —" when Risi spun on him and threw a sucker punch.

Just as Jack had suspected he would.

Since retiring from the ring, Jack had been in a number of scrapes, and every time it came to this, he felt reborn. Maybe he more than understood Andy Baltimore's urge to bust somebody, because he'd thoroughly enjoyed doing just that when he was in the ring

And he enjoyed it now.

He stepped aside and allowed the punch to whistle by his ear, then stepped in and hit Risi with a right hook to the body. The man gasped and started to turn around, away from the direction of the blow, beginning to sink onto one knee. One thing Jack had been known for in the ring was his ability as a finisher. Whenever he got somebody in trouble, he knew just how to finish him. Unfortunately, he was usually the one in trouble.

This time, however, he was in control and he knew how he wanted to finish Risi. He also knew that the man was in fairly good shape, and had — after all — asked for this.

As Risi was sagging, Jack hit him in the right kidney with a wicked right, and the man just screamed and crumpled to the mat.

From behind him Jack heard the door to the center opening. He turned and saw Andy Baltimore entering. Baltimore stopped and stared down at Risi, who was writhing in agony on the mat.

The look on Baltimore's face was a difficult one to interpret. He was sort of glassy-eyed, his mouth open, wearing the same expression as the perverts in Times Square peep shows.

Finally, the man spoke.

"I missed it! I missed it!" he bellowed, and Jack half expected him to stomp his foot. "I could have done something, I could have held him, or hit him —" Suddenly, with a hopeful look in his big, moist, puppy-dog eyes, Baltimore said, "Can I hit him? Please?"

Jack looked down at Risi, who was now making vague, choking sounds, and said, "Andy, I know just how to hit him and just where, because I'm a pro."

"Whaddaya mean? I'm a pro," Baltimore said belligerently.

"Andy, you'd probably kill him."

"I wouldn't —"

"Or paralyze him."

"Well, yeah —"

"And I need to have him talking."

"Well . . ." Baltimore said, almost kicking at the floor with his toe. "Okay."

"You can help me pick him up, if you like."

"Okay."

Together they lifted Risi and supported him between them.

"Can you tell me what you did?" Baltimore asked Jack. "Exactly?"

With both of them craning their necks forward so they could see Risi, Jack described the two-punch combination that effected the TKO.

"Ooh." Baltimore looked as if someone had

just stepped on his foot. "A kidney punch. That's cruel."

"I couldn't help it, Andy," Jack said. "It was just hanging there."

"Ooh," Baltimore said again, "a hanger."

Risi stirred between them, getting his feet beneath him.

"I've got him, Andy."

"Sure you don't need some help inter-rogating him?"

Jack had a vision of laying Risi out on a rack.

"I'm not going to interrogate him, Andy. I'm going to question him."

Baltimore looked sheepish. "Okay," he said, releasing Risi reluctantly, "he's all yours."

"I appreciate your help, Andy."

"I didn't do anything."

"I know, and I appreciate it."

"Sure, Jack," Baltimore said, "anytime."

As Baltimore left, Jack had the uncomfort-able feeling that he had made a new friend.

"Okay, pal, let's find a place for you to sit down."

Jack half dragged and half supported Risi to the stack of mats and sat down on them.

"How do you feel?"

"Get lost," Risi said, leaning forward and rubbing his kidney.

"Hey, friend, you're the one who tried to sucker-punch me, remember?"

"You were a professional boxer," Risi rea-soned. "I needed some kind of an edge."

"An edge is something I don't usually leave lying around."

Risi took a deep breath, let it out easily, and continued to rub his sore kidney.

"I've got some questions for you now, Danny boy, and my advice to you is to answer them."

"I'm not answering anything."

"I could always call my friend Andy back to help me out."

"Okay, okay, so ask," Risi muttered.

"I made a visit to the radio room and checked you out with some friends in New York. You don't have a very good reputation, Dan."

"So? A lot of businessmen don't play fair. That's how you get ahead in the business world."

"Not only in the business world," Jack said, "but in the underworld, as well."

Risi straightened up, then immediately winced at the pain in his kidney.

"What the hell do you mean, underworld? I'm no gangster."

"But you don't always play on the up and up, either."

"Do you?"

Jack was sorry to admit that Risi had a point.

"Keyhole peepers aren't the most reputable of characters in my book."

That was going too far.

"Watch the name-calling, bub," Miles said, prodding Risi's shoulder with stiffened fingers.

"Okay, okay, don't get testy."

Jack almost said, "Testy is my middle name," but it sounded foolish even to him. This character was bringing out the worst in him.

"Getting back to your reputation, a guy with your background doesn't strike me as the kind of guy who would spend money on a cruise just to be near a babe, no matter how exotic she looked."

Risi snorted and said, "Exotic," further illustrating Jack's point.

"You've dealt in hot jewelry before," Jack said. "All you wanted from Susie Tong was the lowdown on Lady Hannah. Admit it."

Risi sulked.

"Kidneys are funny things, Danny," Jack said. "They don't react well to repeating poundings." Jesus! He was starting to sound like a bouncer.

"Okay, so I wanted the jewels. That doesn't mean I didn't enjoy spending some time with Susie. She's real good in the sack, you know."

Jack rapped his knuckles across the bridge of Risi's nose and said, "You are definitely a gentleman."

"Hey!" Risi said, rubbing his nose, then wincing and rubbing his kidney.

"If this doesn't start to go a little more smoothly, you're going to be a mass of bruises and aches."

"What do you want?"

"I want a killer."

"Well, it's not me!"

"Who is it, then?"

"I don't know."

"Then allow me to tell you why I think it might be you."

Risi started to object, but Jack raised his hand, the way one might do to deter a small child, and Risi subsided.

"You've been sniffing after Susie until you could find a way to get close to Lady Hannah through her. When you heard about the cruise ship, you knew that you'd be able to think of a way to get what you wanted. And you finally did." Jack leaned in close to Risi to bring his next word home and said, "Murder!"

"That's ridiculous!"

"Come on, Risi. This whole thing is ridiculous. Help me end it so that the rest of us can enjoy what's left of the cruise. Confess."

"I can't confess, because I didn't do it."

"You stole the jewels, though, didn't you?"

"No." His reply was petulant.

"You know where they are."

Risi shook his head and repeated, "No."

"Yes, you know where they are because you stole them."

"You can't prove that," Risi said boldly.

"Sure I can."

Looking surprised — or alarmed — Risi asked, "How?"

"Come on, let's go." Jack grabbed Risi by the arm and yanked him to his feet.

"Where?"

"To your room. We're going to have us a look-see."

"You can't do that."

"Why not?"

"You don't have a search warrant."

Jack grinned at Risi and said, "Remember me? The disreputable keyhole peeper?"

Risi unlocked the door to his cabin and Jack pushed him inside ahead of him.

"Do you have a gun here?" he asked Risi.

"What would I be doing with a gun? I hate the damned things."

The funny thing was that Jack believed Risi. His distaste for guns seemed genuine, and since Lady Hannah was shot, that meant Jack didn't believe Risi was the killer. Still, if Risi had managed to liberate the jewels from Lady Hannah's cabin, that meant he had visited the murder scene just before, or just after, the actual murder. He must have seen something, but Jack knew that before he'd be able to get any kind of an admission from the man he'd have to find him with the jewels and use them as leverage against him.

"I'm going to look around," Jack said. "Sit on the bed."

There were two beds in the room so Risi said, "Which one?"

Jack put his hand on Risi's chest and pushed him down on one of the beds.

"Sit," he said. "Stay."

Jack began to search the room with one eye on Risi, but he was distressed to see that the man had somehow regained his composure. In fact, he looked downright smug. The jewels were there, and Risi didn't think Jack could find them!

Forty minutes later Jack had searched the

entire cabin — all eighty square feet of it — and, to Dan Risi's everlasting pleasure, had come up empty.

Jack looked at Risi, who placidly stared back, and said, "They're here. I know they're here."

"You're way off base."

Off base? What if the jewels weren't here? What if Risi had taken them and put them in one of the ship's safety deposit boxes that were made available to passengers?

That meant what Jack should be looking for was a key.

"Empty your pockets," Jack said to Risi.

"Why?" Risi sneered. "Are you going to steal my money?"

"Empty them, on the bed."

Risi did so without rising, just leaning one way and emptying a pocket, then the other to do the same.

"Back pockets?" Jack asked.

"There's nothing there."

"Turn them out."

Risi did so, pulling the insides of his back pockets out.

"The others, too."

Risi inverted all his pockets, saying, "Satisfied?"

"I'll let you know."

Jack studied the contents of Risi's pockets, which were unremarkable and contained only one key, and that was his room key.

Once again, Jack went through the room, looking in drawers, under drawers, beneath mattresses, lifting the desk to look under the legs, checking the seams of the curtains, inspecting the life jackets, going through Risi's suitcase, suits, and shoes.

He turned and looked at Risi. The man seemed somewhat less sure of himself, but if there was a key he was probably still fairly certain Jack couldn't find it.

Jack went into the bathroom, ran his fingers underneath the counter, looked at the bottom of the garbage pail, inside the shower, the commode, the sink. He checked to see if Risi had tied a piece of string to the key and lowered it down the drain.

No sale!

On the countertop he went through Risi's toiletry articles. Cologne bottles, after-shave, shaving equipment. He squeezed out the toothpaste tube — out of spite, really, because there was no way the key could have been in there.

Finally, he opened the two red soap holders. Both had perfect bars of soap inside. In the garbage pail he had found a third red holder, empty, and there was a bar of soap in the shower.

And then he remembered the fourth one.

He went outside, opened the desk drawer, and saw the fourth red soap holder. What was it doing in the drawer, and out of the bathroom?

He picked it up and opened it. Even stranger, this bar had obviously been used, since the smooth surface was smeared.

He turned around and faced Risi, who was suddenly engrossed in the cabin's ceiling.

Jack took the used soap bar out of the holder, dropped it to the floor, and ground his heel into it. He bent over, separated the piece, and picked up the key that had been secreted inside.

"Well," he said, holding the key in plain sight for Risi to see, "what have we here?"

Later, after he retrieved the jewels from the safety deposit box, Jack took a totally demoralized Dan Risi to Nate Heller. It was Heller's partner who had been killed — most likely by the same person who had killed Lady Hannah — which meant it was for Heller to question Risi about who he saw coming out of Lady Hannah's room just before he went in, found her dead, and stole the jewels.

There were, after all, certain codes to this business.

DATE: Thursday, May 21, 1938
TIME OF DEPARTURE: 6:00 P.M.
DESTINATION: Charlotte Amalie, St. Thomas
TIME OF ARRIVAL: 10:00 A.M.
DISTANCE: 201 nautical miles
WEATHER CONDITIONS: Overcast sky with
   some rain in the afternoon.

# CHAPTER 18

*Excerpt from operative's report, case file 714, date May 22, 1938. To the attention of George Donahue, vice-president, Cunard Line. Reporting operative: Nathan Heller, president, A-1 Detective Agency, Chicago, Illinois. Written en route during Caribbean cruise aboard Cunard Countess.*

*This will be my final report, George. The details follow.*

*Last night the ex-pug, Miles, recovered your goddamned jewels. So you and the line can rest easy on that score. The import-export "president" (never get too impressed with that title, George — I'm the president of A-1, remember) turned out to be my jewel thief. My jewel thief, however, did not turn out to be the killer. . . .*

*He* did *claim to have seen the murderer leave Lady Hannah's room. My first reaction was that Dan Risi really* was *the killer and was desperately trying to cast the blame off on someone else — a couple of someone elses, actually.*

*But what he said, and who he'd seen, made a certain amount of sense. It clicked with what the other detectives on board had discovered, and with some information that finally reached me via the radio room: some background info on a certain passenger aboard the Cunard Countess.*

*My immediate instinct was to confront the guilty son-of-a-bitch. But my second thought was: What if Risi was lying? What if one of these other detectives — some of whom were less than masters of deduction, George, let's face it — had left something out when they reported back to me, or failed to interrogate the suspects properly, effectively... ?*

*So I spent the rest of the day one on one with each detective, going over in detail what they had found; I spoke to several of the suspects on several muddy points, as well.*

*And by midnight I had put all the pieces together.*

*There was no reason to act like Charlie Chan and gather all the suspects. I knew who had done it. And, despite anything I might have said, I couldn't have done it without the other ops on board. Well, I could have done without that bumbler Trace, but never mind. His lovely associate more than made up for him.*

*I suppose you'd like to know, about now, who did it, and what I did about that "who," right, George? Well, I spent a long week on this tub, suffering through an investigation that made my head and heart hurt, and sea sickness is in there somewhere, too, so I'm going to make you*

's hubby, Hy, had a double indemnity
cy for half a mil, with Sue as the sole heir.
w's that for a murder motive, George?

fter Finestra's death in '29, Hannah packed
nd moved to her husband's villa in Cuba.
retary to Finestra before his death, willowy
la Wright accompanied Hannah to Havana
lent her five grand in return for ten percent
he action. With what remained of her late
band's dough, and what she borrowed from
a, Hannah opened The Perfumed Garden.
was a shrewd businesswoman and soon at-
ted a high-hat clientele. The Perfumed
den became the hot spot in Havana, cater-
to the chic, international set. But if
thing happened to Lady Hannah, Willa
ld inherit everything....

e famous African explorer I. B. Hunter
n taking vacations in Cuba in the early
ies. He went to the best resort on the
d — you got it, George: Hannah's Pered Garden. He and Lady Hannah spent a
f time together during one of his first stays
e, and it was rumored they were an
— though she never admitted it. The truth
'unter was wild about her, and even asked
er hand, and the rest of her as well. For
ile he held Lady Hannah's heart, but then
met that banana-republic politician
sta. Batista was rich and powerful and, ob-
sly, could do a lot for her. So Lady Hannah
Hunter his walking papers — though they
"bloody" row before Hunter stormed out.
l, Hunter just didn't seem to have a

wait. It's time for a formal report — it's time to
lay it out in front of you, all that which my
associates and I assembled.

Here, George, is the story behind the Case of
the Caribbean Blues.

Jonesy was killed with curare, a pinprick
found on his neck. Lady Hannah was the second
to buy the farm — shot in the chest, at close
range, in her cabin, with a .38. All of which
made it seem likely the murderer was somebody
she knew — somebody she willingly invited into
her cabin. A pillow was used as a makeshift
silencer — powder burns and bloodstains were
found on the pillowcase. Traces of curare were
found on the hatpin in Lady Hannah's hat, and
the Caribbean Blues had taken a walk.

We picked up several key clues in Lady
Hannah's room.

There was an empty envelope, postmarked
Boston, addressed to Lady Hannah. It came
from her deceased husband's ex-partner,
Ernest Friendly. This same letter turned up
later, George, as you know — but I'm getting
ahead of myself.

The second clue was left by Lady Hannah
herself — your classic "dying clue." In the few
moments before she was shuffled unwillingly
off this mortal coil, Lady Hannah fanned out
the Tarot deck. She put the Death card on top
of the deck and drew the Lovers card forward.

There were cigarette butts in the ashtray —
Hy Court's; and a cigar as well — Rich
Ledger's. Clues, or red herrings left by the
murderer? Chico missed them but I found them

in the wastebasket. Someone must have dumped the ashtray after they left.

Hy Court courted death next, embracing it in the cool blue water of the pool topside, Wednesday. At first, we all figured he'd drowned. Then the autopsy report came in. Court died from curare poisoning, and (again) a pinprick was found on his neck — this time in back, hidden in his hairline.

The missing-persons op, Baltimore, found Ernest Friendly's letter among Court's effects in the ship's morgue. Friendly wrote that he was dying, after suffering two massive heart attacks, and had instructed his sister to send the letter. In it was a complete confession of the embezzlement of hotel funds, and a detailed account of Finestra's death.

Did Hy Court murder Lady Hannah to keep her quiet about her husband's murder? Or is that just what the real killer wanted us to think? And if Court did kill Lady Hannah, who killed Court? His death had been staged to look like a drowning, but it was murder, by the same curare-tainted hand. . . .

So, George, I reviewed the suspects. Which is to say, anybody on the ship who knew Lady Hannah or had a motive for murder. The two most likely: Hy Court and Rich Ledger. They, along with Ernest Friendly, had been partners of Hannah's deceased husband, Demitrio Finestra, in the Finestra Hotel. According to Friendly's letter, Court and Ledger were responsible for Finestra's death.

Finestra, who did almost nothing hotel, reaped the greatest rewards ners gradually became bitter, resent an unspoken agreement, the three bezzling funds. By the end of 192 crash, Finestra had lost everything to look more closely at the hotel, whi been losing money. He ordered a audit, and soon learned that comp had been embezzled.

Finestra called a conference, s allegations, and threatened to pro three. Finestra promised to dest careers and have them sent up the riv

The partners panicked — Ernest h the-spot nervous breakdown, while Ledger backed Finestra toward the and threw him out. From the top fl hotel.

As for Willa, she was out to lunc time — but then that dizzy dame is fi "out to lunch." Once Finestra had t high dive into the empty pool that street below, Court and Ledger had and think quickly. They destroyed all of embezzlement, and told the po Finestra was depressed over the stoc crash and had committed suicide. Friendly wasn't directly involved murder, but was intimidated into silen other two.

To make matters even cuter, Cou Sue, was having an affair with Led

strong enough motive for killing Lady Hannah.
Too many years under the bridge.

On the other hand, Hunter was in desperate
need of some ready cash. Maybe he asked Lady
Hannah for the dough and got turned down . . .
or did he kill Hannah and take the jewels
instead?

About five years ago, Lady Hannah added
Deena Blue, a so-called "psychic," to her entourage. She hired Deena to work at The Perfumed Garden, reading palms and Tarot cards.
Lady Hannah changed Deena's name to
Madame Deja Bleu and bought her some duds
to suit the part. In her will, Lady Hannah left
one hundred grand to set up a "psychic
research center" in Cuba. Deja, though, never
really believed that she'd see the dough, since
healthy Hannah would no doubt be around for
a good long time. Having seen into the future
in this manner, maybe the Tarot turner decided
to change her destiny — and Hannah's — by
hastening the inheritance. . . .

Reverend Peter Blue (no relation) has his own
looney motive. He wanted the rocks, considered them a "national treasure" that ought
to be returned to Siam. He'd demanded that
Lady Hannah do so, but she'd just laughed at
him. Would he, a man of the cloth, kill to
retrieve those stones?

But the stones didn't really have anything to
do with the murder. Despite their color, the
Caribbean Blues were the biggest red herring of
'em all.

The sky was dark and overcast, as starless as

a movie from Monogram. Tonight even the breeze was muggy. Few people, even honeymooners, found anything to stand on deck and contemplate; only the inky water, with its rolling whitecaps, offered anyone anything to lean on a rail and ponder. Up on Eight Deck, the pool area was empty, the bar closed; the sky was spitting, the sea was choppy, and these upper decks I had to myself.

With one exception.

The top deck, the sun deck, up a short flight of steps from the pool area, was the site of a tearful rendezvous between two lovers.

One might even say "the" lovers.

"Just like the Tarot card, huh, kids?" I asked cheerfully.

The ship groaned, metal whining, as the Cunard Countess took a wave, and Scats Allegro, in his pretentious cape and Zootish tux, was holding a trembling young woman in his arms. She was a beautiful blonde in a classy, clingy black gown. Creamy breasts were spilling out a little, but the edge was off her beauty; her makeup was running. Part of it was the mist. Part of it wasn't.

"What do you want, Heller?" Scats asked. He was sneering, but his voice was strangely tentative — even afraid.

Willa just looked at me, eyes as wet as the night.

"Big party in the Showtime Lounge," I said. "Big-band music, though not up to your level, of course, Scats. Hate to see you sweethearts miss out on it."

"We'd like a little privacy," Willa managed pleadingly.

"Best place for privacy is the ship's morgue," I said, "though I understand it's getting a little crowded."

Willa winced at that, and Scats looked at me with hard, narrow eyes, the sneer turning even uglier.

I moved closer to them. The deck was filled with row upon row of deck chairs; in the background loomed the massive white mast, flags flapping, a string of white lights above us casting a soft-focus glow on the little scene. I couldn't tell if it was romantic or sinister. Maybe both.

They stood near the rail, near the shuffleboard area. "Keep your distance, man," Scats said. The fierceness of his expression wasn't matched by his voice, somehow. As gruff as it usually sounded, there was a tremor undermining it tonight. Good.

"We've been having a little convention this week, Scats," I said. "Some of my op pals and me. And we got a little bored — nothing to do but try and solve your occasional murder. And maybe nail your occasional murderer."

"I ain't your man, Heller."

"You sure aren't, but you are the murderer, all right."

"Like the man says — prove it."

I edged closer. My jacket was unbuttoned. Nine-millimeter under my left arm. Scats wasn't armed — that I could see. But he was a tricky bastard, and graceful for a big man.

"*You met Hannah in Boston in '28,*" *I told him.* "*Spent a wild weekend together, then went your separate ways.*"

"*She was a married lady, man. It was the right thing to do.*"

"*You can always be counted on for that, can't you, Scats? But a few years later, after her husband's death, you got back in touch . . . in Cuba. For old times' sake she gave you a job — as bandleader and singer with the hotel band. And when Hannah made it clear her hots for you had cooled, you made a move on little Willa here, and who could blame you? You were secretly married — and knew very well that Willa was Lady Hannah's heir. . . .*"

"*How often have I gotta play you the same tune, man? Like I said — prove it. It's all talk, man, all talk. . . .*"

"*Maybe Willa is more interested in what I have to say,*" *I said with a benign smile.*

*The girl shivered and clung to the big man. But she said nothing.*

*I said,* "*When Ernest Friendly's letter arrived, you steamed it open, Willa, before you delivered it to Hannah — and you showed it to the Scatman. Were you aware of what you were aiding and abetting, honey? That your big teddy bear here had just seen the perfect opportunity to get rich quick? That he figured Hannah was planning revenge of some sort on her husband's murderers, and all he had to do was make sure that she got caught? He could even*

*provide the corpses, if need be — the Scatman
always could improvise. And the upshot of it
all? You'd inherit, honey. Everything Hannah
owned would belong to you. And you belong to
the Scatman."*

She pulled away from Scats and sat on the
edge of a deck chair; she began to weep into her
hands. I felt sorry for her, a little. A little.

Scats stood there, cape flapping in the misty
night breeze, and he grinned his ersatz Satchmo grin; but the confidence was something
phony he was wearing, like the cape.

"You got nothin', man, nothin' but wind and
air and a little rain."

"I got plenty. I got witnesses and I got hard
physical evidence just waiting for the onshore
labs, and, most important, I got you. You, who
took along a Hannah-like hatpin — tipped in
curare — in case Hannah's revenge was limited
to legal means; if Hannah intended turning
Court and Ledger over to the cops, instead of
pursuing personal vengeance, you'd have to
either kill the partners and frame Hannah, or
vice versa. Vice versa would get you your
precious inheritance faster."

"Shut up," Scats said. His voice was no
longer growly, pseudo-colored; it was distinctly
white, and high-pitched, and unmistakably
frightened.

"Then at that opening-night cocktail party,
you spotted Jonesy. You knew he wasn't a
ship's officer. You knew he was a cop. Maybe

*you knew he was private, maybe not, but more important, you knew he had been a cop back in '34 in Chicago."*

*"So what?" he said. He seemed to be shivering. Not entirely from the cold, either.*

*"You told Baltimore that you went to Cuba in the early thirties. That you hadn't been back to Chicago since. I remembered you from there, but my memory wasn't exact. . . . I would've guessed you were around till at least '34 . . . and you were. You likened a babe in a skimpy outfit to those you saw at the Streets of Paris — which meant nothing to Baltimore, other than maybe you were talking about the real streets of Paris. But you weren't; you were referring to Sally Rand's old showcase, the Streets of Paris, at the Century of Progress Exhibition, the Chicago World's Fair — in 1934. The very year, I've been told, via radio, that you were wanted for questioning in a murder. The murder of an undercover cop investigating narcotics traffic among musicians."*

*"Questioning ain't no big deal," Scats said.*

*Willa's weeping, soft though it was, could be made out over the wind.*

*"You were a prime suspect, pal. Because of the undercover aspect of the investigation, it got no play in the press. And I wasn't a cop, then — I went private in '32. Jonesy, though, was a cop in '34. And he worked that case. You see, Jonesy didn't die saying 'she'; he died saying 'Chi——' for Chicago."*

*Scats swallowed thickly.*

*"You saw your whole future collapsing when you saw Jonesy at that party — and you didn't*

*need Tarot cards to predict it. But you had the hatpin at the ready, for Hannah, or Court and Ledger. . . . Frankly, I don't know which plan you intended to follow. I just know you abandoned it; you improvised again, you rascal, you — you told Willa to douse the lights, maybe without even telling her why, and my partner was dead. Jonesy was dead. Your doing, you lowlife bastard . . . "*

*"If you think I'm gonna crack," Scats said, his voice still white and afraid, "you're wrong. I know you're bluffing. I know you don't really have anything to go on . . . just air . . . just theories . . . unreliable witnesses . . ."*

*"You and willing Willa went to Hannah's cabin that night — around eleven-thirty. Hannah had a meeting with Ledger and Court, a confrontation, one would suppose. Anyway, Willa here kept watch in the hall while you knocked on the door — and your ex-lover let you in her cabin. Why shouldn't she? She didn't know you were there to kill her — until she saw the gun in your hand. No curare for death this time: It had to look like the work of Court and/or Ledger. You grabbed a pillow for a silencer, and then Hannah was on her way to heaven or hell, depending. You went out in the hall, to get Willa, during which time, the few seconds she had left, Hannah must have arranged her 'dying clue' — quickly pulling appropriate cards from the Tarot deck on the dresser nearby . . . implicating 'the Lovers' in her 'Death.' "*

*"That's the lamest riff I ever heard played," Scats said, lapsing into his phony patois.*

*"I don't know how willing Willa was to play*

*along,"* I said as her sobbing jumped in volume, *"but she helped 'set the scene': One of Rich Ledger's cigars and a couple of Hy Court's cigarette butts were dropped in the garbage pail, the Friendly letter was taken from its envelope. . . . Of course, if Court and Ledger had really killed her, they would have taken the envelope, too — but you wanted them implicated, so you left it."*

*"I . . . l-liked Hannah,"* Willa said. *"I wouldn't hurt anybody."*

*"No, but Scats here sure as hell would. And you helped him search the cabin for the jewels, didn't you, Willa? They weren't the object of the killing, but taking them might help throw suspicion elsewhere. After all, you didn't need to steal them — you would have inherited them."*

She swallowed and cried into her lace hanky.

*"Your search was interrupted, though, by a knock on the door . . . Deja Bleu had stopped by, and left when her knock drew no response . . . but this was enough to spook you. You felt you could return later, after the ship was sleeping, to search for the jewels. Then you took a walk on the deck — and Scats, no doubt, took that opportunity to toss the murder gun overboard."*

Scats edged away from me, his back to the railing. I edged closer.

*"What you two didn't know was that the jewel thief aboard — one Dan Risi — saw you leave. He was keeping an eye on Hannah's stateroom, waiting for her to take a late-night*

*stroll she had mentioned to her maid, Susie
Tong — whom Risi was romancing for info.
Anyway, Risi noted your hasty exit, used a
passkey to slip into the stateroom, and found
the body. He also found the jewels — that is,
the key to the jewels. Without touching anything else, Risi slipped out as quietly as he
came."*

"*I say the* jewel thief *killed her,*" Scats said,
some confidence climbing back into his grin.
"*After all, the cat admits he was in that room,
don't he?*"

"*He do, Scats, my man. He do. But he sure
wasn't the one who swam up behind Hy Court
in the pool down there, stabbing him in the
back of the neck with another curare-tipped object, leaving the Friendly letter among Court's
effects, ducking into the steam room to give
himself a damp alibi. You hoped — stupidly,
vainly — that this death would be written off
as a drowning, and the murders written off as
the work of the drowned man. The only one you
fooled was Trace, and that's no great feat.*"

"*A lot of people on this bucket coulda killed
Court,*" Scats said, his voice sounding whiter
and whiter.

"*Not really. Only a few people knew of the
contents of Friendly's letter, and only the
members of Hannah's household knew of
Hannah's penchant for hatpins. That elimi-
nated a lot of suspects, Scats. But not
Willa — and not, through her, you. Besides, I
began to get suspicious of you when you
reacted with concern when Court was killed. It*

*wasn't in character, 'man.' You hated Court and advertised the fact."*

*"You're wrong about one thing, Heller,"* Scats said.

*"Such as?"*

*"I didn't toss the gun overboard,"* he said, *and his hand came out from under the flowing cape and the gun roared, blocking out the sound of waves and the ship's engines and even Willa's sobbing-turned-to-shrieking as I dove for the deck and slid down the shuffleboard alley, yanking my own gun from under my arm, sliding on my stomach as shots ate up the wood around me.*

*My gun was in my hand and I was twisting around, but a shot caught my wrist, cut a red groove in the flesh, and my fingers wouldn't listen to me; they just popped right open and my gun tumbled from my grasp.*

*Then he was looming over me, a dark, massive figure with a Cheshire-white grin in it somewhere, and the glint of gun metal in one hand.*

*"No more!"* someone screamed.

*Not me.*

*Certainly not Scats.*

*Willa.*

*She rode his back, riding him like a demented child playing piggyback with an unwilling and confused daddy, one hand looped around his neck, a fist pommeling the side of his face, and he raised his gun in hand just long enough for me to live awhile, and my hands searched for my gun in the near darkness, didn't find it, but* the fingers that went scrambling over the damp deck found something round and hard — the shuffleboard puck! — and I hurled it like a discus at him.

It caught him in the stomach and he folded in two like a deck chair. She tumbled off and landed unceremoniously on her sweet confused butt, and I got up on my feet and charged him. Somebody was screaming again.

Me.

I grabbed his hand, the one with the gun, and dragged him, all four thousand pounds of him, to the nearby rail and slammed that wrist into the metal, and slammed it again, and the gun fell from his splayed fingers.

But he had recovered from the pain and surprise and was now enraged; his hands went for my throat and somehow my back was to the rail and he was bending over it. I slammed my fists into his side but he didn't seem to feel it; it was like pounding a punching bag in a gym but the response was even less, and the round, crimson, enraged face bearing down on me might scare me to death before my back was broken on the railing.

Then I got my knee where it counts, and his grasp on my throat popped open and so did his eyes and his mouth, and I got out from between him and the rail and then I did something, George, that makes me look a little bad. But you must understand the extremity of the situation. Self-defense it surely was. No court in any land will convict me.

I pushed him over the side.

*His scream was shrill and somehow as feminine as Willa's, which was simultaneous with his and formed an eerie harmony. He bounced off a lifeboat on the way down, turning his scream into a whimper of pain, and then, tangled in his cape, he went in the drink. A little whitecap of his creation followed.*

*Willa was looking over the side; I hung on to her, afraid she would follow her lover overboard. Oddly, she wasn't crying now. She was silent. Stunned into a mute beauty. Nor was she angry with me. Later, perhaps. Now, just numb.*

*The deck began to fill with passengers. The gunfire had been heard by someone, it would seem. Among them were my fellow investigators: Jack Miles, Andy Baltimore, Phil Phlem, Leslie Dither, Trace, and Chico.*

*I told them Scats had gone over the side.*

*Trace, who didn't seem to give a damn, stood with a drink in one hand and, lucky stiff, Chico in the other. Her lovely eyes were filled with compassion, even for the likes of Scats.*

*"He might still be out there!" she said. "We should throw in a life preserver, lower a boat, something. . . ."*

*"No need," I said. "Bastard sank like a stone."*

DATE: Friday, May 22, 1938
TIME OF DEPARTURE: Midnight
DESTINATION: San Juan, Puerto Rico
TIME OF ARRIVAL: 8:30 A.M.
DISTANCE: 72 nautical miles
WEATHER CONDITIONS: Bright sky and
  plenty of sunshine.

# EPILOGUE

The *Countess* has reached her final destination, the port of San Juan, and the cruise is over. The intricate ice sculptures which had drawn appreciative applause at the gala midnight buffet are melting, drop by drop. Cosmetics and toilet articles and jewelry are being hastily tossed into monogrammed carrying cases. The rest of the handsome matched luggage is being whisked ashore.

Hurried farewells are the order of the day. Shipboard friendships end in a flurry of goodbyes as addresses and phone numbers are exchanged. Most of these will be discarded in the coming weeks. The atmosphere of artificial shipboard intimacy evaporates when the passengers return to the outside world of family and familiar companions.

The three bodies will be removed from the freezer-morgue and discreetly wheeled ashore, well out of sight of the departing guests. The handcuffed and manacled notorious jewel thief, the murderous accountant, and the murderer's accomplice wife will be turned over to the custody of the San Juan police.

The other principals in the *Case of the Caribbean Blues* will assess their own lives. Some, like the detectives and the journalist, will have a sense of a mission completed. Others will have to find new employers, new patrons, new well-heeled lovers.

But for now the tale has been told. The last guests have disembarked. The Cunard *Countess* is being scrubbed and vacuumed and freshened for new arrivals. It is their turn to sail this evening through the lovely cerulean waters. *Bon Voyage* to them. Their trip will be pleasant and untroubled.

Our voyage is over. May your journey home be safe. Until we meet again, hail and farewell.

# POSTSCRIPT

~~~~~~~~~~~~~~~~~~~~~~~~~~~~

The United States Private Eye Association was formed before the Cunard *Countess* returned to port in San Juan.

Philip d'Artagnan Phlem was elected the first president.

Before the year was out, he had stolen the dues money from the other members, and the association never met again.

# ABOUT THE AUTHORS*

~~~~~~~~~~~~~~~~~~~~~~~~~~~~~~~~~~~~~~~~~~~

*Members of the Mystery Writers of America.

# MARY HIGGINS CLARK

Mary Higgins Clark was born in New York and is the 1987 President of the Mystery Writers of America. She has written six best-selling suspense novels and claims that when she isn't writing she feels as though she's playing hookey. Her great pleasure is the fact that many young people write to tell her that they began to enjoy reading after they "had to do a book report and your books were on the list and I read one and now I read lots of other books." Her fans also keep her humble. A recent letter from a 13-year-old said, "I like your books so much, I don't even mind the boring parts."

# MOLLY COCHRAN

# Max Allan Collins

Max Allan Collins is the author of the critically acclaimed historical novel *True Detective* (introducing Chicago private detective Nathan Heller), which won the Private Eye Writers of America's Shamus Award for Best Hardcover Novel in 1984. Its sequel, *True Crime*, was nominated for the same award in 1985; a third Nathan Heller novel, *The Million-Dollar Wound* (1986), was similarly acclaimed, with a fourth, *Neon Mirage*, due from St. Martin's Press in January, 1988. His writing credits include: three other suspense series, Nolan, Quarry, and Mallory; his latest book, *The Dark City*, a novel about real-life "Untouchable" Eliot Ness, which initiates yet another series (for Bantam Books). He is also the co-author of a Mystery Writers of America award-winning critical study of Mickey Spillane (*One Lonely Knight*, with James L. Traylor).

Collins has been the writer of the celebrated Dick Tracy comic strip since its creator, Chester Gould, retired in 1977. With cartoonist Terry Beatty, he created comic-book detectives

Ms. Tree and Mike Mist, as well as the recent DC mini-series "Wild Dog."

In his "spare time" he performs with a 1960s-style rock band. He lives in Muscatine, Iowa, with his wife, Barb, and their four-year-old son, Nathan. Of late, Barb has taken over the writing chores on the Crimestopper's Textbook feature in Dick Tracy and the Mike Mist minute mystery feature in the monthly *Ms. Tree* comic book.

# GREGORY MCDONALD

Author of eighteen books, seventeen of which have been fiction, fifteen international best sellers, twelve mysteries (the universally popular nine Fletch and three Flynn novels), twice winner of the Edgar Allan Poe Award (1975, 1977), Mr. Mcdonald is past president of the Mystery Writers of America. The Paramount-Universal film *Running Scared*, based on his 1964 novel, staring Gayle Hunnicutt and Robert Powell, directed by David Hemmings, was released worldwide (except in the United States, where it has never been released), in 1972. The Universal film *Fletch*, starring Chevy Chase, directed by Michael Ritchie, was released in 1985. A second Chase-Ritchie film in a Fletch series is to go before the cameras in 1988. In 1973 Mr. Mcdonald left *The Boston Globe* as Arts and Humanities editor (chief of critics) and critic-at-large columnist. *The Education of Gregory Mcdonald* (Warner Books, 1985) is compiled mostly of close-up sketches of happenings and personalities (John Wayne, Abbie Hoffman, Krishnamurti, Louise

Nevelson, Joyce Grenfell, Joan Baez, Gloria Swanson, Jack Kerouac, etc.) Mr. Mcdonald wrote during his seven years at *The Globe*. Other Gregory Mcdonald titles are: *Safekeeping, Who Took Toby Rinaldi?, Love Among the Mashed Potatoes (Dear M.E.)*. His most recent novel is *A World Too Wide*. In 1987, his mystery/comedy/drama, *Bulls-Eye*, was produced at the Cox and Curry Theater, Giles County, Tennessee. Gregory Mcdonald graduated from Harvard College in 1958. He married Susan Aiken in 1963. The Mcdonalds have two sons, Christopher Gregory and Douglas Gregory. Although they still maintain a home in Massachusetts, the Mcdonalds consider their homeplace to be in Giles County, Tennessee.

# RICHARD S. MEYERS

Richard Meyers has worked in every communications medium except radio. He co-wrote one film, served as special media consultant for the 1986 version of "The Twilight Zone" television show, then wrote and directed four made-for-videotape features in Los Angeles and Hong Kong. Although best known for his column in *The Armchair Detective* magazine and his Edgar Award-nominated *TV Detectives* nonfiction book, he has also served as contributing editor for three film magazines, and is author of infamous volumes concerning exploitation and Kung Fu movies. Under his own name and several others, he has written many popular science fiction, police, and espionage thrillers — all for Warner Books. His recent and upcoming work includes *The Kohga Ritual, The Zanjanko Secret*, and *Death on the Air: The TV Mystery*.

# WARREN MURPHY

Warren Murphy is the author of more than eighty novels, including the Edgar Award-winning *Trace* detective series, and the long-lived *Destroyer* adventure series, which was the basis for the motion picture *Remo Williams: The Adventure Begins*. He also wrote *The Red Moon*, selected by the West Coast Review of Books as Best Adventure Novel of 1984, and *The Ceiling of Hell*, winner of the Private Eye Writers of America's Shamus Award. *Grandmaster*, the first of Murphy's collaborative works with Molly Cochran, was an immediate best seller and earned the authors both the Mystery Writers of America's Edgar Award and the 1985 Fiction Writer's Award.

# BILL AND KAREN PALMER

Bill and Karen Palmer are the owners of Bogie's, the only mystery-oriented restaurant and bar in the world. Murder/dinner parties had their New York debut here, and the monthly events feature participatory whodunits in which everyone can become a detective.

After being involved with mystery weekends for over ten years, the Palmers created "Bogie's Murderous Mystery Tours" in January 1984. They have since perpetrated many murders in domestic and exotic locales. Members of the Mystery Writers of America, The Private Eye Writers of America, and the Crime Writers Association, Karen and Bill write, direct, and produce their analytical, play-fair whodunits.

The Palmers have appeared on TV on "Hour Magazine," "Daytime," the Channel 2 News, and twice with Joe Franklin on WOR. Their mystery weekend, "Murder at the Grand," was televised on WKYC TV. They have been interviewed on radio on the "Voice of America," Canada's "Basic Black Show", WBAI, the

"Patricia McCann Show" on WMCA, the "Warren Pierce Show" in Detroit, and the "Mystery Maize" on WNYE. They were among the winners of Showtime's contest "Murder in Space," and gave a talk on solving mystery puzzles and games at the January 1985 Mohonk Mystery Weekend. Bill has co-authored a radio mystery show which was played in Germany, Switzerland, and on England's BBC.

Both Bill and Karen hold black belts in Kokushiryu Goshinho Jujitsu and have been teaching for over thirteen years. Bill's self-defense class was listed in *New York Magazine* as one of the ten best in New York City. They currently teach at the West Side YMCA.

Bill, a fourth-degree black belt, holds the highest rank awarded in his style, and is the sole recipient of the "Renshi" teaching certificate. Both have also studied judo, aikido, and karate. They have co-authored a book entitled *Martial Arts Movies: From Bruce Lee to the Ninjas*, published by Citadel Press, and are currently working on their second book. They are film reviewers for the cable TV show, "Martial Art Forms," as well as for *Martial Arts Movie Associates* fanzine, and the forthcoming book *TV Key*.

Karen is a licensed psychotherapist/hypnotherapist, in private practice in New York City, and is listed in "Who's Who of American Women." She is a teacher of self-hypnosis, past life regression, and psychic development.

# ROBERT J. RANDISI

Robert J. Randisi is a well-known and respected private eye "activist" who has devoted much time and energy to promoting the Private Eye genre. To this end, some of his major accomplishments have been:

1. the founding, in January 1982, of the Private Eye Writers of America, a writers' organization that was fast in gaining the respect of the industry. He has served as vice-president of PWA, and has been editor of its newsletter, "Reflections in a Private Eye," since the organization's inception, and is now the permanent executive director;

2. He has created the Shamus Award, which is presented each year by PWA to the best in Private Eye fiction;

3. He has instituted the annual PWA Anthology, the first of which was *The Eyes Have It* — for which he was the editor — published in December 1984, by The Mysterious Press — in trade and limited editions — to much critical acclaim. Stories from the collection have won both Edgar and Shamus Awards. The second,

*Mean Streets*, was published by The Mysterious Press in October 1986, and garnered an Edgar nomination. The third, *The Shamus Game*, will be published by The Mysterious Press in 1988.

He is also the co-publisher and co-editor of *Mystery Scene* magazine.

In addition, Mr. Randisi is the author of six private eye novels of his own: *The Disappearance of Penny* (Charter Books, 1980), which features Private Eye Henry Po; and the "Miles Jacoby" series, *Eye in the Ring* (Avon, 1982), *The Steinway Collection* (Avon, 1983), and *Full Contact* (St. Martin's Press, 1984), a series that has received praise from the likes of Elmore Leonard and Harlan Ellison (a new Jacoby novel, *Separate Cases*, is forthcoming from Walker & Co.); and *No Exit from Brooklyn* (St. Martin's Press), which introduces Brooklyn-based P. I. Nick Delvecchio, and has already been praised by the likes of Dean R. Koontz, Charles Willeford, and John Lutz.

His novel *The Steinway Collection* received a PWA Shamus Award plaque naming it as one of the five Best Paperback Private Eye Novels of 1983.

*Full Contact* was nominated for the Shamus Award for Best Hardcover Private Eye Novel of 1984.

His short story "The Snaphaunce" was nominated for a Shamus Award as Best P. I. Short Story of 1985.

Mr. Randisi has also written novels in the

Western, Espionage, and Men's Adventure genres.

Bob Randisi is thirty-five, and lives in Brooklyn, New York, with his wife, Anna, and their sons, Christopher and Matthew.

## JOHN BALL
### AUTHOR OF **IN THE HEAT OF THE NIGHT** INTRODUCING, **POLICE CHIEF JACK TALLON** IN THESE EXCITING, FAST-PACED MYSTERIES.

# HERE IS YOUR CHANCE TO ORDER SOME OF OUR BEST

## HISTORICAL ROMANCES

### BY SOME OF YOUR FAVORITE AUTHORS

\_\_\_\_ **BELOVED OUTCAST** — Lorena Dureau    7701-0508-4/$3.95

\_\_\_\_ **DARK WINDS** — Virginia Coffman    7701-0405-3/$3.95

\_\_\_\_ **KISS OF GOLD** — Samantha Harte    7701-0529-7/$3.50

\_\_\_\_ **MISTRESS OF MOON HILL** — Jill Downie
7701-0424-X/$3.95

\_\_\_\_ **SWEET WHISPERS** — Samantha Harte
7701-0496-7/$3.50

\_\_\_\_ **TIMBERS AND GOLD LACE** — Patricia Werner
7701-0600-5/$3.95

\_\_\_\_ **TIME TO LOVE** — Helen McCullough
7701-0560-2/$3.95

\_\_\_\_ **WAYWARD LADY** — Nan Ryan    7701-0605-6/$3.95

*Available at your local bookstore or return this coupon to:*

- - - - - - - - - - - - - - - - - - - - - - - - - - - - - - - - - - -

## BOOKS BY MAIL

320 Steelcase Rd. E.          210 5th Ave., 7th Floor
Markham, Ont., L3R 2M1        New York, N.Y. 10010

Please send me the books I have checked above. I am enclosing a total of $_____ (Please add 1.00 for one book and 50 cents for each additional book.) My cheque or money order is enclosed. (No cash or C.O.D.'s please.)

Name _____

Address _____ Apt. _____

City _____

Prov./State _____ P.C./Zip _____

*Prices subject to change without notice*
(HIS/ROM)

# FREE!!
# BOOKS BY MAIL
# CATALOGUE

BOOKS BY MAIL will share with you our current bestselling books as well as hard to find specialty titles in areas that will match your interests. You will be updated on what's new in books at no cost to you. Just fill in the coupon below and discover the convenience of having books delivered to your home.

*PLEASE ADD $1.00 TO COVER THE COST OF POSTAGE & HANDLING.*

- - - - - - - - - - - - - - - - - - - - - - - - - - - - -